Rev. Philip R. Bough

838-8127

HANDBOOK OF
DENOMINATIONS

HANDBOOK OF
DENOMINATIONS

IN THE UNITED STATES

New Seventh Edition

Frank S. Mead

Abingdon
NASHVILLE

HANDBOOK OF DENOMINATIONS IN THE UNITED STATES

Library of Congress Cataloging in Publication Data

MEAD, FRANK SPENCER, 1898-
  Handbook of denominations in the United States.
  Bibliography: p. 275
  Includes index.
  1. Christian Sects—United States. 2. Sects—United States. I. Title.
BR516.5.M38 1980   201'.0973   79-20252

ISBN 0-687-16570-9

MANUFACTURED BY THE PARTHENON PRESS AT
NASHVILLE, TENNESSEE, UNITED STATES OF AMERICA

TO THOSE

. . . bishops and brethren, prelates and patriarchs, and plain people, moderators, clerks (stated and without state), superintendents, overseers, secretaries (general, corresponding, recording, executive, and board), statisticians, correspondents, historians, editors (in chief, associate, and managing), canons, elders, chairmen and vice-chairmen of this or that, directors of public relations and offices of information, guardians of records in farm kitchens on RFD 1 and on Riverside Drive;

. . . critics, lay and clerical, official or just interested, caustic and charitable, who read previous editions and suggested changes for this one;

. . . who accepted our plea to distinguish between plain truth and propaganda and who were content to give us the facts and leave the writing to us;

We gratefully dedicate
this book.

CONTENTS

ADVENTISTS

Adventism in general is a Christian faith based upon the conviction that the second advent of Christ is the sole hope of the world. It holds that man's nature is fallen because of sin and that on the basis of neglect or rejection of God's plan of salvation those rebellious against the government of God will be ultimately destroyed, while believers, by God's grace, will be saved. After this cataclysmic event Jesus Christ will reign in triumph through the thousand-year period, or millennium, of Rev. 20:1-6. The whole Adventist thesis rests heavily upon the prophetic and apocalyptic texts of Daniel and Revelation.

As a religious movement, it began with a widespread "awakening" on the question of the advent, which developed spontaneously in the Old World and in the New in the early decades of the nineteenth century. It became strongest and most clearly defined in the United States, at first under the leadership of William Miller (1782–1849) of Low Hampton, New York, a veteran of the War of 1812 and a man respected as a diligent student of the Bible, even though he did not have formal college or seminary training.

The movement under Miller was at first an interchurch (or more accurately, *intra*church) development, with many Methodists, Christians, Baptists, Presbyterians, and Congregationalists among its adherents. It was thus a movement within the existing churches, and in the days of its beginnings there was no intention or attempt to organize a separate denomination. So influential was William Miller that for years his followers were known as Millerites. Miller himself became a Baptist in 1816. He began at once a careful study of the Scriptures, concentrating on the prophecies of Daniel and Revelation. Using only the Bible, its marginal references, and Cruden's *Concordance* as his sources, he came to the conclusion that many Old and New World biblical scholars had already reached—namely, that the symbolic "day" of Bible prophecy represents a year. He also concluded that the 2,300 "days" of Dan. 8:14 started concurrently with the 70 weeks of years of Dan. 9, or from 457 B.C., the year of the command to rebuild and restore Jerusalem; and he believed that the longer of the two periods would end in or about the year 1843 as calculated by Jewish reckoning. Miller thought that the "sanctuary" mentioned in Dan. 8:14 was the earth (or the church) that would be cleansed by fire at the second advent. He came to believe that this cleansing would occur sometime between March 21, 1843, and March 21, 1844.

When the advent expectation failed to materialize by the spring of 1844, many left the movement. Miller's associates, on the basis of meticulous study of Old Testament types, set a second date, October 22, 1844, as the great antitypical Day of Atonement, confident that the "day of the Lord is near, even at the door." By 1844 there were between 50,000 and 100,000 Adventists in North America. Some disposed of their property as the day of expectation approached, gave away their goods, settled all their accounts, and waited prayerfully for the Lord to come. October 22 came and passed with no second coming. Now vast numbers lost all interest in Adventism and went back to their former churches or abandoned the Christian faith altogether.

Those who continued as Adventists formed several smaller bodies. At first a loosely knit Adventist organization came into being at a conference in Albany, New York, in 1845. This group held generally to Miller's positions and theology, emphasizing the personal and premillennial character of the second advent of Christ, the resurrection of the dead—the faithful to be raised at Christ's coming, the rest a thousand years later—and the renewal of the earth as the eternal abode of the redeemed. Known at first as the American Millennial Association, a portion of them later came to be called Evangelical Adventists, a church that has dwindled with the passing of the years to the point of obscurity. Another and larger group in 1861 became known as the Advent Christian Church.

While the general expectation of the advent had united the disparate groups, the disappointment brought all differences to light again. Nearly all Adventists were, at first, agreed that the second advent of Christ will be premillennial—that is, that his return will *precede* the thousand-year period foretold in Rev. 20. Today, however, many of them, including the Advent Christian group, hold the amillennial position.

In other areas there was wide difference of viewpoint also. Just what is the state of the dead—conscious or unconscious—as they await the resurrection? Who are to arise—the righteous *and* the wicked or only the righteous? Is there to be eternal punishment for the wicked or ultimate annihilation? What is the nature of immortality? Does the cleansing of the sanctuary of Dan. 8 refer to a sanctuary in heaven or on earth? When should the Sabbath be celebrated—on the first day or on the seventh, on Sunday or on Saturday? Over these questions the Adventists, as organized bodies, became divided into the four major groups in which we find them today.

Seventh-day Adventists

By far the largest single Adventist body in point of numbers, both in the United States and particularly throughout the world, is the Seventh-day Adventist Church, which traces its beginnings back to the 1840s. It traces its convictions on the Sabbath back to the earlier Seventh Day Baptists of New England and the Old World.

The first major point of disagreement between Seventh-day Adventists and the other Adventist groups was not over the Sabbath question but the question of the "sanctuary" in Dan. 8:14 and the interpretation of that passage. A small group of Adventists became convinced that the sanctuary was in heaven and not on earth and that there would be work of "investigative judgment" in the heavenly sanctuary prior to the second advent. Other Adventist bodies of the period still held that the sanctuary was the earth.

Coupled with this divergence came another, concerning the time of the second advent. The Seventh-day group claimed that the historical and prophetic evidence pointing to October 22, 1844, was correct but that the error lay in a mistaken interpretation of Dan. 8:13-14—that Christ was not at that time to come out of, but was to *enter into,* the Most Holy Place in heaven to complete the second phase of his high priestly ministry before coming to this earth. The group holding these views also came to advocate the observance of the seventh day.

As early as 1844 a small group of these Adventists near Washington, New Hampshire, had begun observing the Sabbath on the seventh day. A pamphlet written by Joseph Bates in 1846 gave the question wide publicity and created great interest. Shortly after this, Bates, together with James White, Ellen Harmon (later Mrs. James White, whose writings Seventh-day Adventists hold "in highest esteem . . . [they] accept them as inspired counsels from the Lord"), Hiram Edson, Frederick Wheeler, and S. W. Rhodes, set out with the aid of regular publications to champion the seventh-day Sabbath, along with the imminence of the advent. Hence their name—Seventh-day Adventists.

The growth of the group around these leaders was slow at first, owing to the general derision in which Adventists were held and to their economic limitations and social handicaps. By 1855, however, they were prosperous and numerically strong enough to set up headquarters at Battle Creek, Michigan, with a publishing house called the Seventh-day Adventist Publishing Association. In 1860 they officially adopted the name Seventh-day Adventists, and in 1903 they moved their headquarters to its present location in Washington, D.C.

Doctrinally the Seventh-day Adventists are evangelical conservatives with a sound Protestant recognition of the authoritative nature of God's revelation of himself through the inspired writings encompassed in the entire Bible. Their standard statement of belief, appearing annually in their *Yearbook,* reveals that they believe in the transcendent, personal, communicating God as revealed in the Father, the Son, and the Holy Spirit, each equally and uniquely divine, personal, and eternal. They believe in creation by divine fiat and recognize the fall of man. Man is by nature mortal but may receive immortality through divine grace and the redemption offered through the total atoning work of Jesus Christ.

They hold the Ten Commandments to be a transcript of the character of God, as exemplified in the life of Jesus Christ, and thus the standard of righteousness for men of all ages. They base their observance of the seventh day as the Sabbath on the fourth commandment—"Six days shalt thou labour, . . . But the seventh day is the sabbath of the Lord thy God." The tithing of incomes provides the entire support of the ministry of the church. Beyond the tithe, they give generously toward missions, local church expenses, and other church enterprises. In 1977 their total per capita giving was $642.75 in North America and $179.37 in the world field.

They believe in the gift of prophecy in the church; that the dead awaiting the resurrection are in an unconscious state; that the whole person will be resurrected on the last day with immortality for the righteous and destruction by fire for the wicked. They seek religious liberty for all and advocate the complete separation of church and state. They consider the body of man to be the temple of the Holy Spirit and, in consequence, rigidly abstain from the use of alcoholic beverages, tobacco, and the promiscuous use of drugs. Likewise, they advocate sound principles of healthful living through diet, exercise, and helpful outlook. They believe in the premillennial, personal, visible return to Christ "at a time unknown but close at hand" and in a new earth to be created out of the ruins of the old as the final abode of the redeemed. They practice immersion as the biblical form of baptism and foot washing as a preparatory service for Communion.

The overall administrative body of the church is the executive committee of their general conference, which is chosen by delegates from the various church groups in the quinquennial sessions of the general conference of Seventh-day Adventists. Working under this general conference are 3 lesser governmental units: (1) the 12 "division" organizations, administering church affairs in different continents; (2) 78 "union conferences" making up the divisional organizations; and (3) 376 "local conferences," or missions, the smallest administrative units.

Each unit has a large amount of autonomy. Local congregations elect lay elders, deacons, and other officers; the local conference office supervises all local pastoral and evangelistic work and pays all pastors and other workers in its territory from a central fund. Theirs is a highly representative form of government.

Evangelism, publishing, educational, health, and welfare work are outstanding and highly successful among Seventh-day Adventists. Regarding themselves not as just another church but as a movement established in the fulfillment of Bible prophecy to prepare mankind for the second advent and to revive and restore neglected truths of the Reformation and of the Apostolic church, they carry forward their work in 590 languages and dialects, 203 with publications and 387 orally. They have 49 publishing houses distributed over the world, with 4 in the United States.

In North America they have 10 liberal arts colleges; 2 universities; a theological seminary; and medical, dental, and physical therapy schools. In the United States and abroad they support 445 medical units and 42 nurses' training schools, 548 colleges and secondary schools, 3,839 elementary schools. There are 3,126 weekly radio broadcasts in 76 languages; 6,040,795 students are enrolled in Bible correspondence schools. An international broadcast, "The Voice of Prophecy," goes out over 895 stations weekly, and a weekly TV program, "Faith for Today," is viewed on 125 outlets. Still another, "It Is Written," is seen on 107 outlets each week.

Inasmuch as Adventists practice adult (age of accountability) baptism, no infants or children are reported in their total membership, which is listed at 2,949,758 in 19,761 churches; it is limited to those who uphold their church standards, including abstinence from liquor and tobacco. There are 551,884 Seventh-day Adventists in the United States and Canada, organized into 3,729 churches, as of 1977.

Advent Christian Church

While William Miller was never active in the founding of the Advent Christian Church, which later became the Advent Christian General Conference of America, his teachings concerning the imminent return of Christ were strongly influential. More important were the teachings, concerning the nature and mortality of man, of such men as Professor Charles F. Hudson and George Storrs. Dissatisfied with what they felt was a purely Platonic doctrine of the immortality of the human soul, they rejected it completely and sought a more biblical emphasis, preaching a new doctrine of "conditional immortality," which declared the unconscious state of all the dead until the resurrection at Christ's return, the establishment of a divine tribunal for the determination of rewards and punishments, the ultimate extinction of all evil, and the inauguration of the everlasting kingdom of God upon this earth as a restored paradise.

The first Advent Christian Association was established at Salem, Massachusetts, in 1860, and its members—still Adventists, though cut off in their new doctrine from other Adventist churches—publicly disclaimed any intent to form a separate denominational group. They founded two colleges—Aurora College at Aurora, Illinois, and the Boston Bible School (now Berkshire Christian College) at Lenox, Massachusetts. Missionary work began in 1891; today there are mission stations in Malaysia, Japan, India, and the Philippines. The church maintains 2 homes for the aged, an orphanage, and a publishing department that issues 5 denominational periodicals.

Congregational in polity, 31,324 members in 381 local churches are grouped in 5 regional districts of the United States and Canada. These conferences, together with various institutions and cooperating societies, are associated under the Advent Christian General Conference of America, which meets in triennial session. The only creedal statement is a declaration of principles adopted by the general conference of 1900, with revisions in 1934, 1964, and 1972. Two sacraments are observed—baptism by immersion and the Lord's Supper. Worship is held on the first day of the week.

In 1964 this church merged with the Life and Advent Union, an Adventist group with 3 churches and 300 members, organized by John T. Walsh in 1848.

Church of God (General Conference)

This church is the outgrowth of several independent local groups of similar faith; some of them were in existence as early as 1800, and others date their beginnings with the arrival of British immigrants in this country around 1847. Many of them organized originally under the name of Church of God in Christ Jesus. The corporate name today is the Church of God General Conference, Oregon, Illinois.

State and district conferences of these groups were formed as an expression of mutual cooperation. A national organization, instituted at Philadelphia in 1888, met again in 1889; however, because of strong convictions on questions of congregational rights and authority, it ceased to function until 1921, when the present general conference was formed at Waterloo, Iowa.

The Bible is accepted here as the supreme standard of faith. Adventist in viewpoint, the second (premillennial) coming of Christ is strongly emphasized. The church teaches that the kingdom of God will be literal, beginning at Jerusalem at the time of the return of Christ and extending to all nations. Emphasis is placed on the oneness of God and the Sonship of Christ; they believe that Jesus did not exist prior to his birth in Bethlehem and that the Holy Ghost is the power and influence of God. They believe in the restoration of Israel, the times of restitution, the mortality of man (asleep in death until the resurrection), the literal resurrection of the dead, the reward of the righteous on earth, and the complete destruction of the wicked in second death. Membership is dependent upon acceptance of doctrinal faith, repentance, and baptism (for the remission of sins) by immersion.

Delegates from each church meet each year to determine church plans and policies and to elect officers who serve as a board of directors. A general conference operates Oregon Bible College for the training of ministers; the printing and publishing of church literature; the Berean Youth Fellowship; the Department of Missions; and the Sunday School Department. The work of the general conference is carried on under the direction of the board of directors, which meets as necessary throughout the year. The executive officer is an executive director who administers the work as a whole. The conference is incorporated as the Church of God, General Conference. Because of the congregational nature of the church's government, the general conference exists primarily as a means of mutual cooperation and for the development of yearly projects and enterprises. There are 7,620 members in 135 churches, divided into 10 state and district conferences. The church periodical, *The Restitution Herald,* is published monthly. Mission stations are located in India, Mexico, the Philippine Islands, Lebanon, Nigeria, and Ghana.

Primitive Advent Christian Church

This is a splinter group from the Advent Christian Church, with 514 members in 10 churches, all of them in West Virginia. As the name implies, it represents an attempt to reemphasize the principles and teachings of earliest Adventism. The group holds a strong pacifist position.

THE AFRICAN ORTHODOX CHURCH

Believing that black Episcopalians should have churches of their own, a Protestant Episcopal rector, the Rev. George Alexander McGuire, withdrew from that church in 1919 to establish independent black churches in the United States, Cuba, and Canada. He called them Independent Episcopal churches, but in 1921 the first general synod of the new body changed the name to The African Orthodox Church and elected McGuire as its first bishop. He was consecrated by Archbishop Vilatte, who took his episcopal orders from the West Syrian Church of Antioch; this put McGuire in the traditional apostolic succession, which he valued highly.

The church lays strong emphasis upon the apostolic succession and upon the historic sacraments and rituals. It has the original 7 sacraments of the Roman Catholic Church; its worship is a blending of Western and Eastern liturgy, creeds, and symbols. The liturgy is usually Western, a mingling of Anglican, Greek, and Roman patterns. Three creeds—Apostles', Nicene, and Athanasian—are used.

The denomination maintains the position that no priest may remarry the guilty party in a divorce, and innocent parties are remarried only after special permission by a bishop. The government is of course episcopal; bishops are in charge of dioceses or jurisdictions, and groups of dioceses form a province, each led by an archbishop and a primate, who in turn presides over the provincial synod. At the head stands a primate archbishop metropolitan who is general overseer of all the work of the church, which now extends over the United States, Canada, Latin America, and the Union of South Africa. Membership, as in the Roman Catholic Church, is counted not by communicants but by the number of persons baptized; in the United States there were 24 churches and 6,000 members in 1957.

AMANA CHURCH SOCIETY

Officially named the Amana Church Society (which from the Aramaic means "to remain faithful"), this group stems from the pietistic movement in early eighteenth-century Germany. In 1714 a small company under the leadership of Johann Friedrich Rock and Eberhardt Ludwig Gruber stirred the German people with their preaching that the days of true and direct inspiration from God had not ended. Both these leaders and others had the divine gift of inspiration. They established new churches in the Province of Hessen, Germany, but were persecuted until 1842, when they came to America, settling near Buffalo, New York. There were approximately 800 of them, and they organized a Christian communal group called the Ebenezer Society.

All property was held and shared collectively; each person did the work for which he was fitted and shared equally in the rewards. Each of the six Ebenezer villages had a common school, meetinghouse, and store, and they farmed the land round and about them that had been purchased through an American land syndicate, who had purchased the area from the Seneca Indians. In 1854 and subsequently they removed to Iowa, where the villages of Amana (East, South, Middle, High, West) and Homestead were established. Here they became incorporated under the laws of Iowa as a nonprofit, religious corporation, taking the name Amana Society.

In 1932 many communal practices were abandoned, and the Amana business society with its own board of directors, and the Amana Church Society with a separate board of 13 trustees were organized, the Amana Church Society remaining nonprofit and the Amana business society operating under a cooperative plan as a pecuniary corporation. The business society conducts 28 different businesses and farms 25,000 acres of land, with stockholders voting for the directors in that $10,000,000 corporation.

The Amana Church Society is still pacifistic in its views, and the traditional garb for church-going is still used by the women. People who work for the Amana business society on the other hand are paid salaries and/or wages.

The purpose of the Amana Church Society is purely religious; it is based upon the salvation of souls in the service of God. They believe that God can now, as well as of old, inspire men, but none has been inspired since the old historic leaders and the two early American leaders, Christian Metz and Barbara Landmann, who died in the latter part of the nineteenth century. The Amana Church Society accepts the teachings of a holy universal church, the remission of sins, the communion of saints, the resurrection of the body, the punishment of the wicked, and life everlasting. It acknowledges baptism by fire and the Holy Spirit. Young members are confirmed and admitted to the church at age 18; the children attend both church-sponsored Sunday schools and the public schools regulated by the State Department of Public Instruction of Iowa. There is no ordained ministry in the church; the services consist of hymn-singing, prayer, readings from the testimonies of Rock, Gruber, Metz, and Landmann, and sermons preached by the elders. The church is separated from the temporal affairs of the community but is still a dominant influence. There are 4 village German congregations (serving all 7 villages) and 1 English service is conducted for all 7 villages. There are 735 members in 7 churches.

AMERICAN ETHICAL UNION

The Ethical Movement in the United States builds its thought and program upon moral philosophy and the ethical traditions of the great religions of mankind; its main emphasis is upon ethics rather than upon creed or ceremony; members include both theists and nontheists. A statement of principles declares that

the search for ethical values and their progressive realization are inherently a religious enterprise. . . . All human beings, however different in their abilities or backgrounds, have an equal right to such fulfillment as encourages the fulfillment of their fellowmen. Such a goal requires diversity in beliefs and practices, and therefore freedom of conscience, thought, and expression. . . . Our attitude toward that which is beyond present knowledge, including questions about cosmic matters, is one of free and cooperative exploration, and respect for individual experience.

Stress is laid upon the development of conscience and a sense of responsibility as great creative forces among men.

There are 25 active Ethical Culture societies in the Ethical Union, the first of which was founded by Felix Adler in 1876. The union is a founding member of the International Humanist and Ethical Union with organizations in some 30 countries around the world. Meetings of the societies feature inspirational music, meditation, readings from Scripture or other inspired poetry or prose, and an address upon some social, political, philosophic, religious, or ethical subject. Ethical Culture leaders serve as counselors, officiate at weddings and funerals, name children, and perform in general the functions of the minister. There are Sunday schools, young people's groups, and study groups; very effective work is done in educational, philanthropic, and social efforts and projects. The New York Society must be given credit for the starting of settlement work in the cities of this country; at the present time societies in New York, Chicago, and Philadelphia sponsor such programs. Free kindergartens, visiting nurses, the Child Study Movement, the abolition of child labor and capital punishment, model tenements, the inauguration of free public legal aid societies, civil liberties, and interracial adoption practices—all constitute Ethical Culture drives.

Outstanding Ethical Culture schools have been developed at Central Park West and Riverdale in New York City and in Brooklyn, attracting many who are not otherwise identified with the movement. There are approximately 5,000 members.

AMERICAN EVANGELICAL CHRISTIAN CHURCHES

Launched in 1944 and first incorporated in Illinois, the A.E.C.C. is described as "an ecclesiastical body or denomination of interdoctrinal character." It seeks to compromise the difference between Calvinistic and Arminian beliefs. Local churches established under its charter are known as American Evangelical Churches and often as American Bible Churches or simply as Community Churches. Each church is sovereign in its management but is obliged to cooperate with the national headquarters if it is to retain membership in the body.

Ministerial applicants must subscribe to seven articles of faith: (1) the Bible as the written Word of God; (2) the Virgin Birth; (3) the deity of Jesus Christ; (4) salvation through the atonement of Christ; (5) the guidance of life through prayer; (6) the return of Christ; (7) the establishment of the kingdom of God on earth. Upon completion of training, ministerial students are granted licenses enabling them to perform all the functions and offices of the ministry with the exception of officiating in marriages. Full ordination is withheld until the licentiate has become pastor of a regular congregation or is engaged in full-time evangelistic or missionary work.

All ordinations must be performed under the supervision of either regional or national officers; 5 regional offices in the United States and 1 in Canada supervise the work of the organization. A training school and missionary home are operated in Pineland, Florida, and an American Bible School in Chicago specializes in home study courses. There are 35 churches operating in the British Isles.

The present ministerial membership is reported at 500, of whom about 50 percent are engaged as full-time pastors. No further statistics are available. Headquarters are in Pineland, Florida 33945.

AMERICAN RESCUE WORKERS

Incorporated in 1896 and with a name amended to the organizational charter in 1913, the American Rescue Workers engage in a typical rescue mission work in offering emergency aid (lodging, clothing, food), half-way houses and rehabilitation centers for alcoholics and drug addicts, workshops and industrial programs for the socially and physically handicapped, and evangelism, yet have the status of a full-fledged nonsectarian church. The rites of baptism and Communion are administered by the officers and ministers in charge of local corps, and regular church and Sunday school services are held in their chapels and mission halls. Ministers are ordained at annual councils.

Their articles of religion include subscription to the Trinity, the inspiration of the Scriptures and their use as the divine rule of faith and practice, the fall of man, redemption through the atoning sacrifice of Christ, restoration through repentance and belief in Christ, regeneration through the work of the Holy Spirit, and the immortality of the soul.

Government is by a board of managers elected by the members of the corporation. Organization is on a military pattern, with William H. Schafer as commander in chief and with territorial commanders in charge. A periodical, *The Rescue Herald*, is published in Philadelphia. There are 750 members in 14 churches.

ANGLICAN ORTHODOX CHURCH

The Rev. James Parker Dees resigned in 1963 from the priesthood of the Protestant Episcopal Church in protest of what he believed to be "its failure to proclaim firmly the Biblical doctrine, and on account of its emphasis on the social gospel and pro-communist program." With a group of former members of the Episcopal Church, he organized the Anglican Orthodox Church to preserve the traditional tenets of Anglicanism—belief in the fundamental (King James) Bible truths and morality, the (1928) Book of Common Prayer, the 39 Articles of Religion, the Homilies, the doctrines of the Anglican Reformers, and the basic Anglican traditions and church government. Dr. Dees was consecrated bishop by Bishop Wasyl Sawyna of the Holy Ukranian Autocephalic Orthodox Church and by Bishop Orlando J. Woodward of the Old Catholic succession.

The fundamentalist doctrines of the Virgin Birth, the atoning sacrifice of the Cross, the Trinity, the Resurrection, the Second Coming, salvation by faith alone, and the divinity of Christ are emphasized. There are 2,630 members in 37 established churches and 5 missions in the United States and missionary congregations in Canada, Europe, and Asia, and 50,000 members are claimed in branches in South India, Madagascar, Pakistan, Nigeria, Rhodesia, Fiji Islands, Colombia, and England. The ministers of the church are trained at Cranmer Seminary at Statesville, North Carolina.

APOSTOLIC CHRISTIAN CHURCH
(Nazarean)

The Apostolic Christian Church (Nazarean) began in this country with the arrival of a Swiss, S. H. Froelich, about the year 1850. Froelich went to work immediately among Swiss and German immigrants, founding a number of small churches among those nationalities in the Midwest.

The theology here is conservative; the church consists of members who have been converted to Christ, reborn, and baptized and who strive for sanctification "and of such friends of the truth who sincerely and earnestly strive to attain adoption to sonship in Christ." They are required to live "according to the Gospel of Christ, subject to the authorities, strive to be at peace with their fellow men, and fulfill their obligations as good citizens." They do, however, refuse to take up arms, since this denies the biblical command to love one's enemies; they will engage in noncombatant service, but they will not kill.

The local churches are independent in polity but united in fundamental organization. Each church is served by elders who are also authorized to baptize, lay on hands, serve the Lord's Supper, and conduct meetings for the exercising of church discipline.

Nearly half the membership is found in Illinois and Ohio; small bodies are located in nearly all the northern states from New England to the West Coast and Canada. With 54 churches and 3,771 members, there are missionaries in Brazil, Argentina, New Guinea, and Ghana. There is also a nonprofit service organization at work, known as the Apostolic Christian Church Foundation.

APOSTOLIC CHRISTIAN CHURCH OF AMERICA

Good

The Apostolic Christian Church of America began with the labors of Benedict Weyeneth, a Swiss who came to America about 1847 and organized a number of Swiss-German churches. Its doctrine is based largely on the teaching of entire sanctification, aiming "solely at the saving of souls, a change of heart through regeneration, and a life of godliness guided and directed by the Holy Spirit." Members are noted for their pacifism but will engage in any service in support of the government "which is compatible with the teachings of Christ and the Apostles." Willful disobedience of church doctrine is punished by expulsion, but membership can be restored. There are no educational institutions, and the ministers are not paid, nor are they expected to study or prepare their sermons but to depend entirely upon the inspiration and revelation of the Holy Spirit. There are more than 10,000 members and 78 congregations, 4 in Japan, 1 in Canada.

APOSTOLIC FAITH

Good

Organized in Portland, Oregon, in 1907, by the Rev. Mrs. Florence L. Crawford "not to promote any new doctrine but rather to reestablish, maintain, and teach all the doctrines as taught by Christ and by his Apostles in the days of the early church," the Apostolic Faith is "Trinitarian, Fundamental and Evangelistic." Arminian in theology, it presents the usual doctrines of fundamentalism, stressing especially justification by faith (as taught by Luther), entire sanctification (as taught by Wesley), and the baptism of the Holy Ghost, as evidenced at Pentecost. There are 49 churches and 5,000 members in the United States (mostly in the South and West), and churches abroad.

Shunning "the swelling of numbers," there are baptismal records but no membership reports; a "born again" experience and subscription to the doctrines of the group are required for membership. It is "a church without a collection plate" (no offering is taken during services); worldly amusements (dancing, theater, card playing, drinking, smoking) are banned; women may not use facial makeup nor bob their hair, and men and women are required to dress conservatively. There is no marriage with unbelievers.

Governing bodies consist of a board of 5 trustees, of which the general overseer of the denomination is chairman, and a board of 24 elders. It was incorporated as "the Apostolic Faith Mission of Portland, Oregon, U.S.A." A headquarters church, a tabernacle, and a publishing house, circulating evangelical literature in more than 70 languages and dialects, are also located in Portland.

APOSTOLIC OVERCOMING
HOLY CHURCH OF GOD

Bishop W. T. Phillips, founder and senior officer of this church and a former member of The Methodist Church, became deeply concerned with the teaching of the doctrine of holiness and in 1916, after 4 years of study and preaching on the doctrine, organized the Ethiopian Overcoming Holy Church of God. The word "Ethiopian" was later changed to "Apostolic."

Active in 14 states and with missions in the West Indies and Africa, the ministers of the body are supported by tithe payments of the membership; the clergy are also required to tithe. Worship includes foot washing and divine healing. Services generally are free, emotional affairs, with the participants speaking in tongues and engaging in ecstatic dances.

It is claimed that this church existed "even from the days of Enos," when Christianity was known to be in existence in Abyssinia. Marriage to unsaved men and women, the use of snuff, foolish talking, jesting, and the use of slang are forbidden.

In doctrine, sanctification and holiness are stressed, with the tenet of the deity of Christ, the final resurrection of the dead, who shall be punished at the time of this Last Death and Last Judgment at the Second Coming of Christ. Women are given the right to preach. A special relief fund provides for the needs of orphans, widows, aged, and disabled members. There is a publishing house in Mobile, Alabama. Bishop Jasper Roby is the Executive Bishop; together with 9 other bishops he supervises the work of the church, which claims more than 100,000 members in 300 local churches.

ARMENIAN CHURCHES

Armenia claims to be the first Christian nation. The apostles Thaddeus and Bartholomew were believed to have been there during the time of Paul, and Christianity was adopted as the state religion in A.D. 301. St. Gregory the Illuminator, preaching in Armenia at that time, became the first head of this national church, with the title of *Catholicos*.

The story of the Christian church in Armenia is written in blood; it suffered in the inevitable conflict between the Byzantine Empire and Persia and in numerous persecutions by the Turks. Thousands escaped to America before and after World War I, and here they functioned under the jurisdiction of the Etchmiadzin See from 1887 to 1933, when a dispute arose over the domination of the church in Soviet Armenia insofar as it affects the American diocese. A split occurred in which one group organized independently and remained so until 1957, known as the Armenian Apostolic Church of America; they went under the jurisdiction of the Holy See of Cilicia in

Lebanon. Those who remained are known as the Armenian Church of America and are under the See of Etchmiadzin.

Today, in spite of the division into two dioceses and still facing the question of loyalty to one or the other jurisdiction, the Armenian churches work in harmony where dogma and liturgy are concerned. Both elect their own primates. Deacons, priests, bishops, and archbishops are ordained and elevated by the hierarchical authorities of their respective jurisdictions. Both the Armenian Church of America (including the diocese of California) and the Armenian Apostolic Church of America claim to be the true American branch of the Ancient Church of Armenia. The former group has a membership of 372,000 in 58 churches, working under the jurisdiction of the Etchmiadzin See; the latter has 125,000 members in 29 churches and is under the jurisdiction of the Holy See of Cilicia, Antelias-Lebanon.

In government, both churches are democratic in that they elect their own officials. Every province and diocese in this country, and indeed in the world, has a constitution adapted to its particular needs but which must be approved by the Catholicos of its respective jurisdiction.

Doctrine is based on the historic writings and declarations of the early church fathers. The saints and the Virgin Mary are venerated; the Assumption of the Virgin is celebrated but not accepted as a dogma. A translation of the Scriptures by St. Sahak and St. Mesrob and of their students is accepted as the only authoritative Armenian Version of the Bible. There are 7 sacraments: baptism by immersion 8 days after birth, confirmation immediately following baptism, Holy Communion even for infants, penance, marriage, ordination, and extreme unction. The principal service is the Holy Sacrifice of the Divine Liturgy; various orders of "hour" services and celebrations of feasts are observed. The Bible is read in Armenian at these services. Language schools, Sunday schools, cultural programs, and libraries help to keep the native tongue alive.

BAHÁ'Í

The Bahá'í faith aims at the universal brotherhood of man, the unity of all religions, and peace for the whole world. Its founder, Bahá'u'lláh, said, "The religion of God is for the sake of love and union; make it not the cause of enmity and conflict." His followers see in his teachings the same universal spirit that spoke in Moses and Jesus, Krishna and Buddha, Zoroaster and Muhammad; to them he is the "return" of all previous prophets, religious leaders, "Manifestations of God," and "The Promised One" of the world's great religions.

Actually, the Bahá'í faith originated with the teachings of Mírzá 'Ali Muhammad, called the Báb (Arabic for "gate" or "door"), who suffered persecution and was martyred in 1850. It is estimated that 20,000 followers of the faith, then known as Babi Faith, were slain during this persecution. His successor was Mírzá Husayn 'Ali, who was given the title of Bahá'u'lláh ("The

Glory of God"), and who died in 1892. He left a vast accumulation of writings that are still treasured as the sacred scriptures of Bahá'í belief. His mantle fell upon his eldest son, 'Abbás Effendi, later known as 'Abdu'l-Bahá. The son spent some 40 years in captivity; released in 1908 at the time of the revolution of the Young Turks, he toured Egypt, Europe, and the United States. In 1912 at Wilmette, a suburb of Chicago, he laid the cornerstone of the first Bahá'í house of worship in the Occident. This is now the seat of Bahá'í national administrative offices in the United States.

The Wilmette temple is a unique religious structure in which the numeral 9, the symbol of unity in Bahá'í, is repeatedly emphasized. There are 9 concrete piers, 9 pillars or pylons, and 9 arches; it is set in a park with 9 sides, 9 avenues, gateways, and fountains. The building was dedicated in 1953 to "the unity of God, the unity of his prophets, the unity of mankind." Services of worship are conducted weekly in the auditorium with *a capella* music and readings from the sacred scriptures of the world's religions. A Bahá'í home for the aged was built in Wilmette in 1958.

Coordination and direction of international Bahá'í activities are now vested in the Bahá'í Universal House of Justice, a body of 9 members in residence at the World Center in Haifa, Israel, elected for a term of 5 years. In addition to administrative and judicial functions for the Bahá'í faith at large, this body legislates on matters not expressly revealed in the Bahá'í writings. To direct the teaching activities, another international institution, known as the Hands of the Cause, functions with auxiliary boards assigned to each continent. Local groups are organized as local Spiritual Assemblies, which in turn are supervised by a National Spiritual Assembly that consists of 9 members. Since 1963 there has been a marked growth in membership; there are more than 17,000 local assemblies, and 130 National Assemblies. Followers of the faith now reside in 5,823 localities in the United States and 70,000 worldwide; within this world fellowship we find men, women, and children of all races and creeds—black, yellow, brown, and white, Europeans, Asiatics, Africans, Americans, former Moslems, Hindus, Christians, and Jews. It is perfect integration in recognition of the truth of their founder's statement, "Ye are the fruits of one tree and the leaves of one Branch."

There are central Bahá'í temples at Frankfurt, Germany; Sydney, Australia; Kampala in (Uganda) Africa; Wilmette, Illinois, in the United States; and Panama City, Panama. Publishing trusts have been established at Wilmette, London, Buenos Aires, Rio de Janeiro, New Delhi, Teheran, Kampala, Frankfurt, and in Belgium. The writings of the Bahá'í faith have been translated into 589 languages.

There is no ritual, no clergy in Bahá'í. Traditional rites and sacraments practiced by the religions of the world are ruled out in the belief that each seeker may receive truth and the Spirit without ecclesiastical mediation. Unpaid teachers and "pioneers" give assistance to students. Marriage and funeral services are simple and flexible. Meetings vary from public lectures, study classes, and discussion groups for inquirers to meetings for the Bahá'í community, assembly meetings, conventions, and summer and winter schools and institutes. Summer schools are located in Maine, California, and

Michigan. Events within their communities are scheduled by a special calendar of 19 months of 19 days each, with the New Year at the vernal equinox. The Bahá'í day starts and ends at sunset.

The chief purpose of Bahá'í is to unite the world in one religion and in one social order; hence, its chief principle is "the oneness and the wholeness of the human race." Among other dominant principles are the following:

1. Independent investigation of the truth
2. The essential harmony of science and religion
3. Recognition of the divine foundation of all religions
4. Universal compulsory education
5. The equality of all men and women
6. The spiritual solution of economic problems
7. The need for a universal auxiliary language
8. Universal peace based upon a world federation of nations
9. The elimination of all prejudice
10. Recognition of the essential unity of mankind

Beyond this, in its effort to develop the spiritual qualities of character, Bahá'í prescribes monogamy; discourages divorce; emphasizes strict obedience to one's government; condemns idleness; exalts any work performed in the spirit of service to the rank of worship; prohibits slavery, asceticism, and monasticism, the use of alcohol and narcotics except for medicinal purposes; and insists upon prayer and fasting as means of elevating the soul.

BAPTISTS

Baptists constitute one of the major Protestant forces in the United States. Twenty-seven Baptist denominations reported an approximate membership of 27,527,471 in 1971; there are approximately 94,508 local Baptist churches, each one independent of the others, with members also completely independent of one another yet bound together by an amazingly strong "rope of sand" in a great common allegiance to certain principles and doctrines based generally upon the competency of each individual in matters of faith.

It is often heard among them that they have no founder but Christ and that Baptists have been preaching and practicing from the days of John the Baptist. That is true in a limited sense; there were certainly men and women holding what have come to be considered distinctly Baptist principles all across the years. But as a church, or as organized churches, they began in Holland and England.

When the Reformation came early in the sixteenth century, scattered groups appeared advocating the convictions of faith that are today the warp and woof of Baptist theology and ideology. We find the name "Baptist" in various forms in Germany and Switzerland: Pedobaptists, among whom, however, there were no "Baptists in the modern sense," inasmuch as they baptized infants and children; Anti-Pedobaptists, who opposed infant baptism; and Anabaptists, who rebaptized adults once baptized as children. The Anabaptists were the left wing of the Reformation and held to a literal application of the Word of God in social matters; they were communistic and pacifistic, opposing capital punishment, oaths in court, the holding of public office, and payment of taxes and interest. They rejected infant baptism as unscriptural, insisted upon the separation of church and state, and defended this belief heroically and to the point of fanaticism and martyrdom. Under persecution they spread all over Europe. Some fled to Norway, others to Italy, Poland, Holland, and England.

In Holland a group of Mennonites, or followers of the former Anabaptist leader Menno Simons (see Mennonites, p. 167), taught Anabaptist principles: that the Scriptures were the sole authority for man's faith and practice, that baptism was a believer's privilege, that church and state should be completely and forever separated, and that church discipline should be rigidly enforced in business, family, and personal affairs. These Mennonites met and perhaps deeply influenced a little group of British Separatists who had taken refuge in Amsterdam from the religious persecutions under James I; many of them lived in Mennonite homes, and one of their leaders, John Smyth, was completely captured by the Mennonite argument. He rebaptized himself and his followers in the Anabaptist, or Baptist, faith and with them organized the first English Baptist church in 1609. When he tried to make Mennonites of them, however, he went too far; Baptist they would be but not Mennonite, for that meant a threat to their British heritage, and they were still good Englishmen and proposed to remain so. Smyth was excommunicated, and he died in 1612, leaving behind him, in a "confession," his convictions that

the magistrate, by virtue of his office, is not to meddle with religion, or matters of conscience, nor to compel men to this or that form of religion or doctrine, but to leave the Christian religion to the free conscience of every one, and to meddle only with political matters.

So died John Smyth, Baptist to the last. His people drifted back across the Channel and, with persecution waning, established yet another Baptist church in London.

These first 2 churches were General Baptist churches, believing in a general atonement for all men. In the course of time there arose a Particular Baptist Church, holding to the predestinarian teachings of John Calvin and preaching a limited atonement. The first Particular (British) Church dates back to 1638. Three years after their founding, a third body, known as Immersion Baptists, broke away and in 1644 wrote a confession of faith that is still held by many modern Baptists. It was this confession that stamped these people popularly for the first time as Baptists.

These early British Baptists wielded a tremendous influence in their time and upon the future; it is claimed for them that "more than any king or Parliament, they set the heart and mind of England free." John Smyth's teaching that "the magistrate . . . is not to meddle with religion, or in matters of conscience" has become one of mankind's great spiritual principles. They sent William Carey to India in 1793, and Carey became the pioneer of modern missions. More than a century earlier, in 1631, Roger Williams had come to America; he was to be the first great champion of freedom for faith and conscience on this side of the Atlantic.

Williams was not a Baptist but a Separatist minister when he arrived. His story is well known: preaching "new and dangerous opinions against the authority of magistrates," he organized a Baptist church at Providence, Rhode Island. John Clarke established another Baptist church at Newport, Rhode Island, at about the same time. The Baptists are still arguing as to which church came first; many scholars put the Providence church in 1639, the Newport church in 1641.

These were Particular, or Calvinistic, Baptist churches. Their strength was challenged by the rise of interest in Arminian theology during the preaching of George Whitefield, but their Calvinism prevailed; it is the theological standard of many, if not most, Baptists in this country today. Their progress was slow; a bitter persecution of their church ennobled them and left one of the darkest blots on colonial history.

Following the tour of Whitefield through the colonies, a dispute arose among the Baptists, dividing them into Old Lights, or Regulars, who distrusted revivals and emotionalism, and New Lights, or Separates, who demanded a reborn membership in their churches. Separate Baptists were outstanding in the fight for religious freedom in the new land. The friction died down with the signing of the Constitution, however, and a new unity was found in a foreign missions crusade. The first Protestant missionary board in America was the American Board, made up of Baptists, Reformed, Congregational, and Presbyterian churchmen. In 1814 the Baptists organized their own separate General Missionary Convention of the Baptist Denomination in the United States of America for Foreign Missions.

This convention, representing a national Baptist fellowship, marked the first real denominational consciousness of American Baptists. It was followed eventually by other organizations which welded them firmly together: a general Baptist convention; a general tract society—later called the American Baptist Publication Society; various missionary societies for work at home and abroad; an education society; and the Baptist Young People's Union.

These organizations were on a national scale. Their unity was disrupted first by a feeling that home missions agencies within the body had failed to evangelize southern territory and later by the question of slavery and the Civil War. The great division over slavery came in 1845, when the Southerners "seceded" to form their own Southern Baptist Convention in order to carry on more effectively the work of the Southern Baptist churches. From this point forward there were to be Northern and Southern Baptist conventions.

Various other Baptist groups, following to the logical end their love of independence, established themselves from east to west. While they differ in certain minor details, they are generally agreed upon the following principles of faith: the inspiration and trustworthiness of the Bible as the sole rule of life; the lordship of Jesus Christ; the inherent freedom of the individual to approach God for himself; the granting of salvation through faith by way of grace and contact with the Holy Spirit; 2 ordinances—the Lord's Supper and baptism of believers by immersion; the independence of the local church; the church as a group of regenerated believers baptized upon confession of faith; infant baptism as unscriptural and not to be practiced; complete separation of church and state; the immortality of the soul; the brotherhood of man; the royal law of God; the need of redemption from sin; and the ultimate triumph of God's kingdom.

These overall doctrines have never been written by the Baptists into any official Baptist creed for all their churches, but they have been incorporated in 2 important confessions of faith for the denomination. The Baptist churches of London wrote a Philadelphia Confession in the year 1689, and this confession was enlarged by the Philadelphia Association in 1742. The New Hampshire State Baptist Convention drew up another confession in 1832. The older Philadelphia Confession is strongly Calvinistic in statement; the New Hampshire Confession only moderately so.

Baptists have insisted upon freedom of thought and expression in pulpit and pew. This has made them one of the most democratic religious bodies in America—and one in which liberal and conservative doctrine is preached freely. They have insisted, too, upon the absolute autonomy of the local congregation; each church arranges its own worship, examines and baptizes its own members. There is no age limit set on membership, but the candidate is usually of such an age that he can understand and accept the teachings of Christ. Candidates for the ministry are licensed by local churches and ordained upon recommendation of a group of sister churches.

Baptist churches are commonly found grouped into associations, local and state, for purposes of fellowship. National conventions are established among many of them to carry on educational and missionary work and to make pension plans. Most state and regional conventions meet annually, with delegates representing all Baptist churches in the given area. They receive reports, make recommendations, and help to raise the national mission budgets, but they have no authority to enforce their decisions. (Some regrouping regionally has taken place in the North among American Baptists.)

In Washington, D.C., there is a Baptist Joint Committee on Public Affairs for American and Southern conventions and other Baptist groups; this committee serves mainly to spread the Baptist conviction on public morals and to safeguard their principle of separation of church and state. Finally, there is the growing Baptist World Alliance, organized in 1905 and now including more than 31,432,130 Baptists all over the globe. The alliance meets every 5 years and is a purely advisory body, discussing the great themes and problems common to all Baptists. Headquarters of the alliance are now located in Washington, D.C.

American Baptist Churches in the U.S.A.

Up to the time of the Revolutionary War, Baptist work in the northern states was in the hands of the local churches, some few of which formed themselves into associations such as the Philadelphia Association or the Warren Association of Rhode Island. Beyond these associations, which were limited to Virginia, New Jersey, Pennsylvania, and Rhode Island, there was no central administrative body to bind the churches together. The association did well, building churches, colleges, schools, and libraries; by the time of the split with the Southern Baptists about 1845, plans for a national coordinating body were under way.

In the early years of the nineteenth century there were 3 Baptist organizations in the North mutually maintained: the American Baptist Home Mission Society; the American Baptist Missionary Union, later known as the American Baptist Foreign Mission Society; and the American Baptist Publication Society. The defection of the Southern Baptists served to intensify the efforts of these 3 bodies; they were separate corporations, but they often called annual meetings at the same time and place.

The women of the northern churches formed their own home and foreign missionary societies in the 1870s. Separate appeals for funds to support all these competing societies created confusion and dissatisfaction and led eventually to the formation of the Northern Baptist Convention in 1907. This convention, actually a corporation with restricted powers in conducting religious work, receiving and expanding money, and affiliating itself with other bodies, changed its name in 1950 to the American Baptist Convention. In 1955 the 2 women's missionary societies joined administratively with their counterparts, the older foreign and home mission societies. Consequently, the 2 foreign societies and the 2 home societies, respectively, function now under identical officers, boards of managers, and administrative staffs, though each of the societies maintains its own corporate identity. In 1968 the Women's Foreign Society was legally merged into the American Foreign Missionary Society. These societies, with the American Baptist Historical Society, the Ministers and Missionaries Benefit Board, and the American Baptist Board of Education and Publication, were known as cooperating organizations of the convention.

State conventions and city mission societies were drawn into closer unity by grouping them into affiliated organizations through which they raised and distributed funds under a cooperative plan with a unified budget. The Division of World Mission Support supervised the collection of money for this unified budget. Numerous other councils and committees carried on the work of the convention under the supervision of the general council, which functioned between the annual gatherings of the convention. In 1950, for the first time, a general secretary was elected.

In 1972 the convention adopted its third and present name, American Baptist Churches in the U.S.A., and restructured to strengthen the representational principle and to develop a much fuller integration of the national program agencies into the structure of the American Baptist Convention. A larger (200-member) general board, representative of election districts, is the policy-making body. A national staff council of executives of national program boards and regional, state, and city units serves   to coordinate the corporate affairs of the denomination under the leadership of the general secretary.

The local church, however, is still the basic and independent unit of American Baptist government and administration. There are 5,937 churches and 1,593,574 members, 27 regional and state conventions, and 9 Baptist city societies. The church is at work in 14 children's homes, 48 homes for the aged, 7 hospitals, 10 theological seminaries, 6 academies, 27 senior colleges and universities, 4 junior colleges, and 1 school for nursing education. The Board of National Ministries has workers in 35 states; it supports Bacone College for Indians in Oklahoma, and carries on a widespread work among blacks, Indians, and oriental residents in the United States. The Board of International Ministries supports missionaries in Burma, Assam, India, Bengal, Thailand, Japan, Okinawa, Hong Kong, the Philippines, and Central America and maintains a cooperative relationship in 10 European countries. American Baptists also support the work of the Burma Baptist Convention, financially.

In matters of faith, every Baptist church speaks for itself, but there are certain Baptist doctrines held in common. The Bible is the foundation of their belief; the individual conscience, the interpreter of the Bible. There is the usual Baptist insistence upon the inspiration and validity of the Scriptures, the lordship of Christ, immortality and the future life, the brotherhood of man, and the need of man's redemption from sin. The ordinances of baptism and the Lord's Supper are considered more as aids than as necessities to the living of the Christian life.

Generally it may be said that Northern Baptists represented in the American Baptist Churches in the U.S.A. are less conservative in thought and theology than those in the Southern Baptist Convention, but this doctrinal difference is not the major cause of the continuing separation of the two groups. Divergent views on the questions of race, open Communion, and especially of the Protestant trend toward ecumenicity are now the major hurdles, with the latter predominant. American Baptists are represented in the National Council of the Churches of Christ in the U.S.A. and in the World Council of Churches; Southern Baptists are represented in neither. American Baptists have made gestures toward union with the General Baptists, the Southern Baptists, the National Baptist Convention, the Seventh Day Baptists, the Disciples of Christ, and the Church of the Brethren and have welcomed the Free Baptists into full fellowship. Unless and until these varying attitudes are changed or reconciled, there does not seem to be any real possibility of the reunion of the two larger Baptist bodies in the United States.

Southern Baptist Convention

It was inevitable that Northern and Southern Baptists should split over the slavery question, even before the outbreak of the Civil War. The friction between the two sections began a quarter of a century before Bull Run. The acting board of foreign missions of the Baptists in the country had its headquarters in Boston. Being located there, it was naturally strongly influenced by the abolition movement. There was bitter debate among the board members, and in the early 1840s it became evident that this board would not accept slaveholders as missionaries. This question of missionaries and of missionary money was the immediate cause of the split. The "brethren of the North" first suggested separation; a month later, in May of 1845, the Southern Baptist Convention was organized, establishing at once its own boards for foreign and home missions.

Southern historians now recognize that in addition to the slavery issue there was a long-standing disagreement between Baptists in the North and Baptists in the South over the nature of denominational organization. Certainly the slave issue precipitated the break, but there was a very significant consequence to it. Baptists in the United States under northern leadership heretofore had no central denominational organization. Instead there were separate and independent organizations (usually designated as "societies") for various phases of cooperative effort such as foreign and home missions and publication. Southerners had desired instead to have one organization controlling these varied activities. From the beginning the Southern Baptist Convention was such an organization. Northern Baptists, on the other hand, waited until 1907 to form a convention uniting their societies. This cohesion of centralized organization and cooperative societies has had much to do, Southern Baptists believe, with their growth.

In Maryland, Virginia, North Carolina, South Carolina, Georgia, Louisiana, Kentucky, and Alabama, 300 churches entered the new organization. Up to the outbreak of the Civil War this convention met biennially; since 1869 it has met annually.

A hard struggle for existence lay immediately ahead. The new convention suffered badly in point of churches, membership, and finances during the war. Homes, schools, churches, the livelihood of citizens, and the very pattern of southern society was destroyed, with devastating effects among all the churches; and antimissionary movement decimated their ranks, and membership—not finances and leadership—was affected when black Baptists withdrew to form their own convention. The recovery of the Southern Baptist Convention was amazing, however. In 1845 there were 351,951 members in the convention, of whom 130,000 were black; by 1890 there were 1,235,908 members, all of them white; in 1972 there were 12,067,284 members in 34,534 churches, including black churches related to the convention.

As previously noted, Southern Baptists generally hold to a more conservative theology than their northern brothers, but the basic items of belief are quite the same. The Southern Baptist faith is more definitely Calvinistic, and it is one of the ironies of Baptist history that the Southern Baptist Convention adheres more firmly to the New Hampshire Confession of Faith than do the American Baptists. Church polity and government are the same in both conventions; membership and ministry are exchanged in harmony and understanding.

Twenty-two denominational agencies work with 33 state conventions in home and foreign missions, Sunday schools, educational institutions, and ministerial retirement. The Home Mission Board works throughout the United States, Panama, and the Panama Canal Zone, with more than 2,186 missionaries active in the field. An additional 1,002 summer missionaries are appointed each year. It cooperates with black Baptists; works among migrants in the South and Indians in the West and Southwest, among several language groups and the deaf; and provides loans for the erection of new church buildings.

Foreign missionaries are at work in 84 countries and on 4 continents; yet in comparison with their huge membership Southern Baptists rank second among Protestant denominations in the number of missionaries sent overseas—with more than 13,083,199 members in 35,255 churches they have 2,694 active missionaries abroad. There are 482 schools supported by foreign missions programs, 7,584 churches and 10,905 chapels, 21 hospitals, and 125 clinics and dispensaries.

The Sunday School Board provides the literature for and supervises the work of 7,430,931 students in 34,363 Sunday schools. The first chair of Sunday school pedagogy was established in 1915 at the Southern Baptist Theological Seminary. There are 6 theological seminaries in the Southern Baptist Convention with 10,688 students, 46 senior colleges and universities, 7 junior colleges, 7 academies, and 5 Bible schools.

Southern Baptists are said to be the fastest growing religious group in the United States; new churches are being established not only in southern but in northern, eastern, and western states as well. Their annual convention is being held increasingly in northern and western cities, and two reasons are given for this: One is that there are few southern cities with hotel accommodations adequate to care for the ever-increasing number of messengers attending conventions; the other is that there are so many Southern Baptists living in northern territory that northern cities from sheer force of numbers are entitled to national conventions within their own state. State and territorial lines are being crossed, and it is more and more evident that the word "southern" in their name is a misnomer. This is fast becoming a national Baptist body in every meaning of the word.

Black Baptists

The first black Baptist church in America was organized at Silver Bluff across the Savannah River from Augusta, Georgia, in 1773; other churches followed in Petersburg, Virginia, in 1776; Richmond, Virginia, in 1780; Williamsburg, Virginia, in 1785; Savannah, Georgia, in 1785; and Lexington, Kentucky, in 1790. It is interesting that Andrew Bryan, a slave, was the first pastor of the First African Baptist Church of Savannah, Georgia, and that its organization came about through the efforts of the Rev. Abraham Marshall (white) and the Rev. Jesse Peter (black).

As early as 1700, white slaveholders in the South were providing religious teaching and places of worship for their slaves; at least most of them did little to prevent it. Usually, however, the black slave sat in the gallery of the white

41

church, identified with the faith of his owner. White ministers, sometimes assisted by black helpers, moved from one plantation to another holding services more or less regularly; occasionally a black minister was liberated to give full time to religious work among his people. These ministers had great influence; they were consulted by the whites as the respected leaders of their people and were a real power up to the time of the slave rebellion of 1831 led by Nat Turner. For a period following this disturbance it was illegal in some sections of the South for blacks to become Christians or to build meetinghouses.

The great majority of blacks in pre–Civil War days were either Baptists or Methodists. When Bull Run was fought in 1861, there were 200,000 black members of the Methodist Episcopal Church, South, and 150,000 black Baptists. In 1793 there were 73,471 Baptists in the United States, and one-fourth of them were black; in 1806 one-third of the Baptists of North Carolina were black. The lack of formality in the Baptist churches, together with the absence of ritual and the freedom and democracy of the local congregation, appealed to blacks more than did the episcopal structure of the Methodists. This was accented at the end of the Civil War; a revival spirit swept the blacks, creating thousands of new churches. Aided by the Freedman's Aid Society and various Baptist organizations, nearly 1,000,000 black Baptists worshiped in their own churches within 15 years.

The first black Baptist association, the Providence Baptist Association of Ohio, was formed in 1836; the first attempt at national organization came in 1880 with the creation of the Foreign Mission Baptist Convention at Montgomery, Alabama. In 1886 the American National Baptist Convention was organized at St. Louis, and in 1893 the Baptist National Educational Convention was organized in the District of Columbia. All 3 conventions were merged into the National Baptist Convention of America at Atlanta in 1895. In 1915 a division arose in this convention over the adoption of a charter and the ownership of a publishing house. The group rejecting the charter continued to function as the National Baptist Convention of America, while the group accepting the charter became known as the National Baptist Convention of the U.S.A., Incorporated (incorporated, that is, under the laws of the District of Columbia). The former is frequently referred to as the "unincorporated" and the latter as the "incorporated" convention, but both trace their beginning to the Foreign Mission Baptist Convention of 1880.

Today, out of approximately 20,000,000 blacks in the United States, better than 10,000,000 are in the South, and 44 percent of the total black population are church members. They are grouped into a large number of churches and denominations. There are more than 30 recognized and entirely different black denominations, some with less than 20 members, but seven-eighths of our total black population is either Methodist or Baptist. Nearly 8,000,000 black Baptists are found in the two major conventions; 5,500,000 in the National Baptist Convention of the U.S.A., Incorporated; and 2,668,799 in the National Baptist Convention of America, usually called the "unincorporated" body.

Black Baptist doctrine runs quite parallel to that of white Baptist churches;

however, it is slightly more Calvinistic. The polity of the 2 larger white conventions prevails; local churches unite in associations, usually along state lines, for the purposes of fellowship and consultation. There are also state conventions concerned with missionary work and often extending beyond state boundaries.

Foreign missionary work is especially strong in Africa, and home missionary efforts are generally those expended in the direction of helping needy churches and schools and in family support and relief. The National Baptist Convention, Inc., has several missionary stations in the Bahamas; the convention has a total abroad of 5 colleges, 1 theological seminary, and 1 training school for women and girls. The convention has stations in Jamaica, Panama, and Africa and gives support to 10 colleges in these countries.

The old enmities between the two conventions are disappearing, but no reunion is expected for some time to come. Moves have been made, however, toward the union of the National Baptist Convention of the U.S.A, Inc., with the American Baptist Convention.

As the outcome of a violent dispute in the National Baptist Convention of the U.S.A, Inc., over procedures in the election of convention officers, a new Progressive Baptist Convention was organized in 1961. No further information is as yet available on this body.

American Baptist Association

Sometimes called Landmarkers because of their historic adherence to the old apostolic order of church polity, the American Baptist Association members deny that those Baptists organized in conventions are faithful to Bible precedent. Maintaining that their own is the true New Testament form, they hold themselves separate from all other religious groups. They "strongly protest the trend of many Baptist groups to identify themselves with Protestantism, believing that their [Baptist] faith preceded the Protestant Reformation."

Starting in 1905 as the Baptist General Association, they organized under their present name in 1924 at Texarkana, Arkansas-Texas. Teaching that the great commission of Christ (Matt. 28:18-20) was given to a local congregation, they believe that the local congregation, or church, is the only unit authorized to administer the ordinances and that it is an independent and autonomous body responsible only to Christ. Thus, every church is equal "with every other like church"; they have been called Church-Equality Baptists.

Their doctrine is strictly fundamentalist. Condemning "so-called modern science," they stand for the verbal inspiration of the Bible, the Triune God, the virgin birth and deity of Christ, the suffering and death of Christ as substitutionary, the bodily resurrection of Christ and all his saints. The second coming of Jesus, "physical and personal," is to be the crowning event of the "gospel age"; this second advent will be premillennial. There is eternal punishment for the wicked; salvation is solely by grace through faith and not by law or works. There must be absolute separation of church and state and absolute religious freedom.

Government of both the local congregations and the annual messenger meetings of the association is congregational in nature. Missionary work is conducted in county, state, interstate, and foreign levels with the program originating in the local church and the missionaries being supported by the cooperating churches. Educational work is pursued though the Sunday schools, 5 seminaries, 2 colleges, and 12 Baptist institutes.

The greater strength of this group is found in the South, Southwest, West, and Southeast; but much new work has been started in recent years in the East and the North. Their 1975 statistics show 3,570 churches with a total combined membership of 1,071,000 and 4,070 ordained clergy with charges. Their membership continues to shift from rural to urban.

A comprehensive publishing program includes 14 monthly and semi-monthly periodicals, a Sunday school literature designed to cover the entire Bible in a 10-year period, and literature for young people's work and vacation Bible schools. National and state youth encampments are held annually, as well as annual pastors' and missionary conferences on a regional and national level.

Baptist Bible Fellowship, International

The Baptist Bible Fellowship is one of the "evangelical independent" groups—perhaps the largest and fastest growing body of independent Baptists in the United States—loosely affiliated with one another in the preaching and teaching of ultraconservative Baptist doctrine. They teach that Jesus was a Baptist in his thinking and work and was baptized by John the Baptist. They are biblical literalists, denouncing all modernists and liberals. They recognize only Baptist (immersion) baptism, participate in Communion only with members of their own church, and are adamant in opposing dancing, drinking, smoking, movies, gambling, and sexual promiscuity. No membership statistics are available.

Baptist General Conference

The history of what is now known as the Baptist General Conference began at Rock Island, Illinois, in the summer of 1852. Gustaf Palmquist, a school teacher and lay preacher, had come from Sweden to Illinois the previous year to become the spiritual leader of a group of Swedish immigrants who had been influenced by the pietistic movement within the state church (Lutheran) of Sweden. At Galesburg, Illinois, he came in contact with the Baptists and early in 1852 was baptized and ordained a Baptist minister. Visiting his countrymen at Rock Island, he won his first converts to the Baptist faith and baptized 3 in the Mississippi River on August 8, 1852. From this humble beginning has come a denomination of 126,000 members, 752 churches, and 16 state or district conferences. In 1879 a national conference—the Swedish Baptist General Conference of America—was organized.

For several decades the American Baptist Home Mission Society and the

American Baptist Publication Society of the American (then the Northern) Baptist Convention aided the new work among the immigrant Swedes, but gradually the church became self-supporting. A theological seminary was founded in Chicago in 1871, and the first denominational paper was launched in the same year. From 1888 to 1944 foreign missionary activities were channeled through the American Baptist Foreign Mission Society; a separation came in 1944, caused largely by a desire to become completely independent. The Swedish Conference set up its own foreign board and today has more than 140 missionaries in India, Japan, the Philippine Islands, Ethiopia, Mexico, Argentina, Brazil, and the Ivory Coast.

Following the First World War, with its intensified nationalistic conflicts, the transition from Swedish to English in church services was greatly accelerated and practically completed in three decades. In 1945 the word "Swedish" was dropped from the name of the conference; it had already been dropped largely by the local churches. With the language barrier removed, the growth of the conference has been rapid and far-reaching. Home missionaries are at work in all northern states, in some of the southern states, and Canada; one of their most effective organizations is the Evangelism Corps, made up of young lay volunteers who spend a year in concentrated home missions work.

The conference owns and controls Bethel College and Seminary at St. Paul, Minnesota (a 4-year college and a 3-year theological school with 1,500 students). Affiliated are 2 children's homes, 7 homes for the aged, and a Hebrew mission. Six periodicals, including *The Standard,* official denominational organ, are issued by the Board of Communication. Harvest Publications offers Bibles, books, and Sunday school materials.

Basically their doctrine is that of "theological conservatives, with unqualified acceptance of the Word of God," holding the usual Baptist tenets. They are a strong fellowship of churches, insistent upon the major beliefs of conservative Christianity but with respect and room for individual differences on minor points.

The conference tends to become more and more inclusive and to appeal to people of all nationalities. Actually about 50 percent of their pastors are not even of Swedish descent, and a large number of their churches contain very few Swedes. The transition has been fast because of the lack of Swedish immigrants and also because of the Swedes's quick assimilation into the American way of life.

Baptist Missionary Association of America

Organized at Little Rock, Arkansas, in May, 1950, as the North American Baptist Association and changing its name to the Baptist Missionary Association in 1968, these Baptists concentrate on fostering and encouraging missionary cooperation. It has had a startling growth, enrolling 1,500 churches and 218,361 members in 25 states. They have 16 workers in the home missions field, and missionary work abroad in Mexico, Japan, Brazil, Formosa, Portugal, Cape Verde Islands, Uruguay, Guatemala, Costa Rica,

Nicaragua, Australia, Italy, France, Africa, India, Bolivia, and the Philippines. A strong publications department issues literature for Sunday school and training classes, pamphlets, books, tracts, and magazines in English and Spanish. They also own and operate a printing business in Brazil, where literature is printed in Portuguese for use in Africa and Europe. A worldwide radio ministry is also maintained.

They are militant fundamentalists, claiming to hold the historic Baptist faith and placing strong emphasis upon the verbal inspiration and accuracy of the Scriptures, direct creation, the virgin birth and deity of Jesus, his blood atonement, justification by faith, salvation by grace alone, and the imminent, personal return of Christ to the Earth. They brand as unscriptural open Communion, alien baptism, pulpit affiliation with heretical ministers, unionism, modernism, modern conventionism, one-church dictatorship, and "all the kindred evils arising from these practices." The Lord's Supper and baptism are accepted as ordinances; baptism is considered "alien" unless administered to believers only and by "divine authority as given to the Missionary Baptist churches."

Churches are completely autonomous in the Baptist tradition and have an equal voice in the cooperative missionary, publication, evangelical, and educational efforts of the association regardless of size or membership. Member churches must, however, conform to the doctrinal standards of the association and deny alien baptism and modernism in all its forms.

There are 3 junior colleges, maintained on a state level, and several orphans' homes. A theological seminary is located at Jacksonville, Texas.

Bethel Ministerial Association

Founded as the Evangelistic Ministerial Alliance at Evansville, Indiana, in May of 1934, this body was incorporated as the Bethel Baptist Assembly under the laws of the state of Indiana on March 16, 1960. There are 4,000 members in 25 churches, 49 ordained clergy, and 5 Sabbath schools with an enrollment of 530. Details on doctrine, organization, etc., are available from headquarters at Box 5353, Evansville, Indiana 47715.

Central Baptist Association

This is an association formed in 1956; it is composed of 40 Baptist churches in Virginia, Tennessee, Kentucky, Indiana, Michigan, and South Carolina. Present membership is approximately 5,000. Following usual Baptist doctrine and polity, its officers have no jurisdiction over the member churches. A tabernacle and children's home are located at Jasper, Virginia.

Christian Unity Baptist Association

The Christian Unity Baptist Association was organized in 1934 as the result of a dispute over the question of open and closed Communion in the Macedonia Baptist Association in North Carolina. The dissenters believed

46

that all Christians in all denominations should be admitted to participation in the Lord's Supper. They are one of the smaller Baptist groups, numbering 345 members in 5 churches.

They believe in one God and the Trinity and in the Bible as the inspired Word of God; that all mankind is fallen and helpless to save itself but can experience regeneration through a universal atonement; in the redemption of "the bodies of the saints," infants, and idiots; that sinners reach God by way of repentance and faith; that the only 2 authorized ordinances are baptism of believers and the Lord's Supper; in foot washing; in the resurrection of the just and the unjust "who shall endure to the end to be saved"; in the everlasting reward of the righteous and the eternal punishment of the wicked.

Government is strictly congregational; there is one association for advisory purposes only. Work centers largely in home missions, evangelism, revivals, prayer meetings, and Sunday schools.

Conservative Baptist Association of America

The Conservative Baptist Association of America is officially described as a

voluntary fellowship of sovereign, autonomous, independent and Bible-believing Baptist churches working together to extend the Baptist testimony. . . . The Association is wholly separated from all other organizations, Baptist as well as non-Baptist. The several churches are held together, not by elaborate machinery, but by a common abiding love for the work and person of Jesus Christ, and the Word of God, as well as love for and confidence in one another.

The founders of the association were active in an earlier organization known as the Fundamentalist Fellowship, which was founded in 1920 within the American (then the Northern) Baptist Convention. This was a group of conservative churchmen who opposed what they considered to be the infiltration of liberal and modernistic tendencies and teachings within that convention. The basic disagreement was doctrinal and had to do with fundamentally different views and interpretations of the Scriptures and of Baptistic theology. The dispute was aggravated by the "inclusive" policy of the American Baptist Foreign Mission Society under which missionaries of conservative and liberal theologies were sent out to home and foreign fields.

Formally organized on May 17, 1947, at Atlantic City, New Jersey, and working under a constitution adopted at Milwaukee in 1948, this is exactly what the name suggests: an *association* of local, conservative Baptist churches. As an association, it must be distinguished from the Conservative Baptist *movement* in the United States. Several conservative Baptist institutions—such as the Conservative Baptist Foreign Mission Society and the Conservative Baptist Home Mission Society and a number of schools and colleges—function as part of the movement but are completely separate and autonomous and in no way officially connected with or controlled by the Conservative Baptist Association of America.

The work of the association includes the building of a fellowship of churches; assisting churches in Sunday school work, evangelism, Bible teaching, missions, organization, and building projects; establishing state associations and aiding in related projects; challenging and aiding established churches in the planting of new churches; encouraging the creation of agencies and institutions; serving in pastoral placement; printing and distributing tracts, pamphlets, and books; endorsing chaplains for the United States armed forces; "presenting a positive testimony to and opposing departure from the Old and New Testaments as God's inspired Word and the historic Baptist distinctives."

Doctrinally they stand for the infallibility of the Scriptures; God as Father, perfect in holiness, infinite in wisdom, measureless in power; Christ as the eternal and only begotten Son of God, his sinlessness, virgin birth, atonement, resurrection, and ascension; the sinfulness of all men and the possibility of their regeneration, sanctification, and comfort through Christ and the Holy Spirit; the church as the living body of Christ, with him as head; the local church as free from interference by any ecclesiastical or political authority; the responsibility of every human being to God alone; and the ordinances of baptism and the Lord's Supper.

Associational and regional officers are elected at annual meetings; a board of directors is made up of the associational officials and 18 regional representatives, elected for 3-year terms. The membership totals 300,000 in 1,111 churches.

Duck River (and Kindred) Associations of Baptists
(Baptist Church of Christ)

Confined to 4 southern states, the Duck River Baptists originated in a protest movement within the old Elk River Association which was strongly Calvinistic. This came in 1825; in 1843 the ranks of the dissenters were broken by a dispute over the legitimacy of missions and the support of a publication society and of a denominational school. Those who withdrew became known as Missionary Baptists and in a few instances as Separate Baptists or the Baptist Churches of Christ. The division persists; there are today 2 Duck River associations.

Doctrinally they are liberally Calvinistic; they hold that "Christ tasted death for every man"; that God will save those who come to him on gospel terms; that sinners are justified by faith; that the saints will "persevere in grace." They stand for believer's baptism by immersion and celebrate the Lord's Supper and foot washing as scriptural ordinances. They admit their close gospel ties with Regular, United, and Separate Baptists.

They are congregational in government, with 8 separate Associations that meet annually for fellowship in a General Association: Duck River, Mt. Zion, Mt. Pleasant No. 1, Mt. Pleasant No. 2, New Liberty, Original East Union, East Union, and Union. The 2 Mt. Pleasant Associations are located in Alabama, Tennessee, Mississippi, and Georgia. The other 6 are located in Tennessee.

There is a "correspondence" relationship with other associations in Alabama, Tennessee, Mississippi, and Georgia. Membership is by vote of local congregations; their ministers are ordained by the vote of 2 or more ministers.

There are, as of 1977, 10,857 members in 101 churches.

Evangelical Free Baptist Church

Incorporated on June 1, 1978, by the state of Illinois, this church withdrew from the Southern Baptist Convention following a doctrinal dispute. It is made up of 22 churches with 2,567 members. The churches, while cooperative, are completely autonomous and self-governing. Church officers and area bishops of the mother church in DuPage County, Illinois, serve a lifetime term of office; trustees are elected for 5-year terms.

Forty-one full-time chaplains serve in state and private institutions and 23 evangelists work part-time as volunteers. The church cooperates in work with hot lines and coffeehouses and has a missionary work in Mexico through the Living Word Outreach. It maintains an elementary school (Providence Bible Academy) in New Jersey.

Free Will Baptists

The rise of the Free Will Baptists can be traced to the influence of Arminian-minded Baptists who migrated to the colonies from England. The denomination organized on two fronts at almost the same time. The southern line, or Palmer movement, began in 1727 when Paul Palmer established a church at Chowan, North Carolina. The northern line, or Randall movement, began with a congregation organized by Benjamin Randall in 1780 in New Durham, New Hampshire. Both groups taught the doctrines of free grace, free salvation, and free will. There were gestures toward union of the northern and southern groups, but the outbreak of the Civil War prevented it. The northern body extended more rapidly in the beginning into the West and Southwest. In 1910 this line of Free Will Baptists merged with the Northern Baptist denomination, taking along 857 of its 1,100 churches, all its denominational property, and several colleges. In 1916 representatives of remnant churches from the Randall movement reorganized into the Cooperative General Association of Free Will Baptists.

The southern churches organized into new associations and conferences and finally into a General Conference by 1921. The division continued until November 5, 1935, when the 2 groups merged at Nashville into the National Association of Free Will Baptists.

Doctrinally, they hold that Christ gave himself as a ransom for all, not just the elect; that God calls all of us to repentance; and that whosoever will, may be saved. Baptism is by immersion. This is one of the few Baptist groups practicing open Communion. They also practice foot washing. Government

49

is strictly congregational. There are 4 Bible colleges, 1 liberal arts college, and 240,000 members in 40 states with 2,500 churches.

General Baptists

The General Baptists claim their name and origin in John Smyth and Thomas Helwys and the group of Baptists organized in England and Holland in 1611 (see general article on the Baptists, pp. 34-35). They hold Roger Williams to be their first minister in the American colonies.

The General Baptists in the colonies along the Atlantic coast were at first overwhelmed by the influence of Calvinism (General Baptists have always been Arminian), but their work was reopened by Benoni Stinson with the establishment of the Liberty Baptist Church in what is now Evansville, Indiana, in 1823. They spread into Illinois and Kentucky, and a general association of General Baptists was organized in 1870. Since that time they have grown steadily; today they are strong in Kentucky, Tennessee, Indiana, Michigan, Illinois, Missouri, and Arkansas, and have located churches in Oklahoma, Nebraska, Kansas, Iowa, Arizona, California, Florida, Ohio, and Mississippi.

Their confession of faith is similar to that of the Free Will Baptists; it is their belief that Christ died for all men; that failure to achieve salvation lies completely with the individual; that man is depraved and fallen and unable to save himself; that regeneration is necessary for salvation except in the case of infants and idiots, who are not responsible for sin; that salvation comes by repentance and faith in Christ; that the Christian who perseveres to the end is saved; that the wicked are punished eternally. The dead, just and unjust, will be raised at the judgment; the Lord's Supper and believer's baptism by immersion are the only authorized Christian ordinances and should be open to all believers. Some of the General Baptist churches practice foot washing.

Church polity is about the same as that found in all Baptist churches. The denomination is congregational in church government. Churches of a common area are organized into local associations that are in turn organized into a general association. Both local and general associations are representative bodies and advisory in power. A peculiar feature of the General Baptists lies in their use of a presbytery, into which the ordained members of local associations are grouped; they examine candidates for the ministry and for the diaconate. Ministers and deacons are responsible to this presbytery, which exists only on the local level.

Current statistics show 866 churches with a total membership of 73,000. They maintain at Oakland City, Indiana, a liberal arts college with a theological department. A publishing house is operated at Poplar Bluff, Missouri, where their monthly paper, *General Baptist Messenger*, is issued together with Sunday school literature.

Foreign missionary work is supported in Guam, Saipan, Jamaica, and the Philippines. They have an active home missionary work in various states.

General Association of Regular Baptist Churches

Twenty-two Baptist churches of the American Baptist Convention left that convention in May of 1932 to found the General Association of Regular Baptist Churches. The protest was against what they considered to be modernist tendencies and teachings in the American Convention, the denial of the historic Baptist principle of the independence and autonomy of the local congregation, the inequality of representation in the assemblies of the convention, the control of missionary work by convention assessment and budget, and the whole convention principle in general.

Any Baptist church coming into this association is required to "withdraw all fellowship and cooperation from any convention or group which permits modernists or modernism within its ranks." Dual fellowship or membership is not permitted. Participation in union evangelical campaigns, union Thanksgiving services, or membership in local ministerial associations where modernists are involved or present is considered to be unscriptural.

Missionary work is conducted through 5 approved Baptist agencies completely independent of any convention and completely orthodox; a close watch is maintained upon these agencies before annual approval is granted. Likewise, only 9 schools are approved; these, too, are "guarded" against any defection from approved practice or doctrine.

The association subscribes to the New Hampshire Confession of Faith with a premillennial interpretation of the final article of that confession. It holds to the infallibility of the Bible, the Trinity, and personality of Satan as the author of all evil, man as the creation of God, and man born in sin. There are doctrines dealing with the virgin birth and the deity of Jesus and faith in Christ as the way of salvation through grace. The saved are in everlasting felicity, and the lost are consigned to endless punishment. There is a bodily resurrection; Christ rose and ascended and will return premillennially to reign in the millennium. Civil government is by divine appointment. There are only 2 approved ordinances: baptism by immersion and the Lord's Supper.

Church government is strictly congregational. Associated churches have the privilege of sending 6 voting messengers to an annual convention; thus a church with 50 members has the same power as a church with 2,500 members. A Council of Eighteen is elected—9 each year—to serve for 2 years. It makes recommendations to the association for the furtherance of its work and implements and puts into operation all actions and policies of the association, and its authority depends completely upon the will and direction of the association.

In 1978 there were 1,544 churches in fellowship with 236,000 members. The 9 approved schools had a total student body of more than 5,000 and 2,026 missionaries were at work in the 5 missionary agencies. State and regional associations have been established across the country; these are supplied with literature published by the Regular Baptist Press, including *The Baptist Bulletin,* a monthly magazine.

General Conference of the
Evangelical Baptist Church, Inc.

The Evangelical Baptists were organized among the members of several Free Will Baptist churches in 1935; they were formerly known as the Church of the Full Gospel, Incorporated.

Their doctrine is Arminian, Wesleyan, and premillennial; organization is similar to that of the Free Will Baptists, with whom they are still in close fellowship. They exchange pastors regularly with the Wilmington Conference of the Free Will Baptist Church. As of 1952, there were about 2,200 members in 31 churches.

Landmark Baptists

"Landmarkism" among Baptists is a position held by some concerning the nature of the church and certain details of church practice. The name originated with the writings of Dr. James Madison Pendleton and Dr. James Robinson Graves in Kentucky and Tennessee in the latter part of the nineteenth century, though Landmarkers insist that their concepts go back to the apostolic period.

There are 4 distinguishing tenets of Landmarkism:

1. The church is only vocal and visible. The expression "the church" is used only when speaking of it as an institution. All saved people make up "the family of God," not "the church." While members of other churches may be saved, they are not members of true churches.

2. The "commission" was given to the church; consequently, all matters covered by it must be administered under church authority. Ministers of other denominations are not accepted in Landmark Baptist pulpits.

3. Baptism to be valid must be administered by the authority of a New Testament (Baptist) church. Baptisms administered by any other authority are not accepted.

4. There is a direct, historic "succession" of Baptist churches back to New Testament times; that is, Baptist churches have existed in practice in every century, though not by name.

These principles are held primarily by the churches of the American Baptist Association, though there are an estimated 1,500,000 members of different Baptist churches that hold to the Landmark position and doctrine.

National Baptist Evangelical Life and
Soul Saving Assembly of the U.S.A.

This assembly was founded in 1920 at Kansas City, Missouri, not as another denomination, but as an evangelical group working within the National Baptist Convention (Unincorporated). It had the endorsement of the parent body for 17 years but became an independent group in 1937.

No new doctrine is set forth by this group; it has no doctrine except the "Bible doctrine as announced by the Founder of the Church, Jesus Christ." Concentration is mainly upon evangelical and relief efforts. The assembly maintains an "automatic" correspondence school offering courses in evangelology, deaconology, missionology, pastorology, and laymanology; degrees are granted in 60, 90, and 120 days.

In 1951, 57,674 members and 264 churches were reported.

National Primitive Baptist Convention of the U.S.A.
(Formerly Colored Primitive Baptists)

The black population of the South all through the years of slavery and the Civil War worshiped with the white population in their various churches. This was true of Colored Primitive Baptists, who attended white Primitive Baptist churches until the time of the emancipation, when their white brethren helped them to establish their own churches, granting them letters of fellowship and character, ordaining their deacons and ministers, and helping in other ways.

Their doctrine and polity are quite the same as in the white Primitive Baptist organization, except that they are "opposed to all forms of church organization"; yet there are local associations and a national convention, organized in 1907. Each church is independent, receiving and controlling its own membership; there is no appeal from a decision of the officers of the local church.

They have a membership of 250,000 in 606 churches. Unlike the white Primitive Baptists, they have since 1900 been establishing aid societies, conventions, and Sunday schools over the opposition of the older and more orthodox members.

North American Baptist Conference

The churches in this conference began in German Baptist churches established on our soil by German Baptist immigrants of more than a century ago. The first of them settled in New Jersey and Pennsylvania—where Penn's Quakers offered them the perfect chance at the religious freedom they sought in flight from the mother country. The scattered German Baptist churches later became the North American Baptist General Conference and organized their first local churches during 1840–51.

The prosperity of these German Baptist churches followed the rise and fall of German immigration. By 1851 they had 8 churches and 405 members, and in that year they organized their churches into an Eastern Conference for fellowship and mutual consideration of common problems.

The local conference idea was enlarged as their churches increased. As their membership moved across the nation, they organized a total of 9 such conferences following geographical lines. In 1865 they held a joint meeting of Eastern and Western Conferences and called it a general conference. The Triennial Conference is now their chief administrative unit.

Twenty-one associations meet annually, elect their own officers and missionary committees, and guide their own work. The general conference meets triennially and is made up of all churches in the 9 local conferences and has clerical and lay representation from all of them. It superintends the work in publication, education, missions, and homes for children and the aged. A general council acts for the conference between its sessions.

The German Baptists participated in the development of what is now Colgate-Rochester Divinity School in Rochester, New York. In 1935 they established a seminary of their own known as the North American Baptist Seminary, which relocated from Rochester to Sioux Falls, South Dakota, in 1949. The North American Baptist College is located at Edmonton, Alberta, Canada. There are 7 homes for the aged. Home missions are conducted among Spanish Americans in the United States; foreign missionaries are located in Nigeria and the United Republic of Cameroon, West Africa, Japan, and Brazil.

Theologically, there is little variance here from the usual Baptist position: North American Baptists in general follow the New Hampshire Confession, stressing the authority of the Scriptures, the revelation of God in Christ, regeneration, immersion, separation of church and state, the congregational form of government, and have a very strong emphasis on missions. There are 57,218 members in 356 churches.

Primitive Baptists

The Primitive Baptists have the reputation of being the most strictly orthodox and exclusive of all Baptists. Unique in that they have never been organized as a denomination and have no administrative bodies of any kind (they believe that each church should "govern itself according to the laws of Christ as found in the New Testament, and that no minister, association, or convention has any authority"), they represent a protest against "money-based" missions and benevolent societies and against "assessing" the churches to support missions, missionaries, and Sunday schools. The position taken was that there were no missionary societies in the days of the apostles, and therefore there should be none now. Apart from this, there was objection to the centralization of authority in these societies. Sunday schools also were unauthorized by Scripture; they believed in the religious training of children but not in Sunday schools. They stood for evangelism as a missionary effort, but on individual responsibility and at individual expense and not under the sponsorship of a money-based society. Spearheading the protest, the Kehukee Association in North Carolina in 1827 condemned all such money-based and authoritarian societies as being contrary to Christ's teachings. Within a decade, several other Baptist associations across the country made similar statements and withdrew from other Baptist churches.

The various associations adopted the custom of printing in their annual minutes a statement of their articles of faith, their constitution, and their rules of order. These statements were examined by every other association, and if they were approved, there was fellowship and exchange of messengers and correspondence among them; any association not so approved was dropped from the fellowship. Added to this was the difficulty of communication in many parts of the South. The result was confusion; there was no chance under such conditions for growth as a denomination and little chance even for a fellowship or quasi unity. This is apparent in the variety of names, some friendly and some derisive, that have been applied to them, such as "Primitive," "Old School," "Regular," "Anti-mission," and "Hard Shell." In general, the term "Primitive" has been widely accepted and used.

A strong Calvinism runs through their doctrine. In general they believe that by Adam's fall all posterity became sinners; that human nature is completely corrupt; and that man cannot by his own efforts regain favor with God. God elected his own people in Christ before the world began, and none of these saints will be finally lost. The 2 biblically authorized ordinances are the Lord's Supper and baptism of believers by immersion. All church societies are the invention of men and are to be denied fellowship; Christ will come a second time to raise the dead, judge all men, punish forever the wicked and reward forever the righteous; the Old and New Testaments are verbally and infallibly inspired.

Ministers must be called of God, come under the laying on of hands, and be in fellowship with the local church of which they are members before they can administer the 2 ordinances; they are to deny to any other clergyman lacking these qualifications the right to administer such ordinances. No theological training is demanded of ministers among Primitive Baptists; while there is no opposition to such education, the position is that the Lord will call an educated man if he wants one, but that lack of education should not bar a man from the ministry. Some Primitive Baptists still practice foot washing, but not all do. In spite of their opposition to money-based missionary societies, they are intensely evangelistic, and their preachers travel widely and serve without charge, except when their hearers wish to contribute to their support.

Membership is granted only after careful examination and vote of the congregation. Membership is estimated at 72,000 in 1,000 churches, but the figure is probably larger. Factionalism, divisiveness, and politics prevent an accurate report on membership.

Reformed Baptists

Reformed Baptists are a fellowship of churches rather than a denomination. The fellowship is made up of some 150 to 200 congregations, not all of which use the name "Reformed," and some do not wish to be called Baptists. The bond that unites them is a strict adherence to "5-point Calvinism": belief in the Calvinistic tenets of total depravity, unconditional election, limited and definite atonement, irresistible (or invincible) calling, and the perseverance of all true saints. They also advocate the doctrines of the Synod of Dordt, the Westminster Assembly, "the Anabaptist doctrines of a called-out church," and the Philadelphia Confession. The churches involved are completely autonomous and independently, as local churches, support an unlisted number of missionaries and the publishing of church literature. No report on membership is available.

Separate Baptists in Christ
(General Association of Separate Baptists)

The first Separate Baptists arrived in the United States in 1695 as one refugee section of the separatist movement in England. They were especially active during the days of the blazing preaching of Whitefield in the early eighteenth century and in the conflict between the Old Light and New Light sects. Separate Baptist churches of this period were marked by their milder Calvinism.

In 1787 Separate and Regular Baptist churches merged in Virginia in the United Baptist Churches of Christ in Virginia. There were other mergers and gestures toward union in New England and other states, but a few Separate Baptist churches maintained their independence. In 1962 they had 84 churches and 7,496 members.

All creeds and confessions of faith are rejected by Separate Baptists; however, there is an annual statement of articles of belief by the several associations and the general association. These include statements of faith in the infallibility of the Scriptures and in the Trinity; 3 ordinances—baptism of believers by immersion only, the Lord's Supper, and foot washing; regeneration, justification, and sanctification through faith in Christ; the appearance of Christ on Judgment Day to deal with the just and the unjust. The "election, reprobation, and fatality" of Calvinism are rejected. Separate Baptists do not claim to be Protestants: "We have never protested against what we hold to be the faith once delivered to the saints."

They are congregational in government, with associations for advisory purposes only. The associations carry on a limited home missions work; there is a full-time missionary stationed in Africa, and individual members and the churches support foreign mission programs in India, and those of other denominations. A missionary periodical called *Christ for the World* is published at Tice, Florida, and a general magazine, *The Messenger*, is circulated from Kokomo, Indiana.

Seventh Day Baptist General Conference

Differing from other Baptists in their adherence to the seventh day as the Sabbath, Seventh Day Baptists (or Sabbatarian Baptists, as they were called in England) first organized themselves as a separate body on this side of the Atlantic in 1672 at Newport, Rhode Island. Stephen Mumford, a member of the Bell Lane Seventh Day Baptist Church in London, had come there knowing well the perils of religious nonconformity and had entered into covenant relation with those who withdrew from "Doctor John Clarke's (Baptist) Church" under the Sabbath persuasion. Other churches were organized in Philadelphia and in New Jersey. From these 3 centers Seventh Day Baptists went west with the frontier; they now have 5,156 members in 60 churches and fellowships.

Belief in salvation through faith in Christ, believer's baptism by immersion, insistence upon intellectual and civil liberty and the right of every man to interpret the Bible "for himself under God" have characterized this people. They hold baptism and the Lord's Supper only as ordinances, practice open Communion, and have fostered 1 university and 2 colleges.

Local churches enjoy complete independence, although all of them support the united benevolence of the denomination known as Our World Mission. For fellowship and service the churches are organized into 8 regional associations, and these often assist local church councils in the ordination of deacons and ministerial candidates. The highest administrative body is the general conference, which meets annually and delegates interim responsibilities to its president, executive secretary, and general council. The conference promotes world mission giving and channels it through mission, publishing, and educational agencies. It also accredits ministers certified to it by ordaining councils and local churches. The denomination participates in the ecumenical movement at local, regional, national, and world levels. The Seventh Day Baptist World Federation, an organization of Seventh Day Baptist conferences, includes conferences in Brazil, Burma, Central Africa (Malawi), England, Germany, Guyana, India, Jamaica, Mexico, Holland, New Zealand, the Philippines, and the United States.

Two-Seed-in-the-Spirit Predestinarian Baptists

Tracing their thought back to the Waldenses, the Two-Seed-in-the-Spirit Predestinarian Baptists in this country began in the late eighteenth century with the protests of Elder Daniel Parker against missions and Sunday schools. Parker opposed the Arminian doctrine of the Methodists and based his dislike of the missionary effort and church schools on what he called his Two-Seed Doctrine. This, briefly, is the conviction that two seeds entered the life stream of humanity in the garden of Eden. One seed was good, planted by God; the other was evil, from the devil. The two seeds have been in conflict in humanity ever since. Every baby is predestined, born with one seed or the other. Nothing can be done for him one way or another. Inasmuch as nothing can be done, missions are useless; they are, moreover, an institution that "usurps the privileges of God."

The seed is in the spirit, not the flesh; this is the cardinal point in the theology of the group. Other points include belief in the resurrection of the body of Christ, which is the church, and salvation by grace alone. The church observes the Lord's Supper and practices foot washing. There is no paid ministry "inasmuch as Christ came to save sinners, and He finished his work." Government is congregational; there are associations for fellowship only. There are no home missions or benevolences. The membership is decreasing; there were 201 members and 16 churches in 1945.

United Baptists

The United Baptists represent a merging of several groups of Separate and Regular Baptists mainly in the states of Virginia, Kentucky, and the Carolinas. While these groups were bodies holding both Arminian and Calvinistic theologies, they maintained a perfect freedom in preaching and polity after their union. As the years passed, many of their members found their way into either the Northern or Southern Baptist conventions; but they are still recognized as a separate denomination with 63,641 members in 568 churches. Their first organization was in Richmond, Virginia, in 1787; a second group organized in Kentucky in 1801. Two associations—Salem and Elkhorn (Regular Baptists) and South Kentucky (Separate Baptists)—joined to form the United Baptists.

Doctrinally there are still traces of Arminianism and Calvinism. Generally they hold that salvation is by grace rather than by works and conditional upon gospel requirements. All men are in a state of general depravity and are commanded to repent; they are led either to repentance through the goodness of God or to rebellion by the devil. It is a matter of individual choice.

There are 26 associations for fellowship and counsel quite independent of one another yet working together closely. They practice closed Communion in some associations and churches, open Communion in others. There are 3 ordinances—baptism, the Lord's Supper, and (in most churches) foot washing.

United Free Will Baptist Church

While they trace their history back to the same original sources of the white Free Will Baptist Church, the United Free Will Baptists (Colored) have been independent since their official organization in 1901. Their members are found largely in North Carolina, Georgia, Florida, Mississippi, Louisiana, and Texas.

Although in general agreement with the congregational polity of other Baptist bodies, this church grants a rather limited autonomy to the local church. There is a system of quarterly, annual, and general conferences, with graded authority. Doctrinal disputes may be carried up to the general conferences; district conferences may exclude members from fellowship.

Doctrinally they are in agreement with white churches of the same faith. There is one institution of higher learning—Kinston College at Kinston, North Carolina. There were 100,000 members in 836 churches in 1952.

BEREAN FUNDAMENTAL CHURCH

The Berean Fundamental Church has its origin in the work of Dr. Ivan E. Olsen in a small independent church in North Platte, Nebraska, in 1936. This became the mother church of a Berean Fellowship. In 1947 the Berean Church Council, Inc., was formed; this is the legal title for the present Berean Fellowship of Churches. Since this time, they have established 52 churches in 9 states: California, Colorado, Kansas, Minnesota, Missouri, South Dakota, Oregon, Wyoming, and, largely, in Nebraska.

They stress the standard fundamental doctrines of the inerrancy of the

Bible in all matters of faith and morals, the Virgin Birth, the literal bodily resurrection, the reality of heaven and hell, etc. Strongly Bible-centered, they are active in evangelistic efforts; unaffiliated with any denomination, it has no Sunday school curriculum or church literature; the churches are left free to choose for themselves from the publications of other (Fundamentalist) churches. They maintain a Bible camp near North Platte, Nebraska, but have no Bible training schools or seminaries.

BIBLE FELLOWSHIP CHURCH

This body, strongly evangelical in purpose and effort, was founded in 1858 and today consists of 43 congregations in Pennsylvania, New Jersey, and New York. Its doctrinal emphases include salvation through the death and resurrection of Christ, transformed life through new birth by the Holy Spirit, the authority and trustworthiness of the Bible as the Word of God, the culmination of history in the second coming of Jesus and "a shared-life in the church of believers, with every member-responsibility for the propagation of the Gospel by evangelism and missions."

The Fellowship churches support missions on five continents, Pinebrook Junior College, Victory Valley Camp for children and youths, a Home for the Aging and Pinebrook-in-the-Pines, a conference and retreat center, in Pennsylvania.

BIBLE PROTESTANT CHURCH

The churches in this body represent a break in the Eastern Conference of the Methodist Protestant Church in 1939, when some 50 delegates (approximately one-third of the Conference) withdrew in protest of the union of the Methodist Protestant Church with the Methodist Episcopal Church and the Methodist Episcopal Church, South, and what the withdrawing group considered to be the modernistic tendencies of those churches. While the church operated under its original charter of the Eastern Conference, the name was subsequently changed to the Bible Protestant Church.

Doctrine here is conservative; this church is a member of the fundamentalist American Christian Churches. Cardinal points in their belief emphasize the verbal inspiration of the Bible; the Trinity; the deity, virgin birth, resurrection, and ascension of Jesus; salvation by faith in his blood and sacrifice, death, and resurrection. There is a strong faith in premillennialism with eternal punishment for the wicked and eternal joy for the righteous believer. Baptism and the Lord's Supper are practiced as divine institutions.

Their churches are confined to New Jersey, New York, Pennsylvania, Massachusetts, Connecticut, Virginia, and Michigan. Actually they are a fellowship of self-governing churches, organized in a conference that meets annually with lay and clerical representation. The chief officer is the president, who holds office for not more than 3 years. All local churches own and control their own property; all contributions to the conference are voluntary and not by assessment; and local churches call their own ministers from the conference roll of ministers or from other churches approved by the Committee on Ministerial Qualifications; formal assignment of the pastor is by a pastoral relations committee of the conference. Candidates for ordination must be graduates of high school and an approved seminary or Bible school. Missionary work is conducted in Japan and among migrant workers in America, and Bible Protestant missionaries are serving in Mexico and Germany under the mission boards of other churches. There are 40 churches, 2,245 members.

BIBLE WAY CHURCH, WORLD WIDE

At a ministerial conference of black Pentecostal ministers in September, 1957, some 70 churches withdrew from the Church of Our Lord of the Apostolic Faith to form the Bible Way Church, World Wide. Their doctrine and teaching remain quite the same as that of the parent body. A phenomenal growth is reported from the original 70 churches to 350 churches and something over 100,000 members, at home and abroad. A general conference is held annually in July; a publishing house at Washington, D.C., circulates periodicals, religious pamphlets, and recordings.

BLACK MUSLIMS

The Black Muslim movement in the United States began with the founding of a Moorish Science Temple in Newark, New Jersey, by Timothy Drew. Drew took the name Noble Drew Ali and preached that the American blacks were actually Moors whose forefathers had lived in Morocco. His followers divided into several groups when he died in 1920; one group was led by Wallace D. Fard in Detroit. Calling himself the reincarnation of Noble Drew Ali, he taught "The Religion of the Black Men of Asia and Africa," a teaching based at first on the Bible and the Mohammedan Koran. But Fard was soon attacking the Bible and announcing himself as a tool in the hands of Allah. The black people, he said, were gods; the white man was the serpent devil and would ultimately be destroyed. He disappeared mysteriously in 1933, and soon after his death his followers were claiming that he was Allah personified—God, the Son of Man, the Savior. He was succeeded by the late Elijah Poole, known as Elijah Muhammad, who traced black ancestry back to men living on the moon 66 trillion years ago.

Elijah Mohammad continued to preach Fard's gospel of black rebellion and revolution which would rid the blacks of white domination and give them their rightful place (as an independent nation) within the United States. Building on the desperate conditions of poverty and underprivilege in the black ghetto areas, the movement spread across the country and increased a militant membership that became of national interest at once religiously, politically, socially, and economically.

Elijah Muhammad went to prison when he advised his younger followers to resist the draft; in prison he converted Malcolm Little (better known as Malcom X) to his cause. (The Black Muslims spurn their "white-given, slave-masters names" and use the X to represent their unknown true names.) The flaming preaching of Malcom X helped build the membership to more than 30,000, but disagreements developed between Malcom X and Elijah Muhammad, and the membership began to decline when Malcom X was murdered in New York City in 1965.

Today membership claims vary from 100,000 to 750,000; some students of the movement think it much less than 100,000. The followers—and nonregistered sympathizers—are generally (nearly 80 percent) young male blacks between 17 and 35 years of age, living in city ghettos, ex-Christian or anti-Christian and anti-white, completely devoted to Elijah Muhammad's idea of the establishment of a separate black state (The Black Nation of Islam) in this country. They are not recognized as a legitimate branch of Islam by the orthodox Middle East Muslims, much as they desire that, but they claim that they accept and practice Mohammedan principles and teachings in everything but their extreme racism. Allah is to them the one true God, and they use the Koran and the traditional Moslem rituals in their temple services.

Marred as it is by violence, their movement has some very definite accomplishments on the positive side. They have established a chain of industries to relieve black poverty—barber shops, supermarkets, bakeries, restaurants, cleaning establishments, and farms. Black Muslims do not gamble, smoke, drink, overeat, or buy on credit. They arrange parole for their convicts and offer postprison guidance. Their claim that they "give black men their self-respect" has at least that element of truth; they have reached many whom the church has been unable to reach, and that may account for much of their popularity among some blacks.

BRETHREN (DUNKERS)

The terms "Brethren" and "Dunkers" have been the cause of much confusion; they call for careful definition. Dunker is a direct derivation of the German word *tunken*, "to dip or immerse." It is a word to be identified with the peculiar method of immersion employed by this group of churches: trine immersion, in which the believer on his knees in the water is immersed not once but 3 times in the name of the Father, Son, and Holy Ghost. Variously through their long history the Dunkers have been called Tunkers, Täufers, or Dompelaars. They were first called Brethren when their first church organization was established at Schwarzenau, Germany, in 1708.

It might be said generally that these Dunker, or Brethren, bodies are former German Reformed who took their theology and much of their practice from the Pietists of the seventeenth and eighteenth centuries in Germany. The Pietists, who were mosly Lutherans, became unhappy with the formalism of worship and ritual in their state church and with the general "barrenness" of German Protestantism. They took the New Testament literally and endeavored to put its teachings into practice in the least detail of their living. They spurned the idea of apostolic succesion, and at the heart of their practice they had a love feast, or agape, which was the serving of the Lord's Supper preceded by a ceremony of foot washing. They saluted one another with a "kiss of peace," dressed in the plainest clothing, covered the heads of women at services, anointed their sick with oil for healing and consecration, refrained from worldly amusements, refused to take oaths, go to war, or engage in lawsuits. These doctrines and practices are held today by many Brethren with certain modifications.

From these German Pietists came the Church of the Brethren (Conservative Dunkers), the Brethren Church (Progressive Dunkers), the Old German Baptist Brethren (Old Order Dunkers), and the Church of God (New Dunkers, disbanded in August, 1962). Another Brethren group, unrelated historically to these and known as the River Brethren, also took its ideology from the German Pietists. This group includes the Brethren in Christ, the Old Order (or Yorker) Brethren, and United Zion Church (formerly United Zion's Children). A third Brethren body known as the Plymouth Brethren has a British rather than a German background.

The Brethren bodies beginning in Germany were known for years simply as German Baptist Brethren; that title has largely disappeared except in the case of the Old German Baptist Brethren (Old Order Dunkers).

Church of the Brethren

The Church of the Brethren began in 1708 with a church of 8 persons in Schwarzenau, Germany. Persecuted and driven from Central Germany into Holland and Northern Germany, one group of the church in Krefeld, Germany, under the leadership of Peter Becker, came to America in 1719 to take up free lands offered them by William Penn. They settled in Germantown, near Philadelphia, where they were joined in 1729 by 59 families brought across the Atlantic by Alexander Mack. From Pennsylvania they spread across the country.

Their German speech, their opposition to war, and their insistence upon the inner Christian life as more important than church organization made them a suspect group from the start. Morally they opposed the Revolution; in the Civil War they opposed slavery. The suspicion and misunderstanding waned as time went on; today historians are generous in their praise of the contributions of the Brethren to American democracy. In our own day the work of their pacifists in World War II and their outstanding efforts in relief to Europe following that war have made them one of the most honored bodies in American Protestantism. In their early days at Germantown the first German Bible in America and the first religious magazine were circulated in 1743 and 1764 respectively, by Christopher Saur I, a friend of the Brethren, and by Christopher Saur II, a Brethren elder.

In 1728 a group under Conrad Beissel left the Church of the Brethren to found the famous Ephrata Community and the Seventh Day Baptists (German); and in 1848 another break resulted in the establishment of the Church of God (New Dunkers). In 1881 a third group withdrew to organize the Old German Baptist Brethren (Old Order Dunkers); and in 1882 came the worst split of all in the organizing of the Brethren Church (Progressive Brethren). In 1926, a smaller group of conservatives withdrew and formed the Dunkard Brethren Church. The original body is known today as the Church of the Brethren and has approximately 178,000 members in 1,042 churches in the United States. Overseas churches that were started as the result of missionary activity in Ecuador, Nigeria, and India are now identified with autonomous churches in those countries, but the church maintains a cooperative relationship with them.

In doctrine this church follows the mainstream of Protestant theology, with considerable freedom of thought for its members and the clergy and great emphasis on practical biblical piety. Its practical teaching is summarized in the following divisions: (1) the doctrine of peace, including refusal to go to war and a positive peacemaking program that makes them more than war resisters; (2) the doctrine of temperance, under which total abstinence is practiced; (3) the doctrine of the simple life, under which unwholesome amusements and luxuries are shunned, and a practical, wholesome, temperate, clean way of personal and family life is stressed; they seek to develop a "concerned stewardship of life rather than prohibition of amusements and overindulgence in luxuries"; (4) the doctrine of brother-hood, under which all class distinctions are opposed as unchristian; and (5) the doctrine that religion means loving and willing obedience to Christ rather than obedience to creeds and cults. Christian living rather than forms is stressed. Baptism is by trine immersion; the love feast is observed, following the pattern of John 13:1-7.

Moderators, lay or clerical, men or women, resident or nonresident, are in charge of local congregations, which enjoy a great deal of autonomy. Pastors are chosen by ballot of the local congregation. Above the local groups stands the district (there are 24) and the annual conference (a legislative body composed of delegates from the churches and an "upper house" known as the Standing Committee, made up of delegates from the districts). The annual conference is an overall unifying body.

A general board, composed of 25 members elected by the annual conference, supervises the general church program. The board administers the overseas church program. It represents the church in the field of social education, social action, relief and rehabilitation, and carries on a worldwide program of peace and human welfare. The program includes a volunteer service in America and abroad for hundreds of young men and women, including conscientious objectors to war, and other older volunteers. It supervises church schools, weekday religious education, and summer camps and is loosely related to higher education in 6 colleges. The board provides leadership and education for the ministry in locating and supporting new churches and in evangelism and carries responsibility for the printing and merchandising interests of the denomination. There is one theological seminary.

The Church of the Brethren cooperates fully with the World Council of Churches, the National Council of the Churches of Christ in the U.S.A., and with local church councils.

Fellowship of Grace Brethren Churches

Born in the 1881–83 split in the original Brethren body in the United States (mentioned above), the Brethren Church is based doctrinally on a statement of faith called the Message of the Brethren Ministry adopted in 1921. The Message included declarations of belief in the infallibility of the Scriptures; the preexistence, deity, and incarnation by virgin birth of Jesus Christ; the vicarious atonement of Christ and his resurrection; justification by personal faith in Christ; the resurrection of the dead; the judgment of the world; believer's baptism by trine immersion; the ordinances of baptism, confirmation, the Lord's Supper, Communion of the Bread and the Cup, foot washing, and anointing the sick with oil.

In 1939 a crisis in the Brethren church divided it into what came to be known as the Ashland group and the Grace group. The latter group is commonly called the National Fellowship of Brethren Churches. Both groups still carry the name of The Brethren Church and operate under one charter, but each group has its own annual conference—the Ashland body at Ashland, Ohio, and the Grace body (usually) at Winona Lake, Indiana. Each conference has its own executives and its own educational institutions and mission boards. The Grace group is more definitely congregational in government than the Ashland group. Both groups claim adherence to the Message of the Brethren Ministry, but it is generally true that the Grace group represents more nearly the Calvinistic viewpoint in theology and the Ashland group, the Arminian viewpoint.

Churches are grouped geographically into districts, which hold annual conferences. The Grace group numbers 38,176 in 242 churches, and the Ashland group numbers 16,357 in 119 churches.

Old German Baptist Brethren (Old Order Dunkers)

While the Brethren Church (Progressive Dunkers) left the Church of the Brethren (Conservative Dunkers) because the latter body seemed too conservative, the Old German Baptist Brethren (Old Order Dunkers) left it because they considered it not conservative enough. The dissenters stood literally for the old order and traditions. The salient point in their opposition lay in their suspicion of Sunday schools, salaried ministers, missions, higher education, and church societies. They withdrew in 1881.

Their basic objections still hold but with certain modifications. Children are not enrolled in Sunday schools, but they are encouraged to attend the regular services of the church and to join the church at an early age—anywhere from 15 to 20, the decision being left entirely to the individual. Many congregations list a majority of members between 15 and 40 years of age. The church today is not completely opposed even to higher education; a few of their youths enter high school and take training in college or professional schools for various professions.

They stand for a literal interpretation of the Scriptures in regard to the Lord's Supper and practice closed Communion, which excludes all but their own membership. While they advocate compliance with the ordinary demands of government, they oppose cooperation in war: "Any member who enters into military service will fall into the judgment of the Church." Noncooperation in political and secret societies is required; their dress is severely plain, and they frown on all worldly amusements. They follow other Brethren bodies in refusing to take oaths or engage in lawsuits, have no salaried ministers, enforce complete abstinence from alcoholic liquors, anoint the sick with oil, veil the heads of their women at worship, and refuse to perform a wedding ceremony for any divorced person. They have no Sunday schools, missions, or educational work. An annual conference that rules on matters "on which the Scriptures are silent" is held each year at Pentecost. There are 4,906 members in 54 churches.

PLYMOUTH BRETHREN

Restless under the close connection of church and state in nineteenth-century England and Ireland and opposing the stereotyped forms of worship in the Established Church, groups of Brethren began to meet for quiet fellowship and prayer. They had no connection, in the beginning, with the Brethren sects in Germany but took their name from the Scriptures; at one time or another they were also called Christians, Believers, or Saints. The largest meeting was held at Plymouth, England—hence the name Plymouth Brethren.

These Plymouth Brethren set up their meetings on strictly New Testament lines. They recognized no division of clergy and laity, inasmuch as they held that they were "a priesthood of all believers." They put strong emphasis upon the imminent rapture of the church—to be expected momentarily—insisted upon the full deity and real humanity of Jesus, and denied fellowship to all who were not "fundamentally sound as to doctrine and godly in walk."

Differences arose over divergent views on the effects of unsound teaching in the Plymouth Assembly, and in 1848 there came a division into Exclusive and Open Brethren. The Open Brethren held that they should receive all persons sound in faith, even though some might come from an assembly in which error was taught—if they personally rejected the error. The Exclusive Brethren held that such reception disqualified the assemblies from participation in the Circle of Fellowship, which was, and is, a joint body of approved assemblies holding a corporate unity and responsibility made up of leaders who make decisions for all constituent assemblies.

The tendencies toward division followed them to America when they came here in the late nineteenth century. Today there are 6 active bodies of Plymouth Brethren in this country, distinguished by Roman numerals.

In doctrine the various bodies are in substantial agreement; their separation is caused mainly by differences in church discipline. Generally they acknowledge no creeds; they take the Bible as their only guide, believing it to be verbally inspired and inerrant. They are Trinitarians; they hold that Christ was begotten of the Holy Spirit and born of the Virgin Mary; that man is created in God's image; that by sin he has incurred physical and spiritual death, which is separation from God; that all men are sinners, whose salvation and justification come through faith in Christ's blood, apart from works; that Christ was resurrected and ascended into heaven to abide there as high priest and advocate for the redeemed. Christ's return will be premillennial; it is imminent and personal, and he will return in glory with all his saints to judge and rule the world. All who receive him by faith are born again and thereby become the children of God. There is a bodily resurrection for the just and for the unjust, eternal reward for the righteous, and everlasting punishment for the wicked.

Plymouth Brethren hold that the true church includes all regenerated believers. There are no specific requirements for membership, but all candidates are expected to give satisfactory evidence of the new birth. They are received as "members of Christ" and do not merely join an organization. There are no ordained or salaried ministers in the usual sense; "personal gift and spiritual power" from the Holy Spirit are sufficient evidence of a call to ministry (I Cor. 12:4-11). In accordance with this they do recognize in certain men gifts of preaching and teaching, and those who devote their time to such work are supported by voluntary contributions. Gifted and godly men are acknowledged as elders and overseers who care for the spiritual needs of the saints.

Government among Brethren I and II is by individual assembly or congregation, under the leadership of their elders; these bodies hold that each assembly is responsible to the Lord alone as head of the church. Brethren III and IV, on the other hand, are joined in Circles of Fellowship, as already described.

The concept of the priesthood of all believers is practiced in their meeting, service, and ministry. There is no ritual. The larger assemblies own church buildings known as Bible, or Gospel, Chapels; smaller assemblies often start in private homes or (as formerly) in rented quarters known as Gospel Halls. Baptism and the Lord's Supper are observed as ordinances; the Supper is celebrated each Sunday, usually in the morning, and the gospel is preached at night. There are other meetings for prayer and Bible study—young people's meetings, missionary activities supported by voluntary subscription, tent meetings, and evangelistic services.

Plymouth Brethren I followed closely the teachings of John N. Darby, the leader of the original Plymouth congregation, who had far-reaching influence on all branches of the movement; strong emphasis is placed upon his teaching that "eternal life in Christ is the common blessing of all believers in every age," yet, among other branches, Plymouth Brethren I is described as "tight" because of its refusal to let anyone take Communion with them unless they have been associated with them for several months and agree with all their doctrines or bring a letter of commendation from some other "tight" assembly. This group does not accept members from other groups unless and until they renounce all affiliation with those groups. "PB-Is" do not wish to be considered a denomination. (Most of those formerly known as PB-I are now found in PB-II, PB-V, and PB-VI.)

Plymouth Brethren II is generally open, in comparison, welcoming anyone who believes in Christ and who has accepted him as Savior. They have fellowship with Christians outside their own membership and hold that "ecclesiastical position in itself does not disqualify anyone." There is actually a broad base of teaching here, some holding that an open ministry is obligatory, others that it is optional, and still others not tolerating it at all. PB-II, known historically as Open Brethren, is the only body to send men for training to graduate theological seminaries proportionately; the Open Brethren send out more missionaries than the Exclusive Brethren and are more likely to have a higher percentage of communicants from non-Brethren family backgrounds.

Plymouth Brethren III is known as the Continental Brethren because of its close relationship to their European counterparts. They are now affiliated with those known as Kelly Brethren, along with PB-VII. (The Kelly Brethren came out of a schism in England in 1881 and was limited to England.)

Plymouth Brethren IV, which has refused to be designated by any name, seems to be disappearing from the scene. Widely known as Raven Brethren and later as Taylorites (following leaders of those names), their differences with other bodies have been largely in the areas of government and discipline.

Plymouth Brethren V follows closely the doctrine of the original British body, is ultraconservative, and probably is the largest of the "Exclusive" Plymouth Brethren.

Plymouth Brethren VI is one of a number of very small Plymouth Brethren groups and is all but extinct.

Plymouth Brethren VII and VIII are comparatively new groups, both of which were part of PB-I up to 1936.

All in all, there are 745 Open Assemblies in the United States and over 350 in Canada, with an estimated 741,000 communicants; there are probably 300 Exclusive Assemblies with fewer than 10,000 members. The Plymouth Brethren support 2 Bible schools and one Missionary Training Center, and an elaborate series of periodicals.

RIVER BRETHREN

A considerable number of post-Reformation Anabaptists and Pietists, fleeing Europe, settled in Lancaster County, Pennsylvania, during the eighteenth century. During the latter third of the century, in cooperation with other mainline denominations, they developed fellowship groups designated as the United Brethren in Christ. A group in a community near the Susquehanna River came into disagreement with the rest of the fellowship over requirements relative to the Christian ordinances, and as a result "The Brotherhood by the River" withdrew from the larger fellowship and formed a new denomination late in the century. The name River Brethren was associated with this body for more than a hundred years.

Other disputes in the new organization brought about the establishment of 2 smaller bodies—the Old Order, or Yorker, Brethren in 1843, and the Brinsers, or United Zion's Children, in 1855. These 3 churches today number about 15,000–16,000 communicant members in the United States and Canada.

Brethren in Christ (Formerly Known as River Brethren)

With the outbreak of the Civil War the draft reached into the ranks of the Brethren, and it became necessary for them to obtain legal recognition as an established religious organization in order to protect their objectors. Nonresistance has always been one of their primary principles. A council meeting in Lancaster County, Pennsylvania, in 1863 adopted the name Brethren in Christ Church; it was not incorporated until 1904.

The Brethren in Christ Church pledges loyalty to the following doctrines: the inspiration of the Holy Scriptures; the self-existent, triune God—Father, Son, and Holy Spirit; the deity and virgin birth of Christ; Christ's death as atonement for our sins, and his resurrection from the dead; the Holy Spirit who convicts the sinner, regenerates the penitent, and empowers the believer; justification as forgiveness for committed sins, and sanctification as heart cleansing and empowerment by the Holy Spirit; observance of the ordinances of God's house; temperance and modesty of apparel as taught in the Scriptures; the personal, visible, and imminent return of Christ; the resurrection of the dead, with punishment for the unbeliever and reward for the believer; the supreme duty of the church as worldwide evangelism.

While the government of this church is largely in the hands of the local churches, there are 6 regional conferences and a general conference, which is the ultimate and final authority. There is also a board of administration; and a board of directors amenable to the board of administration has oversight of the general conference and of general church property and financial transactions.

The church has 2 institutions of learning: Messiah College, Grantham, Pennsylvania, and Niagara Christian College, Fort Erie, Ontario, Canada. Missionaries are at work in Africa, India, Japan, and Nicaragua. There are 13,830 members in 187 churches in the United States and Canada.

Old Order, or Yorker, Brethren

The Old Order, or Yorker, Brethren is the smallest of all River Brethren groups in the United States; they reported only 291 members and 7 churches in 1936. The primary reason for their existence as a separate body lay in their feeling that the Brethren in Christ had become lax in their enforcement of nonresistance and nonconformity to the world. They left the original body in 1843. "Old Order" in their name refers to their desire to keep the old traditions alive; "Yorker" resulted from the fact that most of them at the time of withdrawal lived in York County, Pennsylvania.

Their doctrine is no longer identical with that of Brethren in Christ Church. They refuse to build or meet in church edifices; lacking these, they meet usually in the homes of the members.

United Zion Church

Bishop Matthias Brinser was expelled from the Brethren in Christ Church in 1855, together with about 50 others, for building and holding services in a meetinghouse. They organized under the name United Zion's Children; this was changed in 1954 when the body incorporated under the name United Zion Church.

They are essentially the same in doctrine as the Brethren in Christ. They baptize by trine immersion, observe foot washing as an ordinance along with the Lord's Supper. They encourage the veiling of women and are opposed to divorce and immodest attire.

Located almost exclusively in Dauphin, Lebanon, and Lancaster counties in Pennsylvania, they list 877 members and 16 churches. Church officers are bishops, ministers, and deacons; the top administrative body is a general conference composed of a representation of the various district conferences; the basic unit of government is the district conference.

No foreign missionary work of their own is reported, but they support 2 missionaries working under the Brethren in Christ Church. One home for the aged is maintained, and a monthly magazine, *Zion's Herald,* is published.

UNITED BRETHREN

United Brethren in the United States are found in 2 churches—the Church of the United Brethren in Christ (Old Constitution) and the United Christian Church. The Evangelical United Brethren Church, now merged into The United Methodist Church, was until recently one branch of this body. Originally one group, they were the spiritual descendants of Philip William Otterbein and Martin Boehm (for their early historical background see p. 178). At a general conference of the parent body held at York, Pennsylvania, in 1889, a dispute arose over proposed changes in the church constitution concerned mainly with permitting members to join lodges and secret societies. There was a division into 2 churches: the majority group under the name of the Church of the United Brethren in Christ and the minority in the Church of the United Brethren in Christ (Old Constitution). The larger body merged in 1946 with the Evangelical Church, becoming the Evangelical United Brethren Church, now merged into The United Methodist Church.

Church of the United Brethren in Christ

This is the dissenting group that opposed constitutional changes in 1889; their dissent is still one of discipline rather than of doctrine. In common with other United Brethren they believe in the Trinity; they also believe in the deity, humanity, and atonement of Christ. Observance of strict scriptural living is required of all members, who are forbidden the use of alcoholic drinks, membership in secret societies, and participation in aggressive but not defensive war. Baptism and the Lord's Supper are observed as ordinances of the church.

Local, annual, and general conferences are held; the general conference meets quadrennially and is composed of ministers, district superintendents (presiding elders), general church officials, bishops, and lay delegates. Both men and women are eligible for the ministry and are ordained only once as elders. Missionary societies administer a work in evangelism and church aid in the United States and on foreign fields in Sierra Leone, West Africa, Jamaica, the Republic of Honduras in Central America, Hong Kong, and Nicaragua. A college and seminary are located at Huntington, Indiana, with secondary schools in Jamaica and Sierra Leone. There are 28,035 members in 281 churches. Still insisting upon loyalty to the old constitution, they work in harmony with evangelical groups in other denominations.

United Christian Church

This church separated from the original body in 1862-70 "on account of conscientious convictions" dealing chiefly with questions of infant baptism, the bearing of arms in war, secret societies, and the wearing of fashionable clothes. The Rev. George W. Hoffman was one of its most influential leaders, and for years members were known as Hoffmanites.

Hesitant to create another denomination, this body had no formal organization until 1877. A confession of faith was approved that same year, and the present name was adopted one year later at Campbelltown, Pennsylvania. The confession of faith, constitution, and discipline now in use were approved in 1920.

Orthodox and evangelistic, doctrine in this church emphasizes the inspiration of the Scriptures, the Trinity, total depravity, justification, regeneration, entire sanctification, and strict Sabbath observance. Baptism (the mode of which is optional), the Lord's Supper, and foot washing are observed as ordinances. There are district, annual, and general conferences, and an itinerant ministry; local preachers vote in the annual conference. Foreign missionaries are stationed in Brazil and Japan, and they work jointly with missions in Jamaica, West Indies. There were 430 members and 11 churches, as of 1978.

BUDDHIST CHURCHES OF AMERICA

Buddhism is found in real strength in this country in Utah, Arizona, Washington, Oregon, California, and Hawaii, and it represents the transplanting of the Buddhism of the East. Most of the Buddhists in the United States are Japanese or Japanese-Americans.

The faith is built upon the teaching of the founder, Buddha—Siddartha Gautama, the Enlightened One (566 B.C.)—who attained his enlightenment in India and whose teachings have spread all over the Far East. Often challenged as a system of religious faith, it remains a most complex and involved pattern of thought and action. It is divided into 2 schools—Hinayana, or Theravada, Buddhism, or the Lesser Vehicle; and Mahayana Buddhism, or the Greater Vehicle. These offer, on the one hand, a path of deliverance from suffering and, on the other, a thorough preparation for entry upon that path. Hinayana seems devised for those among its disciples who are satisfied with a comparatively modest attainment of Buddhist virtue, while Mahayana is the way of deliverance through true and real awareness of wisdom and compassion of enlightenment in everyday living as the very ground for the perfection of life. Buddha himself put the essence of his system in these words: "One thing only I teach: sorrow [or pain], the cause of sorrow, the cessation of sorrow, and the path which leads to the cessation of sorrow." These are the Four Truths of Buddhism, the fourth of which includes the actual means of arriving at these truths by way of the "noble eightfold path"—"right views, right intention, right speech, right action, right livelihood, right effort, right mindfulness, right concentration." This description of the 8 paths covers the whole training of the disciple who seeks nirvana, which means literally "blown out" or "extinguished." He strives to extinguish in his living all desire, hatred, and ignorance and thus to attain a nobler life.

There are no theories of creation, no miracles, and no divine being in Buddhism. Supreme reality is neither affirmed nor denied; it is only said to be beyond the comprehension of the human mind. It is actually a system of self-education in the conquering, or forgetting, of pain, sorrow, and suffering. Recognizing that this is a long process, Buddha taught that man has an indefinite number of lives, or reincarnations, in which to accomplish it.

The titular head of American Buddhist churches bears the title of bishop; he is in charge of all religious activities, and he is authorized to transfer or dismiss the clergy under his jurisdiction. The first Buddhist church, or temple, in the United States was consecrated in San Francisco in 1905; the Buddhist Mission of North America was started in San Francisco in 1898 and incorporated in 1942 as the Buddhist Churches of America. There are 9 ministers and 4 churches and about 100,000 members. They represent the Jodo Shinshu Sect of Buddhism in this country, a faith based on "the anatman doctrine, supplemented by the idea of karma and nirvana, the holy ease or a blissful mental state of absolute freedom from evil." Each church is autonomous, holding complete control of its own property. Weekly services are held, and Japanese-language schools are maintained by many of the churches.

A movement known as Zen Buddhism has found some interest among non-Buddhists in this country; it seeks to transmit the spirit of Buddhism without demanding allegiance to all the teachings of Buddha. It makes use of a question-and-answer technique *(mondo)* to reveal truths, not necessarily religious, but truths found within the seeker himself that will bring enlightenment *(bodhi)* and improvement of the condition of man. Wisdom *(prajna)* and love *(karuna)* are major emphases.

CHRISTADELPHIANS

John Thomas came to the United States from England in 1844. He joined the Disciples of Christ but later became convinced that their doctrine made them the apostate church predicted by Scripture and that many other more important Bible doctrines were being neglected. He left the Disciples to organize a number of societies, which under his leadership began preaching the need of a return to primitive Christianity. Loosely organized, these societies bore no name until the outbreak of the Civil War, when their doctrine of nonresistance forced them to adopt a name, and Christadelphians (or Brethren of Christ) was the name chosen.

Christadelphians are both Unitarian and Adventist in theology. They reject the Trinity and belief in a personal devil, maintaining the Scriptures teach that Christ is not God the Son but the Son of God; not preexistent, but born of Mary by the Holy Spirit. Man is mortal by nature with Christ as his only means of salvation. Eternal life comes only to the righteous. Strong millenarians, they believe that Christ will come shortly to reward the saints with immortality and to destroy the wicked; that he will take David's throne in Jerusalem, the faithful will be gathered, and the world will be ruled from the land of Canaan for a thousand years.

The church is congregational in polity; local organizations are known not as churches but as ecclesias. Membership is by profession of faith and immersion. There are no paid or ordained ministers in the usual sense; each ecclesia elects serving brethren, among whom are included managing brethren, presiding brethren, and lecturing brethren. Women take no part in public speech or prayer, though all vote equally. Christadelphians do not vote in civil elections or participate in war, and they refuse to accept public office. There are no associations or conventions, but there are fraternal gatherings for spiritual inspiration. Meetings are generally held in rented halls, schoolhouses, or private homes; there are few church edifices.

Home missions work is local, usually in the form of lectures and instruction in Christadelphian doctrine and righteous living. There are no foreign missions, but ecclesias are found in several countries. There is no educational work with the exception of summer Bible schools in several states. Found in 42 states from coast to coast, they reported 15,800 members in about 850 ecclesias in 1967. Larger numbers are located in Great Britain, New Zealand, Australia, Canada, and Germany.

THE CHRISTIAN AND MISSIONARY ALLIANCE

The Christian and Missionary Alliance originated in 1881 under the leadership of the Rev. A. B. Simpson, a Presbyterian minister in New York City who left that church to carry on independent evangelistic work among the unchurched. It was at first divided into 2 societies, the Christian Alliance for home missions work and the International Missionary Alliance for work abroad. The 2 bodies were merged in 1897 into the present Christian and Missionary Alliance.

Strongly evangelical, the Alliance stands for the literal inspiration of the Bible, the atonement wrought by Christ, the reality of supernatural religious experience, separation from the world, the premillenial return of Jesus Christ, Spirit baptism, and practical holiness. While there is no creed as such, there is a formula of belief built upon a fourfold gospel of Christ as Savior, Sanctifier, Healer, and Coming Lord.

The Christian and Missionary Alliance has ministries in 46 nations and territories. In the United States and Canada, work is carried on in 21 organized districts with 1,561 churches fully or partially organized. Each of these churches or groups is a self-administering and self-governing unit engaged in missionary and evangelical activities. There is an overall conference, called the general council, that meets annually in various parts of the United States and Canada.

Foreign missionary work is carried on in South America, Africa, the Near East, India, Thailand, Japan, Hong Kong and Taiwan, Indonesia including Irian Jaya, and the Philippines. In these areas are found 938 missionaries from the Alliance and 5,526 indigenous workers, and there are 4,453 organized churches with 332,443 members.

In addition to the organized church work in North America, missionary work is carried on among Indians and Eskimos, as well as among other ethnic and minority groups. The Alliance maintains colleges at Nyack, New York; St. Paul; San Francisco; and Regina, Saskatchewan, Canada. In 1977 there were 192,336 members in North America in 1,561 churches. Thus the Alliance has a larger constituency abroad than at home.

CHRISTIAN CATHOLIC CHURCH

The Christian Catholic Movement (Catholic in the sense of "universal," or a church home for all true Christians) began prior to 1896, when John Alexander Dowie, a Congregational preacher educated in Scotland and ordained in Australia, gave it formal organization. Dowie also founded Zion City, Illinois, and when the city opened in 1901, it became headquarters for the new church. Businesses and industries were developed, all controlled and governed by a theocracy of which Dowie was general overseer. He had extensive plans for educational and cultural projects; he criticized both the injustices of capitalism and the excesses of labor leaders, alcoholic beverages, tobacco, medicine and the medical profession, secret lodges and the press. He was also a tireless advocate of racial equality and integration.

Theologically, "CCC" is rooted in evangelical orthodoxy. The Scriptures are accepted as the rule of faith and practice. Other doctrines call for belief in the necessity of repentance for sin and personal trust in Christ for salvation, baptism by triune immersion, the Second Coming of Christ, and tithing as a practical method of Christian stewardship. Dowie emphasized the healing of disease through prayer, and his success in healing led to the establishment of a tabernacle and "divine healing rooms," first in Chicago and later in Zion City.

Several years after the organization of the Christian Catholic Church at Zion, he claimed to be Elijah the Restorer and maintained his leadership of the group until 1906, when he was deposed and followed successively by Wilbur Glen Voliva, Michael J. Mintern, Carl Q. Lee, and currently Roger W. Ottersen.

At first an exclusively religious community, Zion City has a still strong Christian Catholic Church, but independent businesses have been welcomed, and many other churches are at work in the city. Over the past 50 years, the church has sponsored a Zion Conservatory of Music which today has an enrollment of 240 pupils. And for more than 42 years it has had its famous annual Passion Play with a cast of over 200, attracting thousands of visitors to the city. Branches of the church have been established in Chicago, Michigan City (Ind.), Phoenix, and Toronto, Ontario, Canada. Missionary work is conducted in Japan, Australia, Israel, the Philippines, Guyana, and South Africa. In addition, they support missionaries under Campus Crusade, The Navigators, T.E.A.M., the Africa Evangelical Fellowship, Middle East Media, and Wycliffe. In Jamaica they cooperate with The Missionary Church. They are members of the National Association of Evangelicals.

Two radio programs, "Songs of Zion" and "Chapel-Time," are broadcast weekly, and they publish a monthly publication, *Leaves of Healing*, for worldwide circulation. With 6 places of worship in the United States, they have a membership of 2,500.

CHRISTIAN CHURCH (DISCIPLES OF CHRIST)

Among the half dozen largest religious groups in the United States, the Christian Church (Disciples of Christ) might be called the most American; it was born on the nineteenth-century American frontier out of a deep concern for Christian unity. There were four pioneers: Barton Stone, Thomas and Alexander Campbell, and Walter Scott. All of them had Presbyterian background.

Barton Stone believed that Christians could and should unite on the basis of simple faith in Christ and that the divisive doctrines and practices of denominationalism should be abolished. His church at Cane Ridge, Kentucky, became the center of the famous Kentucky Revival; but Stone came out of that movement convinced that salvation had little to do with church affiliation and that "deeds are more important than creeds." Disciplinary action was brought against him and against his followers in the established churches; they withdrew and reorganized under the name Christians and spread across Kentucky, Ohio, and the central states.

Thomas Campbell served as a clergyman in the Seceder branch of the Presbyterian church in northern Ireland; he settled in a Seceder church in western Pennsylvania in 1807, where he advocated closer relations with all Christians, Presbyterian or otherwise, appealed from creeds to the Bible as a basis of faith, and practiced open Communion. Censured, he led in the formation of "the Christian Association of Washington County, Pa.," and published a Declaration and Address that was to become the Magna Charta of the Christian Church (Disciples of Christ). In this declaration he argued that "schism, or uncharitable divisions," in the church were "anti-Christian, anti-Scriptural, anti-natural" and "productive of confusion and every evil work." The church and church membership should be based solely upon the belief and practices of New Testament Christianity; the articles of faith and holiness "expressly revealed in the Word of God" were quite enough without the addition of human opinions or creedal inventions.

Thomas Campbell laid the cornerstone; his son Alexander Campbell gave the movement its formative theology. He left a Seceder church in Scotland to join his father in Pennsylvania in 1810 and enlarged on the concept that every

75

church should be autonomous and completely independent—that creeds, clerical titles, authority, and privilege had no justification in Scripture; that the Lord's Supper should be served at every Sunday service; and that baptism should be by immersion for adult believers (those adult enough to understand the meaning of the ordinance). He argued eloquently for Christian union and freedom of individual faith, and welcomed to his independent church at Brush Run, Pennsylvania, all who came with simple faith in Christ as the Son of God and Messiah. He met the same opposition that his father had met, and with his congregation he joined an association of Particular Baptists, only to be separated from that body in 1830. Barton Stone used the word "Christian" to designate his group, feeling that all God's children should be known so. Campbell used the word "Disciples." In 1832 the Christians and the Disciples merged; both names are still used, but usually and officially the body is known today as The Christian Church (Disciples of Christ).

Early in the movement, Walter Scott popularized the term "restoration," by which he meant the restoration of the New Testament pattern and practice. Like Stone, Scott was suspicious of the values of the current revivalistic frenzies; he related faith more to the mind than to the emotions—it was not a matter of emotional experience but of intellectual acceptance of the truth of Christ's messiahship. He stressed the importance of such faith, together with repentance of sins and baptism by immersion.

The first national convention of the Disciples and their first missionary society (the American Christian Missionary Society) were organized in 1849; state conventions and societies had begun to meet in 1839. They grew rapidly through and following the Civil War period, especially in Ohio, Indiana, Illinois, Tennessee, and Missouri, in spite of conflict within the church over any emphasis on denominationalism or ecclesiastical organization. The differences between conservatives and progressives became acute in such matters as the organization of missionary societies and instrumental music in the churches; the Churches of Christ separated from the Disciples during this debate.

In matters of belief, conservative and progressive attitudes were and still are important, and the church allows for variance of opinion and stands for complete freedom in interpretation, starting from the historic conviction that there is no creed but Christ and no saving doctrines save those of the New Testament. It could be said that the Disciples are "God-centered, Christ-centered, and Bible-centered," but beyond that, faith is a matter of individual conviction. But there are areas of general agreement and acceptance. The Disciples are firm in their belief in immortality but do not accept the doctrine of original sin; they hold that all men are of a sinful nature until redeemed by the sacrifice of Christ; they are not concerned with speculation about the Trinity and the nature of a triune God. They have no catechism, no set orders of worship. Faith in Christ as Lord is the only requirement.

For more than a century the Disciples were strictly congregational in polity—a loosely bound association of local churches. But, increasingly, it was felt that such an arrangement, with overlapping boards and agencies and with no representative voice, needed a restructure in the interest of efficiency and economy. Following a 7-year study and discussion, led by a 130-member Commission on Brotherhood Restructure, a whole new design of governmental organization was adopted at Kansas City in 1968. Under the new plan, the whole church works under a polity of "representative government" on 3 levels—local, regional, and general.

The local church is still the basic unit. All congregations listed in the latest year book are accepted as congregations; each congregation manages its own affairs, has its own charters and by-laws, owns and controls its property, calls its ministers, establishes its own budgets and financial policies, and has voting representatives in regional and national assemblies.

The churches are grouped into 36 regions organized to provide help, counsel, and pastoral care to members, ministers, and congregations. Each region organizes its own boards, departments, and committees. Within policies developed by the general assembly, the regions certify the standing of ministers, provide help and counsel to ministers and congregations in such matters as ordination, licensing, location of ministers, the establishment or dissolution of pastoral relationships, the installation of ministers. Regions have regional ministers as their administrative leaders.

On the location level there is a general assembly made up of voting and nonvoting representatives from the local churches and regions, plus ministers and a few ex-officio members, the chief officers of institutions and the unit boards, and members of the general board. The assembly receives and acts upon proposed programs, policies, reports, and resolutions sent up through the general board, elects the officers of the church and half the members of the general board. The 36 regions elect the other half.

The general board meets annually, processes business going to the assembly, recommends policies, reviews the total program of the church, elects or confirms the governing bodies of the various administrative units and elects the committees of the general assembly and the members of an administrative committee. General board members are laymen, laywomen, and (1/3) ministers.

The administrative committee of the general board is made up of 40 members elected by the board; officers of the church are ex-officio members. Meeting at least twice a year, it provides for long-range planning, implements policies and promotes the causes and units of the church.

Officers of the church are of two classes—voluntary (nonsalaried) officers of the general assembly and salaried officers. There is a volunteer moderator, 2 vice-moderators, a salaried general minister, and a president.

There are now 1,256,849 members in 4,377 churches in the United States and 39 congregations with 5,327 members in Canada. There are 32 colleges, undergraduate schools of religion and foundations; 8 centers for children and retarded persons; and 28 centers for older adults. The Disciples are represented in the National Council of Churches of Christ in the U.S.A, the

World Council of Churches, and the Consultation on Church Union. A World Convention of Churches of Christ has its headquarters in Dallas.

CHRISTIAN CHURCH OF NORTH AMERICA, GENERAL COUNCIL

Originally known as the Italian Christian Churches, this body was incorporated in 1948 at Pittsburg; its first general council was held in 1927, at Niagara Falls, New York. It is described as pentecostal but does not engage in "the excesses tolerated or practiced among some churches using the same name." At least 50 percent of its membership (8,500 in 111 churches) is of Italian nationality or descent.

They have two ordinances—baptism and the Lord's Supper—and in their moral code and teaching they stand against gambling, drunkenness, the use of tobacco, theater-going, and dancing. Intermarriage with unbelievers is strictly forbidden, and they hold to the conservative position ("as outlined in Matthew 19") on marriage and divorce. Their governmental form is congregational.

Foreign missionary work is conducted in India, Africa, South America, Australia, Mexico, Canada, and Europe. The group is an affiliate member of the National Association of Evangelicals.

CHRISTIAN CHURCHES AND CHURCHES OF CHRIST

The churches and members of these independent Christian churches make up not a denomination but a fellowship; there is no formal organization other than that in the local congregations, and there are no denominational societies, officials, or boards. This is a group of churches identified usually with the Disciples of Christ, with a few congregations of the Churches of Christ and the smaller Christian Churches, who preach and teach a conservative, fundamentalist theology, which they feel is being neglected, especially among the Disciples. Their doctrine in general agrees with that of the Disciples and the Churches of Christ, stressing the divinity of Christ, the agency of the Holy Spirit in conversion, the Bible as the inspired Word of God, future rewards and punishments, and God as a prayer-answering deity. They maintain that "all ordinances should be observed as they were in the days of the apostles" and observe the Lord's Supper in open Communion every Sunday.

No official membership survey has ever been made, because of the unusual nature of the fellowship, but various approximations have been made. These approximations are questionable in accuracy. There are said to be 1,040,856 members in 5,436 congregations. Some of these churches withdrew their name from the yearbook of the Disciples in protest against the recent "restructuring" of the Disciples. The group supports at least 32 small Christian Bible colleges in different sections of the country; has over 450 missionaries at work operating dispensaries, hospitals, and Bible colleges; and circulates huge quantities of evangelical literature. Their publishing house—the Standard Publishing Foundation—is located at Cincinnati.

CHRISTIAN CONGREGATION

The philosophy and work of the Christian Congregation, formed in Indiana in 1887, revolve about the "new commandment" of John 13:34-35. It is a fellowship of ministers, laymen, and congregations seeking a noncreedal, nondenominational basis for union. It is pacifistic and opposes all sectarian strife, insisting that according to the new commandment "the household of faith is not founded upon doctrinal agreement, creeds, church claims, names or rites" but solely upon the relationship of the individual to God. The basis of Christian fellowship is love toward one another, the actual relations of Christians to one another transcending in importance all individual belief or personal opinions. Free Bible study is encouraged.

Churches and pastorates are now located in every state in the union; they still remain strongest, however, in the areas in which Barton Stone preached and in which the original Christian Congregation groups were located—Kentucky, the Carolinas, Virginia, Pennsylvania, Ohio, Indiana, and Texas; for the greater part, the work is done in rural, mountain, and neglected areas. In many respects the work of the Christian Congregation is identical with that of the Stone movement and with his original Christian Church, although Christian Congregations were established and at work when the Christian Church was organized.

Polity is congregational. A general superintendent presides over a board of trustees; relations between the superintendent and the board and the people are purely advisory. There are 80,411 members in 1,120 churches.

CHRISTIAN NATION CHURCH, U.S.A.

Originating in a band of independent evangelists called "equality evangelists," the Christian Nation Church was incorporated at Marion, Ohio, in 1895. Membership today stands at 2,000 in 18 churches.

The church teaches a fourfold gospel; justification, entire sanctification, divine healing, and the second coming of Christ. Two ordinances, baptism and the Lord's Supper, are celebrated. Needless ornaments on clothing, worldly organizations and amusements, tobacco and liquor, Sabbath breaking, the remarriage of the divorced, jesting, foolish talking, and the singing of worldly songs are forbidden; and marriage to the unsaved is discouraged. Each family is encouraged to "raise just so large a family of children as God will be pleased to give them," tithing is practiced, and love for friend and enemy is emphasized. Days of fasting and prayer are observed, the sick and needy are assisted, and camp meetings are strongly supported.

Government is by local churches, which are grouped into districts and which meet in annual conferences. The licenses of all pastors expire at the end of each conference year.

CHRISTIAN UNION

Christian Union represents an attempt to unite all Christians in a consciousness of unity on a scriptural basis and to offer a larger unity in thought and worship. Organized in 1864 at Columbus, Ohio, its announced purpose is "to promote fellowship among God's people, to put forth every effort to proclaim God's saving grace to the lost . . . and to declare the whole counsel of God for the edification of believers."

There is no one creed binding upon members of the Union, but 7 principles are stressed: the oneness of the Church of Christ, Christ as the only head of the church, the Bible as the only rule of faith and practice, good fruits as the one condition of fellowship, Christian union without controversy, complete autonomy for the local church, and avoidance of all partisan political preaching. Men and women are ordained ministers; ordinances include baptism—preferably by immersion—and the Lord's Supper.

While church government is congregational, a series of councils meet for fellowship and to conduct such business as concerns the entire church. State councils meet once a year, and a general council meets every 3 years with lay and ministerial delegates. Local missionary work is largely evangelistic and is conducted by state missionary boards; a general mission board oversees home and foreign missions; 40 missionaries are located in Africa, Japan, Alaska, the Philippines, Liberia, Colombia, Algeria, and Ethiopia. In June, 1977, 20 churches and 3,500 members, now called The Church Union of Etinan, Nigeria, West Africa, were received into the church.

A church college is located at Greenfield, Ohio (Christian Union Bible College), and a Christian Union Extension School is established at Excelsior Springs, Missouri. One periodical, *The Christian Union Witness,* is published monthly at Excelsior Springs. There are 150 churches in Oklahoma, Missouri, Arkansas, Iowa, Indiana, and Ohio, with 11,500 members.

CHRIST'S SANCTIFIED HOLY CHURCH

This church began with the preaching of holiness and sanctification in the Colored Methodist Episcopal Church in Louisiana by a small body of white evangelists; it was organized in 1904 as the Colored Church South. Its central theme is sanctification by faith "as a distinct experience from justification by faith in Christ, which is not brought about by a growth in grace but is wrought instantaneously." There is emphasis on "one Lord, one faith, one baptism"; unequal persons, holy and unholy, should not marry; men and women are ordained to the ministry; the strict observance of all church rules is required; no member using or selling tobacco or alcoholic liquors is acceptable; and members pledge that they will "expose all evil" to church officials.

The governing body is a 5-member Board No. 1, which ordains all deacons, deaconesses, and ministers, and which supervises boards of extension, investigation, managers, ministers, and others. An annual conference meets in September, a district conference in June, a Sunday school convention in March. The church, listing 600 members in 30 churches in 1957, is too small to maintain any sizable missionary, philanthropic, or educational work. A summer Bible school, organized in 1940, meets at headquarters during the month of July.

CHURCH OF CHRIST (HOLINESS) U.S.A.

C. P. Jones, a Baptist preacher in Alabama and Mississippi, sought a new church and faith that would make him "one of wisdom's true sons" and "like Abraham, a friend of God." In 1894 he founded the Church of Christ (Holiness) U.S.A., which today reports 9,289 members in 159 churches.

Doctrinally this church emphasizes original sin, the Holy Ghost as an indispensable gift for every believer, and Christ's atonement and second coming. There are 2 sacraments or ordinances: baptism and the Lord's Supper; foot washing and divine healing are employed, not as sacraments, but as aids to the growth of spiritual life. The church is episcopal in government, with final authority vested in a biennial convention. There are 7 dioceses, each under a bishop's charge; a district convention made up of elders, ministers, and local lay representatives meets semi-annually.

Missionary work is conducted at home and in Liberia and Nigeria; there is a college, Christ Missionary and Industrial College, at Jackson, Mississippi, and a national publishing house in Chicago.

CHURCH OF CHRIST, SCIENTIST

At Lynn, Massachusetts, in 1866 Mary Baker Eddy recovered almost instantly from a severe injury after reading in Matt. 9:1-8 the account of Christ's healing of the man sick of the palsy. Profoundly religious and a lifelong student of mental and spiritual causation, she came to attribute causation to God and to regard him as divine Mind. From these roots came Christian Science and the Church of Christ, Scientist.

Generally described as "a religious teaching and practice based on the words and works of Christ Jesus," Christian Science was regarded by Mrs. Eddy as "divine metaphysics," as "the scientific system of divine healing," and as the "law of God, the law of good, interpreting and demonstrating the divine Principle and rule of universal harmony." She believed "the Principle of all harmonious Mind-action to be God"; she wrote most of these definitions and descriptions of her faith in *Science and Health with Key to the Scriptures,* a famous volume which, together with the Bible, has become the twofold textbook of Christan Science.

Like many other religious leaders and pioneers, Mrs. Eddy hoped to work through existing churches. She did not plan another denomination; but organization became necessary as interest in the movement spread, and under her direction the Church of Christ, Scientist, a local church, was established at Boston in 1879. In 1892 she established the present worldwide organization, the First Church of Christ, Scientist, in Boston, and its branch churches and societies. This church in Boston is frequently referred to as the mother church.

Applied not only to the healing of sickness but to the problems of life generally, the tenets and doctrines of Christian Science are often confusing to the non-Scientist and call for careful explanation. They start with the conviction that God is the only might, or Mind; he is "All-in-all," the "divine Principle of all that really is," "the all-knowing, all-seeing, all-acting, all-wise, all-loving, and eternal; Principle; Mind; Soul; Spirit; Life; Truth; Love; all substance intelligence." The inspired word of the Bible is accepted as "sufficient guide to eternal Life." The tenets state: "We acknowledge and adore one supreme and infinite God. We acknowledge His Son, one Christ; the Holy Ghost or divine Comforter; and man in God's image and likeness." Jesus is known to Christian Scientists as Master, or Way-shower. They accept his virgin birth and his atoning mission "as the evidence of divine, efficacious Love unfolding man's unity with God through Christ Jesus the Way-shower." He was "endowed with the Christ, the divine spirit without measure." Man, made in the image of God, "is saved through Christ, through Truth, Life, and Love as demonstrated by the Galilean Prophet in healing the sick and overcoming sin and death." The crucifixion and resurrection of Jesus are held as serving "to uplift faith to understand eternal Life, even the allness of Soul, Spirit, and the nothingness of matter."

This "nothingness of matter" involves the basic teaching of Christian Science concerning what is real and unreal. Says Mrs. Eddy:

All reality is in God and His creation, harmonious and eternal. That which He creates is good, and He makes all that is made. Therefore the only reality of sin, sickness, or death is the awful fact that unrealities seem real to human, erring belief, until God strips off their disguise. They are not true, because they are not of God.

God forgives sin in destroying it with "the spiritual understanding that casts out evil as unreal." The punishment for sin, however, lasts as long as the belief in sin endures.

It is a mistake to believe that the followers of Christian Science *ignore* that which they consider unreal; rather, they seek to forsake and overcome error and evil through Christian discipleship, prayer, and progressive spiritual comprehension of the reality of God's allness and goodness, and of man as his likeness. Error is "a supposition that pleasure and pain, that intelligence, substance, life, are existent in matter. . . . It is that which seemeth to be and is not." As Mrs. Eddy has stated (and this point is fundamental to Christian Science beliefs):

If we would open their prison doors for the sick, we must first learn to bind up the broken-hearted. If we would heal by the Spirit, we must not hide the talent of spiritual healing under the napkin of its form, nor bury the *morale* of Christian Science in the grave-clothes of its letter. The tender word and Christian encouragement of an invalid, pitiful patience with his fears and the removal of them are better than hecatombs of gushing theories, stereotyped borrowed speeches and the doling of arguments, which are but so many parodies on legitimate Christian Science, aflame with divine Love.

She further wrote, "Nothing aside from the spiritualization—yea, the highest Christianization—of thought and desire, can give the true perception of God and Christian Science, that results in health, happiness and holiness."

Certain terms are important in the exposition of Christian Science. *Animal magnetism* is the specific term for the hypnotic error of belief in a mind and power apart from God (typified by the dragon in the Apocalypse; Jesus as the Lamb of God exemplifies the conquering of this sin in every form). Healing is not miraculous but divinely natural; disease is a mental concept dispelled by the introduction of spiritual truth. Heaven is not a locality but "harmony; the reign of Spirit; government by divine Principle; spirituality; bliss, the atmosphere of Soul." Hell is "moral belief; error; lust; remorse; hatred; revenge; sin; sickness; death; suffering and self-destruction; self-imposed agony; effects of sin; that which 'worketh abomination or maketh a lie.'" Mortal mind is "the flesh opposed to Spirit, the human mind and evil in contradistinction to the divine Mind." Prayer is "an absolute faith that all things are possible to God—a spiritual understanding of Him, an unselfed love." Baptism is not observed as a traditional ceremony in this church but is held to be a continuing individual spiritual experience, "a purification from all error."

All local Churches of Christ, Scientist, of which there are approximately 3,000, as branches of the mother church are organized under the laws of the states or countries in which they exist. They enjoy their own forms of democratic government within the general framework of bylaws laid down in the *Manual of the Mother Church* by Mrs. Eddy. Manual articles also provide for the Christian Science college organizations. Reading rooms open to the general public are maintained by all churches. The affairs of the mother church are administered by the Christian Science Board of Directors, which elects a president, the first and second readers, a clerk, and a treasurer. The board of directors is a self-perpetuating body electing all other officers of the church annually with the exception of the readers, who are elected by the board for a term of 3 years.

Important in the Christian Science movement are the reader, teacher, and practitioner. There are 2 readers in each church, usually a man and a woman; in all Christian Science services on Sunday and Thanksgiving Day they read alternately from the Bible and from *Science and Health;* the lesson-sermon of the Sunday service is prepared by a committee of Scientists and issued quarterly by the Christian Science Publishing Society. This system is followed by all Christian Science churches throughout the world. A midweek meeting, which is conducted by the first reader alone, features testimonies of healing from sin and sickness.

Practitioners devote their full time to healing and are authorized by the board of directors to practice. There is a board of education consisting of 3 members—a president, a vice-president, and a teacher of Christian Science. Under the supervision of this board a normal class is held once in 3 years. Teachers are duly authorized by certificates granted by the Board of Education to form classes of pupils in Christian Science. One class of not more than 30 pupils is instructed by each teacher annually.

There is a board of lectureship consisting of nearly 30 members. These members are appointed annually by the Board of Directors. At the invitation of branch churches free lectures are given by these members all over the world. A committee on publication serves as an ecumenical and informational office, representing the denomination to the press and public. The Christian Science Publishing Society is one of the most effective units within the church; it publishes very much and very well-written literature, including the *Christian Science Sentinel,* the *Christian Science Journal,* the *Christian Science Quarterly,* the *Herald of Christian Science* in 12 languages and in braille, and the *Christian Science Monitor.* The *Monitor* is acknowledged in all journalism to be one of the finest newspapers in the world. There is a Christian Science Benevolent Association sanatorium that is maintained by the Christian Science Church. A number of nursing homes for Christian Scientists, relying wholly on spiritual means for healing, are independently maintained throughout the world.

The bylaws written by Mrs. Eddy prohibit the publishing of membership statistics; no comprehensive, accurate, or up-to-date figures are available. The government census of 1936 reported 268,915 members. No count has been reported since that time, but membership has not been as high as some outside writers and publishers have estimated. In deference to the wishes of the officials of the church no estimate will be given here. It is enough to remark upon a strange situation found here and probably in no other church in America: the number of people studying Christian Science and attending its services but not yet admitted to full membership quite likely exceeds the number who have been admitted.

CHURCH OF GOD

At least 200 independent religious bodies in the United States bear the name Church of God in one form or another. Of these, 3 have their headquarters in Cleveland, Tennessee, where the name was first applied in the later years of the last century and where important developments have taken place.

The principal Cleveland body began on August 19, 1886, in Monroe County, Tennessee, as a Christian fellowship, first known as the Christian Union, with 8 members led by Richard G. Spurling. The Union was reorganized under the name of The Holiness Church in May of 1902, and a simple form of government was introduced. A. J. Tomlinson, an American Bible Society colporteur, joined them in 1903 and was elected general moderator in 1906; he was impeached in 1923 and withdrew to form a rival group known as the Tomlinson Church of God; this name was changed to the Church of God of Prophecy in 1953. When Tomlinson died in 1943 his group was divided between his two sons, Milton A. Tomlinson, who remained in Cleveland as head of the Church of God of Prophecy, and Homer A. Tomlinson, who organized his followers under the name Church of God and established headquarters in Queens Village, New York (currently in Huntsville, Alabama). A splinter group left the Church of God of Prophecy in February of 1957 under the leadership of Grady R. Kent to form the Church of God of All Nations in Cleveland, now called the Church of God (New Testament Judaism).

Still another body, known as the (Original) Church of God (see p. 86), was organized in 1886 following a split among the followers of Richard G. Spurling; it claims to be the first church to use the name Church of God and has headquarters in Chattanooga.

Today the Church of God (Cleveland, Tennessee) claims 382,229 members and 8,093 ministers in 4,837 churches in the United States and Canada; the Church of God of Prophecy reports 65,801 members in 1,791 churches and has churches in 50 states and 45 countries; the Church of God (Huntsville, Alabama) claims 75,890 members and 2,737 ministers in 2,635 United States churches; the Kent group makes no report on membership.

In spite of the differences among these bodies, they hold in common doctrines of justification by faith, sancification, baptism of the Holy Spirit, speaking in tongues, being born again, fruitfulness in Christian living, and a strong interest in the premillennial second coming of Christ. The Cleveland Church of God, especially, while "relying upon the Bible as a whole rightly divided rather than upon any written creed," is thoroughly Arminian, stressing pentecostal and holiness tenets; practicing divine healing and condemning the use of alcohol, tobacco, and jewelry; opposing membership in secret societies; and accepting baptism, the Lord's Supper, and foot washing as ordinances. The Huntsville group puts strong emphasis upon the fulfillment of scripture "for the last days" and upon preparation now for the the return of Christ.

The Cleveland churches elect their officers; the Alabama church appoints them. There are differences in licensing and ordaining ministers. The ministry includes 3 orders: ordained minister, licensed minister, and exhorter.

The Cleveland Church of God holds state conventions and a biennial general assembly; operates Lee College at Cleveland; maintains 3 Bible schools and a preparatory school, plus a number of schools abroad, 3 orphanages, and a publishing house. Foreign missions are directed by a missions board, but home missions are in charge of a home missions and evangelism board and a general director.

Church of God (Apostolic)

Organized in 1896 at Danville, Kentucky, by Elder Thomas J. Cox, this body was first known as the Christian Faith Band and was incorporated under its present name in 1919. Its members believe that admission to the church must be only after repentance for sin, confession, and baptism; they teach holiness and sanctification, practice foot washing, and observe the Lord's Supper with unfermented grape juice and unleavened bread.

The general assembly is the governing body; under it serve officers known as the apostle or general overseer, the assistant overseer, district elders, pastors, evangelists, and local preachers. The church is divided into districts, each with an annual ministerial conference. There are 600 members in 22 churches.

The (Original) Church of God, Inc.

This church was organized in Tennessee in 1886 under the name of the Church of God, after a difference of opinion in regard to doctrine and teaching brought about a split among the followers of the Rev. Richard G. Spurling. The faction adhering to the original doctrines added the word "Original" to the name and incorporated in 1922.

The church believes in the "whole Bible, rightly divided"; in repentance, justification, and regeneration as defined by Martin Luther; in sanctification as defined by John Wesley; in divine healing; in the second coming of Christ; in eternal life for the righteous and eternal punishment for the wicked. Christian fruits alone stand as evidence of faithful Christian living; creeds that bind the conscience are considered unscriptural. They believe in the "filling with the Holy Spirit, with the Bible evidence of speaking with tongues as the Spirit gives utterance." Ordinances include baptism by immersion, the Lord's tithing, free-will offerings, the Lord's Supper, and foot washing.

Local churches, following the apostolic pattern, take local names such as the Church of God at Corinth. Each local church is self-governing. The church recognizes the New Testament orders of ministers, apostles, deacons, exhorters, evangelists, bishops, and teachers as given in Eph. 4:11-14. A general convention meets annually; there are a general office and publishing house and denominational headquarters are at Chattanooga; a correspondence Bible school, chartered in Tennessee as Ridgedale Theological Seminary, grants degrees up to master of theology and offers honorary degrees of doctor of divinity and doctor of sacred literature. There are 70 churches, about 20,000 members.

Church of God (Anderson, Indiana)

The Church of God with headquarters at Anderson, Indiana, started about 1880 as a movement within existing churches. It prefers to have its name accepted in an inclusive rather than in a denominational sense and is actually a movement in the direction of Christian unity and of the reestablishment of the New Testament standard of faith and life by realizing the identity of the visible and invisible church in the free fellowship of believers. The founders believed that the church at large was too much restricted and overburdened with organization and ecclesiasticism; it should be "more directly under the rule of God."

Doctrine in this church includes belief in the divine inspiration of the Scriptures; the forgiveness of sin through the atonement of Christ and repentance of the believer; the experience of holiness; the personal return of Christ, which is not connected with any millennial reign; the kingdom of God as established here and now; the final judgment; the resurrection of the dead; the reward of the righteous, and the punishment of the wicked.

Baptism is by immersion. Members of this church also practice foot washing and observe the Lord's Supper but not as conditions of fellowship. They believe the church to be the body of Christ, made up of all Christians, and that all Christians are one in Christ. The confusion of sects and denominations, however, is an obstacle to this unity; being unscriptural, it should be removed. God desires this restoration of the New Testament ideal in his church; it is a restoration based upon spiritual experience and not on creedal agreement.

There are 174,399 members reported in this church along with 120,742 adherents in home and foreign mission stations. They are governed by a congregational system; while they preach the idea of God governing his church, they agree that human instrumentality is quite necessary. Membership is not on a formal basis, and hence no formal membership is kept. Ministers meet in voluntary state and regional conventions, which are chiefly advisory. The general ministerial assembly meets annually in connection with the annual convention and camp meeting held at Anderson, Indiana.

Church of God (Seventh Day)

There are 2 bodies bearing this name, one centered in Denver, with a publishing house in Stanberry, Missouri, and the other in Salem, West Virginia. Both groups were known originally as the Church of God (Adventist). Located first in Michigan, this body established headquarters in Stanberry in 1899, having separated themselves from the Second Advent body (1863–65) during a debate in which the parent body was seeking a distinctive name for a new press they were establishing at Battle Creek, Michigan. This church is still maintained in Denver. Some wanted the name Church of God, others Seventh-day Adventist; when the majority voted for the latter name, the others left. The 2 factions eventually merged in a new body named the Church of God (Adventist). The Salem group split from this new church at Stanberry in 1933 to form the Church of God (Seventh Day); the original group later set up headquarters in Denver. The two groups reunited in 1949, but a dissident group remained in Salem.

The body in Salem traces its organization back to Old and New Testament churches; they choose their leaders by drawing names by lot, convinced that the method of democratic election is unbiblical. They have 12 Apostles "plus 7 and 70" in an apostolic council meeting biyearly, support their ministers by the tithe, observe the seventh day as the true Sabbath, practice foot washing, and abstain from the eating of pork in obedience to the scriptural teaching of "clean and unclean." The Denver group is quite similar in belief and practice, stressing the infallibility of the Bible, the imminent return of Christ, the earth as the eternal abode of the righteous, premillennialism, annihilation of the wicked, reward for the righteous at the final judgment, and abstinence from unclean foods, tobacco, alcohol, and narcotics. The administration of the Denver body uses the biblical example of 12, 7, and 70; their executive board (board of control) is composed of 12 ministers elected to 6-year terms; a united missions board is composed of 7 men (laymen or ministers). An international ministerial congress is composed of 70 leading ministers who consider doctrine for the worldwide body. (Foreign churches are organized in Europe, Africa, Central and South America, India, Mexico, and the Caribbean.) The general conference of the Church of God (Seventh Day) has a U.S. and Canadian membership of 7,000 in 100 churches; the Salem church has 2,000 in 7 churches.

✟ Church of God and Saints of Christ

The Church of God and Saints of Christ was founded in Lawrence, Kansas, in 1896 by William S. Crowdy, a black Baptist deacon who claimed visions from God, a divine commission to bring the truth of God to the world, and a prophetic endowment. He became the first bishop of the church, which today has a membership of 38,127 in 217 churches in the United States, with additional churches in Africa and the West Indies.

Sometimes called Black Jews, members of this church celebrate such Jewish holy and feast days as they feel have biblical authority and support; they observe the Sabbath on the seventh day, the Day of Atonement, and the Jewish New Year. They believe that their church is built upon the patriarchs, prophets, and apostles of the Jewish tradition and that "Jesus the Anointed" is their chief cornerstone. They differentiate between prophetic Judaism ("which seeks to follow the living insight into the spiritual idea to its fullest implication") as opposed to legalistic Judaism. They accept the Decalogue as the standard of conduct for all mankind.

An executive bishop stands at the head of the church and the bishops' council; there is a board of presbytery, which is the law-making body, consisting of 12 men, and an ecclesiastical council made up of all evangelists and ministers; under these officials work general and district officers, deacons, teachers, and missionaries. Local churches are headed by overseers and divided into districts; each district has an appointed evangelist who assists the bishop of that district. The district bishop calls and presides over annual district conferences; a denominational religious convocation called Passover and a national business assembly are held annually, both under the guidance of the executive bishop. The church maintains a home for the aged, an orphans' home, and a school for primary grades.

Church of God by Faith, Inc.

Organized in 1914 and chartered at Alachua, Florida, in 1923, this is a group of 96 churches scattered through Florida, Georgia, Alabama, South Carolina, Maryland, New Jersey, and New York. Doctrine contains items of belief in regeneration, sanctification, the baptism of the Holy Ghost and with fire, speaking in tongues, the Word of God as the communion of the blood and body of Christ, one Lord, faith and baptism, and the isolation of willful sinners from God and the church. Officers consist of a bishop and an executive secretary. A general assembly meets 3 times a year. A school (the Matthews-Scippio Academy) was opened in 1963 at Ocala, Florida. Inclusive membership is reported at 4,500 in 105 churches.

Church of God in Christ

C. H. Mason and C. P. Jones, rejected by Baptist groups in Arkansas for what the Baptists considered overemphasis on holiness, founded the Church of God in Christ in 1897. The name was divinely revealed to Mason, who put strong emphasis upon entire sanctification, and in a revival received the baptism of the Holy Spirit together with "signs of speaking with tongues"; his ardent preaching on these gifts and subjects aroused resentment and subsequent division among his followers.

Doctrine is trinitarian, stressing repentance, regeneration, justification, sanctification, speaking in tongues, and the gift of healing as evidence of the baptism of the Spirit. Holiness is considered a prerequisite to salvation; ordinances include baptism by immersion, the Lord's Supper, and foot washing.

Church organization is held to have its authority in Scripture; there are presiding, assistant presiding, and state bishops; district superintendents, pastors, evangelists, deacons, and departmental presidents. Missionaries are found in South Africa, Thailand, Jamaica, Haiti, Liberia, and on the West Coast in Africa. Saints Junior College is maintained at Lexington, Mississippi; there is a department of publications and a Sunday school publishing house to supply the denomination with literature. There are 425,000 members in 4,500 churches.

Church of God in Christ (International)

Fourteen bishops of the Church of God in Christ (Memphis) withdrew from that church to organize the Church of God in Christ (International) in Kansas City, Missouri, in 1969. Their disagreement with the parent body was not doctrinal but one of polity and the authority of government. The theological background here is Wesleyan but emphasizing 2 works of grace, full baptism by the Holy Ghost, and speaking with other tongues "as the Spirit gives utterance." Membership is reported at 501,000 in 1,401 churches.

CHURCH OF ILLUMINATION

Described as a "church at large rather than a church of congregations," this body was organized in 1908 under the inspiration of the late Rev. R. Swinburne Clymer, now succeeded by his son, Emerson M. Clymer, as director-general of the church. Its stated purpose is to harmonize the teachings of philosophy with the truths of religion, thus offering a spiritual, esoteric, and philosophical interpretation of basic Bible teachings to those in search of spiritual truth. Membership is by written request and does not require severance of membership in any other church.

Much is made of the "priesthood of Melchizedek," which dates from "beyond the year 4255 B.C. and includes all that small body of chosen seekers initiated into the mysteries of the divine law"; this priesthood has come down from the days of Genesis through Jesus, the Gnostics, the early Egyptians, Greeks, Indians, and Persians to the present time, where it is to be found in the Church of Illumination.

The essence of religion here is found in the simple biblical statement that "whatsoever a man soweth, that shall he also reap." This is interpreted as being a matter of inevitable compensation rather than of rewards and punishments at the hands of God. Furthermore:

Religion teaches the Law—the way of Life—a way which makes man aware of the all-important truth that he is, in fact, a child of God, and that within him, buried by much debris, is a spark of the Divine. This Divine Spark is the *Christos*—the unconscious Soul—which may be awakened and brought into consciousness—a second or Rebirth. This is the "talent" entrusted to man and for which he is responsible to his Creator. Neglected, it remains just as it is—a tiny spark. Recognized, aroused, awakened and brought into consciousness, it becomes an inexhaustible source of wisdom and power, lifting man to the heights of Illumination and achievement. The process that makes all this possible is, in reality, the Second Birth. It is the process of Regeneration—mortality taking on immortality—the means whereby the son of man actually and literally becomes the Son of God.

Enlarging upon this, 4 great fundamentals are taught: (1) the law of action and reaction (sowing and reaping), (2) the indebtedness of man to

God for his talents and his obligation to use them well, (3) the practice of the Golden Rule, and (4) the practice of the law of honesty. All this is the means to the fulfillment of man's destiny. It is also taught that we are now in a "manistic" age (*manisis*, the recognition of the equality of man and woman), which will last 2,000 years and in which Revelation will become the "unsealed book of the Bible" and that the world right now is the scene of the final battle of Armageddon. There is also some emphasis upon reincarnation, although belief in this is not required of adherents.

Yearly conferences of ministers and leaders are held in various parts of the country. Officially there are 14 established churches with 9,000 members, but the bulk of the membership is made up of those who are members only in correspondence and not members of any specific church.

THE CHURCH OF JESUS CHRIST

At least 20 independent religious bodies in the United States bear the name Church of Jesus Christ. The largest of these, headquartered in Cleveland, Tennessee, became a charted group in 1927, under the leadership of Bishop M. K. Lawson. There were several splits or divisions in this group from 1934 through the 1960s; the parent church today claims a membership of 37,500.

In spite of their divisions, these several groups hold in common doctrines of justification by faith, the freedom of the individual to accept or reject the plan of salvation, baptism by immersion (in the name of Christ only) and baptism of the Holy Ghost, being born again of water and the Spirit, and the premillenial second coming of Christ. They have two ordinances, baptism and the Lord's Supper (with foot-washing fellowship). They practice divine healing; condemn the use of alcohol, tobacco, and jewelry; and oppose membership in secret societies. Church members marry only church members; while they oppose the taking of oaths before magistrates, they call for obedience to and respect for civil government, except in the use of armed force. Exclusion from church membership is imposed upon those who sin willfully. They refuse to use the term "reverend" and use only the scriptural terms of "bishop," "elder," "evangelist," "deacon," and "pastor."

Foreign missions are found in Africa, India, Haiti, Australia, Jamaica, Israel, Mexico, Panama, the Dominican Republic, and England. A home missions work stresses evangelism. There is one Bible Institute about to open and several academies, the largest of which is located in Terrell, Texas.

CHURCH OF JESUS CHRIST OF LATTER-DAY SAINTS (MORMONS)

Better known as Mormons, the Latter-day Saints have had one of the most tempestuous histories of any church body in the United States. Attacked by mobs and once invaded by United States Army troops, they built a religious community in what was once a desert and established themselves as one of the outstanding religious groups of the nation.

Essentially a laymen's movement in its origin, their church is rooted in the visions of Joseph Smith, who organized the movement in 1830 at Fayette, New York. Smith claimed to have experienced a series of heavenly visitations, beginning with the appearance of God and Jesus Christ to him in 1820, in which he was informed that all existing churches were in error, that the true gospel was yet to be restored, that it would be revealed to him, and that he was to reestablish the true church on earth. He was led by an angel to discover, buried in a hill called Cumorah near Manchester, New York, certain golden plates or tablets left there by an ancient prophet and containing the sacred records of the ancient inhabitants of America and the true word of God. According to the Mormons, America was originally settled by the Jaredites, one of the groups dispersed during the confusion of tongues at the Tower of Babel; the American Indians were direct descendants of the Hebrews who came from Jerusalem in 600 B.C. Jesus himself visited this country after his resurrection.

Smith translated the hieroglyphics on the golden tablets into the *Book of Mormon,* from which the name "Mormon" comes. Oliver Cowdery acted as his scribe. This *Book of Mormon* is considered by the saints as being equal with and "supporting but not supplanting" the Bible and as being equal with 2 other writings of Joseph Smith, the *Book of Doctrine and Covenants* and the *Pearl of Great Price,* which contain the foundation teachings of the church. The golden plates were said to have been returned to the angel by Joseph Smith; their authenticity has been challenged by non-Mormon scholars and as ardently defended by the Mormons, who offer the names of 11 other persons beside Smith who saw them. Smith and Cowdery had the "priesthood of Aaron" conferred upon them by a heavenly messenger, John the Baptist, who instructed them to baptize each other. Later 3 other divine visitants, Peter, James, and John, bestowed upon them the "priesthood of Melchizedek" and gave them the keys of apostleship. This was in 1829, a year before the founding of the church with 6 charter members.

Opposition arose as the church gained strength, and the Mormons left New York in 1831 for Ohio, where headquarters were established at Kirtland. Another large Mormon center developed at Independence, Missouri, where they planned to build the ideal community with a temple at its heart. Friction with other settlers became so acute that the Mormons were expelled from Missouri from 1838-39; they settled at Nauvoo, Illinois. Violence followed them there and reached its peak with the murder of Joseph Smith and Hyrum Smith, the prophet and the patriarch of the church, in jail at Carthage, in 1844.

With Smith's death the Quorum of the Twelve Apostles was accepted as the presidency of the church, and Brigham Young as president of the quorum. A group of the defeated minority, objecting that Young was not the legal successor to Smith, withdrew to form other churches. Some of them followed James T. Strang to Wisconsin to form the sect known as Strangites;

others joined various other splinter groups, but the largest body of "anti-Brighamites" believed that the leadership of the church belonged to direct descendants of Joseph Smith, Jr. and in 1860 these people formed the Reorganized Church of Jesus Christ of Latter-day Saints, led by Joseph Smith III (a church unaffiliated with the Utah-based church). But Young held his office with the vote of the majority, and he had the courage and the administrative ability to save the church from disruption and division.

He led the saints when they were driven out of Nauvoo in February, 1846, and began their epic march to what is now Utah, arriving in the Salt Lake Valley in July of 1847; here they built their famous tabernacle and temple at the heart of what was to become a worldwide Mormonism, creating a self-existent community in the desert. In 1850 the Territory of Utah was formed; it became the state of Utah in 1896.

Based on *The Book of Mormon* and the Bible, which is accepted "as far as it is translated correctly," the faith of the Mormons is a faith to be found in many conservative Protestant churches, plus the revelations of Joseph Smith. However, certain aspects of Latter-day Saints' theology depart from the traditional orthodoxy of Catholic and Protestant churches. They believe that the 3 persons comprising the Godhead are the Father, the Son, and the Holy Ghost; that the Father and the Son have bodies of flesh and bones as tangible as man's but that the Holy Ghost is a personage of Spirit; that men will be punished for their own individual sins and not for Adam's transgression. All mankind may be saved through the atonement of Christ and by obedience to the laws and ordinances of the gospel; these laws and ordinances include faith in Christ, repentance, baptism by immersion for the remission of sins, the laying on of hands for the gift of the Holy Ghost, and the observance of the Lord's Supper each Sunday. They believe in the gift of tongues and interpretation of tongues, visions, prophecy, and healing, and that Christ will return to rule the earth from his capitals in Zion and Jerusalem following the restoration of the 10 tribes of Israel. In addition, it is believed that the Latter-day Saints should adhere to the official pronouncements of the living president (prophet) of the church.

Revelation is not to be regarded as being confined to either the Bible or *The Book of Mormon*; it continues today, in the living apostles, prophets, pastors, teachers, and evangelists of the modern Mormon church. Baptism is necessary to salvation, and obedience to the priesthood is of first importance. Subjection to civil laws and rules is advocated, together with an insistence upon the right of the individual to worship according to the dictates of his conscience.

Two Mormon practices, baptism for the dead and sealing in marriage for eternity, are exclusive with this church. Baptism and salvation for the dead are based upon the conviction that those who died without a chance to hear or accept the gospel cannot possibly be condemned by a just and merciful God. The gospel must be preached to them after death; authority for this is found in I Pet. 4:6: "For this cause was the gospel preached also to them that are dead, that they might be judged according to men in the flesh, but live according to God in the spirit." Baptism is considered as essential to the dead as to the living, though the rites will not finally save them; there must be faith and repentance for salvation. The ceremony is performed with a living person standing proxy for the dead.

Marriage in Mormonism has 2 forms: marriage for time and marriage for eternity (or celestial marriage). Mormons who are married by civil authority only still remain in good standing in the church, but marriage for time and eternity in the church's temples is regarded as a prerequisite for the highest opportunity of salvation. In connection with this, Joseph Smith informed his associates in the 1840s that plural marriage was also sanctioned and commanded by God. Some plural marriages had been secretly contracted for some time before Smith's revelation on the practice was announced publicly by Brigham Young in 1852.

Following the Civil War, the federal government mounted an increasingly intense campaign against Mormon polygamy. In 1882, the Edmunds Act provided stringent penalties for polygamists, and in 1887 the church was disincorporated and its properties were confiscated. In 1890 the U.S. Supreme Court ruled that it was constitutional to deny all privileges of citizenship to all members of the church. Also in 1890, the church president issued a manifesto that officially discontinued the contracting of new plural marriages. Some followers of Joseph Smith, Jr., deny that polygamy was ever sanctioned, but a few in other groups (notably in the Reorganized Church of Latter-day Saints) believe that it will never end. These contemporary polygamists are excommunicated from the Mormon church and are known as Fundamentalists.

Organization and government in the church differ in detail among 5 Mormon denominations but agree in essentials. They are based upon the 2 priesthoods: the higher priesthood of Melchizedek, which holds power of presidency and authority over the offices of the church and whose officers include apostles, patriarchs, high priests, seventies, and elders; and the lesser priesthood of Aaron, which guides the temporal affairs of the church through its bishops, priests, teachers, and deacons.

The presiding council of the church is the First Presidency, made up of 3 high priests—the president and 2 counselors. Its authority is final and universal in both spiritual and temporal affairs. The president of the church is "the mouthpiece of God"; through him come the laws of the church by direct revelation.

Next to the presidency stands the Council of the Twelve Apostles, chosen by revelation, to supervise under the direction of the First Presidency the whole work of the church and to ordain all ministers. The church is divided into stakes (geographical divisions) that are composed of a number of wards corresponding to local churches or parishes. High priests, assisted by elders, are in charge of the stakes. Members of the Melchizedek priesthood hold authority under the direction of the presidency to officiate in all ordinances of the gospel. Seventies work under the direction of the First Seventy (a presiding quorum of 70 men); they are organized into quorums of 70 each, with 7 presidents of equal rank presiding over each quorum. Seventies have a responsibility to proselytize. The duties of the 12 apostles and the seventies carry them into all the stakes, wards, and missions throughout the entire church. The duties of the stake presidents, the ward bishops, the patriarchs, high priests, and elders are to supervise the work within the stakes and wards of the church. The Aaronic priesthood is governed by the presiding bishopric of 3 men, who also supervise the work done in the stakes and wards by members of the priesthood. (In June of 1978, it was ruled that "all worthy male members of the church may be ordained to the priesthood without regard for race or color.")

The church influences every phase of the living of every member; it supplies relief in illness or poverty, assists with education and employment when necessary but does not educate or employ all members. Such a program has resulted in deep loyalty among its members. Almost 28,000 young Mormons currently serve as full-time missionaries throughout the world without compensation; they give 2 years to the work of spreading the teaching of their church at home and abroad. Only about 60 persons in leadership positions in the church receive a salary. Their missionary experience strengthens them and their church and offers a model of church service.

The Church of Jesus Christ of Latter-day Saints

The organization and doctrine of the Church of Jesus Christ of Latter-day Saints has been outlined in the preceeding section; with headquarters in Salt Lake City, it has a membership of 4,200,000 and 10,000 congregations; the membership has increased by 50 percent in the last decade. A general conference is held twice a year at Salt Lake City, and area conferences are held in other countries. The church is supported by the tithes of the membership; each Mormon who earns money is expected to give one-tenth of his income.

The missionary effort of this church is constant and vigorous. There are 170 missionary stations throughout the world. The death rate among Mormons is lower than that of any other group of people of the same size anywhere in the world; this is held by some to be the direct result of Mormon abstinence from liquor and tobacco and of their welfare program. This church maintains storehouses for community food and clothing; members operate vegetable, seed, and wheat farms; orchards; a cotton plantation; dairies; sewing centers; fish canneries; soap processing plants; a vitamin pill factory; and several grain elevators. Most of these products are consumed at home but not all of them; thousands of relief packages have gone to Europe under a church-wide relief plan.

Reorganized Church of Jesus Christ of Latter-day Saints

This church claims to be the continuation of the original church organized by Joseph Smith on April 6, 1830. It has more than 217,000 members located in 37 countries across the world. It bases its claim to be the continuation of the original Mormon church on obedience to the rule of lineal succession and its presidency as found in *The Book of Doctrine and Covenants*. Court actions on 2 occasions, in Ohio in 1880 and in Missouri in 1894, are cited as naming it the legal continuation of the original church. The son of Joseph Smith, it is held, was designated by his father to succeed him, and he became president in 1860.

The Reorganized Church rejected the claims of the Mormons led by Brigham Young, because of their abandonment of this rule and also because of their abandonment of the doctrine of polygamy in 1852, which is held to be contrary to the teachings of *The Book of Mormon* and *The Book of Doctrine and Covenants* endorsed by the original organization in 1835. It also differs on the doctrine of the Godhead, celestial marriage, and baptism of the dead.

At the death of Joseph Smith, Jr., in 1844, the church entered a period of confusion due to certain claims to leadership. Those holding to the "lineal succession" eventually reorganized, the first collective expression of this movement coming at a conference in Beloit, Wisconsin, in 1852. Joseph Smith III was chosen president in 1860 at Amboy, Illinois. His successors have all been descendants of the founder.

Basic beliefs of the Reorganized Church include faith in the universality of God the Eternal Father, Jesus Christ as the only begotten Son of the Father, the Holy Spirit, the worth and dignity of others, repentance for sin, baptism by immersion, the efficacy of various sacramental ordinances, the resurrection of the dead, the open canon of Scripture and the continuity of revelation, the doctrine of stewardship, and the principle of the accountability of all people to God.

The work of the church is supported by tithes and free-will offerings. This is regarded as a divine principle, and the tithe is calculated upon a tenth of each member's annual increase over his needs and just wants.

The church has adherents on every continent in the world and in the islands of the Caribbean and South Pacific. It has 4-year accredited colleges at Lamoni, Iowa (Graceland College), and at Kansas City, Mo. (Park College); a leadership and ministerial school (Temple School) is located at Independence, Missouri.

Church doctrines, policies, and matters of legislation must have the approval and action of a delegate conference held biennially at the auditorium in Independence. General adminstration of the church is by a First Presidency of 3 high priests, a Quorum of Twelve Apostles who represent the presidency in the field, and a pastoral arm under the high priests and elders. The work of their bishops covers church properties, the stewardship of members, and church finances.

Church of Christ (Temple Lot)

Claiming status as a remnant of the church founded by Joseph Smith in 1830, this church has 6,000 members in 32 local congregations. After the death of Smith in 1844, and following the western trek of the Mormons, a number of those who remained in the Midwest became convinced that the church leaders were advocating new teachings quite at variance with the original doctrines; by 1852 there were two protesting groups, one known as the New Organization and the other, centered in Crow Creek, Illinois, functioning under the original name of The Church of Christ. This latter group returned to Independence, Missouri, in the "appointed year" of 1867 and began purchasing "temple lots." The revelation concerning the "return" was given in 1864 through the presiding elder at the time, Granville Hedrick.

The temple lots (the subject of controversy and court action between the Church of Christ and the Reorganized Church of Jesus Christ of Latter-day Saints), finally resolved in favor of the Church of Christ; consist of land dedicated in 1831 by Joseph Smith and other Mormon leaders for the building of the Lord's Temple. The belief here is that the Lord himself will designate the time of building, and that while the men of the church cannot do this until the appointed time, they nevertheless believe that they have a sacred obligation to "hold and keep this land free; when the time of building comes, it can be accomplished as the Lord sees fit."

The Church of Christ puts its faith in the pattern and thought of the church "as it existed at the time of Christ and His apostles." Hence the highest office in the church is that of Apostle, and there are 12 Apostles. They are charged with the missionary work and general supervision of the church. Temporal affairs are directly administered by the general bishopric, under the direction of the general conference and the council of apostles; local churches administer their own affairs but must keep their teachings and practice in harmony with those of the denomination. Most of the membership is described as "Gentile," with several members among the Maya Indians of Yucatan, Mexico.

The church accepts the King James Version of the Bible and *The Book of Mormon* as its standards. It holds that all latter-day revelation, including that of Joseph Smith, must be tested by these scriptures; it does not accept all that was given through him. Because changes were made in the early revelations, this church prefers *The Book of Commandments* to *The Doctrine and Covenants* where these changes are involved. For this reason the doctrines of plural marriage, baptism for the dead, celestial marriage, and plurality of gods are not accepted.

Church of Jesus Christ (Bickertonites)

The founders of this church were at one time members of a Mormon body led by Sidney Rigdon, in Pennsylvania. Rigdon and his followers refused to join the western march under Brigham Young, denouncing Young's teaching of polygamy, the plurality of gods, and baptism for the dead; in 1846 they purchased a farm (later lost at a sheriff's sale) near Greencastle, Pennsylvania. A small group did not go to Greencastle; they remained at West Elizabeth and under William Bickerton, who had been one of Rigdon's elders, were formally organized as The Church of Jesus Christ at Green Oak, in 1862. The name "Bickertonites" is employed to distinguish them from other Mormon groups; they prefer to be known as "the Bickerton Organization." Current president is Dr. Dominic R. Thomas, elected in 1974.

Foot washing is practiced, and they salute one another with the holy kiss.

Monogamy is required, "except in case of death," and obedience of all state and civil laws. They have their own edition of the *Book of Mormon* (in English and Italian), publish a monthly periodical, *The Gospel News,* and other denominational material at headquarters in Monongahela, Pennsylvania, where a general conference meets annually. Missionary work is conducted in Italy, Nigeria, Mexico, and among the Indians of the United States and Canada. There are 2,500 members in the United States and more than 6,000 worldwide, now including Argentina and Ghana. There are 51 churches in North America.

Church of Jesus Christ of Latter-day Saints (Strangites)

The group claims that it is "the one and original Church of Jesus Christ of Latter-day Saints" and that its founder, James J. Strang, is the only legal successor to church leadership with written credentials from Joseph Smith. Strang translated portions of the Plates of Laban; they, together with certain other revelations, are found in *The Book of the Law of the Lord.* Strang also translated what is called *The Voree Record*—a record found under an oak tree near Voree, Wisconsin, dealing in hieroglyphic-like characters with "an ancient people . . . who no longer exist." He was crowned "king" of this church in 1850 and was murdered in 1856 during a wave of anti-Mormonism in the Great Lakes region.

Organized at Burlington, Wisconsin, in 1844, the church denies the virgin birth theory, holds that Adam fell by a law of natural consequences rather than in the breaking of a divine law and that the corruption thus caused could be removed only by the resurrection of Christ. They deny the Trinity and the plurality of gods, celebrate Saturday as the Sabbath day, and believe that baptism is essential for salvation. Due to "lack of prophetic leadership at the present time" they do not practice baptism for the dead.

Chief officer of the church is a high priest in the Melchizedek priesthood, chosen by the general church conference. Membership is given at about 300 in 6 churches or branches.

CHURCH OF OUR LORD JESUS CHRIST OF THE APOSTOLIC FAITH, INC.

Confident that it is "a continuation of the great revival begun at Jerusalem on the day of Pentecost in A.D. 33," this church was organized at Columbus, Ohio, in 1919 by R. C. Lawson. Doctrine is stated to be that of the apostles and prophets with Christ as the cornerstone. Perhaps the basic emphases are those laid upon Christ's resurrection and premillennial second coming, the resurrection and translation of the saints, the priesthood of all believers, and the final judgment of mankind. Baptism is by immersion, and the baptism of the Holy Spirit is necessary to the second birth. Foot washing is practiced but not as an ordinance.

Found in 32 states, the British West Indies, Africa, the Philippines, Haiti, the Dominican Republic, and London, England, the church reports a membership of 45,000 in 155 churches. Twenty-two elementary schools, 1 Bible College, 18 extension schools, 1 clinic, and 1 orphanage are maintained. A national convocation meets every other year at the headquarters church, Refuge Temple in New York City. Officers of the denomination include 5 apostles, 32 bishops, 27 district elders, 3 secretaries, 1 treasurer, and 1 public information officer.

CHURCH OF THE NAZARENE

The theological and doctrinal foundations of the Church of the Nazarene lie in the preaching of the doctrines of holiness and sanctification as taught by John Wesley in the eighteenth-century revival in England. Its physical structure is the result not so much of schism as of the merging of 3 independent holiness groups already in existence in the United States. An eastern holiness body, located principally in New York and New England and known as the Association of Pentecostal Churches in America, joined at Chicago in 1907 with a western (California) body called the Church of the Nazarene; the 2 merging churches agreed on the name Pentecostal Church of the Nazarene. The southern group, known as the Holiness Church of Christ, united with this Pentecostal Church of the Nazarene at Pilot Point, Texas, in 1908. In 1919 the word "Pentecostal" was dropped from the name, leaving it as we know it today, the Church of the Nazarene. This was primarily a move to disassociate in the public mind any connection with other Pentecostal groups that taught or practiced speaking in tongues, a teaching and practice not endorsed by the Church of the Nazarene.

The background of the Nazarenes is definitely Methodist; they adhere closely to the original Wesleyan ideology. Most of the early holiness groups in this country came out of the Methodist Episcopal Church; 2 of the original 7 general superintendents of the Church of the Nazarene were ex-Methodist ministers, and the Nazarene *Manual* has been called a "rewritten and modified Methodist *Discipline*."

The doctrine of the church is built around sanctification as a second definite work of grace subsequent to regeneration; all ministers and local church officials must have undergone this experience. Other doctrines include belief in the plenary inspiration of the Scriptures as containing all truth necessary to Christian faith and living; in the atonement of Christ for the whole human race; in the justification, regeneration, and adoption of all penitent believers in Christ; in the second coming of Christ, the resurrection of the dead, and the final judgment. Members of this church believe in divine healing but never to the exclusion of medical agencies. The use of tobacco and alcoholic beverages is denounced. Two ordinances—baptism by sprinkling, pouring, or most often immersion and the Lord's Supper—are accepted as "instituted by Christ." Members are admitted on confession of faith and on agreement "to observe the rules and regulations . . . of the Church." It is a middle-of-the road church, neither extremely ritualistic on the one hand nor extremely informal on the other; one church historian calls it the "right wing of the holiness movement."

There are 4,867 local congregations grouped into 74 districts in the United States and Canada and an additional 85 districts, or Intercontinental Zones, and mission areas totaling 159 districts throughout the world. Local pastors are elected by local churches; each district is supervised by a district superintendent who is elected for a 4-year term by the members of the district assembly.

The general assembly also elects a general board, consisting of an equal number of lay and ministerial members, which is in turn divided into 8 administrative departments: world missions, home missions, evangelism, publication, pensions and benevolences, education and the ministry, church schools, and youths. A missionary work is conducted in 60 world areas with 580 missionaries. A strong emphasis is laid upon evangelism. Eight liberal arts colleges are maintained, 2 of which were started in 1968. A theological seminary in Kansas City, Mo. and Bible colleges in the United States, Canada, and the British Isles are supported by the church.

The books and periodicals of the church are produced at the Nazarene Publishing House in Kansas City. The annual volume of business exceeds $10,000,000. Membership in the United States is reported at 455,100; in Canada, 8,253; on Intercontinental Zones in overseas stations, 99,204; for a total membership of 562,557. There are 6,900 churches at home and overseas.

CHURCHES OF CHRIST

Seventeen thousand independent congregations with a total membership of about 2,500,000 constitute the Churches of Christ. They are located in 50 states with greatest concentrations in the South and West, have congregations in 75 foreign countries, and in the past 20 years have emerged as one of the top 10 non-Catholic bodies in North America.

There is a distinctive plea for unity at the heart of the Churches of Christ—a unity that is Bible based. It is believed here that the Bible is "the beginning place" in and through which God-fearing people can achieve spiritual oneness; it is an appeal to "speak where the Bible speaks and to be silent where the Bible is silent" in all matters pertaining to faith and morals; consequently, members recognize no other written creed or confession of faith than the Scriptures. In all religious matters, there must be a "thus saith the Lord."

In modern times the churches are related to the restoration movement—in the work and thinking of James O'Kelly in Virginia, Abner Jones and Elias Smith in New England, Barton Stone in Kentucky, and Thomas and Alexander Campbell in West Virginia. (For a detailed discussion, see

"Christian Church (Disciples of Christ).") These 4 movements, all contending that "nothing should be bound upon Christians as a matter of doctrine which is not as old as the New Testament" and all completely independent at the start, eventually became one strong religious stream because of their common purpose and plea.

The leaders among the Churches of Christ in the nineteenth century were more conservative religiously than their counterparts among the Disciples of Christ. They contended for a strict adherence to the New Testament pattern of worship and church organization. Congregations refused to join any intercongregational organization, such as a missionary society. Their worship was simple, and they opposed the addition of instrumental music on the grounds that the New Testament did not authorize it and that the early church did not use it. Around the turn of the twentieth century a recognition of differences between the conservative and more liberal wings of the restoration movements became evident, and in the 1906 Census of Religious Bodies, the Churches of Christ were listed separately for the first time. They disclaim being a denomination but claim to be nondenominational with no headquarters, no governing bodies, and no clergy. They cooperate voluntarily in international radio programs sponsored by one congregation.

Today one of the outstanding features of the Churches of Christ lies in their acceptance of the Bible as a true and completely adequate revelation. This basic concept has resulted in such characteristic practices as weekly observance of the Lord's Supper, baptism by immersion, *a cappella* singing, a vigorous prayer life, support of church needs through voluntary giving, and a program of preaching and teaching the Bible. This concept also explains the autonomy of local churches, governed by elders and deacons appointed under New Testament qualifications, dignified worship services, enthusiastic mission campaigns, and far-flung benevolent programs all financed by the local churches.

The great scriptural doctrines usually classified as "conservative" are received in the Churches of Christ, including the concept of the Father, the Son, and the Holy Ghost as members of one Godhead; the incarnation, virgin birth, and bodily resurrection of Christ; the universality of sin after the age of accountability and its only remedy in the vicarious atonement of the Lord Jesus Christ. Strong emphasis is also laid on the church as the body and bride of Christ. A figurative rather than a literal view is prevalent with reference to the book of Revelation. Membership is contingent upon the faith of the individual in Jesus Christ as the only begotten Son of God, repentance, confession of faith, and baptism by immersion into Christ for the remission of sins. Church attendance is stressed.

While professing identity with the original church established by Christ and the apostles at Pentecost, the Churches of Christ maintain that the final judgment of all religious groups is reserved unto the Lord himself. Members believe they are "Christians only, but not the only Christians." This view, however, still allows for a vigorous evangelism that finds unacceptable the doctrines, practices, names, titles, and creeds that have been grafted into the original Christianity in the long post-apostolic period.

Ministers are ordained rather than licensed, and they hold tenure in their pulpits under mutual agreement with the elders of churches in which they preach. Their authority is moral rather than arbitrary, the actual government of the church being vested in its eldership.

A vigorous missionary program is carried on in 75 nations outside the United States, and in recent years a strong movement to extend the influence of the group in the northeastern United States has developed. Counting native workers in the foreign field and mission activities within the United States, there are over 1,000 missionaries, or evangelists, supported by others than the group to whom they preach. A quota of chaplains is maintained in the air force and the army.

Properties owned by the group probably exceed $2,500,000,000 in value. There are 21 colleges, including 1 in Japan; 70 secondary and elementary schools; 40 homes for orphans or the aged; and 65 periodicals, newspapers, and magazines published throughout the country. Since all official status in these institutions is lacking, none of them being authorized to speak for the entire church, their conformity in ideas and teachings is all the more remarkable.

Another medium of evangelism has been put to use in the publication of articles in a number of big national magazines. Many churches offer correspondence courses. A "Herald of Truth" radio and television program has nationwide coverage; it is sponsored by the Highland Church of Christ in Abilene, Texas, and support is found in hundreds of other churches and individuals throughout the country. The "Amazing Grace Bible Class," conducted by Dr. Ira North and sponsored by the Madison, Tennessee, Church of Christ, the largest of the 17,000 Churches of Christ, is seen and heard on more than 100 television and radio stations and over the armed forces network.

CHURCHES OF CHRIST
IN CHRISTIAN UNION

This church originated in a defection from the Christian Union churches (see p. 80), at the 1909 meeting of the Council of Christian Union churches at Marshall, Ohio. It was organized "to allow a complete freedom in the preaching of full salvation as stated doctrinally by John Wesley"—a teaching and a freedom that the dissenters felt was being neglected in the parent body. Their first annual council was held at Jeffersonville, Ohio, in that year, and annual councils have been held since that date. In 1945 legislation was enacted to provide for the organization of additional councils in other states; it now reaches into 17 states and several countries abroad.

The Churches of Christ in Christian Union are generally evangelistic and revivalistic in faith and work; camp meetings, revivals, and soul-winning campaigns are held regularly throughout the denomination. Worship follows simple forms, with little that is ritualistic or traditional. It is characteristic that they place their emphasis "on the blessing of God rather than on the ingenuity of man." A general council meets every two years at Circleville, Ohio, and district councils meet annually. There is one college, Circleville Bible College, established to train ministers and lay workers. Headquarters are also located at Circleville.

The Reformed Methodist Church merged with this body in September of 1952 and is now known as the North Eastern District of the Churches of Christ in Christian Union. There is a total of 260 churches, with 10,167 members.

CHURCHES OF GOD, GENERAL CONFERENCE

John Winebrenner (1797–1860), a member of the Reformed Church in Maryland, was active in the religious revival that swept this country in the early years of the nineteenth century; his ardent evangelism proved unpopular in the Reformed Church, and he severed relations with it in 1826, forming an independent "church of God" in Harrisburg, Pennsylvania. In 1830 Winebrenner and 6 companion preachers organized the first eldership. The terms "eldership" and "conference" are used interchangeably today in this church. A general eldership was organized in 1845, distinguishing the national body from other local or area elderships organized since 1830. The words "In North America" were added in 1845, and "Church" became "Churches" in 1903. In 1975 the name was changed to "Churches of God, General Conference."

Arminian in theology, these churches consider the Bible to be the sole rule of faith and practice. They believe in justification by faith, repentance and regeneration, the Triune God, the office and work of the Holy Spirit, practical piety, observance of the Lord's Day, and the resurrection of the just and the unjust at the final judgment.

The churches were to be, according to Winebrenner, "spiritual, free, and independent churches consisting of believers only, without any human name or creed or ordinance or law." Each local church today is a Church of God. Sectarianism is held to be antiscriptural. Two ordinances are "perpetually obligatory"—baptism by immersion (the church does, however, accept on transfer the baptismal forms of members from other churches) and the Lord's Supper. The ordinance of foot washing is not obligatory. The Lord's Supper is called Communion in many of the churches and may be observed at any time, "as the time of observance is not of major importance nor is the posture of the communicant."

Organization consists of 15 elderships, or conferences, that meet annually in their respective states; there is also an Indian and Pakistan conference, and there is missionary work in Haiti. The general conference is composed of ministerial and lay delegates in equal numbers, with a proportionate number of youths from the annual conferences; it meets triennially and plans work in evangelism, education, and the other interests of the church. Local churches are presbyterian in government, but ministerial appointments follow a semi-itinerant system. There is a coeducational college (Findlay) and Winebrenner Theological Seminary at Findlay, Ohio, and a publishing house operates in Harrisburg, Pennsylvania. There are 347 churches and 36,016 members.

CHURCHES OF GOD, HOLINESS

The Churches of God, Holiness, began in 1914 with a group of 8 people in Atlanta under the preaching of K. H. Burruss. Large churches were founded in Atlanta and in Norfolk, Virginia, in 1916; and by 1922 there were 22 churches in 11 states, Cuba, the Canal Zone, and the British West Indies. In 1922 these churches were incorporated into what is currently known as the National Convention of the Churches of God, Holiness.

All doctrine within this group is tested strictly by New Testament standards; the Scriptures are accepted as inspired, and the New Testament "gives safe and clearly applied instructions on all methods of labor, sacred and secular," and on the conduct of the whole of life. The churches believe in the Trinity, in justification, entire sanctification and regeneration, and hold that the gift of the Holy Spirit is an act subsequent to conversion. Perfection is both *present* and *ultimate*. One must believe in divine healing to be acceptable as a member, but medicines and doctors are approved for those who desire them, not being expressly denounced by Scripture. Two ordinances, baptism and the Lord's Supper, are observed. The washing of feet is approved but not regularly practiced.

Pastors of all churches are assigned by the one bishop of the denomination; they are assisted in the local congregation by deacons. In direct supervision over the pastors is the state overseer, also appointed by the bishop. State conventions are held annually. The highest administrative body is the national convention, a delegate body that elects the national president, or bishop. The church reports 25,600 members and 32 churches.

CHURCHES OF THE LIVING GOD

Two churches of common origin, similar in type but differing in details, bear the title Church of the Living God. Both came out of an organization formed at Wrightsville, Arkansas, in 1889 by William Christian, who "by virtue of a divine call, created the office of chief." Christian held that "Freemason religion" is the true expression of religion and insisted that his "organism" be known as "operative Masonry and [that] its first three corporal degrees shall be baptism, Holy Supper, and foot washing." Both groups are organized along fraternal lines; members tithe their incomes in support of the church and call their churches temples.

The first body, the larger, is known as the Church of the Living God (Motto: Christian Workers for Fellowship). It claims 45,320 members in 276 churches, stresses believer's baptism by immersion, foot washing, and the use of water and unleavened bread in the celebration of the Lord's Supper. A chief bishop is the presiding officer; there is an annual assembly; and a general assembly meets every 4 years to elect other officers and determine the laws for the church. Membership is biracial.

The second body, called the House of God, Which Is the Church of the Living God, the Pillar and Ground of the Truth, Inc., is also episcopal in polity and generally follows the form and thought of the Workers for Fellowship group. They have 2,350 members in 107 churches.

CONGREGATIONAL CHRISTIAN CHURCHES (NATIONAL ASSOCIATION)

This association was organized in 1955 by a group of churches desiring to "preserve historic Congregational forms of freedom and fellowship (the Congregational Way)." With 387 churches and an estimated 100,000 members, it is the largest of several Congregational bodies that did not participate in the merger of the General Council of Congregational Churches and the Evangelical and Reformed Church in the United Church of Christ in 1957.

The National Association brings local churches together for counsel, inspiration, and fellowship but still preserves the independence and autonomy of the local churches. Member churches are either established Congregational Christian churches or affiliated associations of local churches in sympathy with the purposes of the association. A moderator presides over an annual meeting of all the churches; an executive committee of 12, elected for 4 years, acts for the association between meetings. Eight commissions (Christian education, the ministry, publications, women's work, youth, world Christian relations, and spiritual resources) work under the direction of the executive committee. Four divisions of the Corporation of the National Association provide a Missionary Society, a Building and Loan Fund, a Foundation for Theological Studies, and new church development. A unique feature of the organization is found in its Referendum Council, which on call of 10 percent of the churches and by a two-thirds vote may modify any action or proposal of any of the national bodies or officers of the association.

There is no binding ecclesiastical authority and no required subscription to any creed or program. ("We are bound together not by uniformity of belief but by the acceptance of a covenant purpose to be 'the people of God.' ") The association tends to avoid involvement in controversial social and political questions and action. It does a widespread missionary work at home and overseas in the Philippines, Hawaii, Alaska, Mexico, Hong Kong, Formosa, Greece, Italy, Germany, Brazil, Central America, and South India. *The Congregationalist,* a denominational periodical founded in 1849, was revived in 1958 as the monthly journal of the association. National offices are maintained in Oak Creek, Wisconsin.

CONGREGATIONAL HOLINESS CHURCH

Founded in 1921 by a group of ministers withdrawing from the Pentecostal Holiness Church in an effort to retain holiness doctrines and to establish a more democratic church polity, this church is Trinitarian, emphasizing the inspiration of the Scriptures, justification, sanctification, divine healing (without objection to medicine), the second coming of Christ, eternal punishment and rewards, the merits of the atonement, and the salvation of the entire church.

The Bible is held as the sole rule of conduct; slang, tobacco, membership in oath-bound secret societies, and other forms of worldliness are condemned. Ordinances include baptism, foot washing, and the Lord's Supper. The crowning blessing of religious experience is held to be the baptism of the Holy Ghost and speaking with other tongues "as the Spirit [gives] utterance."

Church government is, as the name suggests, congregational. Local churches are grouped in annual associations from which delegates are elected to a general association. Local church officers, elected annually, consist of deacons, trustees, a secretary, and a treasurer. Pastors are called by a majority vote of the congregation; women are licensed to preach but are not ordained. There are 175 churches and 6,025 members in the United States; newer churches and conferences have been established in Mexico, Honduras, Costa Rica, Brazil, Cuba, Spain, and Guatemala.

CONSERVATIVE CONGREGATIONAL CHRISTIAN CONFERENCE

The origins of the "CCCC" go back to 1935 and the labors of H. B. Sandine, a pastor in Hancock, Minnesota, who was convinced that the denominational establishment of the Congregational Christian Churches had departed from the beliefs, polity, and practices of historic Congregationalism. He carried on a mimeographed educational effort until 1939, when his efforts were consummated in a monthly publication, *The Congregational Beacon,* which later became *The Congregational Christian,* and finally the quarterly *Foresee.* A Conservative Congregational Christian Fellowship was organized at Chicago in 1945. The prospect of still another merger (involving Congregational Christian and Evangelical and Reformed churches) precipitated reorganization into the Conservative Congregational Christian Conference in 1948.

Today there are 132 member churches in the conference, with a total of 23,196 members. There are also 20 "regional" fellowships and associations with some 250 churches, made up of Congregational Christian churches that are in sympathy with the statement of faith and general polity of the conference but not directly involved in its official work and actions.

The statement of faith is conservatively evangelical; it includes items of belief in the infallibility and authority of the Scriptures; the Trinity; the deity, virgin birth, sinlessness, atoning death, resurrection, ascension, and promised return of Christ; regeneration by the Holy Spirit; the resurrection of both saved and lost; and the spiritual unity of all believers in Christ.

Local churches are completely autonomous; national officers include a president, 2 vice-presidents, a recording and an executive secretary (missionary-at-large), a treasurer, an editor, and a historian, all elected for 3 years. A board of directors manages the property and directs the general business of the conference, through an executive committee composed of the officers, with the president as chairman. Under the executive committee there are 13 subordinate committees guiding the various efforts of the conference. Work is largely in the areas of missions, youth, and Christian education, carried on through recognized evangelical home and foreign mission agencies, Bible institutions, colleges, seminaries, and Sunday school publishing houses. An annual meeting is held, usually in August. The CCCC is especially active in the fields of church extension, pastoral placement, and regional activities.

The conference is a member denomination of the National Association of Evangelicals and has recently entered into an international alliance with the Union of Evangelical Congregational Churches of Brazil; the new alliance is known as the International Evangelical Congregational Union, and similarly minded Congregational groups are at work in Brazil, England, and Australia. Headquarters are in Wheaton, Illinois.

DIVINE SCIENCE

Three sisters—Alethea Brooks Small, Fannie Brooks James, and Nona Lovell Brooks—of Denver, and Mrs. Malinda E. Cramer of San Francisco in the late years of the last century worked out independently of one another the principles and practice of Divine Science. They met and joined forces in 1898, incorporating the Divine Science College; their first church—the First Divine Science Church of Denver—was organized in Denver.

The core of its teaching is the principles of the all-inclusive God-mind:

God [is] the Omnipresence, the Universal Presence, Life, Love, Intelligence and Substance; man, a child of God, is of God, is like God; knowledge of this truth frees man into a larger concept of God and the understanding of man's higher nature; the practice of the Presence of God in daily life results in man's right attitude toward negative thinking; evolution is God's method of accomplishing, and love, conscious unity, is the fulfilling of the law.

The founders had all had the experience of divine healing, and the emphasis upon healing naturally persists. Healing comes through an understanding of the nature of God and the Universal Law and is "the cleansing of the inner man from all that is unlike God." Divine Science does not deny the existence of visible matter but interprets form and substance as manifestations of God.

Divine Science further stands for: (1) the Fatherhood of God as Omnipresent Life, Love, Intelligence, and Wisdom; (2) the brotherhood of man; (3) the unity of all life; (4) the higher thought in science, philosophy, and religion; (5) the awareness of man's relation to God released into expression in each individual life of man's divine inheritance—health, abundance, peace, and power; (6) the transcendence and immanence of God manifested in all created things.

For many years local churches and colleges of Divine Science were independent of one another. In 1957 some of the ministers and key workers of existing Divine Science churches and colleges met and organized the Divine Science Federation International. This organization serves its member churches and centers and cooperates with the recently reactivated Divine Science College, which trains ministers, teachers, and practitioners. Churches, centers, and study groups are found in the major cities of the United States and abroad; headquarters are located in Denver, where all publications are printed and a monthly periodical, *Aspire,* is issued.

EASTERN CHURCHES

When in A.D. 330 Constantine moved his capital from Rome to Byzantium and began to rule his vast empire from the new Constantinople, the most important split in the history of Christianity was under way. Up to this time the church in the West, in Rome, and the church in the East, formed one body. In the East there were 4 patriarchs, each traditionally equal with the fifth—the patriarch, or pope, of Rome; all 5 patriarchs accepted the Nicene Creed; all were sacramental and apostolic. There were, however, certain basic differences that made for confusion; racially, socially, linguistically, mentally, morally, and philosophically, there were deep gulfs between the two. The East was Greek in blood and speech; the West was Latin. The transference of the capital from West to East meant a shifting of the center of political, social, and intellectual influence. When the Goths swept down upon Rome, that city turned for help—not to Constantinople, but to the

Franks; in gratitude for his aid the pope crowned Charles the Great as emperor on Christmas Day in 800, and the Roman Church became coterminous with the Holy Roman Empire.

Conflict deepened between the pope at Rome and the patriarch at Constantinople. In 857 Ignatius in Constantinople refused to administer the sacrament to Caesar Bardas on the ground that he was immoral. Tried and imprisoned by the Eastern emperor, Ignatius was succeeded by Photius, an intellectual giant for whom the weaker pope was no match. Their increasing friction broke into flame at the Council of St. Sophia, were Photius bitterly condemned the Latin church for adding the word *filioque* to the Nicene Creed. The Eastern church held that the Holy Spirit proceeded directly from the Father; the Western church had adopted the view that the Spirit proceeded from the Father *and* the Son—*filioque*. Political and ecclesiastical jealousies fanned the flame until, in 1054, the pope excommunicated the patriarch, and the patriarch excommunicated the pope, the result being that there were finally two churches, Eastern and Western, instead of one. The pope remained head of the Western church; at the moment, in the East, there were 4 patriarchs, or heads, guiding the destiny of Eastern Orthodoxy. This is important to an understanding of the Eastern Orthodox Church. It is not a monarchy with one all-powerful ruler at the top: it is "an oligarchy of patriarchs," based on the body of bishops and responsible to local or general (ecumenical) church councils. No one patriarch is responsible to any other patriarch; yet all are within the jurisdiction of an ecumenical council of all the churches in communion with the patriarch of Constantinople, who holds the title of Ecumenical Patriarch.

Today Christendom remains divided into 3 principal sections: Roman Catholic, Eastern Orthodox (frequently referred to as the Greek church), and Protestant. The Eastern Orthodox Church consists of those churches that accept the decisions and decrees of the first 7 general church councils—2 at Nicea, 3 at Constantinople, 1 at Ephesus, and 1 at Chalcedon—and of such other churches as have originated in the missionary activities of these parent churches and have grown to self-government but still maintain communion with them. Certain Eastern church bodies refused to accept the christological definition of the Council of Chalcedon (451) and are generally referred to as the Ancient Eastern Churches, viz., Syrian-Antiochian, Malabar Syrians, the Armenians, the Copts of Egypt, and the Ethiopians.

Claiming to be "the direct heir and true conservator" of the original primitive church, Eastern Orthodoxy has tended historically to divide into independent national and social groups—Syrian, Russian, Serbian, Bulgarian, Romanian, Albanian, Greek, Georgian. These groups have had a bitter struggle for existence, caught as they have been between Arab, Tartar, Turkish, and Western armies in endless wars. Generally it may be said that Greek Christianity became the faith of the people of the Middle East and of the Slavs in Europe, while Latin Christianity became the religion of Western Europe and of the New World.

There are at present the 4 ancient Eastern Orthodox patriarchates (Constantinople, Alexandria, Antioch, and Jerusalem), with the modern patriarchates of the Russians, the Serbs, the Romanians, the Bulgarians, and the Georgians. In 1970, the former Russian Orthodox Greek Catholic Church in North America was granted autocephaly with the new name, Orthodox Church in America. Mount Sinai, Cyprus, the National Orthodox churches of Greece, Albania, Finland, Poland, Japan, and Czechoslovakia have autonomous national status.

The Turkish conquest of Constantinople greatly depleted the power of the patriarchate in that city, although it has retained its primacy among the Orthodox—while the First World War and the Russian Revolution of 1917, with the attendant disruption of the Russian Empire, led the Eastern Orthodox churches in Poland, Finland, Estonia, and Latvia to assert their independence (Lithuania continued loyal to Moscow). After World War II, Estonia and Latvia were reintegrated into the Russian Orthodox Church. Widely separated, they are all still in essential agreement in doctrine and worship, and together they make up what we know as the Holy Eastern Orthodox Church. Nearly all the European and Asiatic bodies of the Eastern Orthodox Church have established dioceses in America, some of which are governed by one or another of the 5 major patriarchates, while others have declared themselves to be independent and self-governing.

In the United States today Albanian, Bulgarian, Greek, Romanian, Russian, Serbian, Ukrainian, Carpatho-Russian, and Syrian churches are under the supervision of bishops of their respective nationalities, mostly related to their respective mother churches in tradition and spirit, if not in administration. A patriarch of Moscow and Alexandria each has jurisdiction over a few parishes in the United States.

Doctrine in Eastern Orthodoxy is based on the Bible, on the holy tradition, and on the decrees of the 7 ecumenical councils. The Nicene Creed is recited in all liturgies and in various other services—the Eastern churches holding that a "creed is an adoring confession of the church engaged in worship"; its faith is expressed more fully in its liturgy than in doctrinal statement. Actually the basis lies in the decisions and statements of the 7 councils that defined the ecumenical faith of the early undivided church against the heresies of the period and in the later statements defining the position of the Orthodox Church of the East with regard to the doctrine and practices of the Roman Catholic and Protestant churches. The Nicene Creed is held in its original form without the "filioque" clause. The dogma of the pope as the sole "vicar of Christ on earth" is rejected, together with the dogma of papal infallibility. Members of Orthodox churches honor the Virgin Mary as *theotokos* but do not dogmatize on the immaculate conception. They also honor the saints and 9 orders of angels. They reject the teaching of the surplus merits of the saints and the doctrine of indulgences but reverence the saints, ikons (consecrated pictures) of revered persons or events, and the cross. The use of carved images is forbidden. Bas-relief is permitted in some Orthodox groups.

They have 7 sacraments: baptism, anointing (confirmation or chrismation), Communion, penance, holy orders, marriage, and holy unction. Infants and adults are baptized by threefold immersion. The sacrament of anointing with chrism, or holy oil (confirmation), is administered immediately after baptism. Holy unction is administered to the sick but not always as a last rite.

The Holy Eucharist is the chief service on all Sundays and holy days, and all Orthodox churches believe and teach that the consecrated bread and wine are the body and blood of Christ. Purgatory is denied, but the dead are prayed for; and it is believed that the dead pray for those on earth. For justification, faith and works are considered necessary.

Government is episcopal. There is usually a council of bishops, clergy, and laymen, and a synod of bishops over which an elected archbishop, metropolitan, or patriarch presides. In the United States each Orthodox jurisdiction is incorporated, with a church assembly of bishops, clergy, and laity. There are 3 orders in the ministry: deacons (who assist in parish work and administering the sacraments), priests, and bishops. Deacons and priests may be either secular or monastic; candidates for the deaconate and the priesthood may marry before ordination, but they are forbidden to marry thereafter. Bishops are chosen from members of the monastic communities; all belong to the same monastic rule, that of St. Basil the Great, and are under lifelong vows of poverty, chastity, and obedience.

Church services are elaborately ritualistic; the liturgy of Holy Communion is a reenactment of the Gospel story. Of their worship Frank Gavin has said:

In the details of Eastern worship is a rough epitome of the history of Eastern Christendom; the *ikons*, about which a bitter controversy once raged; the service in the vernacular as against Latin; the existence of both a married and a celibate priesthood; the strong and passionate loyalty to the national allegiance evidenced by the provision of special prayers for the rulers by name—all these mark the characteristics, peculiarities, and contrasts with the customs of the West.

In the United States they pray for the President, Congress, the armed forces, and for all in places of lawful civil authority.

Membership statistics are confusing and often unreliable, inasmuch as membership is based on baptismal record rather than communicant status. Infants are confirmed (chrismation) immediately after baptism and are given their first Communion; after the age of 7 they must go to confession before taking Communion. Parish membership, however, is more frequently determined by the number of males over 21 than by communicants (often the male head of each family is the voting member in the parish organization). There are probably well over 3,000,000 Orthodox church members in the United States.

It must be kept clear, however, that there are other so-called Orthodox churches in the United States that are not recognized as canonically "Orthodox." These are members and churches that never had or have lost canonical and historical connection with valid, recognized, ancient Orthodoxy. Orthodox churches must be in canonical relationship with the Patriarch of Constantinople and with one another. These irregular Eastern churches might be called autogenic, of self-starting, but they cannot properly be called Orthodox.

Albanian Orthodox Archdiocese in America

The Albanian Orthodox Church in America is the spiritual descendant of the ancient ecclesiastical Western Illyricum (the Holy Illyria) of early

Christianity and the early church, and it has suffered a bewildering series of persecutions and changes in the religio-political struggles of the Balkan area. Under the Peace of Constantine, at the time of the division of the Roman Empire, it was placed under the jurisdiction of the Western church; under the Byzantine (Greek) emperors it was assigned to that of the Patriarch of Constantinople. Christianized by both Latin and Greek missionaries, Albania, as part of Illyricum, had Latin- and Greek-Rite Christians. There were close ties with Rome and Constantinople until the Moslem Turks became the masters of Albania in 1478-79, when half its people became Moslems, and a small minority remained divided between Latin-Rite Christians in the north and Greek-Rite Christians, subordinated to Constantinople, in the south. Four centuries of oppression ended in the political and religious revolts in the nineteenth and twentieth centuries, when Albania became independent, and its people demanded a church independent of Constantinople.

Meanwhile thousands of Albanians had emigrated to America. The Turkish rulers had long refused to allow the maintenance of Albanian language churches by the church authorities in Constantinople, and accordingly the Russian Greek Orthodox Catholic Church in America set up Albanian dioceses here under an Albanian archimandrite-administrator, the Right Rev. Theophan S. Noli, with a liturgy translated into Albanian in 1908. With the outbreak of the Russian Revolution these ties with the Russian Church were severed, and Theophan Noli became the first bishop of a completely independent Albanian-Rite church—a "mother church" that, strangely enough, spread its influence back into the motherland of Albania. Noli was consecrated in the Korche Cathedral in Albania as the Archibishop and Metropolitan of Durazzo, and Albanian candidates for the priesthood in America were ordained in Albania. He returned to America to establish a metropolitan throne, with its see in Boston. All Albanian Orthodox in the New World are under this see; it includes 13 organized territorial parishes and some thousands of unorganized, scattered communicants visited by priests on mission circuits. There are 45,235 members in 2 Albanian church groups: the Albanian Orthodox Archdiocese of America and the Albanian Orthodox Diocese of America. The Archdiocese group is the larger, with 40,000 members.

They have made outstanding contributions in liturgy, the most notable of which is the production of a liturgical literature in a language that has developed as a composite of ancient Pelasgo-Illyrian dialects, Latin, Greek, and Turkish. Their "Albanian Rite" liturgy actually preceded the liturgy of the Albanian-Rite church in Albania. Uniquely, this church has never depended upon the church of its native land. Thanks to communism and the dropping of the Iron Curtain, communication between the two churches is no longer possible, but the strong influence of the American church remains.

American Carpatho-Russian Orthodox Greek Catholic Church

The Carpatho-Russians are Carpatho in that their homeland is in the Carpathian Mountain regions of eastern Czechoslovakia; they are Russian because historically they and their homeland have been a part of the Russian nation, and their religious allegiances have been bound to the Russian and Orthodox churches. Their mother church endured for long years a strife between Eastern Orthodoxy and Roman Catholicism; under political pressure in the seventeenth century it became a Uniate church, with Eastern rites and customs, but under the Uniate or "union" plan, recognizing the supremacy of the Roman pope. The desperate struggle to separate from Rome and to become completely Eastern was transferred to the United States with the immigration of large numbers of their people, especially to our coal-mining and industrial areas. In 1891 the Rev. Dr. Alexis Toth, a Carpatho-Russian Uniate priest, led his church in Minneapolis back to the Orthodox Church, and with several other pastors and parishes was absorbed in the Russian Orthodox Church in America. In 1938 the New Carpatho-Russian Orthodox Greek Catholic Diocese was formed, with the Rev. Orestes P. Chornock as bishop. John R. Martin succeeded Bishop Chornock in 1977 as metropolitan of the church. The diocese was canonized by His Holiness Patriarch Benjamin I in Constantinople.

They now have 68 churches and an inclusive membership of 108,400. Headquarters, a seminary, and a new cathedral are located at Johnstown, Pennsylvania, and there are 2 camps in Mercer, Pennsylvania, and a monastery and retreat center in Tuxedo Park, New York.

American Holy Orthodox Catholic Apostolic Eastern Church
(Affiliated with the Orthodox Catholic Patriarchate of America)

Instituted in 1932 and incorporated in 1933, this church is self-governing, "maintaining the Eastern Orthodox faith and rite for all men indiscriminately." Spiritually it "owns no head but the head of the Christian faith, Jesus Christ our Lord," but considers itself "inseparably joined in faith with the great church of Constantinople and with every other orthodox eastern church of the same profession." The Greek Rite is used in all worship services, but it receives into communion and affiliates with other churches of Eastern Orthodox persuasion and belief that desire to retain their national and individual characteristics.

Government is autocephalous; the archibishop does not acknowledge the authority or jurisdiction of any other church or bishop. He is responsible to the national council, the supreme legislative, administrative, and judicial authority, which is made up of bishops, clergy, and laity. It meets every third year. Two lower ecclesiastical bodies, the holy synod and the supreme ecclesiastical council, manage the affairs of the church between councils.

The work of the church is not only religious but social and educational. It represents an effort, fairly successful, to draw together those of Eastern Orthodox faith into one group regardless of race, nationality, or language. A provisional synod was set up in 1935 to encourage coordination between the national groups in the various Eastern Orthodox churches, and the Patriarchal Holy Synod was fully established in March, 1951, in the state of New York. The church and patriarchate have 10 bishops, 25 clergy, 30 churches, and an inclusive membership of approximately 9,000 members.

Antiochian Orthodox Christian Archdiocese of North America

This church is composed of 2 groups that merged in 1975; the Antiochian Orthodox Christian Archdiocese of New York and All North America (formerly the Syrian Antiochian Orthodox Archdiocese of New York and North America) and the Antiochian Archdiocese of Toledo, Ohio, and Dependencies in North America. It is under the jurisdiction of the Patriarch of Antioch and has a membership of 152,000 in 110 churches.

Bulgarian Eastern Orthodox Church

Before the outbreak of the Macedonian revolution in 1903 there was very little Bulgarian immigration to the United States; in 1940 there were only about 60,000 Bulgarians resident here. Coming out of the Bulgarian Orthodox Church, which is the state church of the country, they brought with them memories of the long struggle for independence of that church from the domination of Constantinople. It was in 1872 that the Bulgarian church won its freedom and self-government.

The church started in this country as the Bulgarian Orthodox Mission in 1909 and established a bishopric in 1938. It is attached directly to the Holy Synod of Bulgaria, with a membership made up of emigrants from Bulgaria, Macedonia, Thrace, Dobruja, and other parts of the Balkan Peninsula. Services are in the Bulgarian and English languages, and doctrine is in accord with that of other Eastern Orthodox churches.

Membership is reported at 86,000 members in 13 churches under the leadership of the Metropolitan Archbishop of North and South America and Australia.

Eastern Orthodox Catholic Church in America

American in background, the Eastern Orthodox Catholic Church began its work in America under the leadership of Bishop Raphael Hawaweeny, who was consecrated by permission of the Holy Synod of Russia. Raphael was succeeded in 1917 by Bishop Aftimos and in turn by Bishop Sophronios and Bishop Morendi, who established (in 1951) what is now known as the Eastern Orthodox Catholic Church in America.

With 265 members in 2 churches, it maintains a mission program, maintains a study center for prospective clergymen, and publishes a monthly periodical, *The American Review of Eastern Orthodoxy.*

The church is governed by what is called the "governing synod." It is the only orthodox jurisdiction in the United States that uses English exclusively in its worship.

Greek Orthodox Archdiocese of North and South America

Greeks arrived in the United States in increasing number between 1890 and 1914, coming from the Greek mainland, the Greek islands of the Aegean Sea, Dodecanese, Cyprus, Constantinople, Smyrna, and other sections of Asia Minor. They asked for and secured the services of Orthodox priests sent to them by the Holy Synod of Greece or the Ecumenical Patriarchate of Constantinople. Each priest maintained his relation with the synod or patriarchate from which he came; there was at first no central organization to unite them.

Following a period of confusion (1908–1922), during which jurisdiction of the American churches was shifted from the Ecumenical Patriarchate of Constantinople to the Holy Synod of Greece and then back again, an act known as the Founding Tome of 1922 established the Greek (Orthodox) Archdiocese of North and South America, consisting of 4 bishoprics under the supervision of the Archbishop Alexander and the Patriarchate of Constantinople. Alexander's successor, Archbishop Athenagoras, was elected Patriarch of Constantinople in 1948, and was succeeded in turn by Archbishop Michael and Archbishop Iakovos, the present incumbent.

Doctrine, polity, and worship are of the usual Orthodox patterns. There are 1,950,000 members in 535 churches and 11 archdiocesan districts, 18 parochial schools, 9 summer camps, 1 seminary, 3 homes for teen-aged boys, and 1 home for the aged.

Holy Apostolic and Catholic Church of the East (Assyrians)

This is the ancient Church of Persia. Its patriarch originally resided in Chaldea, near the Persian Gulf. It is said that at its peak, throughout most of Asia, it had better than 80,000,000 members, but with the exception of the church that still exists in India, it was almost completely annihilated in the wars of Ghengis Khan and Tamerlane and later by the Portuguese and Turks in 1915; they scattered through Iraq, Syria, Persia, and Lebanon.

The church claims as founders Thomas, Thaddeus, Peter, and Bartholomew of the apostles, and Mari and Addai of the seventy. Its theology stresses the 2 natures of Christ, holding that he was "man and God, 2 natures and 2 substances united in one person and one will," and insists that Mary should not be granted the status or name of "Mother of God." ("Mary did not give birth to the divinity, but to the humanity, the temple of divinity.") Accordingly, she is not the mother of God but the mother of Christ. They believe that it was the man in Christ that died, not the God in Christ.

The American branch of this church began during the wave of immigration in 1911, and nearly all its adherents have come here during the last half-century. In 1940 the head of the church, then in exile in England, came to the United States; he is Mar Eshai Shimun XXIII, Catholicos Patriarch of the East and Supreme Head of the Assyrian people in the Republic of Iraq. Some 250,000 members are still active in the

Middle East, Russia, and India; in the United States there are 5,000 members in 10 churches.

Holy Orthodox Church in America (Eastern Catholic and Apostolic)

An interchurch movement rather than a denomination, this body was instituted in 1927–28 to present the Eastern liturgies in the English language, to offset the disadvantages of the use of foreign languages in America, and to establish an autocephalous Orthodox church in America for English-speaking people with American customs and traditions.

The movement stems from the authorization of the late Patriarch Tikhon of the Russian Orthodox Church and the acts of his successors to propagate Orthodoxy among English-speaking people around the world. For its first 15 years in this county it was a program of translating, lectures, classes, and writings.

Services are based on the original liturgy composed by James, first bishop of Jerusalem, as abbreviated and arranged in the fourth century by John Chrysostom into the local usage it has today in all Orthodox bodies, varying only in local custom and language. This liturgy is used throughout the year with the exception of the weekdays of the Great Fast (Lent). The liturgy of Basil the Great is used 10 days of the year.

The faith and order of the Holy Orthodox Church in America rest on the Holy Scripture, holy tradition, the canons of the 7 councils, and the teachings of the anti–Nicene Fathers. Concessions have been made to Western custom in the installation of seats in its churches, in the use of organs and mixed choirs, and in conformity to the Western calendar. It wishes to be known as an independent unit of the Holy Eastern Orthodox Greek Catholic church, following strictly, however, the ancient traditional doctrines and dogmas of that church. There are 260 members in 4 churches.

Romanian Orthodox Episcopate of America

The Romanian Orthodox Episcopate of America was organized at a church congress convened in Detroit on April 25, 1929, by clergy and laity voting as representatives of Romanian Orthodox parishes in the United States and Canada. It was at first under the canonical jurisdiction of the Romanian Orthodox Patriarchate in Bucharest, until political conditions (the advent of communism) forced its separation from that body, and it is now under the jurisdiction of the autocephalous Orthodox Church in America. The Romanian Orthodox bishop is a member of the Holy Synod of the Orthodox Church in America, and the Romanian diocese is recognized as an administratively self-governing body.

The episcopate is headed by a bishop elected for life by a special electoral congress made up of clerical and lay delegates from the parishes of the episcopate. With the aid of an episcopate council composed of 10 laymen and 5 clergymen (elected for 2 years by the church congress), he supervises all matters of administration. The bishop presides at all council meetings, which are held as need arises. The church congress is the chief legislative body; it is composed of 1 clerical and 2 lay representatives from each parish and meets annually in July.

There are 5 "deaneries," or districts, in the United States; some Romanian Orthodox parishes in South America, Western Europe, and Australia are under the jurisdiction of the episcopate. There are 45 churches and 50,000 members in the United States and Canada.

Russian Orthodox Church in the U.S.A.

Eastern Orthodoxy came to Russia with the baptism of Vladimir in A.D. 988. Government of the church at first was ruled by metropolitans appointed or approved by the Patriarch of Constantinople. About 500 years ago Job became the First Patriarch of All Russia. The office of patriarch was suppressed, and a Holy Synod was substituted during the reign of Peter the Great; the other Orthodox churches recognized this synod as being patriarchal in effect. From 1721 to 1917 the Holy Synod was made up of 3 metropolitans and other bishops from various parts of Russia, who sat in rotation at its sessions. A civil officer of the czar, known as the Chief Procurator of the Holy Synod, attended its session as the czar's representative, sitting at a small side desk. This pre-1917 church, like every public organization in Russia, was administratively dominated by the czarist regime.

In 1917 dramatic changes were instituted by the Great Sobor, or church assembly. Administration was changed, the office of chief procurator was abolished, and plans were made to return to the old patriarchal form of government. These reforms were put into effect. As the Great Sobor held its sessions, however, the gunfire of the revolution was heard in the streets, and once the followers of Lenin had taken over the state, they immediately applied their Marxist-Leninist principles: separation of church from state, of school from church, and restriction of church activity in large measure to worship. The patriarch and the synod resisted, but the government found some priests and a few bishops who were ready to support the new regime. These held a rigged assembly that deposed the patriarch, endorsed communism, and declared itself the governing body of the Russian church. Calling themselves the "Renovated," or "Living, Church," they changed the ancient disciplinary rules of the church and instituted liturgical reforms. With the support of the Soviet authorities, who hoped thus to divide and weaken the church, they held control for several years. Although they misled some of the Russian people, they were never recognized by the great body of clergy or people. The government considered opposition to the Living Church a civil offense, and on this basis banished thousands of bishops, clergy, and laymen to hard labor camps. In 1927 the Soviet government again recognized the central administration of the Russian Orthodox Church, but not until 1943 did it permit the holding of a church assembly to elect a patriarch.

When the Germans invaded Russia, it was the aged metropolitan, later

Patriarch Sergius, who called on his people to support the Soviet government in the defense of their country. This marked a turning point in the Soviet government's policy toward the church; the Living Church was discarded and the patriarch's authority was recognized by the state. Many surviving clergy and bishops who had been banished to Siberia were permitted to return, and gradually the patriarchal administration became again the sole authority in the Orthodox Church of Russia.

The main missionary efforts of Russian Orthodoxy were historically directed toward the Moslem, Buddhist, animistic populations of Central Asia and Siberia. In the late nineteenth century an Orthodox mission was begun in Japan. Eight Russian Orthodox monks entered Alaska in 1792; they established headquarters at Kodiak and there built the first Eastern Orthodox Church in America. ("K" is known today as the Orthodox Church in America; it claims a membership of 1,000,000.) Twelve thousand natives were baptized within 2 years' time. Orthodox monks and bishops created an alphabet and printed a grammar in the Aleutian language, translated portions of the Bible, and built a cathedral at Sitka.

A chapel was built in the early years of the century at a Russian trading post near present-day San Francisco. An episcopal see was established in San Francisco in 1872 and moved in 1905 to New York City, as Russian immigration brought thousands of Orthodox to the eastern states. Immigrants from other countries with Orthodox churches—Serbia, Syria, Greece—were for many years cared for by the Russian hierarchy in America. Many Orthodox from the old Austro-Hungarian empire, traditionally having been in a Uniate church that had grown to impressive numbers, came to this country and found themselves in an embarrassing situation, being placed under the direction of Irish and German Roman Catholic bishops. Torn between conflicting demands and loyalties, many of these Uniate parishes returned to the jurisdiction of the Russian Orthodox Church.

Hard days were ahead, however. The Russian revolution of 1917 cut off the financial support that had come from the mother church, which was now fighting for its life. The Living Church faction in Russia, supported by the communist government, sent an emissary to secure control for the church property in the United States, and he succeeded by action in the civil courts in securing possession of the Russian cathedral in New York City. Further seizures were prevented by the declaration of the Russian Orthodox in America at a Sobor (church assembly) at Detroit in 1924, recognizing its spiritual heritage but asserting its administrative, legislative, and judicial independence of Moscow. This church thus became an autonomous Orthodox church and has made great progress in the support and loyalty of its people. It now has 13 archbishops and bishops and reports 755,000 members in 352 churches. Its official title was the Russian Orthodox Greek Catholic Church of America but is now the Russian Orthodox Church in the U.S.A.

In addition to this Russian Orthodox jurisdiction (or administrative unit), with its continuous history in this country since 1792, there are now 2 other Orthodox jurisdictions that have come to America within recent years. No doctrinal differences separate these 3 groups; their disagreement is exclusively on the question of recognizing the authority of the Patriarch of Moscow. A second body, the Russian Orthodox Church Outside Russia, holds that the Moscow patriarchate has forfeited its right to be considered a true Orthodox church because it accepts the authority of the atheist Soviet government. The metropolitan and synod of this body administers all like-minded Russian Orthodox all over the world.

The second body is made up largely of Russian exiles of the revolution and displaced persons of World War II. When armed resistance to the Soviet revolution was finally put down, many sought refuge abroad. A number of bishops and clergy gathered at Constantinople and later transferred to Sremski Karlovici in Yugoslavia, and there they set up a synod to give spiritual leadership to these refugees. After World War II, the establishment of a communist regime in Yugoslavia and the increase in the number of Russian refugees (including some of the bishops of this synod) gathered in displaced-persons camps led the synod to move its headquarters to Munich. Relief programs of the churches brought great numbers of the "displaced persons" to America, and the headquarters of the synod (now called the Russian Orthodox Church Outside Russia) were moved to New York City in 1952. Its complete rejection of the Moscow patriarchate conformed to the attitude of many of these new arrivals and kept them from uniting with the Russian church already established in North America, which claimed in 1951 some 55,000 members and 81 churches. In addition, it maintains bishops and clergy wherever Russian refugees are resettled—in Canada, South America, Australia, Africa, and Europe.

The third body is called the Patriarchal Parishes of the Russian Orthodox Church in the U.S.A. It accepts the full authority of the Moscow patriarchate and is its representative in America. De facto occupancy of the old Russian cathedral in New York City was established when the former emissary of the Living Church faction made his submission to the patriarch's representative. It is governed by 4 bishops appointed by the patriarch and an assembly elected by the parishes. They have 51,500 members in 51 churches.

Serbian Eastern Orthodox Church in the U.S.A. and Canada

The church in Serbia from the seventh century to the thirteenth was under the jurisdiction of the Greek Patriarchate of Constantinople and became the independent National Serbian Church in 1219. It made notable contributions to art and architecture and played an important part in the Serbian struggle for independence all through the long period of Turkish invasion and domination (1389–1876), during which it suffered an unbelievable persecution.

Serbian immigrants to the United States, coming here more for political than economic reasons, began to arrive in large numbers about 1890. They worshiped at first in Russian churches, accepting the ministrations of Russian priests and the supervision of Russian bishops. The Serbian Patriarchate of Yugoslavia approved the organization of the Diocese of the United States and Canada in 1921, and sent its first bishop in 1926. Headquarters are located in

Chicago. There are today 52 parishes and 65,000 members. Doctrine and polity are in harmony with other branches of the Orthodox Church.

Syrian Orthodox Church of Antioch
(Archdiocese of the U.S.A. and Canada)

The word "Antioch" in the name of this church is important, for its origin is traced back to St. Peter, who is believed to have established the first Patriarchate in Antioch. Today this American group is under the jurisdiction of the Syrian Orthodox Patriarch of Antioch and All the East.

Syrians were few in number in the United States until the turn of the last century; their first priest arrived here in 1907; their first patriarchal vicar (Archbishop Mar Athanasius Y. Samuel) was appointed in 1949, and the Archdiocese of the Syrian Orthodox Church in the U.S.A. and Canada was organized in 1957.

At the present time there are 8 archdiocesan parishes in 7 states in the United States and 3 in Canada. As of 1972 there were 50,000 members in 10 churches, and an additional (larger) membership is located in the Middle East, India, Europe, and Australia. They meet annually in an archdiocesan convention.

Ukrainian Orthodox Churches

Eastern Orthodoxy was established as the state religion in the Ukraine by a unique procedure. In the tenth century, Vladimir the Great, ruler of Kiev, sent investigators abroad to study the doctrines and rituals of Islam and Judaism as well as those of Christianity. They came back to report that the Eastern Orthodox faith seemed best suited to the needs of their people. Vladimir was immediately baptized in that faith, and by 988 the entire Ukraine population had become Orthodox Christian.

For more than 600 years the Ukrainian church was under the jurisdiction of the Ecumenical Partriarchate of Constantinople. In 1686 it was placed under the supervision of the Russian Patriarch of Moscow. Rejecting the authority of Moscow after the 1917 revolution, Ukrainians in the United States are still engaged in a bitter dispute among themselves; attempts at union have been made but to date have been unsuccessful. Three groups are in competition. The first, known as the Ukrainian Orthodox Church of the U.S.A., was formally organized in this country in 1919; Archbishop John Theodorovich arrived from the Ukraine in 1924. This group has 107 churches and 87,745 members. The second body is known as the Ukrainian Orthodox Church of America (Ecumenical Patriarchate), was organized in 1928, has 23 churches and 30,000 members. The third body is known as the Holy Ukrainian Autocephalic Orthodox Church in Exile. It broke from the Ukrainian Church in the U.S.A. in 1951 in a dispute over administrative matters and is made up largely of Ukrainian laymen and clergy who came to America after World War II. There are 4,800 members in 15 churches.

EPISCOPAL CHURCH

It is stated in the preface of the *Book of Common Prayer* of the Protestant Episcopal Church (now known generally as the Episcopal Church) that "this Church is far from intending to depart from the Church of England in any essential point of doctrine, discipline, or worship." Therein lies the hint of its origin: The Protestant Episcopal Church constitutes the "self-governing American branch of the Anglican Communion." For a century and a half in this country it bore the name of the Church of England.

Its history runs back to the first missionaries who went to the British Isles from Gaul prior to the Council of Arles in A.D. 314. It is traced down through the days when Henry VIII threw off the supremacy of the pope (Henry, according to Anglican scholars, did not found the Church of England; it was a church that had always been more British than Roman); through the reign of Edward VI, when the *Book of Common Prayer* and 42 Articles of Religion were written; through the period of Catholic restoration under Bloody Mary and through her successor Elizabeth, who put the united church and state under the Protestant banner and sent Sir Francis Drake sailing to build an empire.

Drake came ashore in what is now Virginia in 1578. His Church of England chaplain, Francis Fletcher, planted a cross and read a prayer while Drake claimed the new land for the Virgin Queen. Martin Frobisher had reached Labrador in 1576, also with a chaplain. After them came colonists to Virginia under Sir Humphrey Gilbert and Sir Walter Raleigh; Raleigh's chaplain baptized an Indian named Manteo and a white baby named Virginia Dare before the settlement vanished. With Captain John Smith came Chaplain Robert Hunt, who stretched a sail between 2 trees for a shelter and read the service from the *Book of Common Prayer*.

In the South the transplated Church of England quickly became the established church. It was at heart a tolerant and catholic church, but the control of the crown brought an almost ruthless authority that made the church suspect in the eyes of those colonists who had come here seeking freedom from all such authority. The Virginia House of Burgesses set the salary of the Virginia clergyman at "1,500 pounds of tobacco and 16 barrels of corn." It was a British clergy supported by public tax and assessment and by contributions from the church in England through the Society for the Propagation of the Gospel. And it was technically under the jurisdiction of the Bishop of London. In that fact lay one of its almost fatal weaknesses; colonial ministers had to journey to England for ordination, and few could afford it. This, coupled with the rising tide of the American Revolution, placed the colonial Church of England in an unenviable position.

Yet the church did well. Membership grew rapidly. William and Mary College was established in 1693, and the Church of England became the predominant church in the South. King's Chapel in Boston, the first Episcopal church in New England, was opened in 1689; in 1698 a church was established at Newport, Rhode Island, and another, called Trinity Church, in New York City. In 1702 a delegation from the Society for the Propagation of the Gospel came from England to survey the colonial church and found about 50 clergymen at work from the Carolinas to Maine. The visitors sensed the need for American bishops to ordain American clergymen; they also sensed the increasing opposition of the American patriot to a British-governed church.

The Revolution almost destroyed the colonial Church of England. Under special oath of allegiance to the king, the clergy either fled to England or Canada or remained as Loyalists in the colonies in the face of overwhelming persecution. That many of them were loyal to the American cause meant little; the Rev. William White was chaplain of the Continental Congress, the Rev. Charles Thurston was a continental colonel, and in the pews of the Episcopal Church sat Washingon, Jefferson, Patrick Henry, John Jay, Robert Morris, John Marshall, Charles and "Light-Horse Harry" Lee, and John Randolph. But their presence could not stem the tide. The Anglican house was divided, and it fell. At the war's end there was no episcopacy, no association of the churches, not even the semblance of an establishment. Few thought of any future for this church, which suffered between Lexington and Yorktown more than any other in the colonies.

There was, however, a future—and a great one. In 1782 there appeared a pamphlet entitled *The Case of the Episcopal Churches in the United States Considered*, written by William White. It was a plea for unity and reorganization, and it proposed that the ministry be continued temporarily without the episcopal succession since the latter "cannot at present be obtained." In 1783 a conference of the Episcopal churches met at Annapolis, Maryland, and formally adopted the name Protestant Episcopal Church— "Protestant" to distinguish it from the Roman Catholic Church, "Episcopal" to distinguish it from the Presbyterians and the Congregationalists. In 1967 the general convention adopted the Episcopal Church as an alternate name for the Protestant Episcopal Church in the U.S.A.

Also in 1783 the clergy in Connecticut elected Samuel Seabury as their prospective bishop; he went to England and waited a year for consecration at the hands of English bishops. This was denied, and he then went to Scotland to be consecrated bishop in 1784. Ultimately Parliament and the Church of England cleared the way, and 2 other bishops-elect from New York and Pennsylvania were consecrated by the Archbishop of Canterbury in 1787. In 1789 the constitution of the Protestant Episcopal Church was adopted in Philadelphia, the *Book of Common Prayer* was revised for American use, and the Protestant Episcopal Church became an independent, self-governing body.

There were complete harmony and expansion for the next half century. There were established new churches and church institutions: Sunday schools, Bible, prayer book, and tract societies, theological seminaries, colleges, boarding schools, guilds for men and women, and a domestic and foreign missionary society. Diocesan organizations replaced state organizations; new bishops moved into the new West. Bishop J. H. Hobart in New York, A. V. Griswold in New England, Richard Channing Moore in Virginia, and Philander Chase in Ohio worked miracles in overcoming the revolutionary prejudices against the church. W. A. Muhlenberg, one of the great Episcopal builders, "organized the first free church of any importance in New York, introduced the male choir, sisterhoods, and the fresh air movement, while his church infirmary suggested to his mind the organization of St. Luke's Hospital [in New York], the first church hospital of any Christian communion in the country."

Muhlenberg was a man of wide vision; he inspired a "memorial" calling for a wider catholicity in the Protestant Episcopal Church, which resulted in the famous Lambeth Quadrilateral on Church Unity in 1888 and the movement that produced the further vision of the American *Book of Common Prayer* in 1892.

With the outbreak of the Civil War disruption again threatened the Protestant Episcopal Church, but it did not come. Among the major Protestant churches this one alone suffered no division. New England churchmen may have been abolitionists, and a Louisiana bishop, Leonidas Polk, may have been a general under Lee, but Polk prayed for Bishop Charles Pettit McIlvaine of Ohio in public, and the Ohioan prayed for Polk, and they were still in one church. A temporary Protestant Episcopal Church in the Confederate States was organized to carry on the work in the South, but the names of the southern bishops were called in the general convention in New York in 1862; and once the war was over, the Episcopal house was in 1865 quickly reunited.

The years following Appomattox were years of new growth. A dispute over churchmanship, rising out of the Oxford Movement in England, resulted in the separation of a group into the Reformed Episcopal Church in 1873, but otherwise Episcopal unity held fast. New theological seminaries were established and old ones were reorganized and strengthened. This period saw the organization of a church congress, the Brotherhood of St. Andrew, and numerous other church agencies. The expansion continued into the next century; 2 world wars failed to halt it. In 1830 the Protestant Episcopal Church had 12 bishops, 20 dioceses, 600 clergymen, and 30,000 communicants; in 1930 it had 152 bishops, 105 dioceses, 600 clergymen, and 1,250,000 communicants.

The Episcopal form of government closely parallels that of the federal government. It is a federal union, now consisting of 114 dioceses (originally coterminous with the states of the Union), each of which is autonomous in its own sphere, associated originally for the maintenance of a common doctrine, discipline, and worship, to which objectives have been added the unification, development, and prosecution of missionary, educational, and social programs on a national scale.

Of the 114 dioceses, 21 are overseas missionary dioceses. Most of the overseas jurisdictions will become either independent Anglican churches or parts of existing Anglican churches in their areas.

Each diocese functions through a bishop (elected locally, with the approval of the whole episcopate and of representatives of the clergy and laity of the whole church), who is the spiritual and administrative head. There is a diocesan legislative body (convention, council, or synod) made up of the clergy of the diocese and representatives of the local congregations, meeting annually; a standing committee of clergymen and laymen who are advisers and assessors to the bishop; and, usually, a program board.

The normal pattern for the local congregation is the parish, which elects its own minister (called a rector) who is vested with pastoral oversight of the congregation and who, with the warden and vestrymen (comprising the vestry), administers also the temporal affairs and the property of the parish.

Each parish and parochial district (mission or chapel) is represented in the annual diocesan convention by its clergy and by elected lay delegates of the congregations (usually in proportion to their constituency); each diocese and missionary diocese is represented in the triennial general convention of the church by its bishop or bishops and clerical and lay deputies elected in equal numbers (at present 4 of each). The general convention is a bicameral legislature, and the 2 houses of the convention, bishops and deputies, meet and deliberate separately. Either house may initiate, but the concurrence of both is required to enact legislation.

Between sessions of the general convention, the work of the church is carried on by the presiding bishop (elected for a 12-year term by the house of bishops with the concurrence of the house of deputies) and an elective executive council of 41 members—30 elected by the general convention, 9 elected by the provinces (regional groups of dioceses and missionary districts), and 2 ex officio (the presiding bishop and the president of the house of deputies).

Established in 1919 to unify the work of 3 previously independent boards, the council in 1968 took the further step of abolishing a more or less rigid departmental structure in favor of a collaborative working relationship among the program areas of national and world mission, education for ministry, church in society, communication, administration, finance, and stewardship-development.

The Episcopalian accepts 2 creeds—the Apostles' and the Nicene. The articles of the Church of England, with the exception of the twenty-first and with modification of the eighth, thirty-fifth, and thirty-sixth, are accepted as a general statement of doctrine, but adherence to them as a creed is not required. The clergy make the following declaration:

I do believe the Holy Scriptures of the Old and New Testaments to be the Word of God, and to contain all things necessary to salvation, and I do solemnly engage to conform to the doctrine, discipline, and worship of the [Protestant] Episcopal Church [in the United States of America].

The church expects of all its members "loyalty to the doctrine, discipline and worship of the one holy Catholic and Apostolic Church, in all the essentials, but allows great liberty in nonessentials." It allows for variation, individuality, independent thinking, and religious liberty. Liberals and conservatives, modernists and fundamentalists, find cordial and common ground for worship in the prayer book, which next to the Bible has probably influenced more people than any other book in the English language.

There are 2 sacraments, baptism and the Eucharist, recognized as "certain sure witnesses and effectual agencies of God's love and grace." Baptism by pouring or immersion is necessary for either children or adults; baptism by any church in the name of the Trinity is recognized as valid baptism; baptized children are confirmed as members of the church by the bishop, and those not baptized in infancy or childhood must accept the rite before confirmation. Without stating or defining the holy mystery, the Episcopal Church believes in the real presence of Christ in the elements of the Eucharist. The church also recognizes the sacramental character of confirmation, penance, orders, matrimony, and unction.

Some Episcopalians are high churchmen with elaborate ritual and ceremony; others are described as low churchmen with a ritual less involved and with more of an evangelistic emphasis. All, however, high or low, have a loyalty to their church that is deep and lasting. In more than 300 years this church has known only 1 minor division; today it stands fifth among all denominations: it has 3,070,349 members in 7,494 churches in the United States.

Stanley I. Stuber has called this the "church of beauty," and it is an apt description. Its prayer book is eloquent in the literature of religious worship, containing the heart of the New Testament and Old Testament devotions. Members have built stately cathedrals in this country, among them the Cathedral of St. John the Divine in New York City, which is the third largest cathedral in the world, and the Cathedral of SS. Peter and Paul (national cathedral) at Washington, sometimes called the American Westminster Abbey. Stained-glass windows, gleaming altars, vested choirs, and a glorious ritual give the worshiper not only beauty but a deep sense of the continuity of the Christian spirit and tradition. Next to their stress on episcopacy their liturgical worship is a distinguishing feature; varying in degree according to high or low church inclinations, it has its roots in the liturgy of the Church of England and includes the reading, recitation, or intonation by priest, people, and choir of the historic general confession, general thanksgiving, collects, psalter, and prayers.

National Church financial support is given to 13 U.S. dioceses, to the Navajoland Episcopal Church (an area mission in the Southwest), and to a coalition of dioceses on the East Coast that share a common ministry to the Appalachian mountain people. Special emphasis is placed upon urban ministries, ministry in college communities, and ministry to Black, Hispanic, Indian/Eskimo, and Asian congregations. Overseas missions are located in all American territories—the Panama Canal Zone, Guam, the Virgin Islands, and Puerto Rico—and in the Dominican Republic, Haiti, India, Japan, the Near East, Liberia, Mexico, Okinawa, Taiwan, Central America, and the Philippines. The church sponsors 10 accredited seminaries in the United States plus 2 overseas, 9 colleges, 1 university, about 800 nursery through high schools for boys and girls, 108 homes for the aged, 91 institutions and agencies for child and youth care, 69 hospitals, homes, and convalescent clinics, and work for seamen in 8 dioceses in the United States. The church is unique in Protestantism for its orders of monks and nuns; there are 11 orders for men and 16 for women employed in schools, hospitals, and various forms of missionary work.

Two major developments in the Episcopal Church in the past few years have been subjects of debate: prayer book revision and the ordination of women to the priesthood. The general convention of 1976 gave first approval to a Proposed Book of Common Prayer; this represents the first revision of the American Prayer Book since 1928, and the first revision to use contemporary language. Much of the Tudor idiom, however, has been retained. The Holy Eucharist, Morning and Evening Prayer, the Burial of the Dead, and all the Collects for the Church Year appear in contemporary and traditional language, and Archbishop Cranmer's Great Litany has been somewhat revised, but it appears in its traditional form only. All other services—such as Baptism, Matrimony, Confirmation, Ordination, and the Psalter have been revised and/or rewritten in the contemporary idiom. The Proposed Book is also more comprehensive in such forms as private confession, complete rites for Ash Wednesday and Holy Week, and the addition of 3 more daily offices between Morning and Evening Prayer. The Eucharistic Lectionary has also been revised to include, for the first time, regular readings from the Old Testament at Mass. This Proposed Book was passed by an overwhelming majority at the 1979 convention in Denver.

The issue of women's ordination is extremely complex. Actually it goes back to the historical doctrine of the uninterrupted line of succession in the episcopacy from the apostles to the present—the Apostolic Succession, in which men only have been ordained in the threefold ministries of deacon, priest, and bishop. The controversy has centered basically in 2 opinion groups: those who believe that it is de facto impossible for women to be priests and those who believe that the general convention—even though it is the supreme legislative authority of the Episcopal Church—has no right to decide this question of women's ordination and that such a decision can be made only by Catholic consensus or in some kind of ecumenical council.

The general convention of 1970 authorized the ordination of women to the deaconate, but "priesting" was rejected at the convention and again at the 1973 convention. It passed in 1976 by a narrow margin. But even this did not settle the question. In February of 1978, 3 men were consecrated to the episcopate of a newly formed Anglican Church of North America. This body represents scattered groupings of Episcopalians who feel that they can no longer remain within the Episcopal Church because of the church's stand on women in the priesthood, liturgical revision, and divorce and remarriage. It is estimated, at the moment, that about 100 congregations or parts of congregations have joined ACNA. Some 30 to 40 priests have been defrocked by their bishop for having joined the new church. The great majority, however, though disliking the ordination of women, seem to have no intention of leaving the Episcopal Church. The Archbishop of Canterbury has said that the schismatic group is not to be in communion with the other sister churches of Anglicanism.

The Episcopal Church has an undeserved reputation for exclusiveness and noncooperation with other Protestant bodies; actually it has been most cooperative. The Lambeth Quadrilateral, already mentioned, was adopted by the house of bishops at the general convention of 1886 and accepted with modifications 2 years later. It had 4 points for world unity of the churches: the Scriptures as the Word of God, the Apostles' and the Nicene creeds as the rule of faith, the 2 sacraments of baptism and the Lord's Supper, and the episcopate as the central principle of church government. In 1910 the general convention appointed a commission to arrange for a World Conference on Faith and Order; the first conference was held at Geneva in 1920, the second in 1927 at Lausanne, the third at Edinburgh in 1937. The church is active in the National Council of the Churches of Christ in the U.S.A and in the World Council of Churches. An unusually effective intercommunion has been established among the Anglican and Old Catholic churches and abroad with the Church of Finland, Church of Sweden, Lusitanian Church of Portugal, the Mar Thomas Syrian Church of Malabar, United Church of North India, United Church of Pakistan, Church of South India, the Spanish Reformed Church and the Philippine Independent Churches—all of which may be a first step toward mergers among these bodies.

Reformed Episcopal Church

The Reformed Episcopal Church was organized in New York City in 1873 by 8 clergymen and 20 laymen who formerly had been priests and members of the Protestant Episcopal Church. A long debate over the ritualism and ecclesiasticism of the Protestant Episcopal Church lay behind the separation; the immediate cause of the division lay in the participation of Bishop George David Cummins of Kentucky in a Communion Service held in the Fifth Avenue Presbyterian Church in New York City. In the face of criticism and in the conviction that the catholic nature and mission of the Protestant Episcopal Church were being lost, Bishop Cummins withdrew to found the new denomination.

Doctrine and organization are similar to that of the parent church with several important exceptions. The Reformed Episcopal Church rejects the doctrine that the Lord's Table is an altar on which the body and blood of Christ are offered anew to the Father, that the presence of Christ in the Supper is a presence in the elements of bread and wine, and that regeneration is inseparably connected with baptism. It also denies that Christian ministers are priests in any other sense than that in which all other believers are a "royal priesthood." Clergymen ordained in other churches are not reordained on entering the ministry of the Reformed Episcopal Church, and members are admitted on letters of dismissal from other Protestant denominations.

Worship is liturgical; at the morning services on Sunday the use of the prayer book, revised to remove certain objectionable sacerdotal elements, is required. At other services its use is optional, while at any service extempore prayer may be used by the minister.

Parish and synodical units prevail in the administration of the church; the triennial general council of the Reformed Episcopal Church is not like the general convention of the Protestant Episcopal church, however, as its bishops do not constitute a separate house.

Foreign missions are maintained in India, Congo, Uganda, northern Rhodesia, and Germany. In India and Africa there are 20 primary schools, 2 hospitals, and 1 orphanage. There is a seminary in the United States located at Philadephia. There are 6,532 members in 64 local churches.

EVANGELICAL CHRISTIAN CHURCHES

These churches trace their origin back to the Arminian preaching and teaching of Horace Bushnell (1802–1876). Bushnell criticized the Calvinistic view that grace is irresistible and election unconditional, insisting that man by free will cooperates in his conversion. He is held to be the spiritual father and head elder of the Evangelical Christian Churches until his death in 1876.

Churches variously known as Evangelical Christian Churches, Christian Churches of North America, Christian Missionary, Community and Evangelical Christian Churches were chartered and incorporated as members of the Evangelical Christian Churches in May of 1966.

Their doctrines stress the Trinity, the Virgin Birth, the plenary inspiration of the Bible, Christ's work of atonement, and his second coming. They recognize the many gifts of the Holy Spirit and that one might experience all the gifts, but they do not condone the charismatic movement. There are 12,711 members in 132 churches located in the United States, Canada, and Haiti.

EVANGELICAL CHURCH OF NORTH AMERICA

When The Methodist Church and the Evangelical United Brethren churches merged into The United Methodist Church in Dallas, Texas, in 1968, a number of churches in the Brethren body, dissatisfied with the merger, withdrew to form a denomination of their own—the Evangelical Church of North America. In June of 1968 the new church was incorporated at Portland, Oregon, and eventually came to include congregations across the country, including those of the former Holiness Methodist Church.

The doctrinal position is of the Wesleyan-Arminian persuasion; in organization, there are conference superintendents over each district and annual conferences; the general administration of each conference is carried on by the annual conference sessions, the conference council of administration, and program agencies such as evangelism, missions, Christian education, and stewardship. A general superintendent is the general overseer of the work of the denomination. There is an inclusive membership of 11,909 in 137 churches.

EVANGELICAL CONGREGATIONAL CHURCH

Objecting to the "usurpation of power in violation of the discipline" by bishops, 7 annual conferences, and from 60,000 to 70,000 members of the Evangelical Association—later known as the Evangelical Church—withdrew from that body in 1894 to organize the United Evangelical Church. The 2 churches were reunited in 1922, but again a minority objected and remained aloof from the merger. The East Pennsylvania Conference, together with several churches in the Central, Pittsburgh, Ohio, Illinois, and West Virginia conferences, continued their separate existence under the old name. This was later changed to the Evangelical Congregational Church.

Today the boundaries of the Eastern Conference are larger than at the time of the merger; the Midwest churches are joined in a Western Conference. They are, like their parent Evangelical Church, "Methodists in polity, Arminian in doctrine." There is emphasis upon the inspiration and integrity of the Bible and the "fellowship of all followers of Christ." There are annual and general conferences with equal lay and clerical representation, bishops and district superintendents, and an itinerant ministry. Pastors are appointed yearly by the annual conferences. Local congregations, as the name implies, have more freedom—especially in temporal matters—than congregations in either Evangelical or Methodist churches. The Board of Missions with 2 women's auxiliaries and 2 conference missionary societies supervises the home and foreign missionary programs. There are 50 missionaries abroad and 36 at home, and 328 nationals at work in various lands.

Large summer assemblies are held in 6 campsites strategically located in the conferences. Church headquarters, the publishing house, the infirmary, the home for the aging, and the school of theology are located at Myerstown, Pennsylvania. There are 28,840 members and approximately 161 churches.

EVANGELICAL COVENANT CHURCH OF AMERICA

This church traces its roots to the Protestant Reformation, to the biblical instruction of the Lutheran State Church of Sweden, and to the great spiritual awakenings of the nineteenth century. These 3 influences have in large measure shaped its development and are to be borne in mind in seeking to understand its distinctive spirit.

The Covenant Church adheres to the affirmations of the Protestant Reformation regarding the Holy Scriptures as the Word of God and the only perfect rule for faith, doctrine, and conduct. It has traditionally valued the historic confessions of the Christian Church, particularly the Aposles' Creed, while at the same time it has emphasized the sovereignty of the Word over all creedal interpretations. It has especially cherished the pietistic restatement of the doctrine of justification by faith as basic to its dual task of evangelism and Christian nurture, the New Testament emphasis upon personal faith in Jesus Christ as Savior and Lord, the reality of a fellowship of believers that recognizes but transcends theological differences, and the belief in baptism and the Lord's Supper as divinely ordained sacraments of the church. While the denomination has traditionally practiced the baptism of infants, in conformity with its principle of freedom it has given room to divergent views. The principle of personal freedom, so highly esteemed by the Covenant Church, is to be distinguished from the individualism that disregards the centrality of the Word of God and the mutual responsibilities and disciples of the spiritual community.

The local church is administered by a board elected by the membership; it calls its ministers (ordained by the denomination) generally with the aid and guidance of the denominational pastoral relations commission and the conference superintendent. There are 11 geographical districts known as regional conferences, each of which elects its own superintendent. The highest constituted authority is vested in an annual meeting composed of ministers and laymen elected as delegates by the constituent churches. An executive board, elected by the annual meeting, implements its decisions.

Mission fields are in Africa (Republic of Congo, Kinshasa), Zaire, Alaska, China (Taiwan), Ecuador, Colombia, Japan, Mexico, and Thailand. There is a Bible Institute in Canada, Minnehaha Academy in Minneapolis, and at Chicago the church supports the Swedish Covenant Hospital School of Nursing and North Park College and Theological Seminary. There are 2 homes for orphaned children, 1 sailors' home, 2 hospitals, and 15 retirement centers. There are 74,623 adult members in 536 churches.

EVANGELICAL FREE CHURCH OF AMERICA

The church began with a group of independent congregations and several churches of the old Swedish Ansgarii Synod and Mission Synod, which met together at Boone, Iowa, in 1884 to form a fellowship of "free" congregations, to be known as the Swedish Evangelical Free Mission (later changed to Swedish Evangelical Free Church and still later to Evangelical Free Church of America). In 1950 the Swedish Evangelical Free Church and the Evangelical Free Church Association (formerly the Norwegian and Danish Evangelical Free Church Association) were merged into the present body.

By agreement, in the organization of the fellowship in 1884, this was to be a body of self-governing congregations, each left free to establish its own doctrine; the several churches elected delegates to an annual conference that was purely advisory in character. A society of ministers and missionaries was organized in 1894 to guide the denomination in doctrine and practice. This is still the guiding principle of the church; the only qualification for membership lies in evidence of conversion and the living of a Christian life. Polity is congregational. A 12-point doctrinal statement, in 1950, is incorporated into the bylaws of most local congregations.

There are approximately 700 churches with a constituency of about 100,000, and 14 districts in the United States and 2 in Canada; mission stations in Japan, the Philippines, Hong Kong, Zaire, Singapore/Malaysia, Germany, Venezuela; and 2 new stations in Belgium and Peru. There are 2 schools of higher education—Trinity Evangelical Divinity School in Bannockburn, Illinois, and Trinity Western College in Langley, British Columbia.

The church is a member of the International Federation of Free Evangelical Churches and the National Association of Evangelicals.

FEDERATED CHURCHES

Federated churches in the United States are largely a rural or village phenomenon, strongest in New England and the West. They are churches, 2 or more in number and representing different denominations, that unite for mutual conduct of their work while continuing their connections with the denominations involved. The first federated church of which we have any record was formed in Massachusetts in 1887; another was founded in Vermont in 1899. By 1936 there were 508 federated churches in 42 states, with 88,411 members. There may be double that number now; further statistics are unavailable because of the lack of any national organization or office. Dr. Ralph Williamson, conducting a survey for Cornell University, listed over 800 federated churches in 1952.

Economic pressure, conviction that the community is overchurched, flow of population, the inspiring example of the consolidated school, and the increased cost of church maintenance have been influential in forcing such federations. Ralph A. Felton in *Local Church Cooperation in Rural Communities* (Home Missions Council, 1944) describes the usual circumstances under which the average federated church is created.

Two churches in the same locality begin to have financial difficulties. Their memberships are too small to carry on thriving individual churches. They feel that if they could unite into one local congregation they could provide a more efficient religious program. Neither church wants to give up its affiliation with its denomination. For years they have been saying, "We should unite, but who's going to give up?" Finally they unite locally, hire one minister instead of two, but continue their separate "overhead" or denominational affiliations. The two or more separate churches thus become a federated church.

Usually there are joint religious services and a common Sunday school, and policy is determined by a joint official board. In some cases one minister is chosen to serve continuously; in others the minister is chosen alternately from the denominations represented. In approximately half of the federated churches in this country all the Protestant churches in the community have entered the federation. Presbyterians seem to have the highest percentage of cooperation, with Congregationalists, Christians, Methodists, and Baptists following in that order. There is still a real conflict of loyalties in the federated churches; its conclusion depends upon a slow educational process. There is a noticeable trend toward eventual denominationalization. Majority groups have a way of absorbing minorities; and usually when denominationalization comes, people go to the denomination that continues to provide a minister. It is also clear that if a federated church lasts 5 years, it is seldom abandoned.

Doctrine, polity, and membership requirements correspond in some cases to the standards of the denominations included; in other instances they are completely independent. No blanket statement is possible in these matters.

FIRE BAPTIZED HOLINESS CHURCH

A black pentecostal sect, this church was for the first 10 years of its existence a part of the white Fire Baptized Holiness Association of America; the black membership separated in 1908. In 1922 it became the Fire Baptized Holiness Church.

This church teaches the standard pentecostal and holiness doctrines of repentance, regeneration, justification, sanctification, Pentecostal baptism, speaking with other tongues, divine healing, and the premillennial Second Coming. It stands opposed to the "so-called Christian Scientists, Spiritualists, Unitarians, Universalists and Mormons." Adventism, immorality, antinomianism, the annihilation of the wicked, the glorification of the body, and "many other modern teachings of the day" are denounced as false, wicked, and unscriptural. Government is by a bishop, 2 overseers, a general secretary, treasurer, and a board of trustees. Ruling elders, ordained ministers, and pastors are in charge of local churches; and a general convention is held yearly. In 1958, 988 members were reported in 53 churches. Headquarters are in Atlanta.

FIRE BAPTIZED HOLINESS CHURCH (WESLEYAN)

Preaching on the doctrine of holiness inspired the organization of this church about 1890; its first members were dissenters within the Methodist churches of southeastern Kansas. They called themselves at first the Southeast Kansas Fire Baptized Holiness Association; the present name was adopted in 1945.

Doctrine is primitive Wesleyan, emphasizing sanctification and complete holiness. The church government and organization follow the Methodist Episcopal pattern, and there is strong emphasis upon evangelism. There are 988 members in 53 churches.

FREE CHRISTIAN ZION CHURCH OF CHRIST

Led by E. D. Brown, a local Methodist missionary, a small group of Methodist and Baptist black ministers formed this church in 1905 at Redemption, Arkansas. They objected to the taxing of any church membership to provide support for any ecclesiastical organization, feeling that the care and relief of the needy and the poor were the first responsibility of the church. Such relief activities characterize their local churches today.

Doctrine is completely Methodist and so is government except for minor titles and details. Chiefs or superintendents perform the functions of bishops; a chief pastor is chosen as top administrative officer, making all assignments to pastorates and appointing all church officers. Pastors and deacons head local churches and are responsible for the aid of the poor in their congregations. Laymen share in the conduct of the churches and in the annual general assembly. The latest membership report (1956), listed 22,260 members in 742 churches.

FRIENDS

With a membership in the United States and Canada of only 123,000 and with 200,000 around the world, the Religious Society of Friends, better known as Quakers, has had a deep and lasting influence upon Western society. Contributions in both religious and humanitarian spheres have won the Quakers universal respect and admiration, and their amazing history and loyalty to their quiet faith offer a challenge and inspiration to all the churches.

Their vicissitudes and victories began with George Fox (1624–91), a British "seeker" after spiritual truth and peace. Failing to find such in the churches of his time, Fox found them in a new, intimate, personal relationship with Christ. He said: "When all my hopes in [churches and churchmen] were gone . . . then I heard a voice which said, 'There is one, even Christ Jesus, that can speak to thy condition.' " This is the Inner Voice, or Inner Light, of Quakerism, based upon the description of John 1:9—"the true Light, which lighteth every man that cometh into the world"—a voice available to all men, having nothing to do with outward forms or ceremonies, rituals, or creeds. Every man to the Quaker is a walking church; every heart is God's altar and shrine.

Quakerism was revolutionary, and it was treated as revolution by the state Church of England. To tell this united state and church that they were both wrong, that their theology and dogma meant nothing, that men need not attend the "steeple houses" to find God, and that it was equally wrong to pay taxes in support of state church clergymen—this was rebellion.

Fox and his early followers went even further. They not only refused to go to church but insisted upon freedom of speech, assembly, and worship; they would not take oaths in court; they refused to go to war; they doffed their hats to no man, king or commoner; they made no distinction among people in sexes or social classes; they condemned slavery and England's treatment of the prisoner and the insane. The very names they took—Children of Truth, Children of Light, Friends of Truth, and finally the Religious Society of Friends—roused ridicule and fierce opposition. Fox, hauled into court, advised one judge to "tremble at the Word of the Lord" and heard the judge call him "Quaker." It was derision, but it was not enough to stop them. Persecution unsheathed its sword.

The Quakers were whipped, jailed, tortured, mutilated, murdered. Fox spent 6 years in jail; others spent decades, dying there. From 1650 to 1689 more than 3,000 suffered for conscience's sake, and 300 to 400 died in prison. Thanks to that persecution they prospered, founding the society in 1652. When Fox died, there were 50,000 Quakers.

Some were already in America. Ann Austin and Mary Fisher arrived in Massachusetts from Barbados in 1656, were promptly accused of being witches, and deported. Two days later 8 more came from England. Laws were passed hastily to keep them out; the whipping post worked overtime and failed. Four were hanged in Boston. Quakers kept coming into New England, New York, New Jersey, Maryland, Virginia, and Pennsylvania. Rhode Island and Pennsylvania welcomed them from the start. The long horror in the communities that did not welcome them ended with the passage of the Toleration Act of 1689.

With the Act and Fox's death a new phase began. Persecution waned and died and so did a great deal of Quaker revolutionary zeal. They settled down as businessmen and farmers known for their pacifism and honesty and became quite prosperous.

Yet there were lights in this period of quiet. The meeting organization and community life became well organized. Closely knit family life was emphasized. It was a time of creativeness and mystical inwardness. The period of withdrawal was one in which Quaker philanthropy became widely respected and even admired; their ideas on prison reform began to take effect. Quaker schools increased; as early as 1691 there were 15 Quaker boarding schools in England.

In 1682 William Penn came to Philadelphia. He sat under an elm at Shackamaxon and made a treaty with the Indians—the "only treaty never sworn to and never broken." Treated like human beings, the Indians reacted in kind. If all our cities had been like Philadelphia and all our states like Pennsylvania, our national history would have been vastly different.

But even here the holy experiment had to end. Quakers controlled the Pennsylvania legislature until 1756, when they refused to vote a tax to pay for a war against the Shawnees and the Delawares and consequently stepped down and out of power.

They looked within rather than without and began enforcing discipline on their membership so strictly that they became in fact a "peculiar people." Members were disowned or dismissed for even minor infractions of the discipline; thousands were cut off for "marrying out of Meeting." Pleasure, music, and art were taboo, sobriety, punctuality, and honesty were demanded in all directions; dress was painfully plain, and speech was biblical. They were different and dour; they gained few new converts and lost many old members.

Some few "fighting Quakers" went to battle in the American Revolution, but they were few; most of them remained pacifists. They worked quietly for peace, popular education, temperance, democracy, and against slavery. In 1688 the Friends of Germantown, Pennsylvania, said that slavery violated the Golden Rule and encouraged adultery; they protested the "traffic in the bodies of men" and called it unlawful. Their first attitude of tolerance changed slowly to one of outright opposition; it took nearly a century for the Quakers to rid their society of slavery, but they did it years in advance of any other religious body in America. Sellers or purchasers of slaves were forbidden membership in the society by the close of the eighteenth century. Persistently all across the years the Quakers dropped their seeds of antislavery agitation into the body politic. First John Woolman and then the poet Whittier wielded tremendous influence in the fight; and once the Civil War was over, they threw their strength into such organizations as the Freedman's Aid Society. Ever since, they have been active in education and legislative protection for blacks.

Divisions arose within their ranks during these years: the Hicksites separated in 1827, the Wilburites in 1845; and the Primitives (a small group now extinct) in 1861. Of these separations, the one led by Elias Hicks was of primary concern. Hicks was a rural Long Island Quaker whose liberal and rational theological views brought him into conflict with those of more orthodox and evangelical persuasion. The division came in 1827; basically, while it had personal and sociological emphases, the split was due to the widespread nineteenth-century conflict between liberalism and rationalism on the one hand and an orthodoxy based on Methodist ideas of evangelism and salvation on the other. Two-thirds of the Philadelphia Yearly Meeting withdrew with the Hicksites (a nickname never officially adopted by any

Quaker group) and similar divisions followed in New York, Ohio, Indiana, and Baltimore yearly meetings. A second series of separations resulted from the Wesleyan Methodist influence, led by Joseph John Gurney and John Wilbur (see "Religious Society of Friends [Conservative]," below).

The twentieth century thus far has been a century of Quaker unity and outreach. A Five Years Meeting (now the Friend's United Meeting) was organized in 1902, merging a large portion of the pastoral yearly meetings. The 2 Philadelphia meetings, separated since 1827, were united in 1955. In the same year the 2 New York Yearly Meetings were merged, and the 3 Canada Yearly Meetings came together to form one body. In 1968, 2 Baltimore Yearly Meetings reunited. Southeastern Meeting, newly founded, affiliated with Friends United Meeting and Friends General Conference in 1972.

In 1917, before the guns of World War I had stopped firing, Friends from all branches of the society were at work in the American Friends Service Committee in relief and reconstruction efforts abroad. The A.F.S.C. remains today one of the most effective of such agencies in the world. Its volunteers erected demountable houses, staffed hospitals, plowed fields, reared domestic animals, and drove ambulances. Famine-relief and child-feeding programs were instituted in Serbia, Poland, Austria, Russia, and Germany; at one time the Friends were feeding more than 1,000,000 German children every day; Greek refugees, earthquake victims in Japan, needy miners' families in Pennsylvania, West Virginia, and Kentucky were helped. Thousands would have perished but for the A.F.S.C.

Quakers drove ambulances and served in the medical corps of both world wars, and some were in combat; probably more young Quakers volunteered or accepted military service in these conflicts than resisted on grounds of religious principle. They also worked to relieve our displaced Japanese-Americans, and they cooperated with the Brethren and Mennonites in locating our conscientious objectors in work of real importance on farms, in reformatories, hospitals, and insane asylums. They were in Spain soon after the outbreak of the Spanish Civil War and later fed the child victims in Spain, southern France, Italy, Austria, Holland, North Africa, and Finland. In one year, 1945, they sent 282 tons of clothes, shoes, bedding, and soap to Europe and still more to China and India. Counting gifts, both of cash and materials, the income of the A.F.S.C. is apt to exceed $7,500,000 annually. At home and abroad summer camps of young volunteers have inspired an incalculable goodwill among nations and minority groups within nations.

Nor have they been satisfied with work merely in relief. Peace conferences have been a prominent part of their work, conferences ranging from local to international and covering all age groups. Lake Mohonk in New York was founded by a Friend. Scores of youth conferences and camps at home and in foreign fields testify to their devotion to the way of Christ; it is little wonder that they are known as a "peace church."

Worship and business in the society are conducted in monthly, quarterly, and yearly meetings. The monthly meeting is the basic unit, made up of one or more meetings in a neighborhood. It convenes each week for worship and once a month for business. It keeps records of membership, births, deaths, and marriages; appoints committees; considers queries on spiritual welfare; and transacts all business of the group. Monthly meetings in a district join 4 times a year in the quarterly meeting to stimulate spiritual life and to pass on whatever business they feel should be brought to the attention of the yearly meeting. The yearly meeting corresponds to a diocese in an episcopal system; there are 27 of them in the United States and Canada. They are in touch with Friends all over the world and have standing committees on such subjects as publications, education, the social order, missions, peace, charities, and national legislation; they allocate trust-fund incomes and generally supervise the work of the society.

Group decisions await the "sense of the meeting." Lacking any unity of opinion, the meeting may have a "quiet time" for a few minutes until unity is found, or it may postpone consideration of the matter or refer to a committee for study. Minorities are not outvoted but convinced. Every man, woman, and child is free to speak in any meeting; delegates are appointed at quarterly and yearly meetings to ensure adequate representation, but they enjoy no unusual position or prerogatives. Women have as much power as men and hold a position of absolute equality in Quaker polity.

There are, contrary to popular misunderstanding, church officers—elders and ministers—among the Quakers; they are chosen for recognized ability in spiritual leadership, and they, too, stand on equal footing with the rest of the membership. All members are ministers to the Quaker. A few full-time workers are paid a modest salary, and "recorded" ministers serving as pastors in those meetings having programmed worship also receive salaries (about 1,000 meetings have no paid pastors).

Quaker worship is of 2 kinds: programmed and unprogrammed. The 2, however, are not always distinct. The former more nearly resembles a simple Protestant service, but there are no rites or outward sacraments. While believing in spiritual communion, partaking of the elements is thought unnecessary. In the unprogrammed meetings there is no choir, collection, singing, or pulpit; the service is devoted to quiet meditation, prayer, and communion. Any vocal contributions are spontaneous. There is no uniform practice; some of the so-called churches greatly prefer to be called meetings.

In business meetings there is often frank inquiry into the conduct of business, treatment of others, use of narcotics or intoxicants, reading habits, and recreation. No true Quaker gambles, plays the stock market, bets, owns racehorses, or engages in raffles, lotteries, or the liquor business. Some follow conservative religious or theological patterns, and others are liberal; all are guided by the Inner Light.

The Inner Light is highly important in Quaker belief. Grace, power from God to help man resist evil, is to Quakers universal among all men. They seek not holiness but perfection—a higher, more spiritual standard of life for both society and the individual—and they believe that the truth is unfolding and continuing. They place high evaluation on the Bible but try to rely on individual fresh guidance from the Spirit of God which produced the Bible, rather than to follow only what has been revealed to others. Some modern groups accept the Bible as the final authority in all religious matters.

Rufus Jones says:

They believe supremely in the nearness of God to the human soul, in direct intercourse and immediate communion, in mystical experience in a firsthand discovery of God. . . . It means and involves a sensitiveness to the wider spiritual Life above us, around us, and within us, a dedication to duty, a passion for truth, and an appreciation of goodness, an eagerness to let love and the grace of God come freely through one's own life, a reverence for the will of God wherever it is revealed in past or present, and a high faith that Christ is a living presence and a life-giving energy always within reach of the receptive soul.

No Quaker body has ever departed from the Declaration to Charles II in 1661: "We utterly deny all outward wars and strife and fighting with outward weapons, for any end or under any pretense whatever. . . . The spirit of Christ, which leads us into all Truth, will never move us to fight and war against any man with outward weapons, neither for the Kingdom of Christ, nor for the kingdoms of this world." However, there is great tolerance toward individual variations in this position. In World War II formal Quaker positions favored applying for conscientious objector status, either as noncombatants within the military or in alternate service; during the Vietnam war corporate positions shifted toward encouraging men to practice draft refusal and go to jail if necessary. In both cases a wide variety of positions was seen as acceptable; the emphasis was on following individual conscience. Quakers who enter military service are no longer disowned from membership, but many leave the society and join a church that does not profess pacifism. Conversely, pacifists brought up in other traditions tend to join the Society of Friends in young adulthood.

Marriage is not necessarily a ceremony to be performed by a minister; in cases where the traditional Quaker marriage is observed the bride and groom simply stand before a meeting and make mutual vows of love and faithfulness and are thereby married. In certain sections of the country the pastor of the meeting officiates.

The Friends have never been great proselytizers; they depend almost entirely upon birthright membership and membership by "convincement." In many of their bodies, though not in all of them, every child born of Quaker parents is declared a member of the society. This has resulted in a large number of nominal, or paper, members who contribute little; efforts are being made to correct this custom by establishing a junior, or associate, membership for children. This reliance upon birthright membership has seriously depleted their numbers. There are 30 yearly meetings in America, including 1 in Canada, 1 in Cuba, 1 in Jamaica, and a small group in Mexico. There are also 20 yearly meetings overseas.

If the Friends were ever "exclusive," they are not now; a world outreach has been evident and growing in recent years. The Friend's United Meeting and the Friends' General Conference are members of the World Council of Churches; with the Philadelphia Yearly Meeting it also belongs to the National Council of Churches. A Friends World Committee for

Consultation, organized at Swarthmore, Pennsylvania, following the Second World Conference of Friends in 1937, functions as an agent, or clearinghouse, for the interchange of Quaker aspirations and experiences by way of regional, national, and international intervisitation, person-to-person consultations, conferences, correspondence, and a variety of publications. The committee has headquarters in Birmingham, England, and offices in Philadelphia; Plainfield, Indiana; and Edinburgh, Scotland. The American section has helped some 50 small Friends groups in the United States to monthly meeting status. The F.W.C.C. is a nongovernmental organization related to the Economic and Social Council of the United Nations through cooperation with the A.F.S.C.; it helps operate a program at the U. N. headquarters to forward world peace and human brotherhood. Something of a world brotherhood, or "Franciscan Third Order," has been set up in the organization of the Wider Quaker Fellowship, in which non-Quakers in sympathy with the Quaker spirit and program may participate in the work of the Friends without coming into full Quaker membership. This is not so much an organization as it is "a fellowship of kindred minds—a way of life, a contagion of spirit"; it has 4,200 members, 360 of whom live abroad.

An Evangelical Friends Alliance was formed in 1965 in the interests of evangelical emphasis and denominational unity; it seeks to bring together those interested in an evangelical renewal within Christianity and a renewal of interest in the evangelical emphases of seventeenth-century Quakerism, and includes the Association of Evangelical Friends. Theology· here· is conservative; local pastors are elected. There are 257 churches and 25,531 members.

A further movement toward unity is found in the Religious Society of Friends (Unaffiliated Meetings), which also stresses elements and teachings of early Friends movements. This group is unique in its wide variety and experimentation in worship and polity; it is not associated with the larger bodies in the society. There are 87 churches with 5,696 members.

Friends General Conference

This is a national organization of yearly meetings (Baltimore, Lake Erie, South Central, Canada, New England, Illinois, Indiana, South Eastern, New York, and Philadelphia). It was established in 1968 as a Sunday school conference and matured in 1900 as a general conference for fellowship across yearly meeting boundaries as an instrument for deepening the spiritual and social testimonies of the Society of Friends. One of its main features is an annual conference; in 1978 it had 1,500 members, about one-third of whom were children and young people. There are 22,000 families and 375 meetings in the General Conference, a fraction of whom also belong to the Friends United Meeting (described below); this is explained by the dual membership in Canada, New York, and New England in the General Conference and the Friends United Meeting.

Friends United Meeting (Five Years Meeting)

With 67,362 members and 526 churches in 1976, this is the largest single Quaker body in the United States. (The largest yearly meetings in the world are the East Africa with 35,000 members and London with 19,998.) Organized in 1902, it brought together in one cooperative relationship 12 yearly meetings and 3 yearly meetings abroad—East Africa, Cuba, and Jamaica—with a somewhat different status. They work together in many departments—such as missionary service and the production of Sunday school materials—and while each yearly meeting in the body is autonomous, they come together for spiritual stimulation, business, and conference every 3 years.

The ministries of the "FUM" are carried forward in the interim between Triennial Sessions by 3 planning commissions and the general board, which convene semiannually. Affirming the importance of personal religious experience that goes beyond theory or speculation, it embodies a creative balance of central Quaker accents, evangelism and social concern, mission and service, worship, and ministry. Friends of various persuasions work together within the FUM spectrum.

Religious Society of Friends (Conservative)

Known also as Wilburites, this group resulted from a second division. Joseph John Gurney, a British evangelical Quaker, came to America in the mid 1800s and began preaching and teaching the final authority of the Bible and acceptance of the doctrines of the atonement, justification, and sanctification. John Wilbur, a Rhode Island conservative Friend, while not denouncing the authority of the Bible and its teachings, felt that Gurney's preaching substituted a creed for the immediate revelation of the Divine Spirit available to man. Both men had large followings; the outcome was separation in Kansas, Iowa, Indiana, Ohio, New England, North Carolina, and Canada, between 1845 and 1904.

The conservative pattern, generally, was one "set forth by the Society in the beginning," calling for a silent waiting before God in Quaker meetings, in expectation that his spirit would instruct and move them to speak or pray without program or ritual. In New England in 1945, and in Canada in 1955, differences were resolved between these conservatives, and they were reunited. There are still conservative yearly meetings in Iowa, Ohio, and North Carolina; they cooperate with other Friends groups in various areas of service and in intervisitation. There are 27 Monthly Meetings and 1,728 members.

GENERAL CONVENTION OF THE SWEDENBORGIAN CHURCH

Commonly called Swedenborgian, the Churches of the New Jerusalem are based upon the teachings of Emmanuel Swedenborg and exist in 3 main bodies: the General Convention of the New Jerusalem in the U.S.A (the older U.S. body); the General Church of the New Jerusalem, which broke from the older group in 1890; and the General Conference in England.

Swedenborg, who was born in Stockholm in 1688 and died in London in 1772, was a scientist distinguished in the fields of mathematics, geology, cosmology, and anatomy before he turned seriously to theology. Items in his theology dealing with the nature of the one God, heaven and hell, human freedom, the Bible, marriage, etc., are held to have been revealed of God to man's rational mind through things heard and seen by Swedenborg in the spiritual world; he was "uniquely permitted to have communication with the other world." His writings disclaim spiritism but claim almost daily vision of heaven and hell, which he describes in full detail. He wrote also of frequent conversations with spirits, through whom he learned that a new Christian church was to be born and that his written works would be the basis of its teachings. He died and was buried a Lutheran, but his teachings were definitely different.

Certain that he was divinely commissioned to teach the doctrines of this "New Church," Swedenborg taught that God is man, meaning that the origin of all that is truly human is in one God. The Divine Humanity is, however, Christ's glorified and risen Humanity, in which man is manifested and which is God. These doctrines are accepted and preached by his followers, who consider him to be a divinely illuminated seer and revelator. Against the background of his concept of "correspondence" of the natural world with the spirit world, he expounded an additional sense of the Scriptures considered to be consistent with science and reason. Swedenborg himself never preached, or founded a church, but his followers felt that the need for a separate denomination was implicit in the New Revelation.

The New Church as an organization started in London in 1783 when Robert Hindmarsh, a printer, gathered a few friends together to discuss the writings of Swedenborg; they formed a general conference of their societies in 1815. The first Swedenborgian Society in America was organized at Baltimore in 1792; in 1817 the General Convention of the New Jerusalem in the U.S.A. was established.

The doctrines of the general convention as set forth in the liturgy are as follows:

1. That there is one God, in whom there is a Divine Trinity; and that He is the Lord Jesus Christ.

2. That saving faith is to believe in Him.

3. Every man is born to evils of every kind, and unless through repentance he removes them in part, he remains in them, and he who remains in them cannot be saved.

4. That good actions are to be done, because they are of God and from God.

5. That these are to be done by a man as from himself; but that it ought to be believed that they are done from the Lord with him and by him.

The societies are grouped into a general convention meeting annually; there are also state regulations. Each society is self-regulating. They have ministers and general pastors (in charge of state associations). Services are liturgical but with a wide latitude; based upon the Book of Worship issued by the General Convention. The convention now has 3,500 members active in 45 societies; a theological school is located at Newton, Massachusetts; the Swedenborg Foundation in New York City distributes the writings of Swedenborg.

The General Church of the New Jerusalem accepts the full divine authority of the "Writings," acknowledging them as being not really *his*, but rather "from the Lord alone." There is no fixed constitution in this church; polity is based upon "essential unanimity" in free council and assembly. There are ministers, pastors, and bishops, the latter being chosen by a general assembly meeting every 3 or 4 years; 3,297 members are reported in 21 organized circles and 15 organized groups. Eight of these societies have parochial elementary schools with an enrollment of 627; there is a theological school, a college, and a secondary school. Headquarters are at Bryn Athyn, Pennsylvania, where a cathedral church has been built.

GRACE GOSPEL FELLOWSHIP

Dispensational and premillennial, this Fellowship had its beginnings in a conference of pastors and missionaries in the First Church of the Fundamentals in Evanston, Illinois, in 1944, as a pastor's fellowship. A year later its purpose was defined in a constitution: "The purpose of this organization shall be to promote a fellowship among those who believe the truths contained in [our] doctrinal statement and to proclaim the Gospel of the Grace of God in this land, and through the Worldwide Grace Testimony, throughout the world." Their doctrinal statement includes belief in the Bible as infallibly inspired by God, the total depravity of man, redemption by God's grace on the ground of the blood of Christ through the means of faith, eternal security for the saved, the gifts of the Spirit (as enumerated in Eph. 4:7-16), but that man's nature of sin is never eradicated during this life; they believe in divine baptism but not in water baptism, and they emphasize the resurrection and the second coming of Christ, the lasting suffering of the unsaved dead. Any church may vote to become affiliated with the Grace Gospel Fellowship provided it meets the Fellowship's doctrinal standards.

The Fellowship consists of 48 churches and 3,500 members in the United States; Grace Bible College and Seminary is located in Wyoming, Michigan; there are 6 foreign and 1 home missionary organizations. Abroad, Fellowship churches are found in Africa, Puerto Rico, India, Europe, and Japan.

INDEPENDENT CHURCHES

It is difficult, if not impossible, to classify properly all those churches in the United States calling themselves independent. Generally they may be identified as churches not controlled by any denominational or ecclesiastical organization, but even this does not hold in all cases. The following groupings are possible:

1. Churches called union, community, nondenominational, undenominational, or interdenominational. Community and nondenominational churches together constitute nearly one-half the number of so-called independent churches.

2. Churches using a denominational name but working without denominational supervision.

3. Churches organized by individuals: holiness, evangelistic churches or movements, gospel churches or halls, "storefront" churches, and so forth.

4. United churches of all types.

5. Federated churches (already discussed; see p. 131).

Many of these churches shift from one classification to another; one listed as United one year may be listed as Community (Methodist) the next. Free as they are of denominational control, they are as widely different in doctrine and polity as the preferences of the individuals and groups involved are different.

The most effective community church organization in this country is found in the Council of Community Churches, founded in 1945. This is a fellowship of participating churches, rather than a denominational or ecclesiastical body—a "clearinghouse," or forum for the cooperative activities of the churches. Membership is on an annual basis. Upon invitation the council helps overchurched communities to federate or unite in one community-centered church; it encourages denominations to set up procedures to alleviate overchurched situations, helps to find community-minded ministers, and distributes relevant literature. Many of their churches have a denominational relationship, and some of them have multiple denominational relationships, as in federated churches. There are 203 member churches in the council; services are rendered to about 450 to 500 other churches.

Policies are established by registered delegates of the churches in the council and/or by a board of trustees elected for one year at their annual conference. An executive director is active in field work, correspondence, and as general supervisor or director of various appointed committees. He is liaison officer between the Community Council and the National Council of Churches and the World Council of Churches, in both of which the Community Council is represented as a consultative member.

INDEPENDENT FUNDAMENTAL CHURCHES OF AMERICA

Organized in 1930 at Cicero, Illinois, by representatives of various independent churches anxious to safeguard fundamentalist doctrine, this body has 2 types of membership—one for churches and organizations, the other for ministers, missionaries, evangelists, and Christian workers. The organization membership accounts for 666 churches directly affiliated with 336 other independent churches whose pastors are affiliated. There are 5 Bible camps, 7 Bible institutes, 16 church extension organizations, 2 children's homes, 14 home and 4 foreign mission agencies. More than 1,450 ministers, missionaries, evangelists, and Christian workers are members; total membership is 125,350.

The president of the body presides over an annual conference in which the members have voting power. An executive committee of 12 serves for 3 years; the constituent churches are completely independent but are required to subscribe to the statement of faith of the organization.

The official organ of the I.F.C.A. is the *Voice* magazine, published bimonthly.

INTERNATIONAL CHURCH
OF THE FOURSQUARE GOSPEL

Rising out of the evangelistic work of Aimee Semple McPherson, this church is a tribute to the organizing genius and striking methods of its founder. Born in Ontario in 1890, Mrs. McPherson was converted under the preaching of her first husband, Robert Semple, an evangelist. He died in China, and she returned to the United States in 1911 to tour the country in a series of gospel meetings that were spectacular even in war years. She settled in Los Angeles in 1918, building the famous Angelus Temple, which was opened January 1, 1923, and founding the Echo Park Evangelistic Association, the L.I.F.E. Bible College, and International Church of the Foursquare Gospel religious corporations. The headquarters are still located at Angelus Temple in Los Angeles.

With her great speaking ability and her faith in praying for the healing of the sick, Mrs. McPherson attracted thousands to her meetings. Her more irreverent critics felt that her meetings were too spectacular, but others appreciated her type of presentation. There was great interest in the sick and the poor; "more than a million and a half" are said to have been fed by the Los Angeles organization.

The teaching of the church is set forth in a 21-paragraph Declaration of Faith written by Mrs. McPherson. Strongly fundamentalistic, it is premillennialist, holiness, and Trinitarian, advocating that the Bible is as "true, immutable, steadfast, unchangeable, as its author, the Lord Jehovah." The Holy Spirit baptism, with the initial evidence of speaking in other tongues, is subsequent to conversion, and there is the power to heal in answer to believing prayer. There are the usual doctrines on the atonement, the second coming of Christ "in clouds of glory," reward for the righteous at the judgment, and eternal punishment for the wicked. Baptism and the Lord's Supper are observed.

Mrs. McPherson was president of the church during her lifetime and was, with a board of directors, its ruling power and voice; her son, Rolf K. McPherson, became president at the time of her death. Today the official business of the church is conducted by a board of directors, the missionary cabinet, and an executive council. The highest seat of authority is the convention body, which alone has the power to make or amend the bylaws of the church. District supervisors are appointed for 10 districts, and are ratified by the pastors of the respective districts every 4 years. Each church is governed by a church council and contributes monthly to home and foreign missionary work. There are 230,134 members, 2,637 churches and meeting places in 29 different countries, 3,003 missionaries and national pastors, 30 day schools, 41 Bible schools, 4 orphanages on the foreign field, and a net property valuation of $55,478,854. All members are required to subscribe to the Declaration of Faith. A church flag—red, gold, blue, and purple with a red cross on a Bible background bearing a superimposed "4"—is prominently displayed in the churches and at rallies and assemblies; their radio station, KFSG, broadcasts from Los Angeles.

JEHOVAH'S WITNESSES

The people called Jehovah's Witnesses believe that they have in their movement the true realization of the "one faith" mentioned by the apostle Paul in Eph. 4:5. Their certainty of this and their zeal in proclaiming it have made them, at least in point of public interest, an outstanding religious phenomenon in modern America.

They were not known as Jehovah's Witnesses until 1931. Up to that time they had been called Millennial Dawnists, International Bible Students, and earlier, Russellites, after the man who brought about their first incorporation in 1884. Pastor Charles Taze Russell, their first president, is acknowledged not as founder (there is no "human" founder) but as general organizer; Judge Rutherford, Russell's successor, claimed that the Witnesses had been on earth as an organization for more than 5,000 years and cited Isa. 43:10-12; Heb. 11; and John 18:37 to prove it.

Russell was deeply influenced by belief in Christ's second coming; he studied the Bible avidly and attracted huge crowds to hear him expound it. The first formal group that he organized was in Pittsburgh in 1872; his books, of which 13,000,000 are said to have been circulated, had great influence on the movement. Russell was president; to assist him, a board of directors was elected by vote of all members subscribing $10 or more to the support of the work (a practice discontinued in 1944).

Under Russell's direction headquarters were moved to Brooklyn in 1909, and another corporation was formed under the laws of the state of New York. In 1956 the name was changed to the Watchtower Bible and Tract Society of New York, Inc. When Pastor Russell died in 1916, Joseph F. Rutherford was made president. Known widely as Judge Rutherford, he had been a Missouri lawyer who occasionally sat as a circuit court judge. He wrote tirelessly; his books, pamphlets, and tracts supplanted those of Russell; and his neglect of some aspects of the teaching of Russell brought dissension.

Administration of the group underwent changes in the days of Rutherford's presidency; the governing body of the Witnesses today is in the hands of older and more "spiritually qualified" men who base their judgments upon the authority of the Scriptures. This is considered not a governing hierarchy by the Witnesses but a true imitation of early apostolic Christian organization. Under this governing system, 3 corporations eventually came to serve the society: the Watchtower Bible and Tract Society of New York, Inc., the Watchtower Bible and Tract Society of Pennsylvania; and the International Bible Students Association of England. Judge Rutherford as president was a moving power in all of them.

Under the direction of these leaders at headquarters local congregations of Witnesses (they are always called congregations and never churches) are arranged into circuits with a traveling minister visiting the congregations, spending a week with each. Approximately 22 congregations are included in each circuit. Circuits are grouped into districts, of which there are 38 in the United States. District and circuit organizations are now found in 216 countries and islands across the world.

Meeting in Kingdom Halls and not in churches, they witness and "publish" their faith not only in testimony in their halls but in a remarkably comprehensive missionary effort. They do not believe in any separation into clergy or laity for the simple reason that "Christ Jesus did not make such a separation." They never use titles such as *Reverend* or *Rabbi* or *Father*; this, they feel, is not in accordance with the words of Jesus in Matt. 23:6-10. All of them give generously of their time in proclaiming their faith and teaching in private homes. Called Publishers of the Kingdom, they devote time regularly in kingdom preaching work, preaching only from the Bible. Pioneers are required to give at least 96 hours per month; special pioneers and missionaries devote a minimum of 140 hours per month and are sent to isolated areas and foreign lands where new congregations can be formed. All pioneers provide for their own support, but the society gives a small allowance to the special pioneers in view of their special needs. The headquarters staff, including the president of the society, are housed at the Bethel Home in Brooklyn, engage primarily in editorial and printing work, and receive an allowance of $20 a month in addition to room and board. The literature they write, print, and distribute is of almost astronomical proportions. The official journal, *The Watchtower*, has a circulation of 9,850,000; more than 1,000,000,000 Bibles, books, and booklets have been distributed since 1920; Bibles, books, booklets, and leaflets are available in more than 176 languages. More than 2,220,000 Witnesses are active in this work throughout the world.

In this literature (all of which is circulated without an author's by-line or signature) is contained the teaching of the society. It all rests firmly upon the idea of the theocracy, or rule of God. The world in the beginning, according to the Witnesses, was under the theocratic rule of the Almighty; all then was "happiness, peace, and blessedness." But Satan rebelled and became the ruler of the world, and from that moment on mankind has followed his evil leading. Then came Jesus, "the beginning of the creation by God," as the prophets had predicted, to end Satan's rule; Jesus' rule began in 1914. In 1918 Christ "came to the temple of Jehovah"; and in 1919 when Rutherford reorganized the movement shattered by the war, Jesus, enthroned in the temple, began illuminating the prophecies and sending out his followers to preach.

God, in Witness thinking, will take vengeance upon wicked man in our times; at the same time he is now showing his great love by "gathering out" multitudes of people of goodwill whom he will give life in his new world which is to come after the imminent battle of Armageddon is fought. This is to be a universal battle; Christ will lead the army of the righteous, composed of the "host of heaven, the holy angels," and will completely annihilate the army of Satan. The righteous of the earth will watch this battle but will not participate. After the battle a great crowd of people will remain on the earth; these will be believers in God and will be his servants. Those who have proved their integrity under test in this old world will multiply and populate the new earth with righteous people. A resurrection will also take place and will be an additional means of filling the cleansed earth with better inhabitants. After the holocaust, "righteous princes" are to rule the earth under Christ as "King of the Great Theocracy." One special group—the 144,000 Christians mentioned in Rev. 7 and 14—will become the "bride of Christ" and rule with him in heaven.

Judge Rutherford said often that "millions now living will never die"—which meant that Armageddon was close and that the Kingdom was at hand. He died in 1942, leaving guidance of the movement in the hands of the present president, Nathan H. Knorr; and Armageddon had not yet been fought. But the certainty of its imminence persists.

All this is based upon the Bible; Witnesses quote elaborately from the Scriptures, using it to verify their beliefs. All other teachings and interpretations are to them suspect and unreliable. They oppose and attack the teachings of the various churches as false and unscriptural, insisting as they do so that they are attacking or denouncing not churches or church members as such but only doctrines and interpretations of Scripture that they consider false. They have been especially active in opposing what they consider to be 3 allies of Satan: the false teachings of the churches, the tyranny of human governments, and the oppressions of business. This "triple alliance" of ecclesiastical, political, and commercial powers has misled and all but destroyed humanity, the Witnesses claim, and must be destroyed at Armageddon before the new world can be born. They refuse, for instance, to salute the flag or to bear arms in war or to participate in the affairs of government, not because of any pacifist convictions, but because they consider these to be expressions of Satan's power over men. This attitude has brought them into conflict with law-enforcing agencies; and they have endured jailings, whippings, assault by mobs, even stonings and tar-and-featherings and the burning of their homes. This they have accepted in a very submissive spirit; their position is that they will obey the laws of men when those laws are not in conflict with the laws of God; their guide is Acts 5:29.

The ranks of active "publishers" across the world have grown to 2,220,000, of which approximately 554,000 are in the United States. There are 7,400 congregations in the United States and 41,000 throughout the world. Branch offices are maintained in 95 countries, and work is reported in 216 lands. There are 6,200 who have been trained as foreign missionaries. The Bible School of Gilead was established at South Lansing, New York, in 1943 to train their missionaries and since 1961 has operated at international headquarters at 124 Columbia Heights, in Brooklyn. Since 1959 the society has operated in all the major countries of the world a Kingdom Ministry School, designed to provide a 2-week training course for all congregation elders.

JEWISH CONGREGATIONS

Jews arrived early in the American colonies; some were here before 1650. A small group of Portuguese Jews found safety if not complete understanding in Peter Stuyvesant's New Amsterdam, where they established the first official congregation in North America, Shearith Israel (Remnant of Israel) in 1654. Three years later there was a small group of Jews at Newport, Rhode Island. Jews came to Georgia with Oglethorpe and in 1733 organized a synagogue at Savannah. By 1850 there were 77 Jewish congregations in 21 states, and at the end of the century more than 600 congregations of over 1,000,000 Jews. Today more than 6 million American Jews have a widely varying synagogue membership estimated at anywhere from a minimum of 2,000,000 upward in 5,000 congregations.

The historic sense of unity among the Jewish people soon demonstrated itself here as it had abroad. That unity had defied centuries of dispersion and persecution, and it now welded the followers of Judaism into one of the best organized religious groups in America. In *The Truth About the Pharisees* it has been described by R. T. Herford as a "detailed system of ethical practices by which its adherents consecrated their daily lives to the service of God. The cornerstone of Judaism was the deed, not the dogma."

There are, however, 2 pillars upon which Judaism rests. One is the teaching of the Old Testament, particularly of the Pentateuch, the 5 books of Moses. This is known in Judaism as the Torah. It is the revelation of God, divine in origin and containing the earliest written laws and traditions of the Jewish people. The other is the Talmud, which is a rabbinical commentary and enlargement of the Torah, an elaborate, discursive compendium containing the written and the oral law of the faith.

In Torah and Talmud are the Jewish foundation principles of justice, purity, hope, thanksgiving, righteousness, love, freedom of the will, divine providence and human responsibility, repentance, prayer, and the resurrection of the dead. At the heart of it all lies the Hebrew concept of the oneness of God. Every day of his life the religiously practicing Jew repeats the ancient biblical verse, "Hear, O Israel, the Lord our God is one Lord." All other gods are to be shunned; there is but one Creator of man and the world, holding the destiny of both in his almighty hands.

Man, created by this one God, is inherently good. There is no original sin, no instinctive evil or fundamental impurity in him; he is made in God's image and endowed with an intelligence that enables him to choose for himself between good and evil. He has and needs no mediator such as the Christians have in Christ; he approaches God directly. Men—Jews and Gentiles alike—attain immortality as the reward for righteous living.

Judaism looks forward to the perfection of man and to the establishment of a divine kingdom of truth and righteousness upon the earth. Orthodox Jews believe that this time will come when God sends the Messiah. Reform Judaism speaks of a Messianic age, while Conservative and Reconstructionist doctrine teaches variations of both ideas. To work toward the divine kingdom, the Jews have been established of God as a deathless, unique people, "a kingdom of priests and a holy nation," and as "the servant of the Lord."

Some of their laws provide for the great festivals of the Jewish year: Pesach, or Passover, in late March or early April, a memorial of the Jewish liberation from Egypt; Shabuoth, the Feast of Weeks, or Pentecost, in late May or early June, commemorating the giving of the Ten Commandments to Moses; Sukkoth, or the Feast of Tabernacles, or Booths, in October, marking the years of Jewish wandering in the wilderness; the Feast of Lights, or Hanukkah, in late November or December, celebrating the purification of the temple by the Maccabees after its defilement by Antiochus Epiphanes; the Feast of Lots, or Purim, in February or March, honoring the heroine Esther. Three principal minor fasts are observed: The Fast of Tebeth in January, commemorating the siege of Jerusalem; the Fast of Tammuz in July, observing the breach of Jerusalem's walls; and the Fast of Ab also in July, memorializing the fall of the city and the destruction of the temple. The most important days in the Jewish religious calendar are Rosh Hashanah, or New Year's Day, and Yom Kippur, the Day of Atonement, in September or early October, closing the Ten Days of Penitence which begin with Rosh Hashanah.

Other laws are kept as reminders of God's covenant with Israel; these include the laws of circumcision and Sabbath observance. Still others are held as marks of divine distinction and are kept to preserve the ideal of Israel as a chosen, separate people.

Within the local congregation there is full independence. There are no synods, assemblies, or hierarchies of leaders to control anything whatsoever in the synagogue. The Jews are loosely bound by the "rope of sand" of Jewish unity, with wide variation in custom and procedure. They have been influenced deeply by the many peoples and cultures with which they have come in contact and have made adjustments accordingly. Because of differences in historical background over the centuries some congregations use a German-Polish version Hebrew prayer book; others use a Spanish version. Some use English at various points in their service, such as the sermon; but all use Hebrew in their prayers. Sermons in Orthodox congregations may be in Yiddish, a Jewish language derived from Middle High German with Hebrew-Aramaic and Slavic components. Traditional Orthodox synagogues have no instrumental music in their services; the congregation worships with covered head, and the men and women sit separately. In Reform, Conservative, and Reconstructionist houses of worship, sermons are in English, and there is no segregation by sex.

At the head of the congregation stands the rabbi, trained in college and seminary and fully ordained. He is preacher and pastor. He officiates at marriages and grants divorce decrees in accordance with Jewish law after civil divorce has been granted by the state. He conducts funerals and generally supervises the burial of Jews as Jewish law requires. Congregations usually own their own cemeteries or organize cemetery societies; there are also many private cemetery or burial associations owned and controlled by Jewish benevolent groups. Orthodox rabbis are also charged with the supervision of slaughtering animals for food and with the distribution of kosher meat products in accordance with the Levitical dietary laws. Many congregations engage readers or cantors, but it is the rabbi who is the leader and authority on Jewish law and ritual.

There is no examination for synagogue membership, all Jews being readily accepted as congregants. However, married women and unmarried children are not usually recognized as voting members in Orthodox and Conservative synagogues, but among Reform and Reconstructionist congregations unmarried members, including women, are fully equal in responsibilities and rights. Men and women are almost always the corporate members. There are sometimes also pewholders, who contribute to and engage in the work of the synagogue but without the authority of corporate members. A third class of synagogue members consists of those who merely pay for the use of a synagogue seat during the high holidays. Corporate members are supposed to control all synagogue property and to guide congregational policy and activity, but the other members often participate on almost equal footing.

There are 4 divisions in American Judaism: (1) Orthodox Judaism, represented nationally by The Union of Orthodox Jewish Congregations of America, The Rabbinical Council of America, and the Union of Orthodox Rabbis of the United States and Canada; (2) Reform Judaism, with the Central Conference of American Rabbis and the Union of American Hebrew Congregations—the first national organization of synagogues in the United States, established in 1873—as spokesmen; (3) Conservative Judaism, organized in the United Synagogues of America and the Rabbinical Assembly of America; (4) Reconstruction Judaism, a movement affiliated with Conservative Judaism.

Synagogue membership is difficult to determine; no comprehensive comparison seems available or possible. It is probable that each of the 4 branches has about a million members. In addition to this, many Orthodox congregations are not affiliated with any national organization, and some estimates of their number run as high as 2,000. The smallest in numbers is the Reconstruction group, with about 1,500 members. Percentages of increase are unusually high; congregations are being formed faster than the various seminaries can ordain rabbis to supply their needs.

The multiplicity of Jewish national organizations is bewildering. The American Jewish Year Book lists them in the following categories: community relations and political, 19; overseas aid, 13; religious and educational, including colleges, 130; social and mutual benefit, 19; cultural, 27; social welfare, 25; Zionist and pro-Israel, 47; professional associations, 21; women's organizations, 20; youth and student organizations, 23. In over 225 of the larger cities and towns, the Jewish population maintains at least 1 central local organization, a federation welfare fund or community council. There are at present 200 Jewish periodicals and newspapers in 43 states and the District of Columbia, and 2 Jewish news syndicates. *American Judaism* is the quarterly Reform organ, the monthly *Jewish Life* speaks for the Orthodox branch, and *Conservative Judaism* is a quarterly for the Conservatives. Of general interest are *Commentary, Midstream, The Reconstructionist, Judaism, Jewish Frontier, Jewish Spectator,* and *National Jewish Post and Opinion.*

Education on all levels is a major Jewish concern. Children are enrolled in Sunday schools, weekday schools, all-day schools, Yiddish schools, and released-time schools. In 1966 there was a total of 554,468 children in all weekday and Sunday schools, but it was still estimated that not more than 53 percent of available Jewish children were enrolled in Jewish schools.

Institutions of higher learning are largely limited to schools for the training of rabbis. The most important of these schools are the Rabbi Isaac Elchanan Theological Seminary of Yeshiva University in New York City (Orthodox); the Hebrew Union College in Cincinnati and the Jewish Institute of Religion in New York City (Reformed institutions that were merged in 1948 into what is now called H.U.C.–J.I.R.); and the Jewish Theological Seminary in New York City (Conservative) and the Reconstructionist Rabbinical College in Philadelphia. The Jewish Theological Seminary has a branch in Los Angeles called the University of Judaism; Dropsie College ("a postgraduate, nonsectarian institution of Semitic learning") in Philadelphia and the Yivo Institute for Jewish Research in New York City are the only 2 institutions of higher learning working independently of Jewish seminaries; Yeshiva University in New York City and Brandeis University in Waltham, Massachusetts, are the only Jewish colleges awarding a B.A. degree.

Jewish charity is amazingly efficient. Jewish federations and welfare boards maintain programs costing over $500,000,000 per year; this money is divided among local agencies (health, welfare, education, and recreation), national agencies (civic defense, cultural, religious, and service), and overseas (mainly to help settle refugees in Israel and other countries).

The American Jewish Committee is organized to protect the civil and religious rights of all Jews around the world. It seeks equality for Jews in economic, social, and educational opportunities and gives aid and counsel in cases where intolerance or persecution are evident.

Among the Zionist groups, the Zionist Organization of America still remains the largest single body numerically, except for Hadassah, the women's Zionist group, which is the largest and most active among Zionists in philanthropic and educational programs. In the past decade the most influential spokesman on behalf of aid to Israel has been the Conference of Presidents of major American Jewish organizations, a coordinating body and forum of 22 major American Jewish organizations, on all questions affecting American-Israeli affairs.

Three trends are noticeable: There is a trend toward a relaxation of strict or letter observance of the time-honored Jewish law; one practical expression of this is found in the Reconstructionist movement, a religious-philosophical development of some influence in both Conservative and Reform Judaism. There is also a trend toward "emphasis upon youth," in which young Orthodox Jews are organized as Young Israel in the interests of future leadership in the synagogue. Third, there is a tendency among all groups to consider the inner spiritual strength of Judaism as its only hope for the future; under this drive, American Jews are moving toward fewer divisions and more cooperation and unity.

Orthodox Judaism

Orthodox Judaism has been called "Torah-True" Judaism; it is the branch that preserves the theology and traditions of Old World Jewry in the New World. It assigns equal authority to the written and oral law and to the ancient Jewish codes embodied in the Torah and the Talmud and their commentaries. The Torah is all-important and basic to all the rest: the Torah is of God, given to Moses, and there is no way to God except through obedience to the laws of the Torah; Torah is a revelation of the Fatherhood of God and the brotherhood of man, and it explains the place of the Jews as the chosen people of God. Everything a Jew needs to know is in the Torah; it governs every moment of his life. Moses is believed to have transmitted it down to the time when it was first committed to writing. There are, however, 2 slightly variant emphases in Orthodoxy; the East European, Hasidic Orthodoxy stemming from Hungary opposes resolutely *all* change or innovation in speech, dress, and education; that coming from Germany and western Europe is a bit less severe, attempting to preserve the more important elements of traditional Jewish life but accepting modern changes and ideas in these 3 areas.

Orthodox Jews believe in the political rebirth of their nation, in the return of the Jew to Israel to rebuild his temple on Mount Zion and to reestablish his ancient sacrificial ritual. They look forward to the coming of the Messiah, who is to be a descendant of David. The biblical dietary laws are strictly observed, and the traditional holy days and festivals are faithfully kept. The Hebrew language is used in their synagogue prayers; English, in their sermons. They are the fundamentalists of Judaism.

Reform Judaism

Reform Judaism is liberal Judaism. It began in Germany just after the Napoleonic emancipation, when "reformers" within Judaism shortened the synagogue services, made use of the vernacular and of organs in those services, and established group, in place of individual, confirmation. Some reformers at that time advocated a complete break with Judaistic traditional forms, but that did not come.

Isaac Mayer Wise, one of their outstanding leaders in the United States, founded here the Union of American Congregations (1873), the Hebrew Union College (1875), and the Central Conference of American Rabbis (1889); these important groups sum up the aim of Reform Judaism in their conviction that Judaism should "alter its externals to strengthen its eternals."

Reform holds that there is divine authority only in the written law of the Old Testament; this is its main distinction from Orthodox Judaism. But revelation in Reform is not confined to the Old Testament; it is progressive. The Reform Jew limits himself to the practice of the ceremonial laws of the Pentateuch, with the exception of those laws which, like the law of sacrifice, he regards as having no application or purpose in the present day. The sacrifices of the Mosaic era, he insists, were merely concessions to the customs of the times. Claiming that the mission of Judaism is the spiritualization of mankind, he sees such practices as covering the head at worship, dietary laws, the wearing of phylacteries as anachronisms that isolate the Jew from the rest of mankind and make such spiritualizing impossible, and hence should be abolished. In other words, the Orthodox Jew accepts the entire body of oral and written law as sanctified by tradition; the Reform Jew has simplified the ritual and adapted it to modern needs.

Unlike his Orthodox brothers he does not believe in the Messianic restoration of the Jewish state and return to Jerusalem; he is abandoning belief in a personal Messiah, but he still holds to his faith in the coming of a Messianic age. He does, however, support the return to Israel under the Zionist movement, not so much on spiritual or Talmudic grounds as on the ground that Israel offers a place of refuge for persecuted Jews of the world. He advocates the perservation in the new state of Israel of such Jewish values, customs, and traditions as have inspirational value.

Conservative Judaism

Conservative Judaism holds middle ground between Orthodox and Reform Judaism. It seems to lean closer to Orthodox, but in some areas it resembles Reform thinking and procedure. Established "for the preservation in America of historical Judaism," it takes from Orthodoxy its belief in the Torah and the observance of the dietary laws of traditional Judaism, the use of the Hebrew language, and the historic custom of the men worshiping with their head covered and wearing the *tallis* (prayer shaw) on appropriate occasions in the synagogue and temple (sometimes called Jewish Center).

From Reform comes the tendency to reconcile old beliefs and practices with the cultures in which it finds itself at work: the use of English as well as Hebrew in the prayer service that is read from the *siddur* (Hebrew for the prayer book or service), men and women sitting together in family pews, the optional use of instrumental music and mixed choirs and modern methods of education in their development schools for children and youths. Generally, to the Conservative, Judaism is not static but the deepening, growing, widening faith of a people who take into their culture different influences from other cultures and yet retain their own racial and religious aspects.

Reconstructionism

Within Conservative Judaism there exist Reconstructionist schools of thought that seek to reconstruct Judaism as a natural religion in order to make it relevant to contemporary rational and scientific thought. Originating in 1934 under the leadership of Mordecai M. Kaplan, a member of the faculty of the Jewish Theological Seminary, it is a movement indigenous to America, and it represents an attempt to assure physical and spiritual Jewish survival by indicating how a maximum Jewish life can be lived within the setting of a modern democratic state. Though its program is directed specifically to American Jews, its philosophy applies to Jewish life everywhere.

Reconstructionism defines Judaism as an evolving religious civilization. It sees the need to bring about the spiritual unity of the Jewish people; to reorganize the American Jewish community; to aid in the development of Israel; to revitalize Jewish religion; to encourage the Jewish cultural creativity in education, literature, and the arts; to intensify participation by Jews in all activities that enhance the ideals of democracy. To the ultimate achievement of these objectives Reconstructionists are dedicated. Rabbi Alan W. Miller sums it up in these words:

The Reconstructionist position is a frankly religious-humanist one. It believes that man cooperating with God can move toward a more perfect society. It is a call to action in terms of ethical behavior, rather than to quiescent metaphysical speculation. If it does not appeal to all modern Jews, it may well be that all modern Jews are not thoroughly modern—that is, they have not yet applied to the sphere of religion what they know and practice in all other areas of their lives. To have raised the challenge "Think modern and act modern also" in the sphere of Judaism and Jewish religion, is the lasting contribution which Reconstructionism has made to Jewish life in the twentieth century.

The Federation of Reconstructionist Congregations and Fellowships has a combined membership of 2,300 families and about 1,000 members.

Black Jews

There are a number of small black "Jewish" groups in the United States that claim official recognition by white Jews, but not all of them are recognized. In Judaism, no color line exists, but as in every religion there are rules concerning acceptance or rejection. According to Halacha (the legal portion of the Talmud and of most post-Talmudic literature), only the child of a Jewish mother or one who converts to Judaism according to accepted Jewish principles is Jewish. Sects of any color who do not observe these rules cannot be considered Jewish.

KODESH CHURCH OF IMMANUEL

Sould Be Nazarenes

Formed in 1929 and incorporated in April, 1930, by the Rev. Frank Russell Killingsworth and 120 laymen, some of whom were former members of the African Methodist Episcopal Zion Church, this is an interracial body of approximately 580 members, most of whom are black. The 9 churches of the denomination are located in Pennsylvania, Virginia, and the District of Columbia; a missionary station has recently been established in Liberia, West Africa. Teachings are Wesleyan and Arminian, stressing entire sanctification, or the baptism of the Holy Spirit, and premillennialism. Divine healing is practiced but not to the exclusion of medicine.

As the church was founded for the purpose of "conserving and propagating Bible holiness," the use of alcoholic liquors and tobacco is forbidden; pride in dress and behavior, Sabbath desecration, secret societies, dissolute dancing, and attendance at inferior and obscene theaters are denounced. Divorce is recognized only on the biblical ground of adultery. Water baptism is by the optional modes of sprinkling, pouring, or immersion.

The churches are under the charge of ministers and oversight of supervising elders. Ministers are elected and ordained by annual assemblies, to which they report. Supervising elders are elected and consecrated by general assemblies that meet quadrennially to enact all the laws of the church. The work of the entire church, including the support of foreign missionaries, is maintained by free-will offerings and tithes.

LIBERAL CATHOLIC CHURCH

Tracing its beginnings to the Old Catholic Church movement in Great Britain, which began in Holland, and its orders to an apostolic succession running back to the Roman Catholic Church under the reign of Pope Urban VIII and even to the 12 apostles, the Liberal Catholic Church aims at a combination of traditional Catholic forms of worship with the utmost freedom of individual conscience and thought. It claims to be neither Roman Catholic nor Protestant but still catholic in the broadest sense of the word. The founding bishops were members of the Theosophical Society. International headquarters is located in London; the presiding bishop resides in Sydney, Australia, and the present regionary (president) in the United States lives in Ojai, California.

In the Province of the United States of America, they have 2,393 members in 29 churches, as of 1973.

The Nicene Creed is used in their services generally, but there is no requirement of submission to any creed, scripture, or tradition; they seek not a common profession of belief but a corporate worship in a common ritual. While they give no emphasis to the precepts of the Theosophical Society, they do stress theosophia (divine wisdom) strongly. Paramount in their thinking is a central inspiration from faith in the living Christ, based on the promises of Matt. 18:20 and 28:20. These promises are regarded as "validating all Christian worship," but special channels of Christ's power are found in the sacraments of the church, of which there are 7: baptism, confirmation, the Holy Eucharist, absolution, holy unction, holy matrimony, and holy orders.

The use of the crucifix over the altar is discouraged, but not forbidden, in favor of the Triumphant Christ on the Cross. Crucifixes are found at the church entrances, in symbolism of mortal man on his cross while on earth. Priests and bishops may or may not marry as they choose, and they exact no fee for the administration of the sacraments; many of them are employed in lay occupations. Divine healing is practiced through "the reviving power of the Holy Spirit, the grace of absolution, the sacred oil for the sick and the sacrament of holy unction" but not to the exclusion of physicians and medicines. Bishops elected by a general episcopal synod, and a board of trusteess meet annually.

LUTHERANS

Lutheran was a nickname fastened upon the followers of Martin Luther by their enemies in the days of the Protestant Reformation; today it stands for something far more comprehensive. "It is clear," said Abdel R. Wentz, "that 'Lutheran' is a very inadequate name to give to a movement that is not limited to a person or an era but is as ecumenical and abiding as Christianity itself." Luther's teachings of justification by faith and of the universal priesthood of believers might be called the cornerstone of Protestantism.

The story of Luther's rebellion against the Roman Catholic Church is well-known history. His position was, briefly, that the Roman Catholic Church and papacy had no divine right in things spiritual; that the Scriptures, and not the Roman Catholic priest or church, had final authority over conscience. "Whatever is not against Scripture is for Scripture," said Luther, "and Scripture is for it." Men were forgiven and absolved of their sins, he believed, not by good works or by imposition of church rite—and especially not through the purchase of indulgences offered for sale by the Roman Catholic Church—but by man's Holy Spirit–empowered action in turning from sin directly to God. Justification came through faith and not through ceremony, and faith was not subscription to the dictates of the church but "by the heart's utter trust in Christ." "The just shall live by faith" was the beginning and the end of his thought. He held the individual conscience to be responsible to God alone; he also held that the Bible was the clear, perfect, inspired, and authoritative Word of God and guide of man. God, conscience, and the Book—on these was Lutheranism founded.

In 1529 Luther wrote his Longer and Shorter catechisms. A year later a statement of faith known as the Augsburg Confession was authored by his scholarly associate Philip Melanchthon; 1537 brought the Smalcald Articles of Faith written by Luther, Melanchthon, and other German reformers. In 1577 the Formula of Concord was drawn up. These documents in explanation of Luther's ideology and theology form the doctrinal basis of Lutheranism.

The Reformation resulted not in a united Protestantism but in a Protestantism with two branches: Evangelical Lutheranism with Luther and Melanchthon as leaders; and the Reformed Church, or branch, led by John Calvin, Ulrich Zwingli, and John Knox. Evangelical Lutheranism spread from its birthplace in Germany to Poland, Russia, Lithuania, Czechoslovakia, Austria, Hungary, Yugoslavia, France, and Holland; it became in time the state church of Denmark, Norway, Sweden, Finland, Iceland, Estonia, and Latvia. It was mainly from Germany and Scandinavia that Lutheranism came to the United States.

A Lutheran Christmas service was held at Hudson's Bay in 1619; the first European Lutherans to come here and stay permanently arrived on Manhattan Island from Holland in 1623. They had a congregation worshiping in New Amsterdam in 1649, but they did not enjoy full freedom in their worship until the English took over control of "New York" in 1664. The first independent colony of Lutherans was established by Swedes along the Delaware at Fort Christiana in the colony of New Sweden in 1638.

The New York Lutherans were largely Germans. German exiles from Salzburg also settled in Georgia, where in 1736 they built the first orphanage in America. Lutherans from Württemberg settled in South Carolina. The great influx, however, came to Pennsylvania, where by the middle of the eighteenth century there were 30,000 Lutherans, four-fifths of them being German and one-fifth Swedes. From Philadelphia they swept over into New Jersey, Maryland, Virginia, and North Carolina.

Their first churches were small, often without pastors; and because only a minority of the immigrants joined the church, they were poor churches. The situation was relieved with the coming of Henry Melchoir Muhlenberg from the University of Halle to effect the first real organization of American Lutherans; in 1748 he organized pastors and congregations in Pennsylvania, New Jersey, New York, and Maryland into what came to be called the Ministerium of Pennsylvania; it was the first of many Lutheran synods in America. Other synods followed slowly; New York in 1786, North Carolina in 1803, Maryland in 1820, and Ohio in 1836. Each synod adjusted itself to its peculiar conditions of language, national background, previous ecclesiastical relationship with Lutheran authorities abroad, and geographical location. The need for even further organization, aggravated by the ever-increasing emigration of Lutherans from Europe, resulted in the formation of the General Synod in 1820; with that the last real bonds with European Lutheranism began to break, and American Lutheranism was increasingly on its own.

The General Synod was obliged to extend its efforts farther and farther west as German, Swedish, Norwegian, Danish, Icelandic, and Finnish Lutherans came pouring into the new country. The Missouri Synod was formed in 1847. From 1850 to 1860, 1,000,000 Germans arrived, and the majority of them were Lutherans; the German Iowa Synod was organized in 1854, and in the same year the Norwegian Lutheran Church was established. The Augustana Synod was created in 1860 to care for the Swedes in the new West. By 1870 the Lutherans had the fourth largest Protestant group in the country, with approximately 400,000 members.

The Civil War brought the first serious break in the Lutheran ranks with the organization of the United Synod of the South in 1863; 3 years later a number of other synods led by the Ministerium of Pennsylvania withdrew from the General Synod to form the General Council. To increase the complexity, Lutheran immigrants arrived in larger and larger numbers; from 1870 to 1910 approximately 1,750,000 came from Sweden, Norway, and Denmark; and in those years the Lutheran Church membership leaped from less than 500,000 to nearly 2,250,000. New Lutheran churches, colleges, seminaries, and publications were established from coast to coast.

Since 1910 there has been an almost constant effort toward the unification of Lutheran churches and agencies. Three of the large Norwegian bodies united in 1917 in the Norwegian Lutheran Church of America; some of the Midwest German synods merged in the Joint Synod of Wisconsin in 1918; the synods of Iowa, Ohio, and Buffalo merged in the American Lutheran Church in 1930. The General Synod, the General Council, and the United Synod of the South merged into the United Lutheran Church in 1918, and no less than 8 Lutheran churches were included in mergers in 1960-62. In addition to these, the Lutheran Council in the U.S.A. (consisting of the American Lutheran Church, the Lutheran Church in America, the Lutheran Church—Missouri Synod, and the Synod of Evangelical Lutheran Churches) operates through 5 divisions (Educational Services, Mission and Welfare Services, Public Relations, Service to Military Personnel, and Theological Studies). Perhaps the most cooperative effort in the history of American Lutheranism is found in Lutheran World Action, through which over $300,000,000 in food and cash (inclusive of U.S. government–donated commodities) have been distributed across the world.

In spite of their organizational division there is real unity among American Lutherans; it is a unity based more upon faith than upon organization. All Lutheran churches represent a single type of Protestant Christianity. Their faith is built upon Luther's principle of justification by faith alone in Jesus Christ; it centers in the gospel for fallen men. The Bible is the inspired Word of God and the infallible rule and standard of faith and practice. Lutherans confess their faith through the 3 general creeds of Christendom, the Apostles', the Nicene, and the Athanasian, which they believe to be in accordance with the Scriptures. They also believe that the Unaltered Augsburg Confession is a correct exposition of the faith and doctrine of Evangelical Lutheranism. The Apology of the Augsburg Confession, the 2 catechisms of Luther, the Smalcald Articles, and the Formula of Concord are held to be faithful interpretations of Evangelical Lutheranism and of the Bible.

The 2 sacraments, baptism and the Lord's Supper, are not merely signs or memorials to the Lutheran but channels through which God bestows his forgiving and empowering grace upon men. The body and blood of Christ are believed to be present "in, with, and under" the bread and wine of the Lord's Supper and are received sacramentally and supernaturally. Consubstantiation, transubstantiation, and impanation are rejected. Infants are baptized, and baptized persons are believed to receive the gift of regeneration from the Holy Ghost.

The congregation is usually administered between its annual meetings by a church council consisting of the pastor and a number of elected lay officers, some of whom are called elders, some deacons, and some trustees. There is a growing tendency to call all lay officials deacons. Pastors are elected and called by the voting members of the congregation, but a congregation itself may never depose a pastor from the ministry. As a rule, ministers are ordained at the annual meetings of the synods; they are practically all trained in college and seminary.

Congregations are united in synods; these are composed of the pastors and lay representatives elected by the congregations and have only such authority as is granted by the synod constitution. In some other instances there are territorial districts or conferences instead of a synod, operating in the same manner and under the same restrictions; some of these may legislate, while others are for advisory or consultative purposes only.

Synods (conferences or districts) are united in a general body that may be national or even international and is called variously "church," "synod," or "conference." Some of these general bodies are legislative in nature, some consultative; they supervise the work in worship, education, publications, charity, and missions. Congregations have business meetings at least annually; synods, districts, and conferences hold yearly conventions; the general bodies meet annually or biennially.

Worship is liturgical, centering on the altar. "No sect in Western Christendom outside the Church of Rome," said the late Lutheran Archbishop Nathan Söderblom of Sweden, "has accentuated in its doctrine the Real Presence and the mysterious communion of the sacrament as has our Evangelic Lutheran sect, although our faith repudiates any quasi-rational magical explanation of the virtue of the sacrament."

Non-Lutherans are often critical of the divisions among American Lutherans, but actually they are not as divided as they seem. At one time there were 150 Lutheran bodies in this country; consolidation, unification, and federation have now reduced the number to 12. Six of the bodies in the United States account for about 95 percent of all Lutherans of North America. With the old barriers of speech and nationality disappearing, the tendency toward union becomes constantly stronger. Even on the international front, united efforts are noticeable; groups of lay and ministerial delegates from major Lutheran churches in 22 countries formed a Lutheran World Federation in 1947, for the purposes of relief and rehabilitation among Lutherans on a global scale.

Historically the Lutherans have shown a tendency to remain apart from the rest of Protestantism. In the United States they are identified with churches founded by immigrant groups deeply conscious of their national and linguistic origins, conservative, confessional, nonrevivalistic, and suspicious of anything that might tend to modify their Old World faith and traditions. These traits seem to be vanishing, however, as the older membership passes and an English-speaking generation takes over. The mother tongues of Lutheranism are still used occasionally, but English is predominant. The large Lutheran church in America is a constituent member of the National Council of the Churches of Christ in the U.S.A. Four bodies—the United Lutheran Church, the American Lutheran Church, the Augustana Evangelical Lutheran Church, and the American Evangelical Lutheran Church—participated in the organization of the World Council of Churches. A fifth body, the Evangelical Lutheran Church, affiliated with the World Council in 1957. Lutheran groups participating in interdenominational organizations have always insisted upon the operation of 2 principles within those organizations: the evangelical principle that the churches in the association should be those confessing the deity and saviorhood of Jesus Christ, and the representative principle that the governing and operating units of the organizations should be made up of officially chosen representatives of the churches.

American Lutheran Church

At a constituting convention held April 22-24, 1960, in Minneapolis, 3 major Lutheran churches were formally merged into the body now known as the American Lutheran Church. They were the American Lutheran Church, which had a German background and which began with the formation of the Ohio Synod in 1818; the Evangelical Lutheran Church, of Norwegian heritage, which at the time of the merger was the third largest Lutheran church in America; and the United Evangelical Lutheran Church, founded in 1896 by Danish emigrants. A fourth body, the Lutheran Free Church of Norwegian background, joined these 3 on February 1, 1963, giving the new American Lutheran Church an inclusive membership of 2,499,373 in 5,239 churches. The Evangelical Church of Canada was founded by this group in 1967. Present membership of all stands at 2,390,076 in 4,836 congregations.

This was a merger across ethnic lines, and the problems involved were complex in polity and doctrine, but they were successfully resolved. In government, the highest constitutional authority is vested in a general convention that meets every 2 years and has approximately 1,000 delegates (500 lay, 500 clergy) elected from the 18 districts into which the church is geographically divided. There are 3 national officers—a general president, vice-president, and general secretary. A church council composed of the general officers and a lay and clergy representative from each district together with the district presidents, 2 representatives from the Board of Trustees and 2 youths elected by the Lutheran League serving in advisory capacity, meets as the interim body between general conventions and makes recommendations to the general convention on all matters directed to it by the districts and the boards and standing committees of the church. Five divisions are maintained as churchwide agencies responsible for mission in behalf of or directly in service to member congregations. The Division of Life and Mission in the Congregation is to develop resources for and provide services to the congregations. The Division of Service and Mission in America is to implement the mission of the church within the United States. The Division for World Mission and Inter-Church Cooperation is responsible for the missions of the church abroad. These 3 divisions are the responsibility of 21-person boards with 18 elected by the districts and 3 members elected by the church council. The other 2 divisions are the Division for Theological Education and Ministry and the Division for College and University Services, each directed by a board of 9 members elected by the general convention.

There are 3 service boards established to provide specific services. The Board of Trustees has responsibility for the general management of business affairs, financial controls, and property transactions. The Board of Pensions provides for retirement income and major medical/dental coverage for the clergy and eligible laity. The Board of Publications is a nonbudgetary production and distribution unit. Each of its service boards is composed of 9 members elected by the general convention.

There are 3 administrative offices maintained as agencies responsible to the general president. The Office of Communications and Mission Support is to interpret the mission of the church and to provide support for that mission. The Office of Research and Analysis is organized to keep the church informed regarding the effects of changes in society and to coordinate research efforts. The Office of Support to Ministry is to provide support to the various ministries of the church and to provide staff services to the Council of Presidents. The offices have standing committees to which they relate.

District and national committees on Appeals and Adjudication exercise judicial authority for the church.

The Confession of Faith of this church accepts the Bible as divinely inspired, revealed, and inerrant; the 3 ancient ecumenical creeds (Apostles', Nicene, and Athanasian); the Unaltered Augsburg Confession; Luther's Larger and Shorter catechisms; the Book of Concord of 1580; the Apology; the Smalcald Articles, and the Formula of Concord.

In the field of education there are 3 theological seminaries, 11 senior colleges, 1 junior college, and 1 academy. In the area of social services there are 18 group care homes for the emotionally disturbed, 7 homes for the mentally and physically handicapped, 126 homes for the aged, 2 alcohol treatment centers, 3 homes for unwed mothers, 13 hospitals, 34 multi-service agencies (case work, etc.), and 14 other group services. Foreign missionaries are supported in 15 countries overseas and home missionaries work in 47 states.

Lutheran Church in America

With well over 2,000,000 members, this is the largest Lutheran church in the United States; it represents a consolidation of 4 Lutheran bodies (the United Lutheran Church in America, the Augustana Evangelical Lutheran

Church, the American Evangelical Lutheran Church, and the Finnish Evangelical Lutheran Church) which came about on June 28, 1962.

The United Lutheran Church was the youngest of the 4 uniting bodies, having been formed in 1918 in the uniting of 45 synods previously found in the General Synod, the General Council, and the United Synod of the South. Some 13 of these synods later withdrew or formed along new lines in the following 44 years, but the United Church brought a total of almost 2,500,000 members in 4,600 congregations into the 1962 merger.

The Augustana Evangelical Lutheran Church began in the work of scattered Swedish families and congregations in Iowa and Illinois in the mid-1800s; their Augustana Synod was formed in 1860, with 5,000 communicants and 49 congregations, of which 36 were Swedish and 13 Norwegian. The name "Augustana" affirmed the group's loyalty to the doctrine of the Augsburg Confession (*Augustana*, in the Latin). Ten years later the Norwegians withdrew to form a church of their own; at the time of the 1962 merger the Augustana body had better than half a million communicants in 1,200 congregations.

The Finnish Evangelical Lutheran Church (better known as the Suomi Synod), was organized at Calumet, Michigan, in 1890; it was strictly a confessional church, using the 3 ecumenical creeds and the unaltered Augsburg Confession. Until quite recently the Finnish language was employed in the services of this church, which had 36,000 members and 153 congregations in 1962.

The American Evangelical Lutheran Church was the smallest of the uniting bodies numerically, with 25,000 members in 79 congregations. It was of Danish origin, founded under the direction of ministers sent from Denmark in 1872 and under the name *Kirkelig Missionsforening*. It was a church deeply concerned with the place and meaning of the Bible in Lutheran theology; yet it had a strong tradition of ecumenical interest, and was represented in the National Lutheran Council, the National Council of Churches, and the World Council of Churches.

To bring these 4 churches into 1 body seemed at first impossible, but it was accomplished. A new confession was worked out that preserved the historic creeds and confessions of Lutheranism and yet established a new, broad base of emphasis upon full acceptance of Christ and the Scripture. This statement of faith is found in Article Two of the Constitution of the Lutheran Church in America; it reads; in part:

This church holds that the Gospel is the revelation of God's sovereign will and saving grace in Jesus Christ, . . . acknowledges the Holy Scriptures as the norm for the faith and life of the church, . . . accepts the Apostles', the Nicene, and the Athanasian creeds as true declarations of the faith of the church, . . . accepts the Unaltered Augsburg Confession and Luther's Small Catechism as true witnesses to the Gospel, and acknowledges as one with it in faith and doctrine all churches that likewise accept the teachings of these symbols. . . . [It] accepts the other symbolical books of the evangelical Lutheran church, the Apology of the Augsburg Confession, the Smalcald Articles, Luther's Larger Catechism, and the Formula of Concord as further valid interpretations of the confession of the church. . . . [It] affirms that the Gospel transmitted by the Holy Scriptures . . . is the true treasure of the church, the substance of its proclamation, and the basis of its unity and continuity.

In administration, the chief officer is a president elected for 4 years by a biennial convention; he presides over the convention and over an executive council of 33 members (3 officers, 15 ministers, and 15 laymen) which supervises the work of the synods, and the following churchwide agencies: Division for Mission in North America, Division for Parish Services, Division for Professional Leadership, Division for World Mission and Ecumenism, Office for Administration and Finance, Office for Communication, and Office for Research and Planning.

A full-time president serves each of the 33 synods that coordinate and direct the work of local congregations; these synods hold annual meetings of which each minister, whether active or retired, is a member and in which each congregation is represented by one or more lay delegates; each synod is subdivided into regional districts, under the direction of a pastor-dean.

The LCA is active in missions in 24 foreign countries. Nearly 200 social institutions (hospitals, homes for the aged and children, nurseries, etc.) are supported by the church; there are 28 colleges and seminaries.

Apostolic Lutheran Church of America

Sometimes called the Church of Laestadius after Lars Levi Laestadius, a minister of the state church of Sweden, this church originated with Finnish emigrants in and around Calumet, Michigan, in the middle years of the nineteenth century. They worshiped at first in the Lutheran Church of Calumet under a Norwegian minister; however, differences between the 2 national groups led to the forming, in 1872, of a separate Finnish congregation led by Solomon Korteniemi and called the Solomon Korteniemi Lutheran Society. The first incorporated church in Michigan was incorporated in 1879 under the name of the Finnish Apostolic Lutheran Church of America; this body was actually a merger of independent Apostolic Lutheran congregations into the 1 national body. Spreading over Michigan, Minnesota, the Dakotas, Massachusetts, Oregon, Washington, and California, the new church was divided into 2 districts—Eastern and Western. Foreign missions work in Nigeria, Liberia, and Guatamala.

A scriptural Christian experience is required as a condition for voting membership in spiritual matters; supporting members may vote on temporal matters only. The church accepts the 3 ecumenical creeds and puts strong emphasis upon the confession of sins, absolution, and regeneration. Confession may be made to a Christian brother, but if someone has fallen into sins unknown to other people, private confession is not sufficient, and "he should confess them publicly before the congregation and receive absolution."

The 64 local congregations of this church are quite free to govern themselves; at the annual church convention where every congregation has 1 vote, 3 members are elected to a 9-member executive board for 3-year terms; the board elects a president, vice-president, secretary, and treasurer. Three members are also elected to the Eastern and Western mission boards and to the Elder's Home Board. As of 1961, there were 6,994 members.

Church of the Lutheran Brethren of America

This is an independent church body, with churches located in Minnesota, Wisconsin, North and South Dakota, Iowa, Illinois, and on both East and West coasts. Organized in Milwaukee in 1900, it differs from other Lutheran churches in accepting as members only those who profess a personal experience of salvation and in stressing nonliturgical worship and lay participation. They have 2 years of confirmation instruction, but no vow is used at the confirmation service; they instruct children and wait until there is an individual experience and conversion before receiving them as communicant members. Communion is received in the pew; there are no altars in church buildings. Free prayer and personal testimony are stressed.

The church as a body is the supreme administrative unit, with a president, 2 vice-presidents, secretary, and treasurer. Foreign missions are supervised by a board of 9 members, and home missions by a board of 9. With a total membership of some 9,010 in 97 congregations, the church conducts foreign missionary work in Africa, Japan, and Formosa. There are 58 adult missionaries abroad. On an annual budget of $475,250 (high among Lutherans in proportion to the membership), the church supports a 3-year high school, a 2-year Bible course, a 3-year seminary course—all operated by the synod at Fergus Falls, Minnesota. Sarepta Home for the Aged and the Broen Memorial Home are also controlled by the church. Synodical headquarters are located at Fergus Falls.

Church of the Lutheran Confession

This very conservative Lutheran church is made up of clergy and laymen who withdrew, in 1961, from several synods of the Synodical Conference of North America. Behind the withdrawal was a long debate over conservative and liberal theology; the Church of the Lutheran Confession holds firmly to the fundamentalist approach to the verbally inspired and infallible Bible; they hold without any reservation whatever to all the historic Confessions of the Lutheran Church and faith. They have 9,817 members in 74 churches.

Evangelical Lutheran Synod (Formerly the Norwegian Synod)

The synod was formed in 1918 by a minority group that declined to join the union of other Norwegian groups into the Norwegian Lutheran Church (the former Evangelical Lutheran Church) in 1917. The name was changed as above in 1958.

The jurisdiction of the synod is entirely advisory; all synod resolutions are accepted or rejected by the local congregations. The officers and boards of the synod, however, direct the work of common interest insofar as they do not interfere with congregational rights or prerogatives.

For some years the synod used the facilities of the colleges and seminaries of the Missouri and Wisconsin synods, within the framework of the Synodical Conference; in 1963 the Evangelical Lutheran Synod withdrew from the Synodical Conference because of doctrinal differences with the Missouri Synod. It has maintained Bethany Lutheran College at Mankato, Minnesota, since 1927, and Bethany Lutheran Theological Seminary since 1946. It works in fellowship with the Wisconsin and other smaller synods overseas; there are 12 home mission stations in the United States and 2 foreign missions in South America and Nicaragua, 1 preparatory school, and 19,634 members in 108 churches.

Free Lutheran Congregations, The Association of

Established in 1962, this is a conservative and quite independent church in the Lutheran family. Doctrinally it stresses the inerrancy and supreme authority of the Bible and the conviction that the congregation is actually the final and correct form of the kingdom of God on earth and admits no authority over itself except that of the Word and Spirit of God. They believe that the spiritual union, fellowship, and cooperation of these believers transcends all synodical, racial, and national lines and boundaries; a widespread evangelistic program calls for personal experience with and devotion to Christ and a "wholesome Lutheran pietism" in the religious community. They report 13,946 members in 127 churches.

The Lutheran Church—Missouri Synod

With 2.9 million members and 5,918 churches, this is the second largest Lutheran church in the United States. The "Missouri" in the name comes from the founding of the denomination in that state by Saxon emigrants; these were later joined by Hanoverians in Indiana and Franconians in Michigan. From the start all 3 of these groups were devoted to the maintenance of orthodox Lutheranism. They were Germans who had fought the trend toward rationalism in the old country and who came here for the sake of religious freedom and to establish a synod in which the sovereignty of the local congregation would be recognized.

This synod was organized in 1847 with 12 congregations and 22 ministers under the name German Evangelical Lutheran Synod of Missouri, Ohio, and Other States. Under the constitution adopted at the time, all symbolical books of the Lutheran Church were considered to be the "pure and uncorrupted explanation of the Divine Word," and doctrinal agreement was required for exchange of pulpits and altars with other churches.

The doctrinal standard of the Missouri Synod is strictly observed and enforced. That standard is found in the Bible "as it was interpreted by the Book of Concord," the 3 ecumenical creeds—the Apostles', Nicene, and Athanasian—and the 6 Lutheran confessions: the Augsburg Confession, the

Apology of the Augsburg Confession, the Smalcald Articles, the Formula of Concord, and the 2 catechisms of Martin Luther. All across the years the synod has been unswerving in its allegiance to this conservative Lutheranism.

There are the usual Lutheran districts and district conventions, and the general convention meets biennally.

A startling work is done in education; the Missouri Synod has 1,337 parochial schools, 49 high schools, and 5,889 day schools. The synod's world mission work is done in cooperation with sister churches in India, Ceylon, New Guinea, the Philippines, Taiwan, Korea, Ghana, Nigeria, and Hong Kong. The Middle East Lutheran Ministry, with headquarters in Lebanon, concerns itself chiefly with radio work. The synod serves colleges and universities in North America through its Department of Campus Ministry with 51 full-time pastors and 70 others on a part-time basis.

Also affiliated with the synod are 30 hospitals, 37 family and children's agencies, 14 of which also conduct residential homes; 37 separate residential and nursing-care facilities for the aged; 8 residential care facilities for retarded children and adults; 9 junior colleges; 4 senior colleges; Concordia Seminary in St. Louis, Concordia Seminary in Fort Wayne, and Valparaiso University at Valparaiso, Indiana.

The synod has been troubled in recent years with dessentions of 3 groups over questions of orthodoxy. The Lutheran Churches of the Reformation left the synod in the early 1960s; a Federation for Authentic Lutheranism separated in 1971; currently an Association of Evangelical Lutheran Churches (AELC) was created after a doctrinal dispute within the Missouri Synod and is discussing the possibility of organic union with various other Lutheran churches. This appears to be the largest of the 3 dissenting groups.

Protestant Conference (Lutheran)

A protest against alleged "high-handed" tactics of the church officials and against the inroads of legalism in the life of the Wisconsin Evangelical Lutheran Synod led to the suspension of 47 pastors and teachers in 1927 and to the formation of this conference. Their purpose, as it has developed in the years since their formation, is to "break down within our Lutheran Church, and wherever else it may flourish, the spirit of self-righteousness and self-sufficiency through a re-emphasis upon the Gospel of forgiveness of sins . . . coupled with the warning of the hardening of hearts and of judgment upon those who reject this message and its implications."

A general conference meets 3 times a year, and 1 publication, *Faith-Life,* is issued in Manitowac, Wisconsin. No membership figures are listed for 6 churches and several "home" congregations.

Wisconsin Evangelical Lutheran Synod

Organized in 1850 in Milwaukee under the name of the German Evangelical Lutheran Synod of Wisconsin, this church merged with 2 other synods in 1917—Minnesota and Michigan—and became the Evangelical Lutheran Joint Synod of Wisconsin and Other States. In 1959 the name was changed to the Wisconsin Evangelical Lutheran Synod. The synod stands for an orthodox, confessional Lutheranism committed to the inspired, infallible Holy Scriptures without reservation and is opposed to union or cooperation with other church bodies without full agreement in doctrine and practice.

The synod, which maintains its national headquarters in Milwaukee, is divided into 10 districts. It has a baptized membership of 402,573 in 1,105 congregations in 47 states. World mission fields are supported in Zambia, Malawi, Mexico, Puerto Rico, Colombia, Japan, Taiwan, Hong Kong, Indonesia, India, and among the Apache Indians of Arizona.

For the education of its pastors and Christian day-school teachers, the synod maintains 2 colleges, 4 academies, and a theological seminary. Congregations support 14 area Lutheran high schools with an enrollment of 3,864. There are 340 Christian day schools within the synod with an enrollment of 29,700. Associations of congregations operate 6 homes for the aged and 1 social service agency.

MENNONITES

The first Mennonite congregation of historical record was organized at Zurich, Switzerland, in 1525; it consisted of Swiss Brethren, or *Täufer,* who disagreed with Ulrich Zwingli in his readiness to consent to a union of church and state. They also denied the scriptural validity of infant baptism and hence were labeled Anabaptists, or Re-Baptizers. Anabaptist congregations were organized in Holland by Obbe Philips as early as 1534; Obbe baptized Menno Simons (*ca.* 1496–1561) in 1536.

Menno was a converted Roman Catholic priest; he organized more Anabaptist congregations in Holland, and his contemporaries gave his name to the movement. Many of his Flemish adherents crossed the channel on the invitation of Henry VIII. In England, as well as in Germany, Holland, and Switzerland, they met opposition largely because of their determined distrust of any union of church and state. An impressive martyr roll was created; it might have been much larger had it not been for the sudden haven offered in the American colony of William Penn. Thirteen families settled in Germantown, near Philadelphia, in 1683. Eventually they established a Mennonite congregation there, although many of them had left the Mennonite fold and united with the Quakers before they left Crefeld, Germany. Mennonite emigrants from Germany and Switzerland spread over Pennsylvania, Ohio, Virginia, Indiana, Illinois, farther west, and into Canada; these were later joined by others coming from Russia, Prussia, and Poland. Thanks to their historic insistence upon nonresistance their colonial settlements were comparatively peaceful and prosperous.

The faith of these Mennonites was based upon a confession of faith signed at Dordrecht, Holland, in 1632. In 18 articles the following doctrines were laid down: faith in God as creator; man's fall and restoration at the coming of Christ; Christ as the Son of God, redeeming men on the cross; obedience to Christ's law in the gospel; the necessity of repentance and conversion for salvation; baptism as a public testimony of faith; the Lord's Supper as an expression of common union and fellowship; matrimony as permissible only among those "spiritually kindred"; obedience to and respect for civil government except in the use of armed force; exclusion from the church of those who sin willfully and their social ostracism for the protection of the faith of others in the church; and future reward and punishments for the faithful and the wicked.

The Lord's Supper is served twice a year in almost all Mennonite congregations, and in most of them baptism is by pouring. Most of them observe the foot washing ordinance in connection with the Supper, after which they salute one another with the "kiss of peace." The sexes are separated in the last 2 ceremonies. All Mennonites baptize only on confession of faith, refuse to take oaths before magistrates, oppose secret societies, and follow strictly the teachings of the New Testament. They have a strong intrachurch program of mutual aid and a worldwide relief and eleemosynary service through an all-Mennonite relief organization called the Mennonite Central Committee.

The local congregation is more or less autonomous and authoritative, although in some instances appeals are taken to district or state conferences. The officers of the church are bishops (often called elders), ministers, and deacons (almoners). Many ministers are self-supporting, working in secular employments when not occupied with the work of the church. There are other appointed officers for Sunday school, young people's work, and so forth.

The Amish movement within the ranks of the Mennonites takes its name from Jacob Amman, a Swiss (Bernese) Mennonite bishop of the late seventeenth century who insisted upon strict conformation to the confession of faith, especially in the matter of "shunning" excommunicated members. This literalism brought about a separation in Switzerland in 1693; about 200 years later the divided bodies, with the exception of 3 Amish groups, were reunited.

Amish immigrants to the United States concentrated early in Pennsylvania and moved from there into Ohio, Indiana, Illinois, Nebraska, and other western states; some went into Canada. They have today a common literature. Many of the Amish, distinguished by their severely plain clothing, are found in the Conservative Amish Mennonite Church and the larger Old Order Amish Mennonite Church. They are still the "literalists" of the movement, clinging tenaciously to the "Pennsylvania Dutch" language and to the seventeenth-century culture of their Swiss-German forebears. They oppose automobiles, telephones, and higher education but are recognized as very efficient farmers.

Beachy Amish Mennonite Churches

These churches are made up mostly of Amish Mennonites who separated from the more conservative Old Order Amish over a period of years, beginning in Somerset County, Pennsylvania, in 1927. They were led by Bishop Moses M. Beachy, who died in 1946. There are today 89 congregations and 5,175 members.

They resemble to some degree the Old Order Amish in garb and general attitudes, but their discipline is milder and more relaxed. They worship in church buildings, have Sunday schools, are active in supporting missionary work, and sponsor a monthly publication, *Calvary Messenger*, and an annual 12-week Calvary Bible School.

Church of God in Christ (Mennonite)

This church grew out of the preaching and labors of John Holdeman, a member of the Mennonite Church in Ohio, who became convinced that his church was apostate and in error in many of its teachings and practices. He preached ardently on the necessity of the new birth, Holy Ghost baptism, more adequate training of children in the fundamentals, the discipline of unfaithful members, avoidance of apostates, and the condemnation of worldly minded churches. He separated himself, finally, from the Mennonite Church and in 1859 began holding meetings with a small group of followers who were formally organized into the Church of God in Christ, Mennonite.

The church believes that the same confession of faith must be believed and practiced by all churches, "from the time of the apostles to the end of the world," and that the Bible as the inspired, infallible Word of God must govern all doctrine and teaching. It accepts the Eighteen Articles of Faith drawn up at Dordrecht, Holland, in 1632. It practices the mode form of baptism, and teaches nonresistance and nonconformity to the world in dress, bodily adornment, worldly sports, and amusements. Missions are operated in the United States, Canada, Mexico, Haiti, India, and Nigeria; there are 6,204 members in 38 congregations spread from the United States to Africa.

Conservative Mennonite Conference

Known as the Conservative Amish Mennonite Church until 1954, when the present name was adopted, this conference subscribes to the Dordrecht Confession of Faith and the 1963 Mennonite Confession of Faith. Its first general conference was held at Pigeon, Michigan, in 1910. It separated gradually from the Old Order Amish, installing such innovations as meetinghouses, Sunday schools, evening and "continued" meetings, and the use of English rather than German in worship. Holding strictly to the Mennonite principles of nonresistance and nonconformity, it promotes missions and various types of social work in the United States, Central America, and Europe. There are 6,900 members in 103 mission stations and congregations.

Evangelical Mennonite Brethren Conference

Formerly called the Conference of Defenseless Mennonites of North America, this group now has 3,874 members in 32 churches. It was established by Russian Mennonite emigrants in 1873-74 and concentrates on a strong missionary program under which some 110 missionaries are at work overseas.

Evangelical Mennonite Church

Formerly the Defenseless Mennonite Church, this body was founded about 1865 under the leadership of Henry Egly to emphasize teachings on regeneration, separation, nonconformity to the world, and nonresistance. Their program today is largely one of missions and evangelism. There is a children's home in Flanagan, Illinois; 3,600 members are in 21 churches.

General Conference Mennonite Church

A group of local Mennonite congregations in Iowa, eager to improve upon and enlarge foreign missionary efforts, offer better training for prospective leaders, and to establish a church periodical, organized at Wayland, Iowa, in 1860 to form the General Conference Mennonite Church. The desire to unite all Mennonite churches and conferences was strong among them and still is. They accept established Mennonite doctrine but place strong emphasis upon the autonomy of the local congregation, and in their insistence upon freedom from the traditional Mennonite regulations on dress and attire for men and women they are marked as "liberal in conduct."

Six district conferences meet annually, and a general conference meets triennially for fellowship and the transaction of official business. Elected commissions—overseas mission, home ministries, education, communication, and administration—direct the work of the general conference. The conference maintains 2 liberal arts colleges, 1 Bible college, 1 junior college, 1 theological seminary, several homes for children and the aged, hospitals, and nurses' training schools. There are 36,397 members in 187 churches in the United States, 20,553 members in 103 churches in Canada, and additional churches in Latin America. Mission work is carried on in 10 overseas countries, where the membership totals about 40,000.

Hutterian Brethren

These are disciples of Jacob Hutter, a sixteenth-century Tyrolean Anabaptist who advocated communal ownership of property. He was burned as a heretic in Austria in 1536. Many of the Hutterites came from Russia to Canada and the United States about 1874; they have moved back and forth across the border ever since. Most of them today are of German ancestry and use the German tongue in their homes and churches. Aside from the common-property idea, they are quite similar to the Old Order Amish; they have a Bible-centered faith that they seek to express in brotherly love; they aim at the recovery of the New Testament spirit and fellowship; they feel that this requires nonconformity to the world, and accordingly they practice nonresistance; refuse to participate in local politics, dress differently, make no contributions to community projects, and have their own schools, in which the Bible is paramount. Their exclusiveness has made them unwelcome in certain sections of the country, and their status is uncertain at the moment. There are 20,000 of them in 200 colonies in South Dakota, Minnesota, Montana, Washington, and Canada.

Mennonite Brethren Church of North America

Dutch and German in background, this church was organized in 1860 on withdrawal from the Mennonite Church in the Ukraine of a small group seeking closer attention to prayer and Bible study. Pietistic in orientation, the group adopted a Baptistic polity. Small bodies reached Kansas in 1876 and spread to the Pacific coast and into Canada.

A general conference meets triennially as the chief administrative body, gathering delegates from 2 areas (Canada and the United States). Each area has a number of districts. The area conferences supervise work in home missions, education, and publications. Foreign missions (a department of the general conference) are found in Africa, Asia, Europe, South America, and Mexico.

The Krimmer Mennonite Brethren merged with this church in 1960, bringing the total membership to 38,000 in 260 churches.

Mennonite Church

This is the largest single group of Mennonites in the United States, with 96,092 members in 1,059 churches; it is the church founded by German emigrants in Germantown, Pennsylvania, in 1683. The Dordrecht Confession was adopted at a conference of the Pennsylvania Mennonite ministers in 1725, and this remained the official statement of faith until a 1921 Mennonite general conference adopted a restatement on the Fundamentals of the Christian Faith consisting of 18 articles. In 1963 the general conference of the Mennonite Church adopted a new, revised confession of faith that seeks, without attempting to make Mennonites into a creedal church, to set forth the major doctrines of Scripture as understood in the Anabaptist-Mennonite tradition. The attempt was made to write with simplicity and clarity, to be more biblical than philosophical or even theological. This 1963 Confession of Faith stresses faith in Christ, the saved status of children (without any ceremony), the importance of proclaiming God's Word and "making disciples," the baptism of believers, the ethic of absolute love and nonresistance to injustice and maltreatment, the church as a nonhierarchical brotherhood, and the practice of church discipline.

The general assembly meets every 2 years; ordained persons and others present who are not elected delegates from the district or state conference may debate but not vote; the elected delegates from the district conferences render decisions by a majority vote. The district conferences, in cooperation with their respective congregations, set the disciplinary standards for their constituency. Bishops, ministers, and deacons serve as delegates; most districts also have lay delegates.

Churchwide program boards are in charge of mission, congregational ministries, educational, publishing, and mutual aid work; all are under the coordination of the church's general board. Home missions stress evangelism; overseas missions are found in Asia, Africa, Europe, Central and South America. There are 3 colleges, 2 seminaries, numerous secondary and elementary schools, as well as church-sponsored hospitals, retirement homes, and child welfare services.

Old Order Amish Mennonite Church

Continuous with the Amish emigrants of 1720-40, this church adheres to the older forms of worship and attire, using hooks and eyes instead of buttons, worshiping in private homes, and having no conferences. Members do not believe in conferences, missions, or benevolent institutions and oppose centralized schools; some of them, however, do contribute to the missions and charities of the Mennonite Church. There are 514 Old Amish Church districts listed, and each district averages 110 to 150 members, with approximately half that number baptized.

Old Order (Wisler) Mennonite Church

This church was named for Jacob Wisler, the first Mennonite bishop in Indiana, who led a separation from the Mennonite Church in 1872. Those who separated did so in protest of the use of English in the services and the introduction of Sunday schools. Joined in 1886, 1893, and 1901 by groups with similar ideas from Canada, Pennsylvania, and Virginia, they still maintain their church on the basis of these protests.

Each section of the church has its own district conference, and there are home conferences twice each year in each community. There are no benevolent or missionary enterprises, but some contribute to the work of the Mennonite Church in those fields. There are 8,400 members in 60 churches, 19 bishops, and 76 ministers.

Reformed Mennonite Church

Organized under the leadership of John Herr in Lancaster County, Pennsylvania, in 1812, Reformed Mennonites hold closely to New Testament teachings and believe that there can be but one true church for all believers. They have 4 ordinances: baptism, the Lord's Supper, foot washing, and the kiss of peace; these are "for edification and not a means of salvation." Baptism by pouring or sprinkling is considered an outward testimony of the baptism of the Spirit within the heart, which must precede the reception of water baptism. The Communion service signifies unity with God and with one another and is observed only by members of the church. They practice foot washing as taught in John 13, carry out strictly the instructions in Matt. 18 regarding laboring in love with an erring brother, greet one another regularly with the kiss of peace, insist upon modest and plain uniform clothing, and require their women to wear head coverings.

They are nonresistant, pacificistic, do not vote or hold any governmental office, and refuse to worship with those with whom they are not united in faith and practice. They have 12 churches and a membership of about 500. Their bishops, ministers, and deacons are chosen from the local congregations and are not paid. They have no Sunday schools, believing it obligatory upon the parents to teach their own children.

Unaffiliated Mennonites

A number of small Mennonite groups hold an unaffiliated status with all other Mennonite bodies. These unaffiliated Amish Mennonite and Mennonite churches claim 4,425 members enrolled in 87 churches. There is such a wide variety of emphasis on doctrines and practice that no general statement can be made in respect to their faith and polity.

METHODISTS

England's famed old Oxford University has been called the "cradle of lost causes," but at least one cause was born there that was not lost. This is Methodism. Known and ridiculed at Oxford in 1729, it claims today some 14,000,000 adherents in North America and more than 18,000,000 around the world.

The Oxford Methodists (also dubbed "Bible Bigots," "Bible Moths," and the "Holy Club") were a tiny group of students who gave stated time to prayer and Bible reading; prominent among them were John and Charles Wesley and George Whitefield. They were methodically religious, talking of the necessity of being justifed before they could be sanctified and of the need of holiness in human living, reading and discussing William Law's *A Serious Call to a Devout and Holy Life* and *A Treatise on Christian Perfection*. The 2 Wesleys were sons of a clergyman of the Church of England; with the other members of the Holy Club they stood their ground against jeering students and went out to preach and pray with the poor and desperate commoners of England—prisoners in jail, paupers in hovels, bitter and nearly hopeless "underdogs of a British society that was perilously close to moral and spiritual collapse." Methodism started on a campus and reached for the masses.

The Wesleys came to Georgia in 1736. Charles came as secretary to General Oglethorpe, and John was sent by the Society for the Propagation of the Gospel as a missionary to the Indians. It was an unsuccessful and unhappy 2 years for John Wesley with but one bright spot; on shipboard en route to the colonies he met a group of Moravians and became deeply impressed by their piety and humble Christian living. Later when he returned to London, he went one night to meet with a religious society in Aldersgate Street, heard the preacher read Luther's preface to the Epistle to the Romans and felt his

173

heart "strangely warmed" as the meaning of the reformer's doctrine of "justification by faith" sank into his soul. It was the evangelistic spark that energized his life and started the flame of the Wesleyan revival in England. From the pious Moravians via Wesley came the warmhearted emphases upon conversion and holiness which are still the central themes of Methodism.

Whitefield and the Wesleys were too much afire to be boxed in by the staid Church of England. When its doors were closed to them, they took to the open air, John preaching and Charles writing the hymns of the revival for streets, barns, and private homes and in the mining pits of Cornwall, preaching repentance, regeneration, turning from sin and the wrath to come, justification, holiness, and sanctification. The upper classes laughed, and the lower classes listened to the first words of hope they had heard in many a year. Converts came thick and fast; it became necessary to organize them into societies. The first Methodist society was attached to a Moravian congregation in Fetter Lane, London, in 1739, and later moved to its own quarters in an old, abandoned government building known as the Foundry, where the first self-sustaining Methodist society in London was organized in 1740.

Between 1739 and 1744 the organizational elements of Methodism were instituted; we read of a "circuit system" and of an "itinerant ministry," of class meetings and class leaders, of lay preachers and annual conferences. There was a phenomenal growth in membership; more than 26,000 Methodists were worshiping in England, Ireland, Scotland, and Wales in 1767. Their impact upon British society was startling; the crudities and barbarisms of the times were alleviated, and a "French revolution" averted. It was primarily a lay movement.

Wesley did his best to keep the movement within the Church of England; an evangelical party grew within the church, but the greater numbers recruited from among the unchurched made a separate organization imperative. In 1739 Wesley drew up a set of general rules that are still held by modern Methodists and an ideal delineation of Bible rules and conduct. A Deed of Declaration in 1784 gave legal status to the yearly Methodist conference. But John Wesley was dead in 1791, before Methodism in England had the name of a recognized church, the Wesleyan Methodist Connection.

Meanwhile the movement had invaded Ireland and the American colonies. Wesley had begun to send out leaders; the first of them in this country were Joseph Pilmoor and Richard Boardman. Philip Embury, an Irish lay leader, encouraged by his cousin Barbara Heck, preached in New York and inspired the organization of the first Methodist society overseas about 1766. By 1769 the New York Methodists had built Wesley Chapel, now known as John Street Methodist Church. To the south Captain Thomas Webb, a veteran of Braddock's ill-fated army, established societies in Philadephia, and Robert Strawbridge started a revival in Maryland and built a log-cabin church at Sam's Creek. Devereux Jarratt, a transplanted evangelical Anglican minister, led a revival in Virginia that won thousands.

The true center of Methodism in those days did indeed lie in the South; out of 3,148 Methodists in the colonies in 1775 about 2,000 lived south of Mason and Dixon's Line. Wesley, aware of the rapid spread of the movement in America, sent emissaries to take charge, among them Francis Asbury and Thomas Rankin, the latter as the first full-fledged "superintendent of the entire work of Methodism in America." Rankin presided over the first conference in America, called at Philadelphia in 1773 and attended by 10 ministers.

There were about 1,160 Methodists represented in the conference of 1773; when the Liberty Bell rang in 1776, there were less than 7,000 in all the colonies, and they seemed doomed to disappear as quickly as they had been gathered. The majority of their preachers had come from England and were incurably British; they were so roughly handled by the patriots that by 1779 nearly every one of them had fled either to Canada or home to England. Wesley's pro-British attitude also roused resentment, and Francis Asbury working almost singlehanded had a difficult time keeping some of the churches alive. But a miracle happened; of all the religious groups in the colonies, the Methodists alone actually seemed to prosper during the Revolution. When the surrender came at Yorktown, their membership had grown to 14,000, and there were nearly 80 preachers. They were, after Yorktown, an American church, free of both England and the Church of England. Wesley accepted the inevitable; he ordained ministers for the colonies and appointed Asbury and Thomas Coke as superintendents.

Coke brought with him from England certain instructions from Wesley, a service book and hymnal, and authority to proceed with the organization. A Christmas Conference held at Baltimore in December of 1784 organized the Methodist Episcopal Church, elected Coke and Asbury as superintendents (later called bishops), and adopted the Sunday Service (an abridgment of the Book of Common Prayer) and Articles of Religion as written by John Wesley, adding another article that as good patriots Methodists should vow allegiance to the United States government. The first general conference of the new church was held in 1792, made up solely of ministers. It was not until 1872 that laymen were admitted to what had become by that time a quadrennial general conference. Membership soared: from 37 circuits and 14,000 members at the close of the Revolution there came a membership of 1,324,000 by the middle of the following century.

Methodism not only swept through the cities; it developed an amazing strength in small towns and rural areas. Everywhere there were circuit riders—ministers on horseback riding the expanding frontier and preaching in mountain cabins, prairie churches, schoolhouses, and camp meetings of free grace and individual responsibility and the need of conversion and regeneration. Their itinerant ministry was perfectly adapted to the democratic society of the frontier. The Methodist Book Concern was established in 1789, putting into the saddlebags of the circuit riders a religious literature that followed the march of American empire south and west. The camp meeting, born among the Presbyterians though not always carried on by them, was adopted by the Methodists and exploited to the limit. Its revivalistic flavor and method were made to order for the followers of Wesley and Whitefield. There are still camp meetings in Methodism.

All was not peaceful, however, among all the Methodists; divisions came. Objecting, like good democrats, to what they considered abuses of the episcopal system, several bodies broke away: the Republican Methodists, later the Christian Church, withdrew in Virginia; Methodist Protestants seceded in 1830. Between 1813 and 1817 large black groups formed independent churches: the African Methodist Episcopal Church; the Union Church of Africans, now the Union American Methodist Episcopal Church; and the African Methodist Episcopal Zion Church. In 1844 came the most devastating split of all, the bisecting of the Methodist Episcopal Church into 2 churches, the Methodist Episcopal Church, the northern body; and the Methodist Episcopal Church, South.

The cause of this major split was, of course, slavery. Bishop Andrew, a Georgian, owned slaves through inheritance; and his wife was also a slaveholder. It was not possible for him or his wife to free their slaves under the laws of Georgia. The general conference of 1844, held in New York City, requested him to desist from the exercise of his office so long as he remained a slaveholder. Incensed, the southern delegates rebelled, a provisional plan of separation was formulated, and the southerners went home to organize their own church in 1845. Basic to the separation was the constitutional question of the power of the general conference, which, the southerners maintained, assumed supreme power in virtually deposing a bishop against whom no charges had been brought, who had violated no law of the church, and who had been given no trial. It was a split that concerned neither doctrine nor polity; it was purely political and social, and it was a wound that waited until 1939 for healing. In that year the Methodist Episcopal Church, the Methodist Episcopal Church, South, and the Methodist Protestant Church were reunited at Kansas City, Missouri.

The uniting conference of 1939 adopted a new constitution in 3 sections: an abridgment of the Articles of Religion, drawn up by John Wesley and based on the 39 Articles of Religion of the Church of England; the General Rules, covering the conduct of church members and the duties of church officials; and the Articles of Organization and Government, outlining the organization and conduct of conferences and local churches. This constitution cannot be changed by any general conference unless and until every annual conference has acted on the changes proposed.

In matters of faith there has been very little occasion for confusion or difference among Methodists; heresy trials and doctrinal quarrels have been noticeably absent. Historically they have never built theological fences or walls to keep anyone out; they have stressed the great foundation beliefs of Protestantism and offered common theological ground. Some of the churches repeat the Apostles' Creed in their worship but not all of them, though the discipline of the church provides for its use in formal worship. Their theology is Arminian, as interpreted by Wesley in his sermons, his Notes on the New Testament, and his Articles of Religion.

They preach and teach doctrines of the Trinity, the natural sinfulness of mankind, man's fall and need of conversion and repentance, freedom of the will, justification by faith, sanctification and holiness, future rewards and punishments, the sufficiency of the Scriptures for salvation, perfection, and the enabling grace of God. Two sacraments, baptism and the Lord's Supper, are observed; baptism is administered to both infants and adults, usually by sprinkling. Membership—full, preparatory, or "affiliate" (the latter arranged for people away from their home church who wish to affiliate where they live)—is based upon confession of faith or by letter of transfer from other evangelical churches; admission of children to membership is usually limited to those 13 years of age or over, though in the South the age may be 2 or 3 years younger. There is wide freedom in the interpretation and practice of all doctrines; liberals and conservatives work in close harmony.

The local churches of Methodism are called charges; their ministers are appointed by the bishop at the annual conference, and each church elects its own administrative board, which initiates planning and sets goals and policies on the local level. It is composed of staff people, chairmen of various committees, persons representing various program interests, and members at large. Charge, annual, and general conferences prevail in most Methodist bodies; while Methodist government is popularly called episcopal, it is largely governmental by this series of conferences. The charge conference meets in the local charge, or on the circuit with the district superintendent presiding. It fixes the salary of the pastor, elects the church officers, and sends delegates to the annual conference. The charge conference may delegate to the administrative board of the local church responsibility for many of these duties. Some areas have district conferences between the charge and the annual conference, but it is not a universal arrangement in the church. Annual conferences cover defined geographical areas, ordain and admit candidates to the ministry, vote on constitutional questions, supervise pensions and relief, through action of the bishop exchange pastors with other annual conferences, and every fourth year elect lay and ministerial delegates to the general conference. The general conference is the lawmaking body of the church, meeting quadrennially; the bishops preside, and the work of the conference is done largely in committees, whose reports when adopted by the general conference become Methodist law.

Worship and liturgy are based upon the English prayer book with widespread modifications. The language of the prayer book is much in evidence in the sacraments of the Methodist churches. In many forms of worship, however, each congregation is free to use or change the accepted pattern as it sees fit.

There are 23 separate Methodist bodies in the United States of which The United Methodist Church is numerically the strongest.

The United Methodist Church

Two mergers of major importance produced The United Methodist Church (the largest Methodist church in this country, with 9,861,028 members in 38,795 local churches). The first was actually a rejoining of 3

177

existing Methodist groups; at a uniting conference in Kansas City in 1939, the Methodist Episcopal Church, the Methodist Episcopal Church, South, and the Methodist Protestant Church were reunited under a new name, The Methodist Church. In 1968 The Methodist Church merged with the Evangelical United Brethren Church to form The United Methodist Church.

The history of the Methodist Episcopal Church and the Methodist Episcopal Church, South, have already been outlined above. The Methodist Episcopal Church, South, was organized at Louisville, Kentucky, in 1845, and held its first general conference a year later in Petersburg, Virginia, under the presidency of Bishops James Andrew and Joshua Soule; it brought a membership of 2,500,000 to the reunited church. The Methodist Protestant Church was organized at a conference in Baltimore in 1830, in protest against the almost total rule of the clergy in the Methodist Episcopal Church and the exclusion of laymen from its councils. It had about 200,000 members in 1939.

The Evangelical United Brethren Church came out of a series of mergers in 2 groups: the United Brethren in Christ and the Evangelical Church. The Evangelical Church began with the labors of Jacob Albright (1759–1808) among the German people of Pennsylvania, in what at first was called the Evangelical Association; preaching first as a Lutheran and then as a Methodist exhorter, Albright was made a bishop at the first annual conference of the Association in 1807. He used the Methodist *Discipline* until 1809, preached Methodist doctrine, and was so effective that for some time his followers were known as "the Albrights." A split in the membership in 1891 resulted in a separate denomination known as the United Evangelical Church; the 2 groups were reunited in 1922 under the name of the Evangelical Church.

Another group, known as the Church of the United Brethren in Christ, had a parallel development that began with the preaching of William Otterbein and Martin Boehm among the Germans in Pennsylvania, Maryland, and Virginia; they were elected bishops at a conference in September, 1800, which created the Church of the United Brethren in Christ, and which was also strongly Methodistic in polity, doctrine, and practice. Both groups had a *Discipline* modeled on the Methodist *Discipline*, and had too much in common to remain separated. These 2 bodies—the Church of the United Brethren in Christ and the Evangelical Church—were merged into the Evangelical United Brethren Church at Johnstown, Pennsylvania, in 1946.

Both Methodist and E.U.B. churches, across the years, had been deeply conscious of their common historical and spiritual heritage. Their doctrines were similar; both were episcopal in government; both traced their origins back to John Wesley; both had nearly the same book of *Discipline*. Their preachers exchanged pulpits and congregations, often worked together and shared the same buildings. The only major difference between them was that of language—German among the Brethren, English among the Methodists. As new, native-born generations appeared, this barrier meant less and less. Conversations concerning the merging of the 2 churches began as early as

1803, and were consummated when the 2 came together as The United Methodist Church at Dallas, Texas, on April 23, 1968.

There was some dissent at Dallas; 51 congregations and 79 ministers of the Evangelical United Brethren withdrew from the Pacific Northwest Conference to establish the Evangelical Church of North America; 18 of 23 E. U. B. congregations in Montana left to establish the Evangelical Church of North America in Montana, and 13 other congregations in the Erie and Ohio Southeast Conferences petitioned to leave; these petitions were denied. The split occurred mainly over theological issues and the question of church ownership. But there were still roughly 750,000 Brethren who accepted the merger; their strength gave the new United Methodist Church a membership of nearly 11 million.

In this union no significant changes were made in either doctrine or polity. The Confession of Faith of the Evangelical United Brethren Church, adopted in 1962, was placed beside the Methodist Articles of Religion; Wesleyan standards dominate both statements, and both are used as the congregations of the church elect to use them. The Methodist system of bishops and conferences, already in use in both denominations, is maintained. There are now 73 annual conferences in the United States with a total of 39,395 organized churches and 34,885 ministers. Above the annual conferences are 5 jurisdictional conferences, established for geographical convenience in administrative matters, meeting quadrennially at times determined by the Council of Bishops, to elect new bishops and to name the members of the larger boards and commissions. In lands outside the continental United States, there are central conferences that correspond to the jurisdictional conferences; they meet quadrennially and when authorized to do so, may elect their own bishops. All bishops are elected for life (except in autonomous overseas conferences where the term is 4 years) with retirement set at 72; there are 45 of them in the United States and abroad in charge of the areas of the church, such as the New York Area, the Denver Area, etc. Together they constitute the Council of Bishops, which meets at least once a year and usually twice a year "for the general oversight and promotion of the temporal and spiritual affairs of the entire church."

The general conference consists of over 800 delegates, half laymen and half ministers, elected on a proportional basis by the annual conferences. A judicial council has been created to determine the constitutionality of any act of the general conference that may be appealed, and to hear and determine any appeal from a bishop's decision on a question of law in any district, annual, central, or jurisdictional conference. It is made up of 5 ministerial and 4 lay members, and has become so important that it is often called "the Supreme Court" of the church.

The general conference of 1972 "restructured" the administrative bodies of the church. The Council of Bishops and a Council on Finance and Administration were made responsible to the general conference, and a new Council on Ministries was set up as a coordinating body between the conference and various other commissions, support services, and program boards. The commissions now include those on Archives and History,

Religion and Race, Status and Role of Women; the Support Services include a Board of Publication, United Methodist Communications, and a Board of Pensions. The program boards were rearranged to include boards on church and society, discipleship, higher education and ministry, and global ministries. In this restructuring, the church's 21 major boards and agencies were reduced to 6.

This general conference also broadened the basis of doctrine in the church, in the first restatement on doctrine since the eighteenth century. The classic statements of the merging Methodist and Evangelical United Brethren churches were maintained, but the doctrinal door was left open to theological change and revision. Typical of the openness that has always characterized Methodism is the statement in the *Discipline* that the 4 main sources and guidelines for Christian theology are Scripture, tradition, experience, and reason: "These four are interdependent; none can be defined unambiguously. They allow for, indeed they positively encourage, variety in United Methodist theologizing."

This church has property valued at $8,457,741,470, not including educational plants, hospitals, or homes for the aged. There are 145 institutions devoted to long-term care, 57 to health care, and 58 to child care. There are 81 United Methodist colleges, 7 universities, 13 schools of theology, 19 2-year colleges, 13 secondary schools, 1 elementary school, and 1 medical college. The church is at work in 48 countries; 15 missionary bishops administer the work overseas, where there is a total of 648 missionaries. The United Methodist Publishing House is probably the oldest and largest religious publishing concern in the world; there are 41 periodicals sponsored, exclusive of Sunday school materials.

The World Methodist Council, organized in 1881 and designed to draw the whole Wesleyan movement close together in fellowship and devotion to the Wesleyan heritage, has become increasingly active in recent years. Nine ecumenical conferences have been held by the council since 1881; headquarters are established at Lake Junaluska, North Carolina.

African Methodist Episcopal Church

One of the 3 largest Methodist groups in the United States, this church began with the withdrawal in 1787 of a number of members in St. George's Methodist Episcopal Church in Philadelphia, in protest of what they considered to be the practice of racial discrimination. They built a chapel with the assistance of Bishop William White of the Protestant Episcopal Church. Francis Asbury dedicated their Bethel Chapel in Philadelphia; he also ordained one of their members, Richard Allen, as their minister.

The church was formally organized as the African Methodist Episcopal Church in 1816; in the same year Allen was consecrated as its first bishop, again by Bishop Asbury.

It was a church confined, in the years preceeding the Civil War, to the northern states; following the war its membership increased rapidly in the South, and today it is found all across the nation. They have 13 bishops active in 13 districts, and they hold a general conference quadrennially. Foreign missions are supported in South Africa, West Africa, India, the Caribbean, and South America. They have 8 colleges and 7 theological schools.

Membership statistics are difficult to obtain; their latest report, in 1951, lists 1,166,301 members in 5,878 churches.

African Methodist Episcopal Zion Church

This church dates from 1796, when its first organization was instituted by a group of black members protesting discrimination in the John Street Church in New York City. Their first church, built in 1800, was called Zion; the word was later made part of the denominational name. The first annual conference of the body was held in this church in 1821 with 6 black Methodist churches in New Haven, Philadelphia, and Newark, New Jersey, represented by 19 preachers and presided over by the Rev. William Phoebus of the white Methodist Episcopal Church. James Varick, who led the John Street dissension, was elected for their first bishop at this conference. The name African Methodist Episcopal Zion Church was approved in 1848.

This church spread quickly over the northern states; by the time of the general conference of 1880 there were 15 annual conferences in the South. Livingstone College at Salisbury, North Carolina, the largest educational institution of the church, was established by that conference. Departments of missions, education, and publications were established in 1892; later came administrative boards to direct work in church extension, evangelism, finance, ministerial relief, and so on. Home missions are supported in Louisiana, Mississippi, and in several states beyond the Mississippi, principally in Oklahoma. Foreign missionaries are found in Liberia, Ghana, Nigeria, South America, and the West Indies. There are 5 secondary schools, 2 colleges (Livingstone, in Salisbury, North Carolina, and Clinton Junior College in Rock Hill, South Carolina), several foreign mission stations, and there are 1,342,427 members in 5,000 churches.

African Union First Colored Methodist Protestant Church, Inc.

A black body organized in 1866, this is a union of 2 former churches known as the African Union Church and the First Colored Methodist Protestant Church. Doctrine is in accord with most of Methodism, but there are differences in polity; there are no bishops, and ministers and laymen have equal power in annual and general conferences. There is no foreign missionary program; home missions are maintained by a group of women known as the Grand Body. A general board, with a president, secretary, and treasurer, directs the denominational effort; the board meets annually and the general conference quadrennially.

Christian Methodist Episcopal Church

Known until 1954 as the Colored Methodist Episcopal Church, this church was established in 1870 in the south in an amicable agreement between white and black members of the Methodist Episcopal Church, South. There were at the time at least 225,000 slave members in the Methodist Episcopal Church, South, but with the Emancipation Proclamation all but 80,000 of these joined the 2 independent black bodies. When the general conference of the Methodist Episcopal Church, South, met at New Orleans in 1866, a commission from the black membership asked for a separation into a church of their own. The request was granted, and in 1870 the organization of the Colored Methodist Episcopal Church was realized. They held this name until the meeting of their general conference at Memphis in May of 1954, when it was decided to change it to the Christian Methodist Episcopal Church.

Their doctrine is the doctrine of the parent church; this denomination adds a local church conference to the quarterly, district, annual, and general conferences usual in Methodism. Seven boards supervise the national work, each presided over by a bishop assigned as chairman by the College of Bishops. The general secretaries of the various departments are elected every 4 years by the general conference. There were 466,718 members and 2,598 churches in 1965.

There are 2 periodicals; and 5 colleges, 1 seminary, and 1 nursery care center are maintained.

Congregational Methodist Church

This church was constituted in Georgia in 1852 by a group withdrawing from the Methodist Episcopal Church, South, in objection to certain features of the episcopacy and the itineracy. Two-thirds of its membership in turn withdrew to join the Congregational Church in 1887-88.

Local pastors are called by the local churches; district conferences grant licenses, ordain ministers, and review local reports. District, annual, and general conferences are all recognized as church courts, ruling on violations of church law, citing offending laymen or ministers, and holding the power of expulsion over unworthy members. There is a restricted home and foreign missionary program. A senior college and denominational headquarters and a publishing house are located at Florence, Mississippi. There are 16,000 members in 250 churches.

Cumberland Methodist Church

This is a small Methodist body, listing currently 4 churches and an inclusive membership of 65. Its leaders withdrew from the Congregational Methodist Church in protest against certain elements of polity and doctrine. It was organized at Laager, Grundy County, Tennessee, on May 5, 1950. A general board is the chief administrative body, and a president is elected instead of the usual bishop. The membership is limited to the state of Tennessee.

Evangelical Methodist Church

Organized at Memphis in 1946, this church is "fundamental in doctrine, evangelistic in program, and congregational in government." It represents a

182

double protest against what were considered autocratic and undemocratic government on the one hand and a tendency toward modernism on the other in The Methodist Church from which the body withdrew. There is great emphasis placed upon the protest against modernism.

The church is Arminian in theology and Wesleyan in doctrine. Members seek a return to the original revivalistic thought and program of Wesleyanism; fundamentalist, they oppose the "substituting of social, educational, or other varieties of cultural salvation."

Local churches own and control their own property and select their own pastors. There are 7 districts and 7 district superintendents. Mexico and Bolivia constitute mission conferences. The general conference meets quadrennially. International headquarters are in Wichita, Kansas. There are 138 churches, with a membership of over 10,000.

First Congregational Methodist Church of the U.S.A.

Organized at Forsythe, Georgia, in 1852, this group claims to be the parent body from which the Congregational Methodist Church dissented to form its own organization. Originally under the jurisdiction of the Methodist Episcopal Church, South, they withdrew from that church in disagreement over the episcopal and itinerant systems, claiming that the system lacked biblical authority and democratic principles, to set up a church that would be congregational in government. There are local, district, state, and general conferences, and about 7,500 members in 100 churches, in Alabama, Mississippi, Georgia, Tennessee, Texas, Missouri, Arkansas, and Oklahoma.

Free Methodist Church of North America

This is one of the more conservative among the larger bodies of American Methodism, both in doctrine and in standards of Christian practices. Its founder was the Rev. B. T. Roberts, who with his associates objected to what was called "new school" Methodism, which they considered destructive to the Wesleyan standards of the church. They were "read out" of their churches and organized the Free Methodist Church in Pekin, New York, in 1860. The Genesee Conference, of which Roberts had been a member, restored his credentials to his son in 1910, but no reunion of the group with The United Methodist Church has yet been effected. A merger with the Holiness Movement Church in Canada was approved in 1960.

Doctrinally the Free Methodists call for a return to primitive Wesleyan teaching; they stress the virgin birth and deity of Jesus and his vicarious atonement and resurrection. No one may be received into membership without an experience of confession and forgiveness of sin, and the experience of entire sanctification is sought in all members. Strict adherence to the general rules of Methodism is demanded, and membership in secret societies is forbidden.

The Free Methodist Church has become a world fellowship consisting of 3 general conferences—Egypt, Japan, and North America—with a common constitution formally ratified by each general conference in 1964. All legislative actions are reviewed by a constitutional council with members elected from each general conference. There are 75,305 members in the United States and the United Kingdom in 1,172 churches, and a world membership of 155,189. Foreign missionary work is conducted in Africa, India, Japan, Taiwan, the Dominican Republic, Hong Kong, the Philippines, Indonesia, Egypt, Brazil, Paraguay, Mexico, and Haiti. There are 4 senior colleges in the denomination, 1 Bible college, a cooperative program with other denominations in another senior college, a seminary foundation maintained in cooperation with Asbury Theological Seminary, and Western Evangelical Seminary. Social services include a 177-bed hospital, a home for unwed mothers, 5 retirement and nursing facilities for the elderly, and 1 children's home.

Fundamental Methodist Church, Inc.

Known until August, 1956, as the Independent Fundamental Methodist Church, this church was instituted on August 27, 1942, at Ash Grove, Missouri, organized under its original title in 1944, and chartered under its present title in 1948. Its origin is traced back to the Methodist Protestant Church, of which it was a part until the merging of the 3 major Methodist churches in 1939. Dissatisfaction with the merger and the conviction that the primitive Wesleyan principles and theology would suffer thereby led to the withdrawal and the establishment of the new church. As the name suggests, there is an insistence here upon fundamental teaching.

There are no bishops in this church; it has only a district superintendent and a secretary. Government is more representative than in most Methodist groups, with an annual conference made up of ministers and laymen, voting equally. Conferences are divided into districts, with an annual conference for each district. There are 15 churches, 745 members.

Independent African Methodist Episcopal Church

This group was formed in 1907 at Jacksonville, Florida, by 12 ministers who left the African Methodist Episcopal Church following disputes with the district superintendents of that church. A new book of discipline, doctrines, and laws was written; the *Book of Discipline* is revised from time to time by the quadrennial general conference, but the 25 articles of religion it contains remain unchanged.

There are quarterly, annual, and general conferences. The annual conference ordains ministers as deacons, and the general conference ordains elders and bishops. In 1940 there were 1,000 members and 12 churches.

New Congregational Methodist Church

This church originated in an administrative quarrel in the Georgia conference of the Methodist Episcopal Church, South, over the consolidation of certain rural properties in the southern section of the state. Protesting, the New Congregational Methodist Church was organized in 1881 on the general plan of the Congregational Methodist Church. (There has in recent years been a division of this church, with a number of congregations uniting with the Congregational Methodist Church.) There are at present 773 members in 15 churches—7 of which are in north Florida and 8 in south Georgia. There are 2 smaller groups in central Georgia and Indiana.

Government is a combination of Methodist and Congregational systems; the episcopacy is rejected, and congregations call and elect their own pastors; there are the usual (Methodist) local, district, and general conferences. An unusual feature of this church lies in their practice of foot washing.

People's Methodist Church

Conservative and "holiness," the founders of this church left The Methodist Church in North Carolina at the time of the merger of the 3 major Methodist churches. There are approximately 25 congregations and 1,000 members, and a Bible school in Greensboro, North Carolina. No information on doctrine or polity is available.

Primitive Methodist Church, U.S.A.

This church had its initial organization in England, under the influence of Lorenzo Dow, an American camp-meeting revivalist, who went to England early in the nineteenth century to hold a series of meetings that resulted in the formation of a number of societies among his converts. The leaders of these societies were dropped from the Wesleyan Connection and formed the Primitive Methodist Church in 1810. Four missionaries came to America in 1829, settling in New York City and Philadelphia.

The church has a general conference for both administration and legislation and has 6 districts that are area groups. There is only one salaried official—an executive director. The relationships and assignments of ministers are reviewed annually, and vacancies are filled with student ministers or ordained deacons and elders.

Doctrinally, modified Wesleyan Articles of Religion are accepted. Foreign missionaries are stationed in Guatemala. There are 10,329 members in 88 churches.

Reformed Methodist Union Episcopal Church

This church was started in 1885 at Charleston, South Carolina, in a withdrawal from the African Methodist Episcopal Church, the immediate cause of the division being a dispute over the election of ministerial delegates to the general conference. Intended at first as a nonepiscopal church, the body adopted the complete polity of the Methodist Episcopal Church in general conferences of 1896 and 1916. Its first bishop was consecrated in 1899 by a bishop of the Reformed Episcopal Church. Class meetings and love feasts are featured in the local congregation; there are 3,800 members and 17 churches.

Reformed Zion Union Apostolic Church

This church was organized at Boydton, Virginia, in 1869 by Elder James R. Howell, a minister of the African Methodist Episcopal Zion Church in New York, in a protest against white discrimination and against the ecclesiasticism of other black Methodist churches. This was originally known as the Zion Union Apostolic Church; internal friction completely disrupted the body by 1874, and in 1881-82 it was reorganized under the present name. There are no basic departures from standard Methodist doctrine or polity except that only one ordination, that of elder, is required of its ministers. There are 16,000 members, 50 churches.

Southern Methodist Church

Doctrinally, the Southern Methodist Church remains the same as the body from which it came—The Methodist Episcopal Church, South. They opposed the merger of that church with the northern Methodist Episcopal Church, in 1939, on grounds of "alarming infidelity and apostacy found therein." They regard their Southern Methodist Church not as a separatist body but as a church "brought into existence to perpetuate the faith of John Wesley."

There are no bishops here, but there are the usual Methodist annual (4) and general conferences; a president is elected every 4 years from the elders of the clergy. Laymen and clergy have equal voice and voting privileges in these conferences.

Local churches own and control their own property and buildings and call their own ministers. There are 11,000 members in 169 churches from Virginia to Texas. There is 1 college, Southern Methodist College, and a publishing house (Foundry Press) located at Orangeburg, South Carolina.

Union American Methodist Episcopal Church

This was one of the first black bodies to establish an independent Methodist church. A group of members left the Asbury Methodist Church in Wilmington, Delaware, in 1805; they worshiped out of doors and in private homes until 1813, when they built their first church and incorporated as the Union Church of Africans. Defections from the membership in this church were responsible for the formation of another body known as the African Union Church, which forced the change to the present name—the Union American Methodist Episcopal Church.

General, annual, district, and quarterly conferences are held; general conferences are called only to consider proposed changes in name, law, or polity. There are 2 educational institutions, and the church claims 27,560 members in 256 churches.

METROPOLITAN CHURCH ASSOCIATION

Springing from a revival in the Metropolitan Methodist Church of Chicago in 1894, this association was originated primarily to carry on a local evangelistic work in the poorer and more densely populated sections of the city. It has since grown into a widespread work in this country and abroad.

Foreign missionaries are now stationed in the United Provinces of India, South India (under the ministry of native pastors, serving 7,000 members), the Union of South Africa, and Switzerland. Home missionaries are at work in Mexico.

The founders of the association sought a return to the teaching of primitive Wesleyan holiness, and that emphasis is still strong. There is no creed "except such as may be found in the Scriptures themselves." Inasmuch as this is an off-shoot of Methodism, its government closely resembles the Methodist pattern. The association was chartered under the laws of Wisconsin in 1918. There are 443 members in 15 churches.

MISSIONARY CHURCH

The Missionary Church is made up of 2 groups merged in March, 1969: the Missionary Church Association and the United Missionary Church. The new denomination claims 366 congregations and 26,000 members in 9 districts in the United States and Canada. It has missionaries in 15 countries, and total assets of about $35,000,000.

Up to 1947 the United Missionary Church was the Mennonite Brethren in Christ Church, but in that year it dropped all its Mennonite connections in a new organization. They stressed the Wesleyan-Arminian message of holiness, and were, generally, fundamentalist in theology. The Missionary Church Association was founded at Berne, Indiana, in 1889, and was quite similar to the United Missionary Church in theology and practice.

Local churches in the new Missionary Church will be independent in managing their own affairs, but they will recognize the authority of a general conference made up of ministers, missionaries, and laymen and is held biennially. Working under the general conference is a general board made up of the officers of the administrative boards of the church: Christian education, evangelism and church extension, higher education, overseas mission, publications and social concerns. A president, vice-president, secretary, and treasurer are elected for a term of 4 years.

Missions are highly evangelistic; missionaries are serving in Africa, India, South America, Egypt, Japan, Mexico, Haiti, Hawaii, Jamaica, and Sierra Leone.

The church operates 2 educational institutions in the United States—Bethel College in Mishawaka, Indiana, and Fort Wayne Bible College in Fort Wayne, Indiana, with a combined enrollment of 1,100 students. There are also 2 Bible colleges in Canada.

MORAVIANS

The Moravian Church has roots running as far back as the ninth century and the work, in that century, of Constantine and Methodius among the European Slavs. The Slavic population of Bohemia and Moravia was struggling, at the time, for political and religious freedom. Later, they followed John Hus, who was martyred in 1415, and Jerome of Prague, martyred in 1416. Their first association was formed in Bohemia in 1458, and from this time on we find them called *Jednota bratrska* ("The Union of Brethren") and/or *Unitas Fratrum* ("Unity of the Brethren").

By the middle of the sixteenth century there were about 60 congregations in Bohemia, between 80 and 90 in Moravia, and, somewhat later, 40 congregations in Poland. The number of congregations remained virtually the same (altogether, about 150 congregations in Bohemia and Moravia) until the outbreak of the Thirty Years' War (1618–1648). Fierce persecution under the Hapsburgs, in the war, almost exterminated them, but they survived. In 1722, 2 families named Neisser led by Christian David fled from Moravia, and at the invitation of Nicholas Louis, Count of Zinzendorf, a small band found refuge on his estate in Saxony, where they built the town of Herrnhut. It was the count who called them "Moravians" because they came from northern Moravia.

Zinzendorf was made a bishop in 1737. In America (1741-43) he was active in establishing the church in Pennsylvania, where they founded 3 towns—Bethlehem, Nazareth, and Lititz—following a failure to plant churches in the colony of Georgia. They also established a church in Hope, New Jersey (which proved a failure), and another in Salem, North Carolina, but their largest and most successful efforts have been made in Pennsylvania, where the current Moravian Church *(Unitas Fratrum)* offers a model of one of the finest religious establishments in the nation.

Moravian Church *(Unitas Fratrum)*

It is said of the Moravians that "a unified system of doctrine was never developed." That may be an overstatement, but it is certainly true that the Moravians have no doctrine peculiar to them; they are broadly evangelical, insisting upon a principle of "in essentials unity, in nonessentials liberty, and in all things charity." Their scriptural interpretations agree substantially with the Apostles' Creed, the Westminster and Augsburg confessions, and the Articles of Religion of the Church of England. They hold the Scriptures to be the inspired Word of God and an adequate rule of faith and practice; and they have doctrines dealing with the total depravity of man, the real Godhead and the real humanity of Christ, justification and redemption through the sacrifice of Christ, the work of the Holy Spirit, good works as the fruits of the Spirit, the fellowship of all believers, the second coming of Christ, and the resurrection of the dead to life and judgment. Their main doctrinal emphasis may be said to be upon the love of God manifested in the redemptive life and death of Jesus, the inner testimony of the Spirit, and Christian conduct in everyday affairs.

188

The sacrament of infant baptism by sprinkling, or occasionally by pouring, is practiced. There is a total membership of 54,053 in 145 churches. Members are admitted by vote of the congregational board of elders. The Lord's Supper is celebrated at least 6 times a year, and the old custom of the love feast is preserved. A variety of liturgies is used in worship: the church is notable for an especially beautiful outdoor service held at Easter.

The Moravian Church is divided in the United States into 2 provinces, northern and southern. The highest administrative body in each American province is the provincial synod. Composed of ministers and laymen and meeting every 5 years, it directs missionary, educational, and publishing work, and elects a provincial elders' conference, or executive board, which functions between synod meetings. Bishops are elected by provincial and general synods. They are spiritual, but not administrative, leaders in the church.

Missionary work has always been a first concern of the Moravians; with a comparatively small membership they conducted the most efficient missionary work among the Indians of any of the early colonial churches. The worldwide Moravian Church now supports work in 13 missionary fields, including North, Central, and South America, Africa, and among the Eskimos in Alaska. The church maintains 2 colleges, a theological seminary, and a coed Moravian academy.

Unity of the Brethren

Known until 1962 as the Evangelical Unity of the Czech-Moravian Brethren in North America, this body originated among Czech and Moravian emigrants arriving in Texas in the late nineteenth century. The present name (*Unitas Fratrum,* or *Jednota Bratrska*) is the original name used in 1457.

Their synod meets every 2 years. The church has no colleges or seminaries. In 1964 there were 6,142 members in 32 churches.

MUSLIMS

Islam claims more than 3,000,000 adherents in the United States. There is no national organization (there is, indeed, no titular head or priesthood in all of Islam), but there are Islamic Centers in Washington, Toledo, Detroit, New York, etc. The center in Washington includes a beautiful mosque, library, classrooms for study, and administrative offices; it is open for daily prayer and offers lectures and publications on the literature, philosophy, religion, and art of Islam.

The word *Islam* means "purity, peace, submission to God's will and obedience to his laws." It does not claim to be a new religion formulated by the prophet Mohammed but rather to be "the continuation of all former religious principles decreed by God through his revelations to all prophets," and the prophets include Jesus Christ (they accept him as prophet but not as divine) and many of the Jewish prophets and leaders of the Old Testament, from Noah to Zephaniah.

They revere and honor Mohammed, but they do not worship him; their creed is that "there is no deity worthy of worship except God [Allah], and Mohammed is God's Messenger." This is "the religion of the Book," and the book is the Koran (*Qur´an*, to the Mohammedans), said to have been dictated to Mohammed (born A.D. 571) by the angel Gabriel. The Koran contains the faith of Islam, and describes the manner in which God is to be worshiped; it also outlines legislation concerning civil and criminal laws, laws of war, peace treaties between nations, and laws ruling in such matters as marriage, divorce, inheritance, and wills. The Ten Commandments are embodied in the Koran, and it contains "the Six Articles of Belief" and "the Five Pillars of Faith," which are the heart of Islam. The Five Pillars are: (1) the recital of the creed; (2) recital of prayer 5 times daily, facing Mecca (the Cebba at Mecca is held to be the first house built by Abraham for his son Ishmael, for the worship of God); (3) the giving of tithes for the support of the poor and the expansion of the faith; (4) the observation of Ramadan, the ninth month of the Moslem calendar, fasting during daylight in commemoration of the first revelation of the Koran; (5) a pilgrimage to Mecca, when financially able. The Six Articles of Belief are: (1) God is One, and this is Allah; (2) the Koran is God's truly inspired book; (3) God's angels are heavenly beings created to serve God, and they are opposed to evil spirits; (4) God sent his prophets to earth at stated times for stated purposes; the last of these was Mohammed, and God makes no distinctions between his messengers; (5) the Day of Judgment will find good and evil weighed in the balance; (6) the lives and acts of men are foreordained (predestined) by an all-knowing God. Islam, however, still leaves man as "the architect of his own destiny, free to make or mar his own future through a life of honest endeavor."

Mohammed accomplished his mission, which was primarily to proclaim the unity of God; when he died at 62, the precepts of the Koran became the great unifying force around which, eventually, 500,000,000 people were to become the followers of Islam (Moslems, or Muslims), with Mecca as their holy city and ardent in their faith in the Islamic trinity of the Koran, Moslem tradition, and the Prophet Mohammed. Some divisions and sects have appeared (Shiites, Sunnites, Sufis) with variations in interpretation and practice, but by and large there is and has been a firm allegiance to the Koran and to traditional Moslem practices.

The true Moslem prays 5 times daily, has a service of congregational prayer preceded by a sermon on Friday at noon, eats no pork, drinks no intoxicating liquors, shuns gambling, adultery, and the breaking of one's word. In some countries he practices polygamy and (with less and less insistence) the custom that demands the veiling of Moslem women. He removes his shoes upon entering the mosque and is meticulous in washing feet, hands, head, and arms before prayer. In his mosque there are no icons, statues, symbols, pews, chairs, or musical instruments; there is only a constant repetition and echo of the fundamental Koran approach to prayer: "In the name of God, the Beneficent, the Merciful, praise be to God, Lord of the worlds."

Outside the mosque he is a student. There is a saying that God created the pen as his first creation, and that the first word God revealed to Mohammed was the word *read*. To read and to study and to seek knowledge are obligatory in Islam; the ink of the scholar is more valuable to them than the blood of a martyr.

NATIONAL DAVID SPIRITUAL TEMPLE OF CHRIST CHURCH UNION (INC.), U.S.A.
(The Universal Christian Spiritual Faith and Churches for All Nations)

This is a body founded in 1932 by Dr. David William Short, a former minister of the Missionary Baptist Church. Dr. Short wished to "proclaim the Orthodox Christian spiritual faith"; he was convinced that no man had the right or spiritual power "to make laws, rules, or doctrines for the real church founded by Jesus Christ" and that the denominational churches had been founded in error and in disregard of the apostolic example. He held wisdom, knowledge, faith, healing, miracles, prophecy, discerning of spirits, and diverse kinds of tongues to be spiritual gifts of the Holy Ghost and parts of the church of Christ. He believed that all races should and must be accepted in the true church.

The members of this church consider themselves to be the true and universal church of Christ and not just another denomination. They rely entirely upon the Holy Ghost for inspiration and direction; their church constitution they claim to be found in I Cor. 12:1-31 and Eph. 4:11. Their organization is made up of pastors, prophets, prophetesses, bishops, archbishops, elders, overseers, divine healers, deacons, and missionaries. Archibishop Short is the chief governing officer; there is a national executive board that holds a national annual assembly.

A restricted home missionary work is conducted in hospitals, and a nursing home is maintained. A monthly newspaper, *The Christian Spiritual Voice*, is published at Kansas City, Missouri. Archbishop Short is also founder, president, and mentor of the St. David Orthodox Christian Spiritual Seminary, which was dedicated in 1949 at Des Moines; in 1952 he was elected archbishop and chief apostle of a new Universal Orthodox Christian Spiritual Faith and Church of All Nations, representing a merger of the National David Spiritual Temple, the St. Paul's Spiritual Church Convocation, and King David's Spiritual Temple of Truth Association. The original National David Spiritual Temple has a membership of 40,816 in 66 churches, prayer bands, and missions.

NEW APOSTOLIC CHURCH
OF NORTH AMERICA

The New Apostolic Church of North America is a variant or schism of the Catholic Apostolic Church movement in England. It claims common origin with the Catholic Apostolic Church in the appointment of an apostle in the parent body in 1832. Debate arose in 1860 over the appointment of new apostles to fill vacancies left by death. Insisting on 12 apostles at the head of the true church, Bishop Schwarz of Hamburg was excommunicated from the Catholic Apostolic Church in 1862 for proposing the election of new apostles. A priest named Preuss was elected to the office of apostle "through the spirit of prophecy" to lead the dissenting body; Bishop Schwarz served under him until his own elevation to the apostolic office.

Under Preuss and Schwarz the New Apostolic Church spread from Europe to America, where today it is organized into apostles' districts, bishops' districts, and elders' districts. Each church has a rector and one or more assistants (priests, deacons, and so forth), who serve usually without remuneration. All ministers and other "office-bearers" are selected by the apostleship. The American church is a constituent of the international organization supervised by Chief Apostle Ernst Streckeisen in Zurich, Switzerland.

Just as the true church must be governed on the scriptural pattern by 12 apostles, members of this church believe that only the apostles have received from Christ the commission and power to forgive sin. The New Apostolic Church of North America accepts the Apostles' Creed and stresses the authority and inspiration of the Bible, the apostolic ordinances of the laying on of hands, the necessity of gifts of the Holy Spirit (which include prophecy, visions, dreams, diverse tongues, songs of praise, wisdom, discrimination of spirits, the power of healing and performing wonders), tithing, and the speedy, personal, premillennial return of Christ. Three "means of grace" are found in 3 sacraments: baptism (including children), Holy Communion, and Holy Sealing (the dispensing and reception of the Holy Spirit). Work "along broader interior and missionary lines" is conducted in the United States, Canada, Mexico, and Puerto Rico. The United States has 23,000 members in 297 churches and 65 missions; the international organization about 1,000,000 in 6,000 branches in 46 countries.

OLD CATHOLIC CHURCHES

Old Catholic churches in the United States are outgrowths but unconnected branches of the Old Catholic movement and churches of Europe. The European bodies originated in a protest against the doctrine of papal infallibility adopted by the Roman Catholic Vatican Council of 1870; Roman priests in Germany who refused to accept the doctrine were excommunicated and organized the Old Catholic Church under the leadership of Dr. Ignatz von Döllinger in 1871. A similar break occurred in Holland and Switzerland where other Old Catholic churches were established.

This revolt did not break completely with Roman Catholicism. It rejected papal infallibility, the doctrine of the immaculate conception, compulsory celibacy of the priesthood, and in some instances the filioque clause of the Nicene Creed but kept much of the other doctrine, creeds, customs, and liturgy of the Roman Catholic Church. It was also most anxious to preserve the orders and the apostolic succession of its priests and bishops, inasmuch as they considered apostolic succession as vital in a valid Christian ministry. Much confusion has resulted in conflicting claims of succession and validity of orders, especially in American Old Catholic churches. All Old Catholic bodies in this country were at one time or another connected with European bodies, but that is not true today; most American groups have severed their connections with churches abroad. Someone has said that most of the Old Catholics in America are either dissatisfied Angelicans or former Catholics; and there is some truth in that, if not all the truth. Several attempts have been made, however, to merge Old Catholic churches with those of the Church of England or the Greek Church, and gestures have been made toward membership in the World Council of Churches.

Old Catholic missionaries were in America soon after 1871, establishing scattered congregations. Father Joseph René Vilatte, a French priest ordained by the Old Catholics in Switzerland, attempted to organize these congregations and at once became the storm center of the rising confusion. Vilatte himself vacillated between rival bodies; he studied at a Presbyterian college in Montreal and twice returned to submit to the Roman Catholic Church, dying at last in a French monastery. Vigorously opposed within his own church and by American Protestant Episcopalians, whose ranks he refused to join, he went to Switzerland in 1885 for ordination as an Old Catholic bishop and was finally consecrated as an archbishop by Archbishop Alvarez of Ceylon, who claimed orders through the Syro-Jacobite Church of Malabar. He returned to America to found the American Catholic Church.

Separated and competing as they are, the Old Catholics in the United States have a firm common doctrinal basis. The doctrine is similar to that held by the Greek and Latin churches before those 2 bodies separated; among the Old Catholics it is now more Eastern Catholic than Western. They accept the 7 ecumenical councils of the church held before the division into Eastern and Western bodies. Bible reading is encouraged, and national tongues rather than Latin are used in all worship. There is a strange blend here of orthodoxy and rationalism, both in doctrine and in ritual.

There are 4 main divisions of Old Catholic churches in the United States, with an approximate total of 97,000 members in 100 churches—the American Catholic Church (Archdiocese of New York), the North American Old Roman Catholic Church, Christ Catholic Church of America and Europe (no information available aside from membership, which is 7,100 in 24 churches), and the American Catholic Church (Syro-Antiochian). The African Orthodox Church, a black group, is listed often as an Old Catholic body but is actually Protestant Episcopalian in origin and connection. The Polish National Catholic Church may be said to have certain Old Catholic origins and doctrines, but it has been listed separately in this book in consideration of their distinctively nationalistic character. The Liberal Catholic Church is also related to the Old Catholic movement.

American Catholic Church, Archdiocese of New York

This church was organized by its present archbishop, the Most Rev. James Francis Augustine Lashley, in 1927 and incorporated in 1932. Its orders are derived form the Syrian Church of Antioch through Father Vilatte, and it has a membership of 8,437 in 20 churches, 10 in Manhattan and Brooklyn, 4 in Trinidad, West Indies. Catholic forms of ordination and consecration are followed in the investing of holy orders.

American Catholic Church (Syro-Antiochian)

Deriving its orders from the Syrian Patriarch of Antioch, this church is better known as the Jacobite Apostolic Church. It was organized in the United States in 1915 and is a Monophysitic body. Armenian Coptic and Jacobite Syrian churches are all Monophysitic. The word "Jacobite" was borrowed from the name of Jacobus Baradeus (died in 578), the Syrian monk who founded the movement. Historically, a bitter quarrel has raged between the Jacobites and the Orthodox Christians.

This church is Catholic in worship and discipline and has a Catholic liturgy in the administration of the sacraments; otherwise, it is a self-governing American body.

Syrian Jacobites are found in Mesopotamia, Iran, Syria, India, and Kurdistan, where they claim over 80,000 members. It is from this section of the Middle East that they have migrated to the United States, where they report 750 members in 3 churches.

Mariavite Old Catholic Church

Of Polish origin, the Congregation of Religious of Perpetual Suppliant Adoration was founded on a vision and revelation of Jesus Christ by the Reverend Mother Maria Franciska in 1893. In protest against what she considered the near state of degregation within the Roman Catholic Church, her purpose, and that of her followers, was to establish and maintain a deeper inner life of spirituality; it was comprised, at first, of male priests, known as the Congregation of Mariavite Priests. These priests endeavored to practice an aesthetical-mystical inner religious life according to the First Rule of St. Francis of Assisi.

Surviving periods of ecclesiastical and civil opposition, they are active today in 2 bodies: the Mariavite Old Catholic Church, which started in the United States in 1830, and the Mariavite Catholic Church in Poland. Their work is conducted under the leadership of priests, brothers, and sisters, still adherents to the First and Second rules of Francis of Assisi. They are "dedicated to Christ present in the Most Blessed Sacrament and to Our Lady of Perpetual Help (the Virgin Mary). Each member of the Mariavite Congregation holds a regular daily adoration of one hour before the exposed elements of the Sacrament of the Eucharist. They have 3 creeds (Apostles', Nicene, and Athanasian) and 7 sacraments (baptism, penance, Holy Eucharist, confirmation, matrimony, holy orders, and extreme unction). Beyond this, they reject the dogmas of the immaculate conception and the assumption of Mary as doctrines necessary to salvation, but still accept Mary as the Mother of God.

Mariavite priests and sisters may not accept payment for any service and cannot possess property or gather any assets from the membership, which totals 350,542 in 157 churches.

North American Old Roman Catholic Church

Two Old Catholic groups bear this name, typical of the confusion and debate among Old Catholics. One body, identical in faith, thought, and worship with the Roman Catholic Church, but differing in discipline, was "received into union" with the Eastern Orthodox Church by the Archbishop of Beirut in 1911 and again by the Orthodox Patriarch of Alexandria in 1912.

The second church, still in existence as an Old Catholic Church, claims proven succession of Catholic orders; the Knott Missal is used for all Masses, but the Pontificale is used for all Order Rights. It is not under papal control or jurisdiction. Some 60,000 members are reported in 121 churches.

Old Roman Catholic Church in Europe and America (English Rite)

Archbishop Arnold Harris Mathew, who had been consecrated to the Episcopacy by Archbishop Gerard Gul of the Old Catholic Church of Utrect, Holland, in 1911, consecrated Prince de Landes Berghes de la Rache, a Hungarian, in 1912, and sent him to America to consolidate the small, scattered Old Catholic churches in this country. De Landes settled in Waukegan, Illinois, and on October 3, 1916, consecrated William Henry Francis Brothers as an Old Catholic bishop, and on the following day he also consecrated Carmel Henry Carfora as bishop. Less than a month after, at the suggestion of Msgr. Mathew, and in a dispute over the question of Minor Orders, de Landes excommunicated Brothers. Carfora then organized and incorporated the North American Old Roman Catholic Church, which remained the official name of the church until 1963, when it was changed to the Old Roman Catholic Church (English Rite), following the death of Carfora.

Many Poles and Lithuanians in the country were brought into the membership of this church; in 1972 it had a membership of 65,128 in 186 churches. It is similar to the Roman Catholic Church in worship and discipline (but denies papal infallibility) and differs slightly in doctrine. They celebrate the Mass, have 7 sacraments, teach transubstantiation, "the

Veneration and Invocation of the Glorious and Immaculate Mother of God, of the Angels and of the saints." They offer prayers for the dead, advocate celibacy for their priests but permit them to marry. Worship services are in the English language.

In 1963 the present Archbishop Metropolitan for North America, Robert Alfred Burns, led the church into union with the Old Roman Catholic Church (English Rite) in Great Britain.

OPEN BIBLE STANDARD CHURCHES, INC.

Open Bible Standard Churches, Inc., was originally composed of 2 revival movements: namely, Bible Standard, Inc., founded in Eugene, Oregon, in 1919; and Open Bible Evangelistic Association, founded in Des Moines in 1932. Similar in doctrine and government, the 2 groups amalgamated on July 26, 1935, taking the combined name *Open Bible Standard Churches, Inc.*, with headquarters in Des Moines.

The Pacific Coast group, with activities centered in Oregon, spread through Washington, California, and into the Rocky Mountain areas of the West; the Iowa group expanded into Illinois, Missouri, Ohio, Florida, and Pennsylvania. There are now churches in 24 states, with the main concentration in the central and far western states.

The teachings are "fundamental in doctrine, evangelical in spirit, missionary in vision, and pentecostal in testimony"; they include emphasis on the blood atonement of Christ, divine healing, baptism of the Holy Spirit, personal holiness, the premillennial return of the Lord, and baptism by immersion.

Churches are grouped into 5 geographical divisions, subdivided into 24 districts. Twenty-four district superintendents guide the work under the supervision of divisional superintendents. Individual churches are congregationally governed, locally owned, and are affiliated by a charter with the national organization. The 10 departments function under the leadership of departmental heads with the advice of a committee and are represented on the general board of directors. The highest governing body is the general conference, which meets annually and is composed of all licensed and ordained ministers and 1 lay delegate for each 100 members.

There are 50 missionaries at work in 15 foreign countries, 6 Bible training programs with formal curricula for the training of national workers, 3 Bible institutes and Bible colleges with a total enrollment of about 400 students, located at Des Moines; Eugene, Oregon; and St. Petersburg, Florida.

A board of publications is responsible for the preparation of conference publications. The denomination publishes a monthly periodical, *Message from the Open Bible,* and provides lesson materials for Sunday schools through its Christian education department.

The churches—275 churches with approximately 35,000 members—as a group hold membership in the Pentecostal Fellowship of North America and in the National Association of Evangelicals.

PENTECOSTAL BODIES

"Pentecostalism" is a most inclusive term applied to a large number of revivalistic American sects, assemblies, and churches. Many of them have come out of either a Methodist or Baptist background, and they are primarily concerned with perfection, holiness, and the pentecostal experience.

They offer statements of faith that are often long and involved and highly repetitious, but through them may be traced certain common strains and elements. Most of them believe in the Trinity, original sin, man's salvation through the atoning blood of Christ, the virgin birth and deity of Jesus, the divine inspiration and literal infallibility of the Scriptures, manifestations and "blessings" of the working of the Holy Spirit—the fiery pentecostal baptism of the Spirit, premillennialism, and future rewards and punishments. Two sacraments are found in most of their sects—baptism, usually by immersion, and the Lord's Supper. Foot washing is frequently observed in connection with the Supper. Many practice divine healing, and speaking in tongues is widespread.

Ultrafundamentalistic, varying in size from small group meetings to huge mass meetings, Pentecostalists are found in every state in the Union with their greatest strength in the South, West, and Middle West. They use a great variety of names, and do not always include the word "pentecostal" in their name—for instance, the largest single group of all, the Assemblies of God, with over half a million members, and the Church of God groups. No accurate count of their total membership is possible, as many of them never issue statistical reports of any kind.

Assemblies of God (General Council of)

The largest of the pentecostal bodies, with 1,283,892 members and 9,291 churches, the General Council of the Assemblies of God is actually an aggregation of pentecostal churches and assemblies accomplished at Hot Springs, Arkansas, in 1914. The founders were former ministers and pastors of evangelical persuasion who wished to unite into one body in the interest of a more effective preaching and an enlarged missionary crusade.

Ardently fundamentalist, its theology is Arminian; there is strong belief in the infallibility and inspiration of the Bible, the fall and redemption of man, baptism in the Holy Ghost, entire sanctification, a life. of holiness and separation from the world, divine healing, the second advent of Jesus and his millennial reign, eternal punishment for the wicked and eternal bliss for believers. Two ordinances, baptism and the Lord's Supper, are practiced. Members stand officially opposed to war, but large numbers of their youths accepted noncombatant and even combatant service in World War II. They are especially insistent that baptism in the Holy Spirit is evidenced by speaking in tongues. The Assemblies of God believe that all the gifts of the Spirit should be in operation in the normal New Testament church.

The government of the assemblies is an unusual mixture of presbyterian and congregational systems. Local churches are left quite independent in polity and in the conduct of local affairs. District officers have a pastoral ministry to all the churches and are responsible for the promotion of home missions. Work is divided into 55 districts in the United States, which include 5 foreign-language districts, each with a distinct presbytery that examines, licenses, and ordains pastors. The general council consists of all ordained (not licensed) ministers, and local churches are represented by one lay delegate each. This council elects all general officers, sets the doctrinal standards, and provides for church expansion and development. Missionary work is conducted under the guidance of a central missionary committee; there are 1,193 foreign missionaries at work on a total missionary budget of $26,592,956—unusually high among Protestant churches. A weekly periodical, *The Pentecostal Evangel,* has a circulation of approximately 270,000; and a prosperous church press produces books, tracts, and other religious literature. There are 8 Bible colleges and 1 liberal arts college. The latest school to be established is a graduate school of theology located in Springfield, Missouri. There are 187 Bible institutes abroad, and there is an international broadcast, *Revivaltime,* on 600 stations.

Calvary Pentecostal Church, Inc.

This church was founded at Olympia, Washington, in 1931 by a group of ministers who sought a ministerial fellowship rather than a separate denomination and freedom from the sectarian spirit. The body was incorporated in 1932, and a home and foreign missionary society was incorporated in the same year. Home missions work today consists mainly of evangelistic work, relief to weak churches, and the establishment of new churches. A general superintendent and executive presbytery board administer the work of the church; the general body meets in convention annually or semiannually. Seminary, college, or even Bible school education is considered beneficial but no requisite for ministers of this church, who may be either men or women; those who give evidence of having heard the call of God to preach are qualified by ordination. There are 22 churches and 8,000 members.

Elim Fellowship

Established in 1947, this body is an outgrowth of the missionary-oriented Elim Ministerial Fellowship, formed in 1932, and of the work of graduates of the Elim Bible Institute in Lima, New York (founded in 1924). The organizational pattern is Congregational, and doctrine is basically premillenial, holding the usual tenets of belief in an inspired and infallible Bible, the Trinity, sanctification, the baptism of the Holy Spirit, divine healing, and the resurrection of the saved and unsaved for eternal reward or punishment. Some 5,000 members are found in 70 churches, and 100 missionaries are at work in 18 countries of Africa, Asia, Europe, and South America. Headquarters are located at the institute, on the former campus of Genesee Wesleyan Seminary, purchased in 1951. The assemblies hold membership in the Pentecostal Fellowship of North America and the National Association of Evangelicals.

Emmanuel Holiness Church

The founders of this church had come to a general conference of the Pentecostal Fire-Baptized Holiness Church in 1953 but withdrew from that church in protest of certain positions taken by the conference of doctrine and polity. They now have 1,200 members in 56 churches and tabernacles located in Alabama, Florida, Georgia, North and South Carolina, Indiana, and Michigan; there is missionary activity in Mexico. Their chief administrative body is a general assembly, and their ruling church officer is a general overseer. A periodical, *Emmanuel Messenger*, is published at Franklin Springs, Georgia.

Independent Assemblies of God—International

A holiness and pentecostal group, this is an incorporated association of pentecostal ministers. Sometimes called Philadephia churches, they have a Swedish background and work closely with the Swedish pentecostal movement, with which they conduct an extensive missionary program. It is claimed that their missionary church in Brazil is the largest Protestant church in that country, having "close to half a million followers and really converted people."

Their government follows the autonomous pattern of other pentecostal churches and assemblies. They have 800 churches, 1800 ministers and evangelists, 12 Bible schools, and 200 missionaries in the Philippines.

International Pentecostal Assemblies

This body is the successor to the Association of Pentecostal Assemblies (founded in 1921) and the National and International Pentecostal Union (founded in 1919). Doctrine follows the usual pentecostal standards; the sick are anointed with oil, and prayer is offered for their healing; foot washing is optional; and this group is not opposed to participation in government or in defensive war. There are approximately 10,000 members in 55 churches, under the general supervision of a 9-member general board and several district superintendents who direct the work in 24 states and 13 foreign countries. The entire work is supported by membership tithes and offerings. A Bible college is maintained at Atlanta.

Pentecostal Assemblies of the World, Inc.

This was an interracial body at the time of its organization in 1907; some of the white members withdrew in 1924 to form the Pentecostal Church, Inc., which became a constituent body of the United Pentecostal Church, Inc., in 1945. Origin is traced "directly back to Pentecost, A.D. 33." Doctrine reveals no important departure from that of pentecostalism in general. Secret societies are opposed. Divorce is permitted, but only the grounds of fornication when both man and wife have had the "baptism of the Holy Ghost"; but when the unbeliever in a marriage contract procures a divorce, the believer may remarry.

Organization is similar to that of the Methodists: a general assembly meets annually under a presiding bishop; there is a secretary for foreign missions and 123 district elders. An executive board is composed of bishops (of whom there are 35), 5 directors, the general secretary, and general treasurer. An election of officers is held every 3 years by the ministerial members of the national assembly. Local assemblies are under the direction of the bishop. There are 100,000 members in 825 churches.

Pentecostal Church of Christ

Founded by John Stroup at Flatwoods, Kentucky, in 1917, and incorporated at Portsmouth, Ohio, in 1927, this church subscribes to the usual pentecostal doctrines of the Trinity, regeneration, sanctification, baptism of the Spirit, and puts strong emphasis upon divine healing. They have 1,659 members in 50 churches, missionary work in Brazil, and churches in the United States located in Ohio, Kentucky, West Virginia, Virginia, and Maryland. American headquarters are in London, Ohio.

Pentecostal Church of God

This church was organized in Chicago in 1919, incorporated in Missouri in 1936, and held its first national convention in 1938. It has recently combined with a Colorado Springs body of the same name. Typically pentecostal, it practices baptism by immersion as well as Holy Spirit baptism, physical evidence of speaking in tongues, and divine healing; the second coming of Christ is strongly emphasized.

Officers include a general superintendent, secretary-treasurer, director of world missions, director of Christian education, director of Indian missions, the presidents of their Pentecostal Young People and Pentecostal Ladies Auxiliary, and the district secretaries and presbyters. A general convention meets biennially; the 34 districts have annual meetings.

With 1,300 churches and 135,000 members in 21 countries they maintain 2 Bible colleges and 12 Bible colleges abroad. A large publishing house is located at Joplin, Missouri.

Pentecostal Fire-Baptized Holiness Church

This church was organized in 1911 by a small group who declined to continue in the union of the Fire-Baptized Holiness Church and the Pentecostal Holiness Church; their objection had to do mainly with matters of discipline in the wearing of ornaments and elaborate dress. They withdrew from the union in 1918.

Members of this church are forbidden to buy or sell or to engage in any labor or business for which they may receive "pecuniary remuneration." They are also forbidden "filthiness of speech, foolish talking or jesting, slang, attendance at fairs, swimming pools, or shows of any kind, the use of jewelry, gold, feathers, flowers, costly apparel, neckties."

The sect is strongly premillennialist and perfectionist; "joyous demonstrations" are prominent, finding expression in hand clapping, crying, and shouting. State conventions support convention evangelists, and there is a general convention that elects a 7-member board of missions. Foreign missions are supported in Mexico. There are 545 members and 41 churches.

Pentecostal Free-Will Baptist Church, Inc.

As the name suggests, this is a Pentecostalist group with a Free-Will Baptist background; it came into existence through the merging of 3 Free-Will Baptist conferences in North Carolina in 1959. Doctrine is, naturally, a mixture of Baptist and Pentecostalist beliefs; they include regeneration through faith in the shed blood of Christ, sanctification as a second definite work of grace (subsequent to regeneration), pentecostal baptism of the Holy Ghost, divine healing, and the premillennial second coming of Christ. Heritage Bible College was opened in September, 1977.

Officials include a general superintendent, general secretary, and general treasurer. A general meeting is held annually in August, composed of lay and ministerial representatives.

There are 15,000 members and 150 churches.

Pentecostal Holiness Church

This church was organized in 1898 at Anderson, South Carolina, by a number of pentecostal associations which at the time used the name Fire-Baptized Holiness Church. A year later another group organized as the Pentecostal Holiness Church; the 2 bodies united in 1911 at Falcon, North Carolina, under the latter name. A third body, the Tabernacle Pentecostal Church, joined them in 1915. There are 86,103 members in the United States, in 1,374 churches, and 49,307 in 966 churches in foreign mission fields.

The theological standards of Methodism prevail here, with certain modifications. It accepts the premillennial teaching of the Second Coming and believes that provision was made in the Atonement for the healing of the body. Divine healing is practiced but not to the exclusion of medicine. Three distinctive experiences are taught: 2 works of grace—justification by faith and sanctification, as a second work of grace—and the Spirit baptism, attested by speaking in other tongues. Services are often characterized by "joyous demonstrations."

Polity is also Methodistic. A general executive board of 11 members is elected by a quadrennial conference for a 4-year term and is limited to 2 consecutive terms in any 1 office. There are a general superintendent (bishop) and 3 assistant general superintendents, 1 secretary-treasurer, 6 board members, representing geographical areas and the church at large. Conferences are quadrennial instead of annual; there are 13 quadrennial conferences in the United States and 1 each in Haiti and the Philippines. Foreign mission stations are located in Hong Kong, India, South and Central America, Central and West Africa, Mexico, and Cuba.

Emmanuel College and Oklahoma City Southwestern College are accredited junior colleges, both offering also a 4-year ministerial training program. Holmes Theological Seminary is located at Greenville, South Carolina. There is a children's home at Falcon, North Carolina, a children's convalescent center at Bethany, Oklahoma, and homes for the aged are located at Falcon and Carmen, Oklahoma.

United Pentecostal Church International

The product of a union of 2 Pentecostal organizations (the Pentecostal Assemblies of Jesus Christ and the Pentecostal Church, Inc.) at St. Louis in 1945, this church stresses the necessity of repentance, water baptism in the name of Christ, and the receiving of the baptism of the Holy Ghost with the initial sign of speaking in tongues. It has 405,000 members in 2,701 churches; the superintendents of geographical districts make up their general board, which is the international administrative body. One hundred fifty thousand missionaries are supported in a foreign missions program which has 2,450 ministers and 2,670 congregations in 64 countries; 37 summer campgrounds are maintained in the United States and Canada. Headquarters and a publishing house that issues the official *Pentecostal Herald* are located in St. Louis.

The church also sponsors an international radio broadcast on 275 stations, maintains a Youth Redemption Training Center for drug addicts in Lincoln, Nebraska, has 8 affiliated Bible colleges, and a children's home in Tupelo, Mississippi.

PILLAR OF FIRE

The Pillar of Fire originated from the evangelistic efforts of its founder, Mrs. Alma White. The wife of a Methodist minister in Colorado, Mrs. White often preached from her husband's pulpit. Her fervent exhortations on regeneration and holiness—and especially her habit of organizing missions and camp meetings on her own authority—brought her into sharp conflict with the bishops and other leaders of Methodism, and she withdrew to become an evangelistic free-lance. She established the Pentecostal Union in 1901 and changed the name to Pillar of Fire in 1917.

Mrs. White's first headquarters were located at Denver; they were later moved to Zarephath, near Bound Brook, New Jersey. In Denver and Zarephath the body has a college, preparatory school, Bible seminary, radio station, and publishing house. Other schools are located in Cincinnati; Los Angeles; Jacksonville, Florida; Pacifica, San Francisco, Seattle, Philadephia, Liberia (Africa), and London.

Modernism in theology is condemned by Pillar of Fire; its teaching is based upon primitive Wesleyanism, with doctrines on the inspiration and inerrancy of the Scriptures, repentance, justification, second blessing holiness, premillennialism, and future judgment. Sacraments include baptism and the Lord's Supper; marriage is a "divine institution."

Mrs. White was the first bishop of Pillar of Fire; on her death, authority passed to her 2 sons. (Bishop White's granddaughter, Arlene White Lawrence, a bishop, is now president and general superintendent of Pillar of Fire.) The membership is divided into 4 classes: probationary, associate, regular, and full, with only regular and full members being allowed to vote on administrative matters. There are deacons and deaconesses, and men and women are ordained as ministers; there are also consecrated deaconesses, licensed preachers, and missionaries and, as in Methodism, presiding elders (district superintendents) and bishops. Considerable literature is printed and distributed in the United States, and there are regular broadcasts from WAWZ, Zarephath, KPOF, Denver, and WAKW, Cincinnati. There were approximately 5,000 members and 61 branches as of 1949.

POLISH NATIONAL CATHOLIC CHURCH OF AMERICA

A strictly American church born on American soil, the Polish National Catholic Church of America was formally organized at Scranton, Pennsylvania, on March 14, 1897; behind this formality lay a long period of conflict between the Roman Catholic Church and many of the Poles who had immigrated to the United States around the turn of the century. Roman Catholic in homeland background, they objected that in the United States they had no bishops and few priests who were Polish, that they could not teach in Polish in their parish schools, and that under the ruling of the Roman Catholic Council of Baltimore in 1884 they had no right to establish parishes of their own. All this, they felt, gave the Roman hierarchy and priesthood an unwarranted religious, political, financial, and social power over their parishioners and permitted "an unlawful encroachment upon their right to private ownership and paved the way for the political and social exploitation of the Polish people." (Some scholars feel that the cause of dissension has roots further back, in the demand in Poland in the Reformation era for a Polish National church.) Resentment smoldered gradually into open revolt in Chicago, Detroit, Cleveland, Buffalo, and Scranton, and gradually resulted in the founding at Scranton of an independent Polish body with approximately 20,000 members mainly in the eastern states. This is the only break of any considerable size from the Roman Catholic Church in the

United States; but there are other groups among Slovaks, Lithuanians, Ruthenians, and Hungarians that have also broken away. Several of the Slovak and Lithuanian parishes have merged with the Polish National Catholic Church.

A constitution for the new church was adopted by the Scranton parish in 1897, claiming the right for the Polish people to control all churches built and maintained by them, to administer such church property through a committee chosen by the parish. The first synod was held at Scranton in 1904, with 146 clerical and lay delegates representing parishes in Pennsylvania, Maryland, Massachusetts, and New Jersey. The Rev. Francis Hodur, the organizer and dominant figure in the group, was chosen bishop-elect; he was consecrated bishop in 1907 at Utrecht, Holland, by 3 bishops of the Old Catholic Church. This synod also approved of the establishment of a seminary at Scranton. Following the synod, Polish gradually replaced Latin as the liturgical language.

The doctrine of this church is founded in the Holy Scripture, holy traditions, and 4 ecumenical synods of the undivided church. However, the following 3 councils are not rejected. The Apostles' and Nicene creeds are accepted. Doctrine is expanded in a confession of faith that includes belief in the Trinity, the Holy Spirit as the ruler of the world and the source of grace, the necessity of spiritual unity of all Christians, Christ's one body (the church), apostolic and universal, the church as teacher, steward of grace and a light unto salvation, the equal right of all men to life, happiness, and growth in perfection and equal responsibility toward God of all people and nations, immortality and the future justice and judgment of God. The doctrine of eternal damnation and punishment is supplanted in the church's Eleven Great Principles by an expressed hope and surety of universal salvation as taught in the church by Gregory of Nyssa and Clement of Alexandria. The seventh of their Eleven Great Principles reads:

We cannot conceive that God created man out of sheer caprice, nor selfishness . . . nor for the purpose of delivering him to devils for them to abuse and treat him cruelly by physical and spiritual torment and torture . . . but He created man that he should live his own life according to his creator's image.

Faith is necessary to salvation, but it must be manifest in good works. Sin is

a misunderstanding of the being and purpose of God on the part of the individual, the nation, and even all humanity. Left to himself . . . sinful man . . . deteriorates, wastes away; and surely would perish if not for the help of the Father Creator who does not desire the death of a sinner but rather that he be converted and live.

Seven sacraments are observed, with baptism and confirmation as one sacrament (confirmation is regarded as a completion of baptism). The seventh sacrament here is the hearing of the Word of God proclaimed by the church from the Scriptures. Two forms of confession are in general use—a private confession for children and youths and a general confession for adults only.

A general synod is the highest legislative authority in the government of the church. It meets every 4 years, except for such special sessions as may be considered necessary, and is composed of active bishops, clergy, and lay delegates from every parish. The administration and destiny of this church, according to its constitution, rests with the prime bishop. A supreme council meets annually, or on call, and is composed of all active bishops, 6 clerical and 14 lay delegates approved by the general synod. In like manner the authority of the diocese is vested in a diocesan bishop and diocesan synod that meets every 4 years. Each parish is governed by an elected board of trustees. There are approximately 282,400 members in about 160 parishes in the United States and Canada, divided into 5 dioceses: Buffalo, Pittsburgh, Canadian, Eastern, and Western. Polish and English are used in worship and in the educational programs of parish schools, taught largely by pastors. The clergy may marry, but only with the knowledge and permission of the bishops.

The Polish National Union, a fraternal and insurance organization established by Bishop Hodur in 1908, is set up on parish lines as an adjunct to parish life. It consists of 12 districts divided into 224 branches and has approximately 32,000 members, all of whom are not required to be members of the church.

A missionary work was begun in Poland in 1919, and by 1939 it had over 50 parishes and a theological seminary in Krakow. Missionary bishop Padewski was arrested by the Communists and died in prison during the same year; since that time the church in Poland has become autocephalous, but the 2 churches remain in theological and ideological harmony. In the United States there is a theological seminary in Scranton, Pennsylvania, and a home for the aged at Spojnia Farm, Waymart, Pennsylvania.

In 1912 the Lithuanian National Catholic Church was established under the jurisdiction of the Polish National Catholic Church. This church has a missionary work among the Poles in Brazil. As the only member of the Old Catholic Union of Utrecht, it has in recent years strengthened its ties with the European Old Catholics.

PRESBYTERIANS

Presbyterianism has 2 firm and deep roots: one goes back to the Greek word *presbuteros* ("elder") and has to do with the system of church government of ancient and apostolic times; the other goes back to John Calvin and the Protestant Reformation and has to do with the form of government used by all people calling themselves Presbyterian and holding the faith of the Reformed churches.

Calvin (1509-64) was a Frenchman trained for the law. Turning to theology, his keen, legalistic mind and his lust for freedom from the rigid, confining forms of Roman Catholicism drove him as a fugitive from Roman reprisal to the city of Geneva where he quickly grasped the reins of leadership in the Reformed sector of the Reformation. Resolute and often harsh with those who opposed him, he established himself and his theological system at the heart of a "city of God" in the Swiss capital, making it, according to Macaulay, the "cleanest and most wholesome city in Europe."

Calvin's whole thought revolved about the concept of sovereignty: "the sovereignty of God in his universe, the sovereignty of Christ in salvation, the sovereignty of the Scriptures in faith and conduct, the sovereignty of the individual conscience in the interpretation of the Will and Word of God."

His system has been summarized in 5 main points: human impotence, unconditional predestination, limited atonement, irresistible grace, and final perseverance. God, according to Calvinism, is sovereign and eternal ruler of the world; man is completely dominated by and dependent upon him.

The doctrine of God's eternal decree is held in harmony with the doctrine of his love to all mankind, his gift of his Son to be the propitiation for the sins of the whole world, and his readiness to bestow his saving grace on all who seek it; that concerning those who perish, the doctrine of God's eternal decree is held in harmony with the doctrine that God desires not the death of any sinner, but has provided in Christ a salvation sufficient for all, adapted to all, and freely offered in the gospel to all; that men are fully responsible for their treatment of God's gracious offer; that his decree hinders no man from accepting that offer; and that no man is condemned except on the ground of his sin. All dying in infancy are excluded in the election of grace, and are regenerated and saved by Christ through the Spirit, who works when and where and how he pleases. (Quoted from the declaratory statement in the Constitution of the United Presbyterian Church)

Out of this Calvinism came miracles of reform. Few reformers have made as many contributions as John Calvin in so many fields at once—in education, in the building of an intelligent ministry, in the liberation of the oppressed and persecuted, and in the establishment of democratic forms of government in both church and state. In his thought lay the germ that in time destroyed the divine right of kings. He gave a new dignity to man, and representative government to man's parliaments and church councils. He struck the final blow at feudalism and offered a spiritual and moral tone for dawning capitalism.

Strictly speaking, John Calvin did not found Presbyterianism; he laid the foundations upon which it was reconstructed in Switzerland, Holland, France, England, Scotland, and Ireland. He inspired fellow Frenchmen out of whose ranks came the Huguenots; by 1560 there were 2,000 churches of Presbyterian complexion in France. He influenced the Dutchmen who established the Dutch Reformed Church in Holland. He gave courage to British Presbyterians in their bitter struggle against Catholic Bloody Mary. To him came Scots who became Covenanters; to him came John Knox who went home to cry "Great God, give me Scotland, or I die." Knox and the Covenanters set Scotland afire and made it Protestant and Presbyterian.

A delegation of Scots sat in the Westminster Assembly of Divines along with 121 English ministers, 10 peers, and 20 members of the House of Commons, resolved to have "no bishop, and no king." This Westminster

Assembly is a milestone in Presbyterian history. Meeting at the call of Parliament to resolve the struggle over the compulsory use of the Anglican *Book of Common Prayer*, it sat for nearly 5 years (1643-48) in 1,163 sessions, produced a Larger and a Shorter Catechism, a directory for the public worship of God, a form of government, and the Westminster Confession of Faith, which, built upon the Old and New Testaments, became the doctrinal standard of Scottish, British, and American Presbyterianism.

Dominant in the Westminster Assembly, the Presbyterians soon dominated the British government. Cromwell completed the ousting of a monarch and established a commonwealth; the commonwealth crashed, the monarchy returned, and the fires of persecution flamed again. British Presbyterians fled to America with the Puritans; an attempt to establish episcopacy in Scotland after 1662 sent many Presbyterians out of Scotland into Ireland, where economic difficulties and religious inequalities drove them on to America. The Presbyterian British, and even more the Presbyterian Scotch-Irish, became the founders of Presbyterianism in America. Beginning in 1710 and running into midcentury, from 3,000 to 6,000 Scotch-Irish came annually into the American colonies, settling at first in New England and the middle colonies, then spreading out more widely than any other racial group ever to reach our shores.

There were Presbyterian congregations in the colonies long before the Scotch-Irish migration of 1710-50. One was worshiping in Virginia in 1611; others were worshiping in Massachusetts and Connecticut in 1630. Long Island and New York had congregations by 1640 and 1643. Francis Makemie ranged the coast from Boston to the Carolinas, planting churches and giving them unity with one another; 6 groups were united into the first presbytery in Philadelphia in 1706; in 1716 this first presbytery had become a synod made up of 4 presbyteries and held its first meeting in 1717.

United Presbyterian Church in the U.S.A.

Overwhelmingly the largest single body of Presbyterians in America, this church is the result of a merger (1958) of 2 groups in the United States: the Presbyterian Church in the U.S.A and the United Presbyterian Church of North America. We shall consider them first separately, under their original names, and then as a united church.

The Presbyterian Church in the U.S.A dates back to the organizing of the general presbytery in 1706. The first general synod of its spiritual forefathers, meeting in 1729, adopted the Westminister Confession of Faith with the Larger and Shorter catechisms "as being, in all essential and necessary articles, good forms of sound words, and systems of Christian doctrine." The same synod denied to the civil magistrates any power whatever over the church or any right to persecute anyone for his religious faith.

Free in the new land with their Scotch-Irish fire and Covenanter background, the Presbyterians quickly set about procuring trained ministers; creeds and colleges have been their stock in trade from the earliest days. William Tennent, Sr., organized a "log college" in a cabin at

Neshaminy, Pennsylvania. He started with 3 of his 4 sons as his first pupils, and this family school grew into the most important Presbyterian institution of higher learning in America. Out of it came the College of New Jersey (now Princeton University) and a stream of revivalistic Presbyterian preachers who played leading roles in the Great Awakening of the early eighteenth century. Prominent among them were William Tennent, Jr., and his brother Gilbert, who met and liked the British revivalist George Whitefield and followed him in preaching an emotional "new birth" revivalism, which came into conflict with the old creedal Calvinism. The camp-meeting revival grew out of the Great Awakening enthusiasm; it was born as a Presbyterian institution and was continued by the Methodists when the Presbyterians dropped it.

Presbyterian objection to emotional revivalism went deep; it split their church. Preachers took sides; those of the "old side" opposed revivalism, while those of the "new side" endorsed it, claiming that less attention should be paid to college training for the ministry and more to the recruiting of regenerated common men into the pulpit. The 2 sides quarreled until 1757, when they reunited; in 1758, the first year of the united synod, there were 98 ministers in the Presbyterian Church in the colonies, 200 congregations, and 10,000 members. One of the ablest of the new-side preachers was John Witherspoon, president of Princeton (founded in 1746), member of the Continental Congress, and the only ministerial signer of the Declaration of Independence.

Witherspoon may have been instrumental in the call of the general synod upon the Presbyterian churches to "uphold and promote" the resolutions of the Continental Congress. The Scotch-Irish accepted the revolution with relish; the persecution they had experienced in England and Ulster left them as natural dissenters and solidly anti-British. Their old cry, "No bishop and no king," was heard as far off as England; Horace Walpole supposedly remarked that "Cousin America" had run off with a Presbyterian parson.

The Presbyterians moved swiftly to strengthen their church after Yorktown, meeting as a synod at Philadelphia in 1788 at the same time that the national constitutional convention was in session in the same city. The national administrative bodies of American Presbyterianism were known as The Presbytery from 1706-16; as The Synod from 1717-88, and as The General Assembly from 1789 to the present time.

From 1790 to 1837 membership in the Presbyterian Church in the U.S.A increased from 18,000 to 220,557. This growth was due to the revival that swept the country during those years and to the plan of union with the Congregationalists. Under this plan Presbyterian and Congregational preachers and laymen moving into the new western territory worked and built together; preachers of the 2 denominations preached in each other's pulpits, and members held the right of representation in both Congregational association and Presbyterian presbytery. The plan worked well on the whole, absorbing the fruits of the national revivals and giving real impetus to missionary work both at home and abroad. Then came disagreements between Old School and New School factions within the church over matters of discipline and the expenditure of missionary money. The general assembly of 1837 expelled 4 New School presbyteries, which promptly met in their own convention at Auburn, New York. The Presbyterian Church in the U.S.A was split in two between New School men who wanted to keep the plan of union and Old School men who were suspicious of the "novelties of New England [Congregational] theology."

These years promised to be an era of expansion for the Presbyterians. Marcus Whitman drove the first team and wagon over the south pass of the Rockies into the great Northwest. After him came hosts of Presbyterian preachers and laymen building churches, schools, colleges, and seminaries. From 1812 to 1836 the Presbyterians in the United States built their first great theological seminaries: Princeton, Allegheny, Auburn, Columbia, Lane, McCormick, Union in Virginia, and Union in New York City. They also set up their own missionary and educational societies. But the era of unity suddenly became an era of schism. Even earlier than the Old-School–New-School division the Cumberland presbytery had broken away in 1810, following a dispute over the educational qualifications of the ministry, to form the Cumberland Presbyterian Church. Antislavery sentiment was increasing. A strong protest was made in 1818, but it was later modified. In 1846 the Old School assembly regarded slavery in the southern states as no bar to Christian communion; but the New School assembly took action in the same year, condemning it without reservation. By 1857 several New School southern synods had withdrawn to organize the United Synod of the Presbyterian Church, and the greater and final break came in 1861 when 47 Old School southern presbyteries formed their General Assembly of the Presbyterian Church in the Confederate States of America. In 1865 the United Synod and the Confederate churches merged into what is now known as the Presbyterian Church in the United States. The Synod of Kentucky united with it in 1869 and the Synod of Missouri in 1874.

The Old School and New School bodies, holding separate assemblies since 1837, were united in 1870 on the basis of the Westminster Confession; they were joined in 1906 by a large majority of the Cumberland churches and in 1920 by the Welsh Calvinistic Methodists.

From the 1920s through the 1950s, 2 strong emphases were noticeable in this church: one was the emphasis upon theology, seen in the struggle between liberals and conservatives; and the other was the emphasis upon Presbyterian unity. The latter was evident in the proposed merger with the Protestant Episcopal Church, which was not realized, and in the 1958 merger of the Presbyterian Church in the U.S.A. with the United Presbyterian Church of North America.

The United Presbyterian Church of North America was formed by the merging of the Associate Presbyterian Church and the Associate Reformed Presbyterian Church at Pittsburgh in 1858. The doctrines, traditions, and institutions of the 2 combining bodies were preserved; government in the united church followed the Presbyterian form with session, presbytery, synod, and a general assembly that met annually.

In matters of faith this church rested upon the broad foundation of the

Westminster Confession with certain modifications, one of which amended the chapter in the confession on the power of civil magistrates. A confessional statement of 44 articles was drawn up by the United Presbyterian Church in 1925; it contained the substance of the Westminster standards and symbols but restricted divorce cases to marital unfaithfulness, denied infant damnation, extended sacramental privileges to all who professed faith in Christ and led Christian lives, withdrew the protest against secret or oath-bound societies, abandoned the exclusive use of the psalms, maintained insistence upon the verbal inspiration of the Scriptures, affirmed the sufficiency and fullness of the provisions of God for the needs of Christ, emphasized the renewing and sanctifying power of the Holy Spirit, and held salvation to be free to all sinners.

There were no insurmountable doctrinal differences when the United Presbyterian Church of North America and the Presbyterian Church in the U.S.A. merged in 1958; there were the usual disagreements between theological conservatives and liberals, but on the whole they found agreement and unity in the doctrine of the Westminster Confession, which had been the accepted doctrinal statement of Presbyterianism in the United States since its adoption here in 1729. But as time passed, the conviction grew in the united church that a new statement or confession written, not against the background of seventeenth-century language, thought, and culture, but in the language of the twentieth century was needed and necessary to proclaim the gospel. The Westminister document was 300 years old; many felt that it was too much "bound by time." Accordingly, a special committee was appointed to prepare and present a new statement. Climaxing nearly 8 years of study and discussion, the 179th General Assembly of the church, meeting at Portland, Oregon, approved the committee's new "Confession of 1967" as a contemporary statement of faith. It was the first major change in 3 centuries.

Presbyterians now have a *Book of Confessions* containing not 1 creed or confession but 9: The Nicene Creed of 325, the second-century Apostles' Creed, the Scots Confession of 1560, the Heidelberg Catechism of 1563, the Second Helvetic Confession of 1566, the Westminster Confession of 1647, the Shorter Catechism of 1647, the Theological Declaration of Barmen (1934), and the Confession of 1967. The purpose of this arrangement of creeds and confessions was to trace the development of the great affirmations of the Christian faith, particularly through the Reformed tradition, to make clear the great common confessional belief of the majority of Christians in the world and to offer common ground for unity among those churches holding the Reformed position.

The Confession of 1967 is brief (4,200 words), avoids the confusing terminology of the Westminster Confession, and stresses the concepts of love, sin, eternal life, and (especially) the work of reconciliation in God, Christ, and the church. It is Christ-centered, emphasizing faith in Christ as Messiah and Lord and, generally, repeats in modern speech the standards of the Westminster Confession. While there is still some opposition (on the ground that it waters down some of the traditional statements of the

Westminster Confession), an overwhelming majority in the church has accepted it, convinced that it not only reflects the mind and faith of true Presbyterianism but offers as well a wide theological base upon which all Presbyterians can stand together.

Under the Presbyterian system of government, each congregation has its local session, which acts in receiving and disciplining members and in the general welfare of the church. Congregations in limited districts are grouped in presbyteries that examine, ordain, and install all ministers; review reports from the sessions and hear cases of complaint brought before them. The synod supervises the presbyteries of a larger district, reviews the records of its constituent presbyteries, organizes new presbyteries, and functions in an administrative capacity in all denominational matters lying within its jurisdiction. The highest judiciary is the annual general assembly, made up of clerical and lay delegates elected by the presbyteries on a proportional plan. The general assembly settles all matters of discipline and doctrine referred to it by the lower bodies, establishes new synods, appoints agencies and commissions, and reviews all appeals. Its decisions are final except that it cannot of itself amend the constitution of the church. The officers of the general assembly are the stated clerk (the chief executive officer), elected for 5 years with the privilege of reelection, and the moderator, chosen each year to preside over the session of the general assembly.

On the national level, a program of restructure concentrated direction of the work of the denomination in 3 new agencies—the Program Agency, the Vocation Agency, the Support Agency—and the General Assembly Mission Council. The General Assembly Mission Council recommends goals, objectives, policies, and the best possible use of all resources to the general assembly; oversees the implementation of decisions made by the general assembly; appropriates funds to agencies and synods; assesses the effectiveness of mission undertakings; coordinates policies, procedures, and practices established by the assembly. The Program Agency trains and deploys people in mission on all 6 continents—missionaries, fraternal workers, volunteers, church leaders, service people in human ministries; provides money and consultation that enable other units of the church at home and abroad to conduct programs in church development, evangelism, church education, and issue-responsive ministries; serves people with particular needs—refugees, disaster victims anywhere in the world, and people with needs related to military service; maintains relationships with Presbyterian education and health-care institutions around the world, with world and national ecumenical groups, and relates to other UPC councils and agencies at the national level. The Vocation Agency works in developing new ministries, providing placement counseling, training judicatory staff, setting guidelines for enlistment, career counseling, remuneration, and retirement (pensions). The Support Agency works in the general areas of communication, research, and finance; it provides news and information through the channels of press, radio, and television; is associated with *A.D.*, a magazine serving both the United Presbyterian Church in the U.S.A and the United Church of Christ; provides accounting counsel and functions and budget operations, oversees treasury functions, including payments made to and by all agencies, foreign accounting, banking and insurance management, supervises and informs on property management, the sale, rental, lease, and assigned use of property records management, central purchasing, marketing and distribution, office services, travel and overseas shipping, renders legal services such as property transfers, mortgages, church loans, and legal opinions.

Historically it is interesting to note the Presbyterian concern with Christian higher education. From the start, in this country, this church has insisted upon high standards of academic training for its ministers and has developed an admirable educational program for both clergy and laity. Today there are 53 United Presbyterian-related colleges and universities, 7 theological seminaries in the United States and 21 abroad, and a total of about 120 ministers and chaplains serving on college campuses.

The membership of the church stands at 2,569,437 in 8,656 churches as of 1977. There are 10 different Presbyterian denominations in the United States, with a total membership of over 4 million. Of these, well over 3 million are found in the United Presbyterian Church and the Presbyterian Church in the U.S. (southern). (This figure already needs revision, due to the recent defection of some 400 churches from the southern group.) Of the 10 groups, 5 are working together in the North American area of the Alliance of Reformed Churches Throughout the World Holding the Presbyterian Order, organized in 1875.

Presbyterian Church in the United States

The establishment and historical background of this church have already been described (see p. 207). Popularly known today as Southern Presbyterians, they are still separated from the Northern Presbyterians in the United Presbyterian Church in the U.S.A., in differences that are theological, ecclesiastical, administrative, and social in nature, but there are still evidences of cooperation in missionary planning, in 2 colleges and 1 theological seminary. Probably more than either of the other 2 churches in "the big 3," (Presbyterians, Methodists, and Baptists), the Presbyterian Church in the U.S. has led the effort to integrate black churches into the denomination and to open the doors of their conferences, colleges, and seminaries to those of all races.

Through all its history, the Presbyterian Church in the United States has been characterized by a continuing demand for freedom and intelligence in both politics and religion—a fundamental concept and drive brought here by the Scotch-Irish Presbyterian dissenters who migrated from the north of Ireland to settle in the American South. Their influence in the establishment of the American commonwealth has run wide and deep. Virginia and North Carolina presbyteries were calling for American independence long before the Boston riots and the Liberty Bell; the Mecklenberg (North Carolina) presbytery was the first ecclesiastical body in the colonies to approve the Declaration of Independence. Presbyterian civic leaders brought law and order to many areas of the South before colonial officials could be appointed or elected; with their distinguishing passion for education, Presbyterian ministers taught school before there was any organized system of public education in the region. In parallel patriotic passion they were prominent in both French and Indian and Revolutionary wars and in the long struggle for religious liberty and the rights of religious dissenters. With the Baptists they laid in church and school the spiritual, political, moral, and intellectual foundations of the famous Jeffersonian "Act for Establishing Religious Freedom" in Virginia, which preceded similar statements concerning the same rights and freedoms in the Constitution of the United States. Their missionary zeal was evident in their presence in the first wagons and wagon trains that moved out through the Mississippi Valley to the West.

Doctrinally they are of course Calvinistic. As in most Reformed churches, ministers, elders, and deacons are required to give adherence to a confessional statement. Women are now admitted to the ministry and eldership and are encouraged to enlist in other government fields of Christian work. Polity government and doctrine follow the Presbyterian pattern.

The are 7 synods and 59 presbyteries, 4,036 churches, and 877,664 members in 18 states. The church supports 4 theological seminaries—Austin, Columbia, Louisville, and Union (Richmond)—15 colleges and 1 other affiliated college, 5 junior colleges, 4 secondary schools, 2 missions schools, and 1 school of religious education, 18 children's homes, and 20 homes for the aged. Home missionary work is conducted among the Indians and Latin Americans in Texas and Oklahoma, in the Ozarks and Appalachians; the work is marked not only by financial support but by concern for comity in churching the several areas, in urban problems, etc. Abroad, a missionary force of 519 is at work in Mexico, Ecuador, Brazil, Taiwan, Korea, Japan, Portugal, Iraq, Vietnam, and the Congo; they serve not only Presbyterian churches and missions but many indigenous projects as well. There are 29 periodicals published by the Board of Education, which also operates the John Knox Press.

The Presbyterian Church in America

Organized at a constitutional assembly in December, 1973, this church was known first as the Continuing Presbyterian Church, then as the National Presbyterian Church, and finally as the Presbyterian Church in America. It represents a separation from the Presbyterian Church in the United States (southern). The dissenting group stood in opposition to what they considered to be a long-developing liberalism in that church, a liberalism that did not emphasize the historic Presbyterian positions on the inerrancy and infallibility of Scripture. Also involved were questions of the position of the church on marriage and divorce, the admission of women to church offices, the affiliation of the parent body with the National Council of the Churches of Christ in the U.S.A. and the World Council of Churches and the movement toward merger with the more liberal United Presbyterian Church in the U.S.A. (northern).

Basic in the debates that led to the separation was the question of firm subscription to the Westminster Confession of Faith and the Larger and Shorter catechisms of the Westminster Assembly with their distinctive doctrines. The dissenting body "readopted" the confession and the catechism; they hold firmly to a conservative Calvinism in doctrine and theology.

The "PCA" maintains the historic Presbyterian polity and the rule of the church by elders; there is the usual session, presbytery, and general assembly, but it puts a new emphasis on the parity of the teaching ministers, elders, and the ruling elders; these are viewed as of equal authority in all the church courts. The work of the church is carried on by 3 major committees—Mission to the World, Mission to the United States, and Christian Education and Publications. At the present time it has no centralized headquarters but has administrative offices in Columbus, Georgia; Jackson, Mississippi; Decatur, Georgia; and Montgomery, Alabama. Their stated clerk is located in Clinton, Mississippi.

Statistics of December, 1977, reveal 66,461 members in 405 churches.

Associate Reformed Presbyterian Church

This is a synod of the former Associate Reformed Presbyterian Church; it is a body of Covenanter origins and traditions. ("Covenant" here refers to the Reformed branch of the church. The Associate Presbyterian Church of North America, in distinction, is of Seceder origin; the Associate Reformed Church is a result of the union of the Associate and Reformed groups.) Feeling that the distances that separated them from their fellow members in the North were too great, the synod of the Carolinas withdrew in 1822 from the Associate Reformed Church to form the Associate Reformed Synod of the South. Following the creation of the United Presbyterian Church in 1848 (which this group never joined), they dropped the phrase "of the South," thereby becoming the Associate Reformed Presbyterian Church. They became a general synod in 1935.

The standards of the Westminster Confession are followed. For some years the only music in this church was the singing of the psalms; this was modified in 1946 to permit the use of hymns. Foreign mission stations are located in Pakistan and Mexico. *The Associate Reformed Presbyterian* is published weekly at Greenville, South Carolina; Erskine College and Erskine Theological Seminary are located at Due West, South Carolina. The William Dunlap Orphanage is located at Brighton, Tennessee. There is an assembly ground, "Bonlarken," at Flat Rock, North Carolina. Total membership is placed at 31,854 in 157 churches.

Bible Presbyterian Church

In 1936 during the fundamentalist-modernist controversy in the Presbyterian churches, a group of about 100 ministers, led by Dr. J. Gresham Machen of Princeton Theological Seminary, withdrew from the

Presbyterian Church in the U.S.A. to establish the Presbyterian Church in America, later renamed the Orthodox Presbyterian Church. Two years later, with the controversy still raging and complicated by the formation of an American Council of Christian Churches and an International Council of Christian Churches, a group led by Dr. Carl McIntire withdrew from this Orthodox Presbyterian Church to organize the Bible Presbyterian Church; the group also withdrew from both councils in 1955. A majority of the local churches, however, continued in the councils through the Bible Presbyterian Church Association. The general synod of the next year, 1956, divided into 2 synods—the Bible Presbyterian Church (Columbus Synod) and the Bible Presbyterian Church (Collingswood Synod). So from 1956 to July, 1961, there were 2 separate Bible Presbyterian churches representing the 2 different synods. In 1961 the Bible Presbyterian Church (Columbus Synod) changed its name to the Evangelical Presbyterian Church, which later (1965) united with the Reformed Presbyterian Church in North America to become the Reformed Presbyterian Church, Evangelical Synod. In the same year the Collingswood body dropped that name and continued as the Bible Presbyterian Church.

The word "Bible" is included in the name of this church to emphasize its conservative, Bible-based position. It is thoroughly fundamentalist, subscribing to the Westminster Confession of Faith (including the Larger and Shorter catechisms); it opposes all "social gospel" teaching and refuses to have fellowship with "that which compromises and which represents unbelief " in such doctrines as those of the verbal and infallible inspiration of the Bible, the virgin birth, the blood atonement, and the bodily resurrection of Christ. Through the American Council of Christian Churches it carries on a continuing debate with the National Council of the Churches of Christ in the U.S.A., which it considers apostate, and through the International Council of Christian Churches it stands opposed to the ecumenical policies and liberal doctrine of the World Council of Churches.

There are distinct breaks here with the usual Presbyterian polity. The property of the local church is guaranteed to the church itself. Local congregations may call their pastors "without interference" (by presbyteries, synods, etc.). Any church may withdraw at any time "for reasons sufficient to themselves." The work of the church is carried on through independent agencies, such as the Independent Board for Foreign Missions and Faith Theological Seminary, "leaving the presbyteries and synods as places for fellowship." There are about 8,000 members.

Cumberland Presbyterian Church

An outgrowth of the great revival of 1800, the Cumberland Presbytery was organized on February 4, 1810, in Dickson County, Tennessee, by 3 Presbyterian ministers, the Revs. Finis Ewing, Samuel King, and Samuel McAdow. Contributing factors to the organization were a rejection by the founders of the doctrine of fatality of the Westminster Confession of Faith and an insistence that the rigid standards of the Presbyterian Church for the education of the clergy be relaxed in the light of extraordinary circumstances existing on the American frontier. A union with the Presbyterian Church, U.S.A, in 1906 was only partially successful. A considerable segment, to whom the terms of union were unsatisfactory, perpetuated the Cumberland Presbyterian Church as a separate denomination.

This church reports 87,649 members in 857 congregations located for the most part in 11 southern states, with some congregations in the states of Indiana, Illinois, Ohio, Michigan, Iowa, Kansas, New Mexico, and California.

The church sponsors missionaries in Colombia, Japan, and Hong Kong. Memphis Theological Seminary of the church is located at Memphis and Bethel College at McKenzie. There is a children's home at Denton, Texas. Frontier Press, denominational headquarters, and a resource center are also at Memphis.

Second Cumberland Presbyterian Church in the United States
(Formerly Colored Cumberland Presbyterian Church)

This church was built on the 20,000 black membership of the pre–Civil War Cumberland Presbyterian Church with the full approval of the general assembly of that church held in 1869. The first 3 presbyteries were organized in Tennessee, where the first synod, the Tennessee Synod, was organized in 1871. In doctrine this church follows the Westminster Confession with 4 reservations: (1) there are no eternal reprobates; (2) Christ died for all mankind, not for the elect alone; (3) there is no infant damnation; and (4) the Spirit of God operates in the world coextensively with Christ's atonement in such manner "as to leave all men inexcusable." There were 19 presbyteries, 4 synods—Alabama, Tennessee, Kentucky, and Texas—121 churches, and 30,000 members found in all sections of the country in 1949. In May of 1940 the general assembly accepted an overture from a presbytery of 17 churches and 1 school in Liberia, Africa, and voted to make it a part of the Second Cumberland Presbyterian Church.

Orthodox Presbyterian Church

This church was organized June 11, 1936, in protest against what were believed to be modernistic tendencies in the Presbyterian Church in the U.S.A. (now the United Presbyterian Church in the U.S.A.). Led by Dr. J. Gresham Machen, the dissenters had formed a foreign missionary society that they were ordered to disband; refusing, they were tried, convicted, and suspended from the Presbyterian Church in the U.S.A. They organized the Presbyterian Church of America; an injunction brought against the use of that name by the parent body resulted in the change in 1938 to the name Orthodox Presbyterian Church.

The Westminster Confession and the Westminster Larger and Shorter catechisms are accepted as subordinate doctrinal standards or creedal statements. Strong emphasis is laid upon the infallibility and inerrancy of the

Bible (the books of the Bible were written by men "so guided by Him that their original manuscripts were without error in fact or doctrine"); original sin; the virgin birth, deity, and substitutionary atonement of Christ; his resurrection and ascension; his role as judge at the end of the world and the consummation of the Kingdom; the sovereignty of God; and salvation through the sacrifice and power of Christ for those "whom the Father purposes to save." Salvation is "not because of good works, [but] it is in order to do good works."

The Presbyterian system of government is followed; a general assembly meets annually. The church constitution contains the creedal statement of the group, a form of government, book of discipline, and directory for the worship of God. The church has published the *Trinity Hymnal*, which is probably the only hymnal designed as a worship supplement to the Westminster Confession of Faith. Committees appointed by the general assembly conduct work in home and foreign mission, Christian education, and general benevolence. With 15,800 members in 133 churches and 36 chapels, the church is a constituent member of the Reformed Ecumenical Synod, an international association of churches holding the Reformed faith.

Reformed Presbyterian Church, Evangelical Synod

A Reformed Presbyterian Church was founded in 1774 in Dolphin County, Pennsylvania; in 1965 it merged with the Evangelical Presbyterian Church, which had split from the Orthodox Presbyterian Church in 1937.

It is biblical in theology and subscribes to the Westminster Confession and catechisms. It operates Covenant Theological Seminary in St. Louis and Covenant College at Lookout Mountain, Georgia. Their National Missions Board assists in establishing new local churches in the United States and Canada, and a Board of Home Ministries and Christian Training is active in educational work. They have 10 chaplains on active duty with the armed forces. There are 19,669 members in 154 churches and 21 missions. The church is currently exploring possibilities of merger with the Presbyterian Church in America and/or the Orthodox Presbyterian Church.

Reformed Presbyterian Church of North America

A body of direct Covenanter lineage, its first minister came to this country from the Reformed Presbytery of Scotland in 1752. Most of the early membership joined the union with the Associate Presbytery in 1782, but a small group remained outside the union and reorganized at Philadelphia under the name Reformed Presbytery in 1798. A synod was constituted at Philadelphia in 1809, only to split in 1833 into Old Light and New Light groups in a dispute over citizenship and the right of its members to vote or participate generally in public affairs; the general synod of the Reformed Presbyterian Church (New Light) imposed no such restriction. This restriction was finally removed in 1964; members are free to participate in civil government and to vote on issues and for candidates who are committed to Christian principles of civil government.

Special emphasis is given to the inerrancy of Scripture, the sovereignty of God, and the Lordship of Christ over every area of human life. The government is thoroughly Presbyterian, except that there is no general assembly. Members use only the psalms in their worship services, and no instrumental music is permitted. Members cannot join secret societies.

Home missionaries are opening new work in 7 states under a Board of Home Missions and Church Extension; foreign missionaries are stationed in Japan and Taiwan. There is a college at Beaver Falls, Pennsylvania (Geneva College), a theological seminary at Pittsburgh, and one home for the aged. The denomination is a member of the National Association of Evangelicals and of the North American Presbyterian and Reformed Council. There are 5,155 members in 69 congregations and 7 mission stations.

This church was merged with the Associate Presbyterian Church of North America in 1969.

REFORMED BODIES

When the Belgic Confession was written in 1561 as the creedal cornerstone of the Reformed churches in Belgium and Holland, the "Churches in the Netherlands which sit under the Cross" gave thanks to their God in the preface of that document, where they said, "The blood of our brethren . . . crieth out." There was real cause for crying out, but the Reformation was spreading into the Netherlands from Switzerland in the midst of the long Dutch struggle against Catholic Spain. The Dutch Reformed Church was cradled in cruelty.

Those Reformation-founded churches called Reformed, as distinguished from those called Lutheran, originated in Switzerland under Zwingli, Calvin, and Melanchthon; they were Reformed in Switzerland, Holland, and Germany; they were Presbyterian in England and Scotland, and Huguenot in France; still others in Bohemia and Hungary used national names. As they moved overseas to the American colonies, they formed into 40 groups of churches; 2 from Holland became the Reformed Church in America and the Christian Reformed Church; 1 from the German Palatinate became the Reformed Church in the United States, later known as the Evangelical and Reformed Church and now merged with the Congregational Christian churches in the United Church of Christ; the fourth, coming from Hungary, became the Free Magyar Reformed Church in America. All of them were and still are Calvinistic and conservative, basing their doctrine generally upon the Heidelberg Catechism, the Belgic Confession, and the Canons of the Synod of Dordrecht, and using a modified Presbyterian form of government.

Reformed Church in America

This church had an unorganized membership along the upper reaches of the Hudson River in the neighborhood of Fort Orange (Albany), New York, in 1614. Members had no regularly established congregations or churches; but they were numerous enough to require the services of Reformed ministers, 2 of whom came from Holland in 1623 as "comforters of the sick." By 1628 the Dutch in New Amsterdam had a pastor of their own in Dominie Jonas Michaelius and an organized Collegiate Church, which was to become the oldest church in the middle colonies and the oldest church in America with an uninterrupted ministry.

When the English took New Amsterdam in 1664, Dutch churches were thriving in Albany, Kingston, Brooklyn, Manhattan, and at Bergen in New Jersey. As the immigration from Holland ceased, there were perhaps 8,000 Dutch churchmen and churchwomen in the country, holding their services in Dutch and served by either native clergymen or pastors sent from Holland. It was difficult and expensive to send native-born ministerial candidates to Holland for education and ordination; the question rent the Reformed Church and was finally resolved in the building of a college and seminary at New Brunswick (Queen's College, later Rutgers). It was the first theological seminary to be built in this country, and it was fathered by the famous Dominie Theodore Frelinghuysen, who also took a leading part in the revival called the Great Awakening.

A sharp controversy disputing the authority of the classis of Amsterdam resulted in the complete independence of the Dutch churches in America; a general body and 5 particular bodies were created, a constitution was drawn up in 1792, and the general synod was organized in 1794. The names Dutch Reformed Church in North America and Reformed Dutch Church in the United States of America were both in use in 1792; in 1819 the church was incorporated as the Reformed Protestant Dutch Church, and in 1867 it became the Reformed Church in America.

The American Revolution had little effect upon the Reformed Church in America except to offer the Dutchmen a chance to even matters with the English. Once the war was over, Scottish, English, and Germans began joining the church, creating a problem in the use of the Dutch tongue which took years to resolve. A second Dutch emigration from the Netherlands started in the middle of the nineteenth century, bringing whole Dutch congregations with their pastors. One group, led by Dominie Albertus van Raalte, settled in western Michigan and established the community called Holland, known today for Hope College, Western Theological Seminary, and an annual tulip festival. Van Raalte and his group became part of the Reformed Church in America in 1850. Another colony, led by Dominie Scholte, settled in Pella, Iowa, in 1847-48 and in 1856 merged with the Reformed Church in America except for a small dissenting group.

Domestic missions began in 1786; actually, missionary work among the Indians had begun much earlier. Needy and destitute churches in New York, Pennsylvania, and Kentucky were assisted by the domestic missionaries of the classis of Albany for many years, and in 1806 the general synod took over administration of all missionary agencies. This church cooperated with the American Board of Commissioners for Foreign Missions. In 1832 the Board of Foreign Missions was created but continued to work through the American Board until 1857, from which time it has operated independently. Insisting from the start upon 7 years of college and seminary training for its ministers, the church established the Education Society of the Reformed Church in America in 1828 and changed it to the Board of Education of the General Synod in 1831.

The explicit statements and principles of the Belgic Confession, the Heidelberg Catechism, and the Synod of Dordrecht are still the doctrinal standard of the Reformed Church in America. The mild and gentle spirit of the confession with its emphasis upon salvation through Christ is a central theme; the primacy of God and his power in human life are at the heart of the preaching of the church, as they are at the heart of the canons of Dordrecht; and the Heidelberg Catechism, based as it is on the Apostles' Creed, is employed in many catechetical classes. The divine authority of the Scriptures is important here; "the final authority in the Reformed faith is the Holy Scripture, the living Word of God, spoken to every man through the Holy Spirit of God."

Worship is semiliturgical, but it is an optional liturgy; only the forms for baptism and the Lord's Supper, the 2 recognized sacraments of the church, are obligatory. It is a corporate, or congregational, way of worship, blending form and freedom and distinguishing this church from other Protestant communions. A new edition of the liturgy and psalter was published in 1968.

Government of the church stands midway between the Episcopal and Presbyterian forms; it might be called "modified Presbyterian." The governing body in the local church is the consistory, made up of elders, deacons, and the pastor, who is always president. Elders are charged with the guidance of the spiritual life of the church, and deacons are in charge of benevolences; but they generally meet and act as one body. A number of churches in a limited area are grouped into a classis, which has immediate supervision of the churches and the ministry and is composed of all the ministers of the area and an elder from each consistory. Classes are grouped into particular synods, of which there are 6, meeting annually and made up of an equal number of ministers and elders from each classis and supervising the planning and programming of the churches within the area. The higher court of the church is the general synod, representing the entire church, meeting once a year and composed of delegations of ministers and elders from each classis; the size of the delegation depends upon the size of the classis.

In 1968 this church underwent a process of "restructure" that drastically changed its form of government. Formerly there were 4 national boards (world missions, North American missions, education, and pensions) together with agencies working under these boards; the boards have now been unified in a general program council, which has taken over their responsibilities. There are fewer board members under this plan, but each of the 44 classes in the United States has a representative on the council. The program staff is assisted by 3 "service offices" (administration and finance, promotion and communications, and human resources). As of 1973 a further process of decentralization is taking place: new "centers" will be organized on a regional basis, to expedite work peculiar to those regions.

Foreign missionaries are appointed to work in 11 areas abroad; home missionaries work among Dutch immigrants in Canada, and among Chinese, Japanese-Americans, blacks, Indians, migrants, and sharecroppers. Scholarships and student aid are provided in 3 colleges and 2 theological seminaries. Membership in 1978 stood at 350,734 in 902 churches.

Christian Reformed Church

With a membership of 287,114 in 750 churches, this Reformed group began in Michigan in 1847 and was affiliated with the Reformed Church in America from 1850 to 1857, when they found themselves in disagreement with the parent church on matters of doctrine and discipline. A conference held at Holland, Michigan, in 1857, effected the separation of the True Holland Reformed Church from the Reformed Church in America. Through a series of changes in name, the True Holland Reformed Church became the present Christian Reformed Church. Emigration from Holland brought several other groups into the new organization and rapidly increased its membership.

The Christian Reformed Church today is largely an English-speaking church, although Dutch, German, Navajo, and Spanish are used in some of their churches. Doctrine shows no important differences from accepted Reformed standards; the 3 historic creeds are accepted. Organization bears the usual Reformed markings, including 37 classes that meet every 4 months (in some cases every 6 months) but with no intermediate or particular synods between the classes and a general synod made up of 2 ministers and 2 elders from each classis meets annually.

One hundred eighty-five home missionaries in Canada and the United States maintain ministries among the unchurched, Navajo and Zuni Indians, blacks, Chinese, Spanish-Americans, and on many university campuses. One hundred fifty-eight foreign missionaries are stationed in Japan, South America, Northern Nigeria, Cuba, Taiwan, Mexico, Guam, Korea, Puerto Rico, the Philippines, Australia, Honduras, and Liberia. The Christian Reformed World Relief Committee carries on a worldwide relief program.

The "Back to God Hour" radio broadcast from a chain of stations in the United States and superpower stations abroad reaches Canada, Europe, Africa, and Asia as well as North and South America; a TV ministry known as CRC–TV also broadcasts in the United States and Canada. There are 3 colleges—Calvin College and Seminary in Grand Rapids, Dordt College in Sioux Center, Iowa, and Trinity College in Palos Heights, Illinois. A publishing house is located in Grand Rapids, providing literature for the church at large and for the unique Christian school societies made up of parents who work to support a national educational program.

221

Hungarian Reformed Church in America

The Hungarian Reformed Church in America is the successor to a work begun in the United States by the Reformed Church of Hungary in 1904. Work among Hungarian Reformed people had actually begun in 1891 under the auspices of other interested Calvinistic groups, but that sponsored by the parent body in Hungary soon became the most vital and popular, and by 1912 there were 2 classes affiliated with the church in Hungary. With the break-up of the Austro-Hungarian Empire and the impoverishment of Hungary, the Reformed Church in that country transferred jurisdiction of its churches in the United States to the Reformed Church in the United States, in an agreement reached at Tiffin, Ohio, in 1921. Three of the original congregations and 4 more recently organized refused to accept the agreement, and united to form the Free Magyar Reformed Church in America at Duquesne, Pennsylvania, in 1924. The present name was adopted in 1958.

The church's polity is a combination of Synod-Presbyterian elements developed in Hungary in the eighteenth century. It is made up of 3 classes—New York, Eastern, and Western—that form a diocese headed by an elected bishop and lay curator. Doctrinal standards are those of the Heidelberg Catechism and the Second Helvetic Confession. Synodical meetings are held annually, and a "constitutional" meeting is held every 3 years. There are 23 congregations with 4,878 baptized members in 10 states: Connecticut, New York, New Jersey, Pennsylvania, Ohio, Michigan, Florida, Kansas, Colorado, and California. There are also 2 congregations in Ontario, Canada. The church is a constituent member of the World Alliance of Reformed Churches, the National Council of Churches, and the World Council of Churches.

Netherlands Reformed Congregations

This is the smallest of all Reformed groups in the United States; it has 22 churches and 7,319 communicants and 4,195 baptized members. Its short history began with a secession from the state church in Holland; Dutch emigrants formed their first 2 churches in South Holland, Illinois (1865), and Grand Rapids, Michigan (1870), basing their belief on the Belgic Confession, the Heidelberg Catechism, and the Canons of Dordrecht. There are 9 additional churches in Canada, with a total of 8 Sunday schools and 7 clergymen; a synod meets every 2 years.

Protestant Reformed Churches in America

Three consistories of the Classis Grand Rapids East and Grand Rapids West of the Christian Reformed Church, with their pastors, were deposed from that church as the result of a disagreement over the doctrine of common grace (Arminianism). The debate began in 1923; the dissenters were formally organized as Protestant Reformed Churches of America in 1926. They stand for particular grace, for the elect alone, and hold to the 3 Reformed confessions—the Heidelberg Catechism, the Belgic, or Netherlands, Confession, and the Canons of Dordrecht—as the basis of their belief in the infallible Word of God. In government they are Presbyterian, subscribing to the 87 Articles of the Church Order of Dordrecht. Their general synod meets annually in June.

A small theological seminary is maintained at Grand Rapids. An association of Protestant Reformed men in the same city publishes a bimonthly periodical known as *The Standard Bearer*; and another publication, a monthly called *Beacon Lights*, issued by the denomination's young people's federation. There are 4,000 members in 21 churches located in Michigan, Illinois, Iowa, Wisconsin, Minnesota, Colorado, California, Washington, North and South Dakota, Texas, and New Jersey.

Reformed Church in the United States

This body, originally, was made up of Swiss and German emigrants arriving in this country in the 1700s, formerly operating under the auspices of the Dutch Reformed Synod of South and North Holland. It separated from the synod in 1793. The name "German" was dropped in 1869, and it has since been known as the Reformed Church in the United States. It merged into the Evangelical and Reformed Church in 1934 and in 1957 merged with the Congregational and Christian churches into the United Church of Christ. One group, the Eureka Classis in South Dakota, refused to become a part of the united church, and continued as the Reformed Church in the United States. Their doctrines are those set forth in the Heidelberg Catechism; they have 26 churches and an inclusive membership of 4,008 baptized and communicant members and 27 active ministers.

ROMAN CATHOLIC CHURCH

For the first 1,500 years of Christendom up to the time of the Protestant Reformation, the Western world was almost solidly Roman Catholic. The eleventh-century separation left the faith divided between Roman Catholic and Eastern Orthodox sectors. The Reformation left continental Europe and the British Isles divided among Roman Catholic, Lutheran, Anglican, and Reformed churches, with the prospect of still further division as denominationalism increased.

The Roman Catholic Church dates its beginning from the moment of Christ's selection of the apostle Peter as guardian of the keys of heaven and earth and as chief of the apostles, and it claims this fisherman as its first pope. It gained temporal authority and power when it arose as the only body strong enough to rule after the fall of the city of Rome in A.D. 410. A house of terror ravaged first by Goths, Vandals, and Franks, and then by Saxons, Danes, Alemanni, Lombards, and Burgundians, Europe found its only steadying hand in the church. Without the church, anarchy would have been king from Britain to the Bosphorus.

The first mention of the term "Catholic" (meaning "universal") "Church" was made by Ignatius about A.D. 110-15, but the first real demonstrations of its Roman authority came as it won the barbarians to its banners while it kept the flame of faith burning in its churches and the candle of wisdom alive in its monastic schools. Augustine deeply influenced its theological and philosophical structure, and he gave papacy its finest justification and defense. He left it strong enough to give crowns or deny them to Europe's kings.

The church beat back the threats of its enemies at home and from afar; it converted the barbarian, won against the Saracen, and employed the Inquisition against the heretic boring from within. It brought the hopeful interval known as the Peace of God; it also supported chivalry and feudalism, fought the Crusades, built schools, created a noble art and literature. For long centuries the Benedictine monasteries guarded and preserved learning and culture in Europe; this order of monks was founded in 529 in Italy by St. Benedict; since its founding, more than 4 million men have practiced the Benedictine rule of life. Centuries later (1209) St. Francis of Assisi established the Franciscan order, and at about the same time St. Dominic began his Order of Friars Preachers (Dominicans).

Inevitably there came the temptations of power and prosperity from without. Then came the Reformation. Roman Catholic scholars readily admit that there were corrupt individuals within the church and that reform was necessary. Indeed, reform was underway before the Reformation broke; Martin Luther himself was a Catholic reformer within the church before he became a Protestant. Erasmus and Savonarola wrote and preached against the corruption and worldliness of certain Roman Catholic leaders and laymen, but they stayed within the church. That all these reformers had a case against the members of the Roman church is not denied by the Roman Catholics; they do, however, maintain that while priests and bishops and even popes may err, the one true church cannot err, and that Luther was wrong in rebelling against the church. But rebel he did, and the Roman church suffered its most fateful division.

There were, too, other reasons for the revolt. There was the growth of nationalism and secularism, the ambitions of political princes and rulers with great personal ambitions who wanted no interference from the church. And there was the Renaissance, with its revival of Greek and Roman pagan influences and emphases. All these forces worked together to produce the Reformation. The counter Reformation was effective in halting the spread of the new Protestantism in Europe and effective in halting the spread of the new Protestantism in Europe and won back some areas to the Roman Catholic Church and faith; one of its chief instruments was the Society of Jesus (Jesuits), an educational and missionary order founded by Ignatius of Loyola in 1534.

But long before Luther, Roman Catholics had reached America. The first Roman Catholic diocese on this side of the Atlantic was established in Greenland in 1125; there were bishops in residence there until 1377. Priests of Catholic Spain came with Columbus in 1492; missionaries came with Coronado and with the other early Spanish explorers. Most of them perished; one of them started the first permanent parish in America at St. Augustine, Florida, in 1565.

French explorers, *voyageurs*, and colonizers—Cartier, Joliet, Marquette, and others—were generally Roman Catholics accompanied by missionary groups. Among them were the Recollects, Jesuits, Sulpicians, Capuchins, and the secular clergy. New France became a vicariate apostolic in 1658 with Bishop Laval at its head. The See of Quebec (1675) had spiritual jurisdiction over all the vast province of France in North America, reaching down the valley of the Mississippi to Louisiana.

In 1634 the Roman Catholics founded Maryland; later they were restricted by law in Maryland and in most other colonies, and the restrictions were not removed until after the Revolution. In the face of these restrictions and in view of the fact that most of the colonial immigrants were Protestants, the Roman Catholic Church grew slowly. In 1696 there were only 7 Catholic families in New York, and 80 years later they were still traveling to Philadelphia to receive the sacraments. In 1763 there were fewer than 25,000 Catholics out of a population of 2,200,000 in the colonies; they were under the jurisdiction of the vicar apostolic of London.

Among the signatures on the Articles of Confederation, the Declaration of Independence, and the Constitution are found those of Thomas Fitzsimmons, Daniel Carroll, and Charles Carroll of Carrollton, all of whom were Catholics. The Revolution brought them religious as well as political freedom; religious equality became the law with the adoption of the Constitution in 1787.

There was no immediate hierarchal superior in the United States when the war ended, and the vicar apostolic in London refused to exercise jurisdiction over the "rebels." After long investigation and delay and an appeal to Rome, the Rev. John Carroll was named superior, or prefect apostolic, of the church in the 13 original states. At that time there were 15,800 Catholics in Maryland, 700 in Pennsylvania, 200 in Virginia, and 1,500 in New York, unorganized and with no priests. At the turn of the century there were 80 churches and about 150,000 Roman Catholics; by 1890 there were 6,231,417—a growth due primarily to the flood tide of emigration from the Catholic countries of Europe. Today the nearly 50 million members of the Roman Catholic Church make up about one quarter of the population of the United States.

Baltimore became the first American diocese in 1789 and an archdiocese in 1808; other dioceses and archdioceses were formed as the church expanded. Three plenary, or national, councils were held at Baltimore in 1852, 1866, and 1884. Archbishop John McCloskey of New York became the first American cardinal in 1875, and Archbishop James Giggons of Baltimore was elevated to the same rank in 1877.

The Civil War and 2 world wars failed to disturb the work of the church or to interrupt its growth; indeed World War I produced one of the ablest hierarchal Roman Catholic agencies in the country—the National War Council, now known as the United States Catholic Conference. There were

18,608,003 Catholics in the United States in 1926; by 1977 the Roman Catholic Church had become the largest church in the United States, with 49,325,752 members in approximately 18,250 churches. About 23 percent of the American people identified themselves as Roman Catholics.

The faith and doctrine of Catholicism are founded upon "that deposit of faith given to it by Christ and through his apostles, sustained by the Bible and by tradition." Thus, they accept as official creeds the Apostles' Creed, the Nicene-Constantinople Creed, the Athanasian Creed, and the Creed of Pius IV, also called the Creedal Statement of the Council of Trent.

Roman Catholics, like the Eastern Orthodox, believe in 7 sacraments. Baptism, necessary for membership in the church, is administered to infants and adults by pouring or immersion, and all baptized persons are considered to be members of the church. Confirmation by the laying on of hands and anointing with the holy chrism in the form of a cross follows baptism; the ordinary minister of this sacrament is the bishop, but priests may also confirm. The laity usually receive the Eucharist (Lord's Supper) in the form of bread alone; the body and blood of Christ are considered as actually present in the eucharistic elements. The sacrament of penance is one through which postbaptismal sins are forgiven. The anointing of the sick is for those seriously ill, injured, or aged. The sacrament of holy orders is one of ordination for deacons, priests, and bishops. Marriage is a sacrament that "cannot be dissolved by any human power"; this rules out divorce with remarriage. Members are required to attend Mass on Sundays and obligatory holy days, to fast and abstain on certain appointed days, to confess at least once a year, to receive the Holy Eucharist during the Easter season, to contribute to support of pastors, and to observe strictly the marriage regulations of the church.

The government of the Roman Catholic Church is hierarchal and authoritarian, but laymen are frequently consulted. (The trend is toward more and more lay participation, since Vatican Council II.) At the head of the structure stands the pope, who is also Bishop of Rome and "Vicar of Christ on earth and the Visible Head of the Church." His authority is supreme in all matters of faith and discipline. Next to him is the College of Cardinals. Although laymen were once chosen to be cardinals, the office has been limited to priests since 1918; the last lay cardinal died in 1876. Many of the cardinals live in Rome, acting as advisors to the pope and as heads or members of the various congregations or commissions supervising the administration of the church. When a pope dies, the cardinals elect his successor; they hold authority in the interim. The Roman Curia is the official body of papal administrative offices through which the pope governs the church; it is composed of congregations, tribunals, and curial offices.

In the United States there are 9 active cardinals, 55 archbishops (8 also are cardinals), 346 bishops, and over 58,000 priests. The archbishop is in charge of the archdiocese and has precedence in his province. There are 32 archdioceses and 137 dioceses. Bishops are the ruling authority in the dioceses, but appeals from their decisions may be taken to the apostolic delegate at Washington and even to Rome. The parish pastor is responsible to the bishop; he is appointed by the bishop or archbishop and holds authority to celebrate Mass and administer the sacraments with the help of such other priests as the parish may need. Bishops are appointed from Rome, usually upon suggestions from the hierarchy in the United States.

The clergy of the church includes deacons, priests, and bishops. Candidates for orders studying in divinity schools are called seminarians; there are 15,943 of them in diocesan and religious-order seminaries. The usual seminary course covers a period of 8 years of study after high school—4 years of philosophy and 4 years of theology. Those in religious orders also spend 1 or 2 years in a novitiate.

Since the restoration of the permanent deaconate in 1967, more than 1,900 men have completed the training course and been ordained deacons. Most of these men are married and over 35. They are empowered to preach, baptize, distribute Holy Communion, and officiate at weddings. Most deacons support themselves in secular jobs and exercise their ministry on weekends and evenings.

In 1977 there were 35,904 diocesan or secular priests in the United States and 22,395 priests who belonged to religious orders and congregations. Add to these the 9,740 lay brothers and the 146,914 sisters engaged in the work, and their importance in the overall task of the church becomes clear. The official *Catholic Directory* lists a total of 101 religious orders of priests and brothers, 24 religious orders for brothers only, and over 400 orders of women. They differ widely in their work. Some are "contemplative" orders, remaining in their monasteries or cloistered convents. Those in active or mixed religious orders engage in teaching, care of the sick, missionary work, writing, or social work. Those in brotherhoods or sisterhoods are required to take vows of poverty, chastity, and obedience but are not ordained; they engage primarily in educational, philanthropic, and charitable work. (Technically the only orders for ordained men are the Dominicans, Carmelites, Benedictines, Augustinians, and Jesuits, but ordinarily any religious community of men or women is called a religious order.)

Besides religious orders and congregations, Catholics may join secular institutions whose members also observe poverty, chastity, and obedience but do not wear any distinctive garb or live together in a community; before receiving approval as secular institutes engaged in apostolic work, these groups may operate as approved "pious unions." Worldwide membership in these institutes and unions exceeds 15,000. Some members are also ordained priests.

Three ecclesiastical councils form an important part of the Catholic system; they are known as general or ecumenical; plenary, or national; and provincial councils. A general council is called by the pope or with his consent; it is composed of all Catholic bishops of the world, and its actions on matters of doctrine and discipline must be approved by the pope. Plenary councils are made up of the bishops resident in a given country; their acts, too, must be submitted to the Holy See before promulgation. Below them are diocesan and provincial councils that make further promulgation and application of the decrees passed by the other councils and approved by the pope. Pope John

XXIII summoned the bishops of the church to the twenty-first ecumenical council known as the Second Vatican Council. Following his death Pope Paul VI reconvened the council, which stimulated liturgical reform, Catholic participation in the ecumenical movement, updated many church practices, and inaugurated the idea of collegiality among the bishops. In 1968 Paul VI reaffirmed the official church position against any form of birth control except total or partial abstinence from sex relations in marriage; many theologians, priests, and laymen protested this, voicing opposition to the encyclical *Humanae Vitae*, and the hierarchies of such countries as France, Canada, Belgium, Holland, Switzerland, Austria, and West Germany interpreted the papal position in the light of the freedom of the individual conscience.

The central act of worship is the Mass; its 2 principal parts are the Liturgy of the Word and the Eucharistic Liturgy. Some of the chief parts of the Liturgy of the Word are the readings from the Old and New Testaments; the homily, or sermon; the Nicene Creed; and the Prayer of the Faithful. The Eucharistic Liturgy includes the offering of the bread and wine, the consecration, the Lord's Prayer, and the Communion. From the third century to 1963 the Western Church prescribed Latin as the liturgical language; now the entire Mass is recited in the vernacular by both priest and people. Besides the Mass, Catholics may participate in popular devotions such as the benedictions, rosary, stations of the cross, novenas, and Bible vigils.

With the most centralized government in Christendom, the Holy See at Rome has representatives in many countries of the world. Roman Catholic churches have been established in 217 countries with a total membership of over 633,000,000. The majority of Italians, Spanish, Irish, Austrians, Poles, Latin Americans, Belgians, Hungarians, Southern Germans, Portugese, French, and Filipinos are baptized Roman Catholics. The Society for the Propagation of the Faith is the overall representative missionary body. In 110 foreign countries there are 7,699 missionaries sent out from the United States.

Education has been a primary concern of American Catholics ever since the establishment of a classical school at St. Augustine, Florida, in 1606. As of 1977 there are 8,375 elementary parochial and private schools in this country, with 2,478,229 students, 1,601 Catholic high schools with 895,775 students. More than 442,000 students attend 241 Catholic colleges and universities, including Notre Dame, Fordham, Georgetown, Boston College, St. Louis, Marquette, Catholic, Loyola, and Villanova. There are 167,836 full-time teachers in Catholic schools, of whom 6,009 are priests, 3,537 are brothers, 50,121 are sisters, and 107,856 are lay teachers. An estimated total of 1,400,000 Catholics attend non-Catholic colleges and universities.

Almost every diocese publishes a weekly newspaper; a total of 461 Catholic newspapers and magazines are published in the United States and Canada. Some of the largest and most influential periodicals are *The National Catholic Reporter*, *Commonweal*, *America*, *Columbia*, *U.S. Catholic*, *St. Anthony Messenger*, *Catholic Digest*, *Catholic World*, and *Ligourian*. Periodicals reflecting a more conservative position include *The Wanderer*, *Twin Circle*, and *The National Catholic Register*.

Roman Catholic charity and welfare work is conducted by many different organizations, religious and otherwise. The National Conference on Catholic Charities helps to coordinate work on state and national levels; work is also conducted by several religious orders of men and women devoting full time to the relief of the poor in homes or in institutions; there are also bureaus of charities in many of the dioceses. The Society of St. Vincent de Paul is perhaps the largest and most effective charity organization; numerous others—the Little Sisters of the Poor, the Sisters of Charity, the Daughters of Charity of the Society of St. Vincent de Paul, the Sisters of Mercy, and the Third Order of Franciscans—are active among the poor in Catholic hospitals, orphanages, and homes for the aged. There are 730 general and special hospitals treating over 31,000,000 patients annually; 1 out of every 3 beds in the nation's private hospitals has been provided by the Catholic hospital system. There are 461 homes for the aged and 219 orphanages.

The members of the hierarchy are also members of the United States Catholic Conference, which operates as a clearinghouse of information; this is not a council or a legislative body; so the resolutions of its meetings do not have the force of law. It facilitates discussion of all policies affecting the interests and activities of the church and unifies, coordinates, and organizes work in social welfare, education, and other activities. Every bishop in the United States and its territories and possessions has a voice in this conference.

A new phenomenon of the church will have important effect in the shaping of future structures: parish councils, created to aid the priests in the management of the parish and composed of laity, have consultative powers; while new diocesan senates, composed of priests, assist the bishop in the setting of policies in the diocese.

While most Roman Catholics belong to the Latin Rite, there are at least 20 groups of churches and an estimated 10 to 12 million other Catholics belonging to the Eastern Rites. These Catholics hold identical doctrinal beliefs and recognize the authority of the pope, but they differ in language, liturgy, customs, church laws, and tradition. Generally they follow 1 of 5 historic rites: Byzantine, Alexandrian, Antiochian, Armenian, or Chaldean. Across the world the main Eastern Rite bodies are the Catholic Copts, Ethiopian Catholics, Syrians, Chaldeans, Catholic Armenians, Malabar Catholics, Byzantine Catholics, and Maronites.

Some 605,000 Eastern Rite Catholics, mostly Ukrainians and Ruthenians, live in the United States. Smaller groups include the Maronites, Melkites, Romanians, Russians, and Armenians. All these rites are jurisdictionally related to one or another of the Eastern Patriarchs.

The Roman Catholic Church today finds itself in an era of change, tension, and some dissension. Pope John XXIII and Vatican II brought about new programs and approaches in the fields of ecumenism, religious liberty, the liturgy, biblical studies, and social action. Priests now face their people as they say Mass; Masses once said only in Latin are now said in the modern vernacular of the people. Many Catholics may choose to practice confession by sitting down and discussing their sins and spiritual problems face-to-face with the priest, and many of them may choose one of several forms of penance. Before Vatican II, Catholics were forbidden to attend meetings of the World Council of Churches; now Catholic observers attend council sessions as observers, and Catholic bishops have entered into theological dialogue with several of the larger Protestant denominations. A Catholic Pentecostal Movement stressing the charismatic gifts of speaking in tongues, healing, interpretation, and prophecy now claims 300,000 Catholics meeting in charismatic prayer groups across the country. Dissension is found in the questioning of the authority of the bishops, celibacy, birth control, abortion, and the anti-sex positions of many of the Fathers of the early church.

Vatican II opened the way for many of these changes and reforms; it now remains to be seen what the newly elected Pope John Paul II will do with or about them. It is a crucial day for this great, historic church.

SALVATION ARMY

William Booth, an ordained minister in the Methodist New Connexion body in England, regretfully left the pulpit of that church in 1861 to become a free-lance evangelistic preacher. This step led him, in 1865, to the slum areas in London's East End and to a dedication of his life to the poverty-stricken, unchurched masses in that area. His first plan was to make his work supplementary to that of the churches, but this proved impractical because many converts did not want to go where they were sent; often they were not accepted when they did go, and Booth soon found that he needed his converts to help handle the great crowds that came to his meetings. He began his work in Mile End Waste under the name of the Christian Mission; in 1878 the name was changed to The Salvation Army.

Being a Methodist, Booth first organized his movement along lines of Methodist polity, with annual conferences at which reports were made and programs planned. With the changing of the name to The Salvation Army, the whole organization became dominated by the new title. "Articles of War" (declaration of faith) were drawn up, and soon the mission stations became corps, members became soldiers, evangelists became officers, and converts were listed as seekers. Booth was designated as "general," and gradually he set up his organization on a military pattern that provided a direct line of authority and a practical system of training personnel for effective action. The leader reasoned that it was "just as valid to build an army of crusaders to save souls as it has been to send armies to recover a sepulchre."

The work spread quickly over England, Scotland, and Wales, and in 1880 it was officially established in the United States by a pioneer group under the direction of Commissioner George Scott Railton. Once committed to a policy of expansion, Booth lost no time in sending pioneering parties in different directions, reaching Australia and France in 1881; Switzerland, Sweden, India, and Canada in 1882; New Zealand and South Africa in 1883; and Germany in 1886. Today the Salvation Army is working in 82 lands with approximately 25,000 officers; preaching the gospel in some 111 languages, 15,450 evangelical centers; and operating more than 3,038 social institutions, hospitals, schools, and agencies. There is a general membership of about 2,000,000 in the Army.

Administratively, the Army is under the command of "the General of the Salvation Army," with top leaders in charge in 82 countries and colonies. In the United States the Army conducts its religious and social program in all 50 states, implementing its purpose of preaching the gospel and effecting the spiritual, moral, and physical reclamation of persons coming under its influence through 9,559 centers of operation and including 6,930 service extension units. They are administered by more than 5,000 officers, assisted by about 20,000 employees. The unit of the Army is the corps, of which there may be several in a city. Each corp is commanded by an officer, ranging in rank from lieutenant to brigadier, who is responsible to divisional headquarters. The 39 divisions in the United States each consists of a number of corps, and the work of each division is under the direct supervision of a divisional commander. The divisions are grouped into 4 territories—Eastern, Central, Southern, and Western—with headquarters in New York City, Chicago, Atlanta, and Rancho Palos Verdes, California. Territorial commanders are in charge of the work in each territory, and the 4 territorial headquarters are composed of departments to facilitate the supervision and direction of all phases of Army work. National headquarters is the coordinating office for the entire country, and the national commander is the chief administrative officer, official spokesman, and president of all Salvation Army corporations in the United States. Property and Revenues are in the custody of a board of trustees or directors, and citizens' advisory boards assist in interpreting the work of the Army to the general public.

Within the structure of the Army, converts who desire to become soldiers (members) are required to sign the Articles of War, after which, as members, they give volunteer service. The function of officers is similar to that of ministers of other churches, and officers are commissioned to full-time Salvation Army service.

Basic training for each officer is a 2-year-in-residence course at 1 of the Army's 4 schools for officers' training located in New York, Chicago, Atlanta, and Rancho Palos Verdes. The chief source of officer candidates is the Salvation Army corps. After a soldier has served actively for at least 6 months, he may make application for officership and, if accepted, may enter the School for Officers' Training where his curriculum, in addition to formal study, includes practical field experience in corps and social service institutions as well as orientation in all possible areas of Salvation Army service. He is graduated from the school as a lieutenant and, following additional studies, is eligible thereafter to attain the ranks of captain, major, lieutenant colonel, colonel, and commissioner.

The motivating force of the Salvation Army in all its work is the religious faith of its officers and soldiers; and the fundamental doctrines of the organization are stated in its Foundation Deed of 1878 in 11 cardinal affirmations. These statements document the Army's recognition of the Bible as the only rule of Christian faith and practice; of God who is the creator and

Father of all mankind; the Trinity of Father, Son, and Holy Ghost; Jesus Christ as Son of God and Son of man; sin as the great destroyer of man's soul and society; salvation as God's remedy for man's sins and man's ultimate and eternal hope made available through Christ; sanctification as the individual's present and maturing experience of a life set apart for the holy purposes of the kingdom of God, and an eternal destiny that may triumph over sin and death. While the Army has a dual function of church and social agency, its first purpose is the salvation of men "by the power of the Holy Spirit combined with the influence of human ingenuity and love." To the Salvation Army, its social services are merely a means of putting the socially disinherited—the needy in both the physical and spiritual realm—into a condition to be physically and spiritually uplifted. In meeting the needs of the "whole man," the Army has established a widespread social welfare program.

The work of the Army in the United States includes 116 adult rehabilitation centers aiding almost 58,000 annually. In 28 homes and hospitals, over 4,500 unwed mothers are cared for. A total of 21,799 were admitted last year to the Army's 2 general hospitals and related institutions, 72,855 persons were given outpatient care; 57 camps provided camping facilities for over 32,000 children, mothers, and senior citizens; the Army maintained over 2,100 boys' and girls' clubs; 1,115 corps community centers with over 700,000 members; 1 Red Shield club for servicemen with a total attendance of 44,795; 264 canteens serving over 700,000 persons in emergencies; family service bureaus serving 812,912 families; hotels and lodges for men and women, settlements, missing persons' bureaus, and day-care centers, care for alcoholics, correctional service bureaus with prisoners and their families, community centers for all ages, and other allied services. These services are given without respect to race, color, creed, or condition; the whole work is financed largely through voluntary subscriptions, federal funds, and annual maintenance appeals from each service.

SCHWENKFELDER CHURCH

Caspar Schwenckfeld von Ossig (1498–1561), a Silesian nobleman, was baptized and reared in the Roman Catholic Church and experienced a spiritual awakening in 1519. Disappointed in his hope to help reform the Roman Catholic Church from within, he played a leading role in the Reformation, advocating wider reading of the Bible by laymen, urging the need of the power, guidance, and leading of the Holy Spirit, and preaching that the sacramental eating in the Lord's Supper is a mystical partaking of Christ as food for the soul; the food is really bread. This interpretation of the Lord's Supper, together with his insistence upon complete separation of church and state, led him into disagreement with Luther and Lutheranism.

He founded a number of spiritual brotherhoods whose members in time came to be known as Schwenkfelders.

The body has disappeared in Europe but persists in the United States in a church of 2,250 members in 5 local congregations. A large body of them arrived in this country in 1734; their first formal society of Schwenkfelders was organized in 1782. Their 5 churches today are all located within a radius of 50 miles of Philadelphia.

All theology, they hold, should be constructed from the Bible, but the Scriptures are considered as dead without the indwelling Word. Christ's divinity was progressive, his human nature becoming more and more divine without "losing its identity"; faith, regeneration, and subsequent spiritual growth work a change in human nature; but justification by faith is not to be permitted to obscure the positive regeneration imparted by Christ.

Their theology is thus Christocentric. In polity they are congregational, each church being incorporated, self-sustaining, and conducting its affairs through its district or local conference. A general conference composed of all the local churches meets twice a year to develop the larger program of education and missions. The general conference sponsored the founding of the Perkiomen School for boys at Pennsburg, Pennsylvania, in 1892; and a majority of the board of trustees of the school are still members of Schwenkfelder churches. A home for the elderly is located at Lansdale, Pennsylvania.

SOCIAL BRETHREN

This is a body organized in Illinois in 1867 by a small group of persons from various denominations, holding quite orthodox doctrines but disagreeing in certain matters of interpretation of Scripture, discipline, and decorum. In 1975 they reported 3 associations, each meeting annually, 1 general assembly meeting biennially, 30 churches located in Illinois, Michigan, and Indiana, and 1,784 members.

Their confession of faith emphasizes the following points:

The infinite power, wisdom, and goodness of God, in whom are united 3 persons of one substance, power, and eternity, the Father, Son, and Holy Ghost.

The authority and consistency of the Scriptures, comprising the Old and New Testaments, as containing all things necessary to salvation, "so that whatsoever is not read therein nor may be proved thereby is not required of any man that it should be believed as an article of faith or thought to be requisite or necessary to salvation."

Regeneration and sanctification through Christ.

Eternal salvation of the redeemed and eternal punishment for apostasy.

The ordinances of baptism and the Lord's Supper for true believers only. Baptism may be by sprinkling, pouring, or immersion.

Lay members of the church should have the right of suffrage and free speech, but ministers are called to preach the gospel and not for political speeches.

Polity is a fusion of Baptist and Methodist structures and customs; and the

233

work of the Social Brethren, aside from efforts in mutual aid and assistance, is largely evangelistic.

SPIRITUALISTS

The movement is known popularly for its mediums, séances, clairvoyance, and so on. Ouija boards, table tipping, and spirit rappings and conversations have attracted thousands anxious to communicate with their departed ones. But Spiritualism has genuine religious bases and connotations as well as psychic experiments. The movement has become a church. The N.S.A. offers a Declaration of Principles, which reads as follows:

1. We believe in Infinite Intelligence.

2. We believe that the phenomena of Nature, both physical and spiritual, are the expression of Infinite Intelligence.

3. We affirm that a correct understanding of such expression and living in accordance therewith constitute true religion.

4. We affirm that the existence and personal identity of the individual continue after the change called death.

5. We affirm that communication with the so-called dead is a fact scientifically proven by the phenomena of Spiritualism.

6. We believe that the highest morality is contained in the Golden Rule. . . .

7. We affirm the moral responsibility of the individual, and that he makes his own happiness or unhappiness as he obeys or disobeys Nature's physical and spiritual laws.

8. We affirm that the doorway to reformation is never closed against any human soul, here or hereafter.

9. We affirm that the practice of Prophecy, as authorized by the Holy Bible, is a divine and God-given gift, reestablished and proven through mediumship by the phenomena of Spiritualism.

The teaching of God as love is central in Spiritualism; the Lord's Prayer is used in both public worship and private séance. Christ is recognized as a medium; the Annunciation was a message from the spirit world, the Transfiguration was an opportunity for the materialization of the spirits of Moses and Elias, and the Resurrection was evidence that all men live on in the spirit world. Man's soul is often called the "astral body"; at death the material body dissolves, and the soul as the body of the spirit progresses through a series of spheres to a higher and higher existence. There are 2 lower spheres in which those of lower character or sinful record are purified and made ready for the higher existences. Most of the departed are to be found in the third sphere, called the summer land; above this are the philosopher's sphere, the advanced contemplative and intellectual sphere, the love sphere, and the Christ sphere. All reach the higher spheres eventually; Spiritualists do not believe in heaven or hell, or that any are ever lost.

Services and séances are held in private homes, rented halls, or churches. Most Spiritualist churches have regular services with prayer, singing, music selections read from the *Spiritualist Manual,* a sermon or lecture, and spirit messages from the departed. The churches and ministers are supported by free-will offerings; mediums and ministers also gain support from classes and séances in which fees are charged. The attendance at church services is invariably small; one authority estimates the average congregation at 20 to 25. But membership cannot be estimated on the basis of church attendance; for every enrolled member, there are at least 15 who are not enrolled but are interested in the movement and in attending its services. Nearly 180,000 Spiritualists were reported as members of their churches in 1954, but this is not comprehensive or inclusive of all using the services of the church.

Administration and government differ slightly in the various groups, but most of them have district or state associations and an annual general convention. All have mediums, and most have ministers in charge of the congregations. Requirements for licensing an ordination also differ, but a determined effort is being made to raise the standards in education and character in the larger groups.

International General Assembly of Spiritualists

Organized at Buffalo, New York, in 1936, this is a cooperative body endeavoring to establish cohesion and unity in the Spiritualist movement. It had an inclusive membership of 164,072 and 209 churches in 1956 and was organized originally as an auxiliary of the General Assembly of Spiritualists in New York to care for churches outside that state. Its present purpose is to charter new Spiritualist churches; headquarters are located at Norfolk, Virginia.

National Spiritual Alliance of the U.S.A.

This body was founded in 1913 by the Rev. G. Tabor Thompson and has its headquarters at Lake Pleasant, Massachusetts, where it was incorporated. Holding general Spiritualist doctrines, the alliance stresses subnormal and impersonal manifestations and intercommunication with the spirit world. Salvation is held to be through the development of personal character; "one reaps as he sows, yet . . . all things are working together for good and evolution obtains perpetually in all persons."

The local churches of the alliance elect their own officers and choose their own ministers; a 3-day convention is held annually with delegates from all the churches electing their national officers—president, secretary, and treasurer. An official board of directors directs the missionary work of ministers and certified mediums; college training is not required of a minister, but he must have passed a course of study arranged by the alliance. Mediums may baptize, but only ministers may officiate at the ceremonies of ordination and marriage. The work of the alliance is mainly in benevolent, literary, educational, music, and scientific activities. There are 3,230 members and 34 churches.

National Spiritualist Association of Churches

This association is influential far beyond its immediate membership, furnishing literature for the whole movement and advocating higher qualifications in mediums and ministers. It has a seminary, the Morris Pratt Institute, for the training of its ministers; a great deal of the work of the seminary is by correspondence. A national director of education directs a training course for members, licentiates, lecturers, mediums, and ordained ministers. The N.S.A. holds an annual legislative convention that elects officers triennially. This is the orthodox body of American Spiritualism.

Progressive Spiritual Church

This church was founded in Chicago in 1907 by the Rev. G. Cordingley and has its own confession of faith. It was organized "to lift spiritualism above mere psychic research, to establish it upon a sound, religious basis, and to secure its recognition among other Christian denominations." The confession of faith states the members' belief in the communion of spirits, in man's restoration to everlasting life, in God as an absolute divine Spirit, and in angels who as departed spirits communicate with the living by means of mediums. Jesus Christ is recognized as a medium controlled by the spirit of Elias and the spirit of Moses and the spirit of John the Baptist. "The fingers of the hand of a medium under control can write and deliver divine messages and vision. . . . A divine understanding of dreams can be had. . . . The stars divine the pathway of life of every character." The Bible is acknowledged as the inspired Word of God, a guide to the spirit life as well as to the phases and phenomena of Spiritualism—prophecies, spiritual palmistry, spiritual automatic writing, spiritual materialization, spiritual trumpet speaking, spiritual healing by magnetized articles, and so forth. Heaven and hell are believed to be conditions, not locations.

Four sacraments—baptism, marriage, spiritual communion, and funerals—are observed. Ministers, who may be of either sex, must pass a course of instruction in the church seminary. Church officers include a supreme pastor, secretary, treasurer, and board of trustees. Local churches elect their own officers but are subject to the constitution and bylaws of the mother church. The work of the church is largely benevolent, social, literary, scientific, and psychical. There are 11,347 members and 21 churches.

THEOSOPHY

Some call Theosophy a religion, and some call it a philosophy; it is both—a blending of Eastern and Western philosophical and religious teaching. Its founder was Madame Helena Petrovna Blavatsky, who was born in Russia in 1831 and who traveled over the world in search of "a knowledge of the laws which govern the universe." She arrived in the United States in 1872 and with Henry Steel Olcott and William Q. Judge founded the Theosophical Society of New York in 1875. Her purpose and aim in Theosophy was "to form a nucleus of the Universal Brotherhood of Humanity, without distinction of race, creed, sex, case or color; to encourage the study of comparative religion, philosophy and science; and to investigate the unexplained laws of Nature and the powers latent in man."

Mrs. Blavatsky made use of the teachings of the great thinkers of various religions, but her system depended mainly upon the precepts and teachings of Buddhism and Hinduism. Proceeding from the premise that God is "immanent" in the hidden forces of nature and that man can attain perfection through his own powers, she described God as impersonal. God is the Absolute Principle of pantheistic Hinduism, a creator (like Brahma), a preserver (like Vishnu), and a destroyer (like Shiva). He is also supreme over an earthly hierarchy that includes Jesus and other master thinkers who have experienced a series of rebirths or reincarnations to ultimately attain divinity. Reincarnation is a great central theme in Theosophy; it is the experience through which men rid themselves of all impurities and reach the true heaven.

When Mrs. Blavatsky died in 1891, Mrs. Annie Besant took over leadership of the movement, with headquarters established in Adyar, India. Conflicts developed during this period between Mrs. Besant as leader of the Adyar Society and the leaders of other Theosophical groups in Europe and the United States; in 1895 William Q. Judge, one of the 3 founders and president of the American Society, established the independent Theosophical Society in America; those loyal to Mrs. Besant worked in the Theosophical Society of New York. Other splits developed in the years following, and the fragmentation is still evident, but the basic teachings of Mrs. Blavatsky still hold in all the rival groups.

No accurate report of membership seems possible among these groups but it is estimated that there are upwards of 40,000 Theosophists worldwide, and perhaps 5,000 of them in the United States. Their influence, thanks to the current interest in oriental philosophy and religion, is felt in many other occult groups unconnected with any Theosophical Society, here or abroad.

TRIUMPH THE CHURCH AND KINGDOM OF GOD IN CHRIST

Founded in Georgia in 1902 by Elder E. D. Smith, this church teaches the cleansing from sin in all "justified" believers through the shed blood of Christ; entire sanctification as an instantaneous, definite work of second grace obtained through the faith of the consecrated believer; the second coming of Christ; and baptism by fire as a scriptural experience also obtainable by faith. General overseers are the chief officers of the body; they meet quadrennially in what is called the International Religious Congress;

otherwise the work of the church is carried on by state, county, and local officers. There are 54,307 members and 475 churches.

UNITARIAN UNIVERSALIST ASSOCIATION

In May, 1961, the Unitarian and Universalist churches in the United States and Canada were consolidated as the Unitarian Universalist Association of Congregations in North America. As one of the most influential liberal churches in this country they have separate and interesting origins and history.

It has always been claimed by the Unitarians that their thought reaches back into the early Christian centuries, before the concept of Trinitarianism was developed. Unitarianism as we know it today, however, began with the Protestant Reformation, among Arminians and Socinians. The movement spread from independent thinkers and Anabaptists in Switzerland, Hungary, Transylvania, Holland, Poland, and Italy to England, where it found champions in such leaders as Newton, Locke, and Milton. No attempt was made to organize the movement in England until late in the eighteenth century.

American Unitarianism, however, developed independently out of New England Congregationalism. Members of the liberal wing of the Congregation Church in eastern Massachusetts, asked only to join a covenant in that church and never to subscribe to a creed, were branded as Unitarian while still within the Congregational membership. The first organized church to turn to Unitarianism as a body, however, was not a Congregational church but the Episcopal King's Chapel in Boston in 1785.

In the second half of the eighteenth century many of the older and larger Congregational churches moving toward Unitarianism were known as Liberal Christian churches or groups; the name Unitarian was finally accepted in 1819.

The split within Congregationalism came into the open in 1805 with the appointment of Henry Ware as professor of theology at Harvard; it was made certain when William Ellery Channing of Boston preached his famous Baltimore sermon in 1819 and in it outlined the Unitarian view. In that sermon the liberals had their platform. A missionary and publication society known as the American Unitarian Association was formed in 1825, and with it began an activity looking forward to the formation of a separate denomination. A national conference was established in 1865.

Channing defined the true church in these words:

By his Church our Savior does not mean a party bearing the name of a human leader, distinguished by a form or an opinion, and on the ground of this distinction, denying the name and character of Christians to all but themselves. . . . These are the church—men made better, made holy, virtuous by his religion—men who, hoping in his promises, keep his commands.

The Unitarians proceeded from this to formulate their views. They have no creed; the constitution of the general conference stated that "these churches accept the religion of Jesus, holding in accordance with his teaching that practical religion is summed up in the love to God and love to man." Cardinal points in their doctrinal attitudes are those of the oneness of God (as opposed to Trinitarianism), the strict humanity of Jesus, the perfectibility of human character, the natural character of the Bible, and the ultimate salvation of all souls. They deny the doctrine of total depravity and believe in the divine nature of man; Trinitarianism is rejected as unscriptural, and they reject the deity of Christ but say that they believe in his divinity as all men are divine as the sons of God. Salvation is by character; character is not an end but a means, and salvation lies in being saved from sin here, not from punishment hereafter. Hell and eternal punishment are held to be inconsistent with the concept of a loving and all-powerful God; to admit that God would permit eternal punishment would be to admit that he was powerless to save. Heaven is a state, not a place. Unitarians do not accept the doctrine of the infallibility of the Bible; they believe that the Bible is not a book but a library of books, all of which cannot be accepted as of equal value and importance. These ideas have been prominent in Unitarianism, but within this ideological framework the widest possible freedom is encouraged in personal interpretation and belief; even students and teachers in Unitarian theological schools are not required to subscribe to any dogmatic teaching or doctrinal tests. Emphasis upon individual freedom of belief, democratic principles, hospitality to the methods of science in seeking truth, and less concern with traditional doctrinal matters characterize the Unitarian movement.

In accordance with its charter, the American Unitarian Association considered itself to be devoted to certain moral, religious, educational, and charitable purposes which to the non-Unitarian may be as enlightening as an analysis of their religious or doctrinal statements; under these purposes, the association felt obligated to:
(1) diffuse the knowledge and promote the interests of religion that Jesus taught as love to God and love to man;
(2) strengthen the churches and fellowships that unite in the association for more and better work for the kingdom of God;
(3) organize new churches and fellowships for the extension of Unitarianism in our own countries and in other lands; and
(4) encourage sympathy and cooperation among religious liberals at home and abroad.

Organization has always been liberally congregational; independent local churches were grouped in local, county, district, state, and regional conferences, and were united in an international association for purposes of fellowship, counsel, and promotion of mutual interests.

At the time of merger, there were 2 denominational seminaries and 2 preparatory schools, 386 churches, and approximately 115,000 members.

Foreign work was conducted through the International Association for Liberal Christianity and Religious Freedom with headquarters at Utrecht, Holland; the International Association has correspondents in 22 countries.

The Universalists draw their inspiration and find evidence of their thinking and philosophy in many cultural streams; much that is basic with Universalism is discovered throughout the world's several religions. Universalism is not exclusively a Christian denomination, having roots in both pre-Christian and contemporary world faiths, yet within the Christian frame of reference Universalists claim roots in the early Christian gnostics, Clement of Alexandria, Theodore of Mopsuestia, the Anabaptists of Reformation times, and the seventeenth- and eighteenth-century German mystical universalists. American Universalism has its direct origin in the work of Dr. George DeBenneville, one of the German mystics; in John Murray, the British anti-Calvinist; and in Hosea Ballou, an original universalist thinker.

DeBenneville, the English-educated son of French Huguenot *émigrés*, studied medicine in Germany, came under the influence of the early Brethren and Friends of God and the German pietists in Pennsylvania in 1741, and preached his gospel of universal salvation as he practiced medicine among the settlers and the Indians.

In 1759 James Relly of England wrote a book entitled *Union* in which he opposed the Calvinistic doctrine of the election of the few. Relly's conviction of universal salvation deeply influenced John Murray, a Wesleyan evangelist who came to New Jersey in 1770; Murray found groups of universalist-minded people scattered along the Atlantic coast, and became minister to one such group in Gloucester, Massachusetts. The Independent Christian Church of Gloucester became the first organized Universalist church in America in 1779. One of its charter members was Gloucester Dalton, a black. Murray served briefly as a Revolutionary War chaplain in the armies of Washington and Greene.

The Universalists met at Philadelphia in 1790 to draft their first declaration of faith and plan of government. Government was established as strictly congregational; doctrinally, they proclaimed their belief in the Scriptures as containing a revelation of the perfections and the will of God and the rule of faith and practice, faith in God, faith in Christ as a mediator who had redeemed all men by his blood, in the Holy Ghost, and in the obligation of the moral law as the rule of life. War was condemned; statements approving the settlements of disputes out of the courts, the abolition of slavery and the education of blacks, testimony by affirmation rather than by oath, and free public education were approved. This Philadelphia declaration was adopted by a group of New England Universalists in 1793; at about the same time Hosea Ballou, a schoolteacher and itinerant preacher in Vermont, was ordained to the Universalist ministry.

Ballou broke radically with Murray's thought; in 1805 he published a book, *Treatise on Atonement*, that gave Universalists their first consistent philosophy. Ballou rejected the theories of total depravity, endless punishment in hell, the Trinity, and the miracles. Man, said Ballou, was potentially good and capable of perfectibility; God, being a God of infinite love, recognized man's heavenly nature and extraction and loved him as his own offspring. The meaning of the Atonement he found not in bloody sacrifice to appease divine wrath but in the heroic sacrifice of Jesus, who was not God but a Son of the eternal and universal God revealing the love of God and anxious to win all men to that love. It was an avowedly Unitarian-Universalist statement of theology that deeply influenced American Universalism. Ballou made another lasting contribution with his insistence that the base of Christian fellowship lay not in creeds but in mutual good faith and goodwill; from this principle came 2 consistent aspects of modern Universalism—a broad liberalism in theology and a universal concern for persons.

It must be kept clear that the Universalists have never had an *official* statement of faith or covenant. From time to time they have set down their basic principles, not as tests of membership nor to be used in any official way, but only to examine their emphases at a given moment in history. Accordingly, in 4 successive statements, they have grown progressively liberal and inclusive. The Philadelphia statement of 1790, for instance, had obvious Trinitarian overtones and spoke in prevailing orthodox terms on the Scriptures, God, the Mediator, and the Holy Ghost; the Winchester Profession of 1803 humanized Jesus and thus directly opposed Trinitarianism and reemphasized salvation for the whole family of mankind; it also saw the Bible as one revelation of the character of God. A statement of 5 Universalist principles in Boston in 1899 liberalized their doctrine still further, and in 1935, in Washington, D.C., they adopted their latest statement, which reads as follows:

The bond of fellowship in this Convention shall be a common purpose to do the will of God as Jesus revealed it and to cooperate in establishing the kingdom for which He lived and died.

To that end we avow our faith in God as Eternal and All-Conquering Love, in the spiritual leadership of Jesus, in the supreme worth of every human personality, in the authority of truth known or to be known, and in the power of men of good will and sacrificial spirit to overcome all evil and progressively establish the kingdom of God. Neither this nor any other statement shall be imposed as a creedal test, provided that the faith thus indicated be professed.

In 1942 the character of the Universalist Church of America was changed to read: "To promote harmony among adherents of all religious faiths, whether Christian or otherwise." This was the last of a long series of steps calculated to meet the challenges of intellectual and social developments, and to safeguard the Universalist conviction that no doctrinal statements should be employed as creedal tests. Consequently Universalism has become a harmonious body of theists, naturalists, humanists, mystics, Christians, and non-Christians, who find great significance and meaning in a universal approach to life.

A keen sense of ethical responsibility has accompanied this sense of the importance of freedom among Universalists. They were very early active in movements of reform for prisons and working women; they opposed slavery from their earliest days, stood for separation of church and state, maintained a continuing interest in the fields of science, labor management, civil rights, and human concern. They have placed medical workers in West Berlin and South German refugee centers in modern times; international student work-camp teams are serving underprivileged children and refugee youths in Europe. American Universalists are feeding children in Japan; developing community centers in India; providing child care for black children in Virginia and a social center at an interracial public housing developent in Chicago; and doing work in various state mental hospitals. They have founded several colleges or universities—Tufts, St. Lawrence, Lombard (now part of the University of Chicago), Goddard, California Institute of Technology, Akron, Dean Junior College, and Westbrook Junior College. Through membership in the International Association for Religious Freedom, they contributed to the support of liberal religious groups in 22 countries abroad, and they maintain a close affiliation with Universalist groups in Holland, Japan, Korea, and the Philippines. At the time of the formation of the Unitarian Universalist Association, they had 68,949 members in 334 churches.

Joined now in their new association, neither Unitarians nor Universalists seem to have lost anything of their original ideology, theology, or purpose. Except for matters of organization and government, the churches involved will continue as they have been across the years; no minister, member, or congregation "shall be required to subscribe to any particular interpretation of religion, or to any particular religious belief or creed." The aims and purposes of the association are set forth in a revised (1974) statement:

The Association, dedicated to the principles of a free faith, shall:

(a) Support the free and disciplined search for truth as the foundation of religious fellowship;

(b) Cherish and spread the universal truths taught by the great prophets and teachers of humanity in every age and tradition, immemorially summarized in the Judeo-Christian heritage as love to God and love to humankind;

(c) Affirm, defend and promote the supreme worth of every human personality, and the use of the democratic method in human relationships;

(d) Implement the vision of one world by striving for a world community founded on ideals of brotherhood, justice, and peace;

(e) Serve the needs of member societies;

(f) Organize new churches and fellowships and otherwise extend and strengthen liberal religion;

(g) Encourage cooperation among people of good will in every land.

Under the constitution a general assembly is the overall policy-making body for carrying out the purposes and objectives of the association. Ministers and laity are represented in this assembly. The general assembly meets annually, or in such special sessions as may be called by the board of trustees. The elected officers of the association (a moderator, president, 2 vice-moderators, secretary, and treasurer—all elected for 4-year terms), together with 24 other elected members, constitute a board of trustees, which appoints the executive and administrative officers and generally carries out the policies and directives. Members of this board have the usual powers of corporate directors as provided by law. The trustees meet 4 times a year, between regular meetings of the general assembly. A series of committees is appointed to facilitate and coordinate the association's work. Under the general assembly there are a nominating committee, program and business committees, and a commission on appraisal; under the board of trustees, an executive committee, a ministerial fellowship committee, finance committee, and investment committee.

Among its most notable and successful achievements are its publishing house, Beacon Press, which produces and circulates over 1 million books every year to students, teachers, libraries, counselors, bookstores, Unitarian Universalists, and the world at large, a newspaper, *The UU World,* which is sent out 16 times a year to more than 100,000 Unitarian Universalist families; a Unitarian Universalist Service Committee provides suggestions and materials in the field of social change to some 45,000 people, and a religious education curriculum that ranks as one of the best in the United States.

Continental headquarters are in Boston; 23 district offices have been established on regional or geographical bases. There are 186,153 members in 1,000 churches.

UNITED CHURCH OF CHRIST

Four churches of historic importance constitute the United Church of Christ: the Congregational Church, the Christian Church, the Evangelical Synod, and the Reformed Church. The first 2 were merged into the Congregational Christian churches in 1931 and were joined by the by-then merged Evangelical and Reformed Church in 1957. The union was completed in the adoption of a constitution at Philadelphia in July, 1961.

The backgrounds of these 4 churches are important enough to be studied separately.

Congregational Church

Congregationalism has been an issue in Christianity from the beginning; it began, as Gaius Glenn Atkins suggests, "without a name and with no sense of its destiny." Even before the Reformation broke over Europe, there were little dissenting groups of churchmen in England "seeking a better way" than that of the established church (Anglican Church or Church of England). As the Reformation developed in England, dissent took corporate form in the Puritan movement, of which Congregationalism was the most radical wing.

Until a few years ago it was generally believed that Congregationalism had

243

its rise in separatism, a movement that began in the days of Queen Elizabeth and that held that the Church of England was unchristian; that to attempt to reform it from within was hopeless; and that the only course for a true Christian to take was to separate himself from it completely. Recent historians, however, have proved that though Robert Browne and other separatist leaders developed sundry ideas that were identical with those of early Congregationalism, the 2 groups were wholly distinct, the former being perfectionists who refused cooperation with other branches of the church, the latter being as cooperative as possible without giving up their principles.

John Robinson, one of their most influential early leaders first enters church history as a separatist; in 1609 he fled persecution in England and settled at Leiden in the Netherlands with the exiled congregation from Scrooby in Nottinghamshire. There he met William Ames, Congregationalism's first great theologian, and Henry Jacob, its first great pamphleteer and organizer. These men were also fugitives from the ecclesiastical courts of Britain. By them Robinson was converted from rigid separatism to the position of Congregationalism.

For 12 years Robinson and his congregation enjoyed peace and freedom under the Dutch; but haunted by the conviction that their sons would not grow up as Englishmen, a large part of the company sailed for America in 1620 aboard the historic *Mayflower*. In a hostile new world with the wilderness before them and the sea at their backs, they helped lay the foundations of the American commonwealth; the democratic ideals of their Plymouth Colony, worked out slowly and painfully, were the cornerstone of the structure which gave us our free state, free schools, and free social and political life.

Other Congregational churches were established at Barnstable, Salem, and elsewhere along the Massachusetts coast. Between 1630 and 1640, 20,000 Puritans came to Massachusetts Bay. It was inevitable that the "Bay People" who came direct from England and the "Plymouth People" from the Netherlands should join forces, which they did, establishing thereby an all-powerful theocratic government over both settlements.

Church and commonwealth were this theocracy's 2 instruments. It was a stern—and at times an intolerant—regime. Suffrage was limited to church members; Anne Hutchinson and Roger Williams were banished; Baptists were haled into court; and 4 Quakers were hanged on Boston Common. It was a dark, but a comparatively short, period, ending with the Act of Toleration in 1689.

In 1636 Thomas Hooker led a company of 100 to what is now Hartford, Connecticut; the freeman's constitution drawn up by Hooker and his associates became the model of the American Constitution. Dissenting from the rigidity of current church worship, Congregationalists such as Jonathan Edwards of Northampton played leading roles in the Great Awakening which broke in 1734; that revival was marked not only by the eloquence of George Whitefield but by the vigorous writings and preaching of Edwards, whose books are now regarded as American classics.

Emerging stronger than ever from the Revolution, in the preparation of which it played a great heroic part, Congregationalism was concerned for the next century with 5 significant developments: higher education, missions, the Unitarian separation, the formation of a national council, and the production of a uniform statement of belief. In the field of education this church had already made tremendous contributions: it had founded Harvard in 1636; Yale (1707) was a Congregational project for the education of its clergy; Dartmouth (1769) developed from Eleazer Wheelock's School for Indians. These, with Williams, Amherst, Bowdoin, and Middlebury, were among the first colleges in New England. By 1953 there were 48 colleges and 10 theological seminaries in the United States with Congregational Christian origin or connection.

Interest in missions among American Congregationalists began the day the Pilgrims landed at Plymouth. The Mayhews, David Brainerd, and John Eliot were soon at work among the Indians. Eliot spent 7 years mastering the Indian tongue, put the Bible in their language, and published an Indian catechism in 1653, the first book to be printed in their language. By 1674 there were 4,000 "praying Indians" in New England, with 24 native preachers. When the wagon trains went West after the Revolution, the families of Congregational ministers and missionaries were prominent. Manasseh Cutler, a preacher from Hamilton, Massachusetts, was instrumental in framing the famous Northwest Territory Ordinance of 1787; and other ministers led in the founding of Marietta, Ohio, the first permanent settlement in the Northwest Territory.

The American Board of Commissioners for Foreign Missions was organized in 1810 and was concerned at first with both home and foreign missionary work. On it served not only Congregationalists but representatives of Presbyterian, Dutch Reformed, and Associate Reformed churches. This was the first foreign missionary society in the country, and it was interdenominational. The first 5 men ordained were the 5 young men who had participated in the famous "haystack" meeting at Williams College. After them came missionaries to more than 30 foreign countries and in American territories, not the least of which was Hawaii, where Congregational missionaries within 25 years taught a whole nation of people to read and write, laid the foundations of a constitutional democratic government, and made of their beautiful islands a sociological laboratory filled with many races. The Congregational achievement in Hawaii is one of the greatest in the whole history of Protestant missions.

The rise of denominationalism worked against the interdenominational complexion of the American Board, and by mid-century the non-Congregationalists had all withdrawn to go their separate ways. The American Board was no longer interdenominational.

Moving westward, Congregationalists from New England came into contact with Presbyterians moving out from the middle and southern states. To avoid competition and duplication of effort, a plan of union was worked out under which ministers and members from both churches were exchanged and accepted on equal basis. Adopted in 1801, the plan eventually worked out to the advantage of the Presbyterians; it was discontinued in 1852, leaving the Presbyterians stronger in the West and the Congregationalists with a virtual church monopoly in New England. But the plan did much to inspire new Congregational missionary work. In 1826 the American Home Missionary Society was founded; it was active in the South before the Civil War and especially effective there toward the end of that conflict with its "contraband" schools for blacks, one of which became Hampton Institute.

Meanwhile differences of opinion between theological liberals and conservatives were developing within the church. Strict Calvinists and Trinitarians were opposed by Unitarians, and a famous sermon by William Ellery Channing at Baltimore in 1819 made a division inevitable. The American Unitarian Association was established in 1825. Almost all the older Congregational churches in eastern Massachusetts went Unitarian; only one Congregational church was left in Boston. Debate and legal action over property and funds were not finished until about 1840.

In spite of the Unitarian defection Congregationalism continued to grow. It assumed such proportions that a national supervisory body became necessary, and a series of national conventions or councils evidence the growing denominational consciousness of the widely scattered independent local churches. A national council held at Boston in 1865 was so effective that a regular system of councils was established. Following conferences between the associations into which the churches had grouped themselves, the first of the national councils was called at Oberlin, Ohio, in 1871. Known as the General Council of the Congregational Christian Churches, it met biennially and acted as an overall advisory body for the entire fellowship.

The council of 1913 at Kansas City adopted a declaration on faith, polity, and wider fellowship that has been accepted by many churches as a statement of faith. While it did not in any way modify the independence of the local churches, it did give a new spiritual unity to the church. It read as follows:

Faith—We believe in God the Father, infinite in wisdom, goodness, and love; and in Jesus Christ, His Son, our Lord and Savior, who for us and our salvation lived and died and rose again and liveth evermore; and in the Holy Spirit, who taketh of the things of Christ and revealeth them to us, renewing, comforting, and inspiring the souls of men. We are united in striving to know the will of God, as taught in the Holy Scriptures, and in our purpose to walk in the ways of the Lord, made known or to be made known to us. We hold it to be the mission of the Church of Christ to proclaim the Gospel to all mankind, exalting the worship of the true God, and laboring for the progress of knowledge, the promotion of justice, and reign of peace, and the realization of human brotherhood. Depending, as did our fathers, upon the continued guidance of the Holy Spirit to lead us into all truth, we work and pray for the transformation of the world into the kingdom of God; and we look with faith for the triumph of righteousness and the life everlasting.

Polity—We believe in the freedom and responsiblity of the individual soul and the right of private judgment. We hold to the autonomy of the local church and its independence of all ecclesiastical control. We cherish the fellowship of the churches united in district, state, and national bodies, for counsel and cooperation in matters of common concern.

The Wider Fellowship—While affirming the liberty of our churches, and the validity of our ministry, we hold to the unity and catholicity of the Church of Christ, and will unite with all its branches in hearty cooperation; and will earnestly seek, so far as in us lies, that the prayer of our Lord for His disciples may be answered that they all may be one.

The "wider fellowship" is taken seriously; unity and cooperation across denominational lines have been outstanding characteristics of Congregationalism all through its history. Christian Endeavor, the largest young people's organization in all Protestantism, was founded by a Congregationalist, Francis E. Clark, in 1881; by 1885 it had become an interdenominational organization known all over the world as the United Society of Christian Endeavor. In 1924 the Evangelical Protestant Church of North America was received into the National Council of Congregational Churches as the Evangelical Protestant Conference of Congregational Churches; the 2 mergers with the Christian churches and the Evangelical and Reformed churches coming comparatively close together, again witness to the widening fellowship and vision of the Congregationalists. Into the most recent merger they brought 47 church-related (not church-*controlled*) colleges, 11 theological seminaries, foreign mission stations in Africa, Mexico, Japan, the Philippines, India, Ceylon, Greece, Lebanon, Syria, Turkey, Korea, and Micronesia, and home missionaries in every state in the Union and Puerto Rico.

Christian Church

The Christian churches, like the Congregational, were born in protest against ecclesiasticism and the denial of individual freedom in the church. There were actually 3 revolts which resulted in the establishment of Christian churches in New England and in the South.

The first came in 1792, when James O'Kelly, a Methodist minister in Virginia, withdrew from that church in protest against the development of the superintendency into an episcopacy, especially insofar as it gave the Methodist bishops absolute power in appointing ministers to their charges. O'Kelly and his followers organized under the name Republican Methodists; this was later changed to "Christian," with the new church insisting that the Bible be taken as the only rule and discipline, and that Christian character be made the only requirement of church membership.

Abner Jones, convinced that "sectarian names and human creeds should be abandoned," left the Vermont Baptists to organize at Lyndon, Vermont, in 1801 the First Christian Church in New England. This was done not so much in objection to Baptist organization or doctrine as from a desire to secure a wider freedom in religious thought and fellowship. Like O'Kelly, Jones insisted that piety and character were to be the sole test of Christian fellowship.

In the Great Awakening which swept Tennessee and Kentucky in 1801 there was a great deal of preaching that either ignored the old emphasis on

247

the doctrines of the various denominations involved or was often in direct contradiction to them. Barton W. Stone, accused of anti-Presbyterian preaching, led a number of Presbyterians out of the Synod of Kentucky to organize a Springfield Presbytery. This presbytery was discontinued as its members gradually came to accept the ideology of James O'Kelly and Abner Jones, and adopted the name "Christians." Stone, an ardent revivalist, was deeply influenced by the preaching of Alexander Campbell and led many of his followers and churches into the fold of the Disciples of Christ. But the large majority of his Christian churches remained with the original Christian body.

The groups under O'Kelly, Jones, and Stone engaged in a long series of conferences which resulted in their union on 6 basic Christian principles:

1. Christ, the only head of the Church.
2. The Bible, sufficient rule of faith and practice.
3. Christian character, the measure of membership.
4. A right, individual interpretation of the Scripture, as a way of life.
5. "Christian," the name taken as worthy of the followers of Christ.
6. Unity, Christians working together to save the world.

No council or other body in the Christian church has ever attempted to draw up any other creed or statement. Their creed is the Bible. Their interpretation of Bible teaching might be called evangelical, but no sincere follower of Christ is barred from their membership because of difference in theological belief. Open Communion is practiced; baptism is considered a duty, but it is not required; immersion is used generally, but any mode may be employed.

The union of the Congregational and Christian churches has been thoroughly democratic, leaving both free to continue their own forms of worship and each with its own polity and doctrine. Adhering strictly to the congregational idea, each local church is at liberty to call itself either Congregational or Christian, and the same choice is found in the self-governing district and state associations into which the churches are organized.

Evangelical and Reformed Church

The Evangelical and Reformed Church was the product of a union established at Cleveland, Ohio, on June 26, 1943, between 2 bodies of Swiss and German background with basic agreements in doctrine, polity, and culture—the Evangelical Synod of North America and the Reformed Church in the United States.

The Evangelical Synod was the younger of the 2 bodies, originating with 6 ministers who met at Gravois Settlement near St. Louis in 1840 to form the Evangelical Union of the West. They were ministers of Lutheran and Reformed churches in the Evangelical United Church of Prussia. Two had been sent to America by the Rhenish Missionary Society and 2 by the

Missionary Society of Basel; the other 2 were independent, one coming from Bremen and the other from Strasbourg.

The Evangelical Union of the West was a cooperative ministerial association until 1849, when the first permanent organization was established. As the movement spread to the east and northwest among German-speaking Lutheran and Reformed peoples, headquarters were established at St. Louis and a new name, the German Evangelical Synod of North America, adopted. A series of amalgamations with 4 other bodies of similar belief and polity—the German Evangelical Church Association of Ohio, the German United Evangelical Synod of the East, the Evangelical Synod of the Northwest, and the United Evangelical Synod of the East—resulted in the formation of the Evangelical Synod of North America, giving it a membership of 281,598 at the time of the merger with the Reformed Church in the United States.

The Reformed Church in the United States had its origin in Switzerland and Germany, and particularly in the flood tide of German immigration to Pennsylvania in the eighteenth century. More than half the Germans in Pennsylvania in 1730 were of the Reformed persuasion; their congregations were widely separated along ther frontier; and lacking ministers, they often employed schoolteachers to lead their services. Three of their pastors, Johann Philip Boehm, George Michael Weiss, and Johann Bartholomaeus Rieger, were deeply influenced by Michael Schlatter, who had been sent to America by the Synod (Dutch Reformed) of South and North Holland; with him they organized in 1747 a coetus (synod) in Philadelphia. It was a synod directly responsible to and in part financially supported by the synod in Holland, from which it declared its independence in 1793, taking the name of the German Reformed Church; and in that year it reported 178 congregations and 15,000 communicants. The word "German" was dropped in 1869; from that time on the denomination was called the Reformed Church in the United States.

Reformed church missionaries went early across the Alleghenies into Ohio and south into North Carolina. An overall synod of the church divided the country into 8 districts or classes in 1819, and an independent Ohio classis was formed in 1824. Franklin College (now Franklin and Marshall) was founded at Lancaster, Pennsylvania, with the support of Benjamin Franklin; a theological seminary was opened at Carlisle and later moved to Lancaster; an academy that later became Marshall College was established in 1836. The Synod of Ohio established a theological school and Heidelberg University at Tiffin, Ohio, in 1850. The mother synod in the east and the Ohio synod were united in the general synod in 1836, which functioned until the merger with the Evangelical Synod of North America in 1934.

Difficulties arose in the early years of the last century over the languages used in the Reformed Church; the older Germans preferred the use of German, and the second-generation members demanded English. Inevitably in a church of such mixed membership there were conservatives and liberals in conflict. Some of the churches withdrew and formed a separate synod but returned in 1837 as wiser heads prevailed and compromises were made. New district synods of both German-speaking and English-speaking congregations were created, and 2 Hungarian classes were added in 1924 from the Old Hungarian Reformed Church.

By 1934 the boards of the church were directing a widespread home missions work and foreign missionary work in Japan, China, and Mesopotamia. There were 12 institutions of higher learning, 3 theological seminaries, and 3 orphanages. There were 348,189 members in the Reformed Church at the time of the 1934 merger, largely concentrated in Pennsylvania and Ohio.

Few difficulties were encountered in reconciling the doctrines of the 2 bodies when the union was finally accomplished. Both churches were German Calvinistic; the Reformed Church had been based historically on the Heidelberg Catechism, and the Evangelical Synod on the Heidelberg Catechism, the Augsburg Confession, and Luther's Catechism. These 3 standards of faith were woven into one in the new constitution of the Evangelical and Reformed Church in these words:

The Holy Scriptures of the Old and New Testaments are recognized as the Word of God and the ultimate rule of Christian faith and practice.

The doctrinal standards of the Evangelical and Reformed Church are the Heidelberg Catechism, Luther's Catechism, and the Augsburg Confession. They are accepted as an authoritative interpretation of the essential truth taught in the Holy Scriptures.

Wherever these doctrinal standards differ, ministers, members, and congregations, in accordance with the liberty of conscience inherent in the Gospel, are allowed to adhere to the interpretation of one of these confessions. However, in each case the final norm is the Word of God.

Two sacraments—baptism, usually administered to infants, and the Lord's Supper—were accepted; confirmation, generally before the thirteenth or fourteenth years, ordination, consecration, marriage, and burial were considered as rites. Although hymns and forms of worship are provided for general use, a wide freedom of worship is encouraged.

Church polity, when this church joined the Congregational Christians in 1957, was modified Presbyterian; each local church was governed by a consistory or church council elected from its own membership. Local churches formed a synod, of which there were 34, each made up of a pastor and lay delegate from each charge; the synod met twice a year and had jurisdiction over all ministers and congregations, examined, licensed, and ordained all pastors, and elected its own officers—a procedure quite different from that of the Congregational Christian churches. It led many to wonder whether a union between 2 such different forms of government could possibly work; their wonder or hesitancy is a root cause for the dissension of the few churches that have thus far refused to cooperate in the merger.

The Evangelical and Reformed Church was a thriving church in 1957-60 when the details of union were being worked out. There were 810,000 members in 1959, in 2,740 churches; 8 colleges, 3 theological schools, 2 academies; foreign missionaries in India, Japan, Hong Kong, Iraq, Africa, and Honduras; and a widespread home missionary work in the United States among the people of the Ozarks, the American Indians, the Volga Germans, Hungarians, and Japanese.

United Church of Christ

On July 8, 1959, representatives of the Congregational Christian Churches and the Evangelical and Reformed Church adopted, at Oberlin, Ohio, a statement of faith for the United Church of Christ, into which they were merging. It reads as follows:

We believe in God, the Eternal Spirit, Father of our Lord Jesus Christ and our Father, and to his deeds we testify:

He calls the worlds into being, creates man in his own image and sets before him the ways of life and death.

He seeks in holy love to save all people from aimlessness and sin.

He judges men and nations by his righteous will declared through prophets and apostles.

In Jesus Christ, the man of Nazareth, our crucified and risen Lord, he has come to us and shared our common lot, conquering sin and death and reconciling the world to himself.

He bestows upon us his Holy Spirit, creating and renewing the Church of Jesus Christ, binding in covenant faithful people of all ages, tongues, and races.

He calls us into his Church to accept the cost and joy of discipleship, to be his servants in the service of men, to proclaim the gospel to all the world and resist the powers of evil, to share in Christ's baptism and eat at his table, to join him in his passion and victory.

He promises to all who trust him forgiveness of sins and fullness of grace, courage in the struggle for justice and peace, his presence in trial and rejoicing, and eternal life in his kingdom which has no end.

Blessing and honor, glory and power be unto him. Amen.

This is "a testimony rather than a test of faith"; it is not intended to set forth doctrinal positions (the doctrines and theological positions of the 4 churches now within the United Church of Christ remain as they were before the union was accomplished), not to stand as a substitute for the historic creeds, confessions, and covenants of the churches involved. It is not binding, in any creedal or theological sense, upon any local church in the denomination; no congregation is required to subscribe to the statement. But it does stand as a tribute to the faith, charity, and understanding of the merging groups.

Equally impressive is the understanding and cooperation evident in the governmental provisions of the constitution. The United Church of Christ represents a union of Congregationalism and Presbyterianism—"it establishes congregationalism as the rule for the local congregation and presbyterianism as the basis for organization of the connectional life of the churches" (Harold E. Fey). The constitution is explicit: "The autonomy of the local church is inherent and modifiable only by its own action. Nothing . . . shall destroy or limit the right of each local church to continue to operate *in the way customary to it."* But beyond the local church, protected as it is, are associations, conferences, and the general synod. Local churches in a geographical area are grouped into associations. The association is concerned with the welfare of the churches within its area; assists needy churches; receives new churches in the United Church of Christ; licences, ordains, and installs ministers; adopts its own constitution, by-laws, and rules of procedure; and is made up of the ordained ministers and elected lay delegates of the area. The association meets annually, and is related to the general synod through its conference.

Associations are grouped into conferences, again by geographical areas. The voting members of the conference are ordained ministers of the associations in the conference and lay delegates elected from the local churches. The conference acts on requests, counsel, and references from the local churches, associations, general synod, and other bodies. It meets annually, and its main function is one of coordinating the work and witness of the local churches and associations, rendering counsel and advisory service, establishing conference offices, centers, institutions, and other agencies.

The general synod is the top representative body of the church; it meets biennially and is composed of 675 to 725 delegates chosen by the conferences, and of ex officio delegates (the elected officers of the church, members of the executive council, the moderator, and assistant moderators). The conference delegates are clergymen, laymen, and laywomen, in equal numbers; there are also associate delegates, with voice but without vote. The general synod has no power to "invade" local churches, associations, or conferences; it nominates and elects the officers of the church (a president, secretary, director of finance, and treasurer) for 4-year terms, a moderator and 2 assistant moderators who preside over the session of the general synod and hold office for 1 year only. (The duties are quite similar to those of a moderator among the Presbyterians).

The major boards, commissions, councils, offices, and "other instrumentalities" of the church are established by the general synod; these include the Board of World Ministries (foreign missions spread from Europe to Southern Asia and Latin America), made up of 225 ministers, laymen, and laywomen; the Board for Homeland Ministries (home missions), also with 225 ministers, laymen, and laywomen; the Council for Higher Education, composed of the executive heads of the 2 academies, 31 colleges, and 14 schools of theology of the church; the Council for Health and Welfare Services, administered by the heads of 65 church institutions in these fields; the Office for Church in Society, the Office for Church Life and Leadership, the Commission for Racial Justice and the Stewardship Council, which is responsible for program development, information, promotion, and social audiovisual resources. Pension and relief activities are administered by a nonprofit corporation responsible to and reporting annually to the general synod. Two committees (nominating and credentials) are also appointed by the general synod, and the synod is authorized to appoint other necessary committees.

An executive council of 43 voting members and 9 ex officio members (ministers, laymen, and laywomen) is elected by the general synod to act for the synod in the interims between synod meetings. It determines the salaries of the officers of the church, appoints the editor of *A.D.*, a joint publication of the United Church of Christ and the United Presbyterian Church in the U.S.A., prepares the agenda for all meetings of general synod, and appoints committees not otherwise provided; it also submits to general synod "any recommendation it may deem useful" to the work of the church.

As of 1959, there were 1,419,171 members and 5,500 churches in the Congregational Christian Churches; there were approximately 810,000 members in 2,740 churches in the Evangelical and Reformed Church. While some local churches in both groups declined to enter the merger, there are today 1,785,652 members and 6,512 churches in the United Church of Christ.

The national church holds membership in the National Council, the World Council of Churches, and the World Alliance of Reformed Churches.

UNITED HOLY CHURCH OF AMERICA, INC.

A pentecostal church organized at Method, North Carolina, in a meeting held by the Rev. Isaac Cheshier in 1886, this body was successively called the Holy Church of North Carolina, the Holy Church of North Carolina and Virginia, and finally (1918) the United Holy Church of America. Its purpose is to establish and maintain holy convocations, assemblies, conventions, conferences, public worship, missionary and school work, orphanages, manual and trade training, and religious resorts, with permanent and temporary dwellings.

Articles of faith contain statements of belief in the Trinity, the record of God's revelation of himself in the Bible, redemption through Christ, justification and instantaneous sanctification following justification, the baptism of the Holy Spirit, divine healing, and the ultimate reign of Christ over the earth. Baptism by immersion, the Lord's Supper, and foot washing are observed as ordinances.

The chief officer is the president; the board of bishops supervises the general work of the church. There are 28,980 members in 470 churches, as of 1960.

UNITY SCHOOL OF CHRISTIANITY

Charles Fillmore, bankrupt and a cripple, and his wife Myrtle, seriously ill with tuberculosis, discovered in 1886 "a mental treatment that is guaranteed to cure every ill that the flesh is heir to." The treatment, or system, is offered today in the Unity School of Christianity as a curative in many areas beyond physical healing. Unity is not a church or denomination, but a nonsectarian religious educational institution devoted to demonstrating that the teaching of Jesus Christ is a practical, seven-day-a-week way of life.

The Fillmores held that "whatever man wants he can have by voicing his desire in the right way into the Universal Mind," and this emphasis upon Mind they found originally in Christian Science. Both studied Christian Science, though neither was ever a part of the movement. They also studied New Thought, Quakerism, Theosophy, Rosicrucianism, Spiritism, and Hinduism; out of their studies came an ideology both old and original, built on ancient truth and concepts but moving in new directions.

Unity teaches that all thought goes back to God, who is "Principle, Law, Being, Mind, Spirit, All Good, omnipotent, omniscient, unchangeable, Creator, Father, Cause and Source of all that is." In the attribute of Mind is found the "meeting ground of man and God." Unity has a Trinity: "The Father is Principle, the Son is that Principle revealed in a creative plan. The Holy Spirit is the executive power of both Father and Son carrying out the creative plan." Jesus Christ is "Spiritual man, . . . the direct offspring of Divine Mind, God's idea of perfect man." Man is a son of God filled with the Christ consciousness. It is through Christ, or the Christ consciousness, that man gains eternal life and salvation, both of which terms have meanings different from those in orthodox Christianity. Salvation here may be said to mean the attainment of that true spiritual body which replaces the physical body when man becomes like Christ. This transformation takes place not in any hereafter but "here in this earth" through a series of reincarnations and regenerations. Man suffers no final death but only changes into increasingly better states until he becomes as Christ. All men will have this experience.

Unity has been described as "a religious philosophy with an 'open end,' seeking to find God's truth in all of life, wherever it may be." It has no strict creed or dogma; it finds good in all religions, and we should keep our minds open to receive that goodness. Each man must do for himself. Others may help, but ultimately it must be a relationship between God and the individual. Knowing and loving God is the key to peace and success: "To them that love God all things work together for good."

Unlike Christian Science, Unity recognizes the reality of matter, the world, sin, and sickness. Sin and sickness are real but may be overcome. Health is natural; sickness is unnatural. Anything that injures the body is to be avoided—such emotions, for instance, as strife, anger, hatred, or self-interest. But all this is strictly personal, and a matter of individual decision; Unity lays down no laws concerning health but concentrates on spiritual goals, knowing that healthful living habits will follow. Some Unity students are vegetarians in the interests of health; many are not. Unity is personal; there are no social or health "programs" as such, no hospitals or relief agencies.

Solutions are suggested for every human want and illness. The follower is told to repeat over and over certain affirmations, which develop the all-powerful mind and bring to him from the Divine Mind whatever he needs. Mr. Fillmore once wrote a revised version of the twenty-third psalm calculated to help in the area of economic struggle and success:

> The Lord is my banker; my credit is good . . . ;
> He giveth me the key to His strongbox;
> He restoreth my faith in riches;
> He guideth me in the paths of prosperity for His name's sake.*

He does, however, stress the importance of giving above receiving and condemns the greed of mere money-getting as sinful and destructive.

The Bible is used constantly in Unity, but it is not considered the sole or final authority in faith and practice; man must be in direct, personal communion with God and not be dependent upon such secondary sources as the Scriptures.

Unity insists that it is not a church. "The true church is a state of consciousness in man." Unity does have annual conferences, a statement of faith, pulpits supplied with ministers who must be approved by Unity headquarters, and rituals for baptism, Communion, weddings, and funerals. Local groups are organized into centers, which are linked to members of the Association of Unity Churches (a separated organization affiliated with Unity School). More than 600 radio and 270 TV stations broadcast 250 Unity programs per week.

The real work of Unity School is done through what is called Silent Unity. A large staff of workers in Unity Village, near Kansas City, is available for consultation day and night, answering telephone calls, telegrams, and letters—an average of 10,000 calls a week. It is a service of counsel, prayer, and affirmation, offering help on every conceivable problem. Each case or call is assigned to one of this staff, who suggests the proper affirmations. The whole staff joins in group prayer and meditation several times a day. All calls and requests are answered. There is no charge for this service, but love offerings are accepted. In 1 year Unity answered 600,000 such calls for help, most of them coming from members of various Christian churches. No correspondent is ever asked to leave the church to which he belongs. In addition to the services of Silent Unity some 4,000,000 books, booklets, tracts, and magazines are published and undoubtedly used by many who never contact headquarters at all and never in any sense become members of the school.

VEDANTA SOCIETY

The members of the Vedanta Society base their faith and philosophy upon the writings of the Vedas, the scriptures of the Indo-Aryans. This Indian

*From *Prosperity*. Used by permission of Unity School of Christianity.

philosophy, explaining the nature and end of all wisdom, harmonizes the findings of modern science, offers a scientific and philosophical basis for religion—rational, nondogmatic, and liberal—and stresses the oneness of all religions as taught in the Upanishads and the Bhagavad Gita. It was first expounded in this country by Swami Vivekananda at the World's Parliament of Religions held in Chicago in 1893; he founded the Vedanta Society of New York in 1894.

There are 12 Vedanta centers, 3 monasteries, and 2 convents in the United States; all belong to and are under the management of the Ramakrishna Math and Mission founded by Swami Vivekananda, with headquarters in Belur Math, near Calcutta. Each center is an independent, self-supporting unit with its own board of trustees made up mostly of American citizens. The swamis are ordained monks, and come as guest teachers. There are public lectures and classes for instruction that seek not to convert but to enlighten. There are 1,600 members in 13 societies.

VOLUNTEERS OF AMERICA

The Volunteers of America is a religious social welfare organization founded in 1896 by the late Ballington and Maud Booth and incorporated in the same year under the laws of the state of New York; more than 30,000 members were reported in 1973, but this figure hardly tells the whole story of services rendered to hundreds of thousands of people in the principal cities of the United States.

Religious services are offered in missions, Volunteer churches, Sunday schools, companionship leagues, prisons, and on the streets; the organization has its own rituals for baptism, the Lord's Supper, and marriage. Doctrine is evangelical, with strong emphasis on the saving grace of God, the Trinity, the atonement of Christ, regeneration through the Holy Spirit, the necessity of repentance and conversion, immortality, and future rewards and punishments.

The social welfare programs include departments of family welfare, salvage, health camps, day nurseries, hospices for working girls, maternity homes, homes for mothers and children, adoptive placements, clubs and homes for the aged, rehabilitation workshops, family counseling centers, transient men's homes, and boys' and girls' clubs. There is an excellent prison department, assisting discharged and paroled prisoners, men and women in prison, and their families; more than 100,000 prisoners are enrolled in the Volunteer Prison League—a self-help group organized by inmates in various correctional institutions with VOA consultation and guidance. Recent program developments include 2-score prerelease centers or half-way house facilities. There are also 28 housing projects for low and moderate income families and senior citizens, constructed during the past five years. These facilities provide more than 7,500 units serving nearly 30,000 families and individuals. VOA is also guiding the development and operation of nursing home care and presently operates 17 nursing homes with a 1,500-bed capacity.

Operation of the Volunteers is based on a semimilitary organization structure. All officers bear military titles and wear uniforms. The chief governing body is called the Grand Field Council and is composed of those officers bearing the rank of lieutenant major or above. There is a board of 10 members known as the National Executive Board that functions when the Grand Field Council is not in session. The incorporation has a directorate of 9, who are the responsible financial officers and who act as trustees and custodians of all property. Military regulations do not apply in the selection of these top officers; they are chosen by democratic election. The commander in chief is elected for 5 years and is also president of the corporate body. There are 4 administrative regions—Eastern, Western, Midwestern, and Southern. National officers and staff are located in New York City.

During 1972 nearly 6,000,000 people received material assistance through various departments, exclusive of religious service. There were 9,000,000 meals and 2,000,000 lodgings furnished; in addition, more than 6,500 children were cared for in such child service centers as day care centers, foster day care, group homes, summer camps, etc. Nearly 100,000 elderly persons participated in the Sunset Club program; more than 16,000 interviews were held in prisons; 160,000 prisoners attended Volunteer religious services; and 2,000 prisoners were paroled in their custody. Nearly 60,000 men were given job opportunities in the Men's Rehabilitation Centers, and 30,000 unemployed men were aided in securing work in business and industry. Over 30,000,000 articles such as furniture, household appliances, and clothing were distributed free or at a nominal cost to low income families and individuals. The annual budget of the Volunteers is in excess of $45 million.

WESLEYAN CHURCH

Until 1968 this was the Wesleyan Methodist Church of America; it represented, at the time of its founding in 1843, a protest against slavery and the Methodist episcopacy that predated by 1 year the historical division of the Methodist Episcopal Church and the Methodist Episcopal Church, South. With the slavery issue settled by the Civil war, other differences of a spiritual or reform nature—entire sanctification and opposition to the liquor traffic—seemed important enough to continue the separate existence of the Wesleyan Methodist Church.

In June of 1968 the Wesleyan Methodist Church merged with the Pilgrim Holiness Church, giving it a membership total of 96,337 in 1,735 churches in the United States and 134,052 worldwide. With this merger, the body became the Wesleyan Church.

The Pilgrim Holiness Church was close in doctrine and polity to the Church of the Nazarene, and thus close to Methodism and in agreement with Wesleyan doctrines. There was no shift or change in doctrinal emphases when the 2 churches joined. The time-honored teaching of santification is still central. Candidates for membership are required, in the Wesleyan Church, to disavow the use, sale, or manufacture of tobacco and alcoholic beverages, and to refrain from membership in secret societies.

An enlarging evangelistic and missionary activity is directed from world headquarters in Marion, Indiana. As of June, 1969, 49 conferences had missionaries at work in Australia, Haiti, Honduras, India, Jamaica, Japan, Mexico, Nepal, New Guinea, Puerto Rico, Taiwan, Sierra Leone, Rhodesia, South Africa, South America, and among the Indians in South Dakota. There are 4 colleges, 2 Bible colleges, 2 academies, and 1 seminary foundation (associated with Asbury Seminary in Wilmore, Kentucky).

Also Wesleyan in doctrine is another denomination, the Wesleyan Holiness Association of Churches. Founded in 1959 in Indiana by a group of clergymen and laymen from various churches who sought to conserve "sweet, radical and scriptural holiness," it has a general conference that meets every 2 years and has its headquarters in Tempe, Arizona. No statistics on membership are available.

HEADQUARTERS OF DENOMINATIONS

(Addresses of denominational headquarters are given wherever possible; otherwise, the names of chief and preferably permanent officials are listed.)

Adventists:
  Seventh Day Adventists: 6840 Eastern Avenue, Washington, DC 20012
  Church of God (General Conference): Oregon, IL 61061
  Primitive Advent Christian Church: Sec., Hugh W. Good, Elkview, WV 25071
African Orthodox Church, 122 West 129th Street, New York, NY 10027
Amana Church Society: Pres., Charles L. Selzer, Homestead, IA 52236
American Ethical Union: 2 West 64th Street, New York, NY 10023
American Evangelical Christian Churches, Pineland, FL 33945
American Rescue Workers: 2827 Frankford Avenue, Philadelphia, PA 19134
Anglican Orthodox Church: Bishop James Parker Dees, 323 East Walnut Street, Statesville, NC 28677
Apostolic Christian Church (Nazarean): P.O. Box 151, Tremont, IL 61568
Apostolic Christian Church of America: Elder Roy L. Sauder, 3528 North Linden Lane, Peoria IL 61604
Apostolic Faith: Northwest Sixth and Burnside, Portland, OR 97209
Apostolic Overcoming Holy Church of God: Sec., Mrs. Juanita R. Arrington, 514 10th Avenue, Birmingham, AL 35204
Armenian Churches: St. Varton Cathedral, 630 Second Avenue, New York, NY 10016
Bahá'í: 536 Sheridan Road, Wilmette IL 60091
Baptists:
  American Baptist Churches in the U.S.A.: Valley Forge, PA 19481
  Southern Baptist Convention: 460 James Robertson Parkway, Nashville, TN 37209
  National Baptist Convention U.S.A. Inc.: Sec., the Rev. T. J. Jemison, 915 Spain Street, Baton Rouge, LA 70872
  National Baptist Convention of America: Sec., the Rev. Billy H. Wilson, 2620 South Marsallis Avenue, Dallas, TX 77020
  American Baptist Association: 4605 North State Line Avenue, Texarkana, TX 755011
  Baptist Bible Fellowship, International: 730 East Kearny, Springfield, MO 65800
  Baptist General Conference: 1233 Central Street, Evanston, IL 60201
  Baptist Missionary Association of America: Sec., the Rev. Ralph Cottrell, P.O. Box 2866, Texarkana, AR 75501
  Bethel Ministerial Assn.: Box 5353, Evansville, IN 47715
  Central Baptist Assn.: Dana M. Crawford, 726 Hollis Street, Kingsport, TN 37660
  Conservative Baptist Assn. of America: P.O. Box 66, Wheaton, IL 60187
  Duck River (and Kindred) Assns. of Baptists: Clerk, Marvin Davenport, Auburntown, TN 37061
  Free Will Baptists: 1134 Murfreesboro Road, Nashville, TN 37202
  General Assn. of Regular Baptist Churches: 1300 North Meacham Road, Schaumburg, IL 60185
  General Baptists: Poplar Bluff, MO 63901

General Conference of the Evangelical Baptist Church, Inc.: Kevetter Bldg., 2400 East Ash Street, Goldsboro, NC 27530

Landmark Baptists: Dr. I. K. Cross, P.O. Box 848, Bellflower, CA 90706

National Baptist Evangelical and Soul Saving Assembly of U.S.A.: 441 Monroe Avenue, Detroit, MI 48226

National Primitive Baptist Convention, U.S.A: P.O. Box 2355, Tallahassee, FL 32301

North American Baptist Conference: 1 South 210 Summit Avenue, Oakbrook Terrace, IL 60181

Primitive Baptists: Elder W. H. Cayce, South Second Street, Thornton, AR 71766

Reformed Baptists: Gene Rice, 1919 Division Street, Nashville, TN 37203

Separate Baptists in Christ: Floyd Wilson, 59 Greenspring Street, Indianapolis, IN 46224

Seventh Day Baptist General Conference: 510 Watchung Avenue, Box 868, Plainfield, NJ 07061

United Free Will Baptist Church: Kinston College, 1000 University Street, Kinston, NC 18501

Berean Fundamental Church: North Platte, NB 69101

Bible Protestant Church: 84 Clementon Road, Gibbsboro, NJ 08206

Bible Way Church, World Wide: 1130 New Jersey Avenue, NW, Washington, DC 20001

Brethren (Dunkers):

Brethren Church: 524 College Avenue, Ashland, OH 44805

Church of the Brethren: 1451 Dundee Avenue, Elgin, IL 60120

Fellowship of Grace Brethren Churches: 1108 Chestnut Avenue, Winona Lake, IN 46590

Old Baptist German Brethren: Elder Clement Skiles, Route 1, Box 140, Bringhurst, IN 46903

Plymouth Brethren: P.O. Box 294, 218 West Willow, Wheaton, IL 60187

River Brethren:

Brethren in Christ Church: Sec., Arthur M. Climenhaga, 4208 Southeast Jennings Avenue, Portland, OR 97222.

United Zion Church: Sec., the Rev. J. Paul Martin, Box 212 D, Route 1, Annville, PA 17003

United Brethren:

Church of the United Brethren in Christ: 302 Lake Street, P.O. Box 650, Huntington, IN 46750

United Christian Church: Elder Henry C. Heagy, Lebanon, R.D. 4, Lebanon County, PA 17042

Buddhist Churches of America: 1710 Octavia Street, San Francisco, CA 94109

Christadelphians: H. P. Zilmer, 1002 Webster Lane, Des Plaines, IL 60016

Christian and Missionary Alliance: 350 North Highland Avenue, Nyack, NY 10960

Christian Catholic Church: Dowie Memorial Drive, Zion, IL 60099

Christian Church (Disciples of Christ): 222 South Downey Avenue, Indianapolis, IN 46206

Christian Church of North America: 1818 State Street, Sharon, PA 16146

Christian Churches and Churches of Christ: 3533 Epley Road, Cincinnati, OH 45231

Christian Congregation: Supt., the Rev. Ora Wilbert Eads, 708 South Bragg Street, Monroe, NC 28110

Christian Nation Church: Gen. Sec., the Rev. W. F. Clark, 345 Cedar Drive, Loveland, OH 45140

Christian Union: P.O. Box 38, Excelsior Springs, MO 64024

Christ's Sanctified Holy Church: South Cutting Avenue & East Spencer Street, Jennings, LA 70546

Church of Christ (Holiness) U.S.A.: 329 East Monument Street, Jackson, MS 39202

Church of Christ, Scientist: Christian Science Center, Boston, MA 02115

Church of God:

    Church of God (Anderson, Ind.): Box 2420, Anderson, IN 46011

    Church of God (Apostolic): St. Peter's Church of God (Apostolic), 11th & Hickory Street, Winston Salem, NC 27101

    Church of God (Cleveland, Tenn.): Keith Street at 25th NW, Cleveland, TN 37311

    Church of God (Seventh Day, Denver, Colo.): P.O. Box 2370, Denver, CO 80201

    Church of God (Seventh Day, Salem, W. Va.): 79 Water Street, Salem, WV 26426

    Church of God (New Testament Judaism): P.O. Box 1207, Jerusalem Acres, Cleveland, TN 37311

    Church of God (Tomlinson): 2504 Arrow Wood Drive, Huntsville, AL 35803

    Church of God and Saints of Christ: Belleville, Portsmouth, VA 23704

    Church of God by Faith: 3220 Haines Street, Jacksonville, FL 32206

    Church of God in Christ: 938 Mason Street, Memphis, TN 38126

    Church of God in Christ (International): 1905 Columbia Avenue, Philadelphia, PA 19121

    Church of God of Prophecy: Bible Place, Cleveland, TN 37311

    (Original) Church of God: P.O. Box 3086, Chattanooga, TN 37404

Church of Illumination: Beverly Hall, Clymer Road, Quakertown, PA 18951

Church of Jesus Christ: Cleveland, TN 37311

Church of Jesus Christ of Latter-day Saints: 50 East North Temple Street, Salt Lake City, UT 84111

    Reorganized Church of Jesus Christ of Latter-day Saints: Saints Auditorium, Independence, MO 64051

    Church of Jesus Christ (Bickertonites): Sixth and Lincoln, Monongahela, PA 15063

    Church of Jesus Christ of Latter-day Saints (Strangites): Elder Vernon D. Swift, P.O. Box 522, Artesia, NM 88210

    Church of Jesus Christ (Temple Lot): Temple Lot, Independence, MO 64000

Church of Our Lord Jesus Christ of the Apostolic Faith, Inc.: 2081 7th Avenue, New York, NY 10027

Church of the Nazarene: 6401 The Paseo, Kansas City, MO 64131

Churches of Christ: Ed., J. Roy Vaughan, Gospel Advocate, 1006 Elm Hill Road, Nashville, TN 37210

Churches of Christ in Christian Union: 459 East Ohio Street, Box 30, Circleville, OH 43113

Churches of God, General Conference: P.O. Box 926, Findlay, OH 45840

Churches of God, Holiness: 170 Ashby Street, NW, Atlanta, GA 30314

Churches of the Living God:

    Church of the Living God (Christian Workers for Fellowship): Bishop F. C. Scott, 801 NE 17th Street, Oklahoma City, OK 73105

House of God, Which Is the Church of the Living God: Bishop A. H. White, 6107 Cobbs Creek Parkway, Philadelphia, PA 19143

Congregational Christian Churches, National Assn. of: P.O. Box 1620, Oak Creek, WI 53154

Congregational Holiness Church: Route 1, Box 325, Griffin, GA 30223

Conservative Congregational Christian Conference: 25 West 626 Street, Charles Road, Wheaton, IL 60187

Divine Science: 1819 East 14th Avenue, Denver CO 80218

Eastern Churches:

Albanian Churches: 54 Burroughs Street, Jamaica Plain, MA 02130

American Carpatho-Russian Orthodox Greek Catholic Church: Johnstown, PA 15906

American Holy Orthodox Catholic Apostolic Eastern Church: His Holiness Patriarch Clement, 247 East 126th Street, New York, NY 10035

Antiochian Orthodox Christian Archdiocese of North America: 358 Mountain Road, Englewood, NJ 07631

Bulgarian Eastern Orthodox Church: 312 West 101 Street, New York, NY 10025

Eastern Orthodox Catholic Church in America: 1914 Highway 17-92, Fern Park, FL 32730

Greek Orthodox Archdiocese of North and South America: 8-10 East 79th Street, New York, NY 10021

Holy Apostolic and Catholic Church of the East (Assyrians): 554 Arball Drive, San Francisco, CA 94132

Holy Orthodox Church in America (Eastern Catholic and Apostolic): See House, 321 West 101st Street, New York, NY 10025

Romanian Orthodox Episcopate of America: 2522 Grey Tower Road, Jackson, MI 49201

Russian Orthodox Church in the U.S.A.: St. Nicholas Patriarchal Cathedral, 15 East 97th Street, New York, NY 10029

Russian Orthodox Church Outside Russia: 75 East 93rd Street, New York, NY 10028

Serbian Eastern Orthodox Church in the U.S.A. and Canada: 5701 North Redwood Drive, Chicago, IL 60656

Syrian Orthodox Church of Antioch: 292 Hamilton Place, Hackensack, NJ 07601

Ukranian Orthodox Churches: South Bound Brook, NJ 08880

Episcopal Church: 815 Second Avenue, New York, NY 10017

Reformed Episcopal Church: Sec., the Rev. D. Ellsworth Raudenbush, 560 Fountain Street, Havre de Grace, MD 21078

Evangelical Church of North America: Supt., Dr. V. A. Ballantyne, 8719 John Drive, Indianapolis, IN 46234

Evangelical Congregational Church: 100 West Park Avenue, Myerstown, PA 17067

Evangelical Covenant Church of America: 5101 North Francisco Avenue, Chicago, IL 60625

Evangelical Free Baptist Church, Inc.: P.O. Box 529, Addison, IL 60101

Evangelical Free Church of America: 1515 East 66th Street, Minneapolis, MN 55423

Federated Churches: National Council of Community Churches, 89 East Wilson Bridge Road, Worthington, OH 43085

Fire Baptized Holiness Church (Wesleyan): 600 College Avenue, Independence, KS 67301

Free Christian Zion Church of Christ: 1315 Hutchinson Street, Nashville, AR 71852

Friends:

Friends General Conference: 1520-B Race Street, Philadelphia, PA 19102

Friends United Meeting: Gen Sec., Lorton G. Heusel, 101 Quaker Hill Drive, Richmond, IN 47374

Religious Society of Friends (Conservative): George C. Parker, North Carolina Yearly Meeting, Route 1, Box 10, Woodland, NC 27897

General Convention of the Swedenborgian Church: Pretty Prairie, KS 67570

Grace Gospel Fellowship: 1011 Aldon Street, SW, Grand Rapids, MI 49509

Independent Churches: See Federated Churches

Independent Fundamental Churches of America: 1860 Mannheim Road, Westchester, IL 60153

International Church of the Foursquare Gospel: 1100 Glendale Boulevard, Los Angeles, CA 90026

Jehovah's Witnesses: 117 Adams Street, Brooklyn, NY 11201

Jewish Congregations: American Jewish Committee, 165 East 56th Street, New York, NY 10022

Kodesh Church of Immanuel: 1509 S Street, NW, Washington, DC 20009

Liberal Catholic Church: Krotona 62, Ojai, CA 93023

Lutherans:

American Lutheran Church: 422 South 5th Street, Minneapolis, MN 55415

Lutheran Church in America: 231 Madison Avenue, New York, NY 10016

Apostolic Lutheran Church of America: Sec., James Johnson, Route 2, Box 99, L'Anse, MI 49916

Church of the Lutheran Brethren of America: Fergus Falls, MN 56537

Church of the Lutheran Confession: Markesan, WI 53946

Evangelical Lutheran Synod: The Rev. Alf Merseth, 106 13th Street, Northwood, IA 50459

Free Lutheran Congregations: 3110 East Medicine Lake Boulevard, Minneapolis, MN 55441

Lutheran Church—Missouri Synod: 500 North Broadway, St. Louis, MO 63102

Protestant Conference (Lutheran): Sec., the Rev. Gerald Hinz, Shiocton, WI 54170

Wisconsin Evangelical Lutheran Synod: Pres., the Rev. Oscar Nauman, 3512 West North Avenue, Milwaukee, WI 53208

Mennonites:

Beachy Amish Mennonite Churches: Ervin N. Hershberger, R. D. 1, Meyersdale, PA 15552

Church of God in Christ (Mennonite): 420 Wedel Street, Moundridge, KS 67107

Conservative Mennonite Conference: Sec., Daniel Yutzy, Two Rod Road, Marilla, NY 14102

Evangelical Mennonite Brethren Conference: 5800 South 14th Street, Omaha, NB 68107

Evangelical Mennonite Church, Inc.: 1420 Kerrway Court, Fort Wayne, IN 46805

General Conference Mennonite Church: 722 Main Street, Newton, KS 67114

Hutterian Brethren: Joseph J. Waldner, P.O. Box 628, Havre, MT 59501

Mennonite Brethren Church of North America: Dr. Frank C. Peters, Winnipeg, Man., Canada

Mennonite Church: 528 East Madison Street, Lombard, IL 60148

Old Order Amish Mennonite Church, % Raber's Book Store, Baltic, OH 43804

Old Order (Wisler) Mennonite Church: Henry W. Riehl, Route 1, Columbiana, OH 44408

Reformed Mennonites: Bishop Earl Basinger, 1036 Lincoln Heights Avenue, Ephrata, PA 17522

Unaffiliated Mennonites: Dr. J. C. Wenger, Goshen Biblical Seminary, 3003 Benham Avenue, Elkhart, IN 46514

Methodists:

United Methodist Church, 475 Riverside Drive, New York, NY 10027

African Methodist Episcopal Church: Sec., the Rev. Richard A. Chappelle, 3526 Dodier, St. Louis, MO 63107

African Methodist Episcopal Zion Church: Sec., Herman L. Anderson, P.O. Box 1401, Charlotte, NC 28232

Christian Methodist Episcopal Church: 564 East Frank Avenue, Memphis, TN 38006

Congregational Methodist Church, Sec., the Rev. A. F. O'Connor, P.O. Box 555, Florence, MS 39073

Cumberland Methodist Church: Pres., the Rev. Charles A. Shadrick, Whitwell, TN 37397

Evangelical Methodist Church: 3036 North Meridian, Wichita, KS 67204

Free Methodist Church of North America: 901 College Avenue, Winona Lake, IN 46590

Fundamental Methodist Church, Inc.: 1034 North Broadway, Springfield, MO 65801

Primitive Methodist Church, U.S.A.: Sec., the Rev. G. Kenneth Tyson, 7202 Jonquil Drive, Orlando, FL 32808

Reformed Methodist Union Episcopal Church: Charleston, SC 29407

Reformed Zion Union Apostolic Church: Deacon James C. Feggins, 416 South Hill Avenue, South Hill, VA 23907

Southern Methodist Church: Pres., the Rev. J. B. Gamble, P.O. Box 132, Orangeburg, SC 29115

Union American Methodist Episcopal Church: The Rev. David M. Harmon, 774 Pine Street, Camden, NJ 08123

Metropolitan Church Association: 333 Broad Street, Lake Geneva, WI 53147

Missionary Church: 3901 South Wayne Avenue, Fort Wayne, IN 46807

Moravians:

Moravian Church in America (*Unitas Fratrum*): 69 West Church Street, P.O. Box 1245, Bethlehem, PA 18018

Unity of the Brethren: Pres., the Rev. Milton Maly, 2205 Carnation Lane, Temple, TX 76501

Muslims: The Islamic Center of Washington, 2551 Massachusetts Avenue, NW, Washington, DC 20008

New Apostolic Church of North America: 3753 North Troy Street, Chicago, IL 60618

HEADQUARTERS OF DENOMINATIONS

Old Catholic Churches:

American Catholic Church, Archdiocese of New York: Most Rev. James Francis Lashley, 457 West 144th Street, New York, NY 10030

American Catholic Church (Syro-Antiochian): St. Peter's Cathedral, 1811 NW 4th Court, Miami, FL 33136

Mariavite Old Catholic Church: 2803 10th Street, Wyandotte, MI 48192

North American Old Roman Catholic Church: 236 Wyona Street, Brooklyn, NY 11207

Open Bible Standard Churches, Inc.: Sec., O. Ralph Isbil, P.O. Box 1737, Des Moines, IA 50306

Pentecostal Bodies:

Assemblies of God (General Council of): 1445 Boonville Avenue, Springfield, MO 65802

Elim Fellowship: Carlton Spencer, Elim Fellowship, Lima, NY 14485

Emmanuel Holiness Church: Sec., J. Robert Hicks, Route 3, Anderson, SC 29621

Independent Assemblies of God—International: 3840 Fifth Avenue, San Diego, CA 92103

International Pentecostal Assemblies: 892 Berne Street, Atlanta, GA 30316

Pentecostal Assemblies of the World: 3040 North Illinois Street, Indianapolis, IN 46208

Pentecostal Church of Christ: Box 263, London, OH 43140

Pentecostal Church of God: 221 Main Street, Joplin, MO 64801

Pentecostal Fire-Baptized Holiness Church: Taccoa, GA 30577

Pentecostal Free Will Baptist Church, Inc.: P.O. Box 1081, Dunn, NC 28334

Pentecostal Holiness Church: P.O. Box 12609, Oklahoma City, OK 73157

United Pentecostal Church International: 8855 Dunn Road, Hazelwood, MO 63042

Pillar of Fire: Zarepath, NJ 08890

Polish National Catholic Church of America: 529 East Locust Street, Scranton, PA 18505

Presbyterians:

United Presbyterian Church in the U.S.A.: 475 Riverside Drive, New York, NY 10027

Presbyterian Church in the United States: 341 Ponce de Leon Avenue, NE, Atlanta, GA 30308

Presbyterian Church in America: P.O. Box 256, Clinton, MS 39056

Associate Reformed Presbyterian Church: 300 University Ridge, Ste. 206, Greenville, SC 29601

Bible Presbyterian Church: Haddon Avenue and Cuthbert Boulevard, Collingswood, NJ 08108

Cumberland Presbyterian Church: 1978 Union Avenue, Memphis, TN 38104

Second Cumberland Church in the U.S.: Clerk, the Rev. R. E. Thomas, 1404 North Grand Avenue, Tyler, TX 75701

Orthodox Presbyterian Church: 7401 Old York Road, Philadelphia, PA 19126

Reformed Presbyterian Church, Evangelical Synod: Clerk, Dr. Paul R. Gilchrist, 107 Haedy Road, Lookout Mountain, TN 37350

Reformed Presbyterian Church of North America: Clerk, Louis D. Hutmire, 7418 Penn Avenue, Pittsburgh, PA 15208

Reformed Bodies:

Reformed Church in America: 475 Riverside Drive, New York, NY 10027

Christian Reformed Church: Stated Clerk William P. Brink, 2850 Kalamazoo Avenue, SE, Grand Rapids, MI 49508

Hungarian Reformed Church in America: Bishop Dezso Abraham, 18700 Midway Avenue, Allen Park, MI 48101

Netherlands Reformed Congregations: Pres. of Synod, the Rev. W. C. Lamain, 2115 Romence Drive, NE, Grand Rapids, MI 49503

Protestant Reformed Churches in America: 16515 South Park Avenue, South Holland, IL 60473

Reformed Church in the U.S.: Clerk, the Rev. D. W. Treick, 2604 West 8th Street, Hastings, NE 68901

Roman Catholic Church: U.S. Catholic Conference, 1312 Massachusetts Avenue, NW, Washington, DC 20005

Salvation Army: 120-130 West 14th Street, New York, NY 10011

Schwenkfelder Church: Pennsburg, PA 18073

Social Brethren: The Rev. John Bailey, R. R. 1, Box 122, Simpson, IL 62985

Spiritualists:

International General Assembly of Spiritualists: 1809 East Bayview Boulevard, Norfolk, VA 23503

National Spiritual Alliance of the U.S.A.: Lake Pleasant, MA 01347

National Spiritual Association of Churches: Sec., the Rev. Alice M. Hull, P.O. Box 128, Cassadaga, FL 37206

Theosophy: Theosophical Publishing House, 306 West Geneva Road, Wheaton, IL 60187

Triumph the Church and Kingdom of God in Christ (International): 213 Farrington Avenue, Atlanta, GA 30318

Unitarian Universalist Association: 25 Beacon Street, Boston, MA 02108

United Church of Christ: 297 Park Avenue, South, New York, NY 10010

United Holy Church of America, Inc.: 159 West Coulter Street, Philadelphia, PA 19144

Unity School of Christianity: Unity Village, MO 64063

Vedanta Society: 34 West 71st Street, New York, NY 10023

Volunteers of America: 340 West 85th Street, New York, NY 10024

Wesleyan Church: Gen. Sec., the Rev. D. Wayne Brown, P.O. Box 2000, Marion, IN 46952

GLOSSARY OF TERMS

The definitions rendered here depend largely upon 6 sources: *The Dictionary of Religion and Ethics,* edited by Shailer Mathews and Gerald B. Smith (Macmillan); *Funk and Wagnall's College Standard Dictionary; Webster's Dictionary* (Merriam); *The Oxford Dictionary of the Christian Church* (Oxford); *Dictionary of Ecclesiastical Terms,* by J. S. Purvis (Nelson); *Dictionary of Religious Terms,* by Donald T. Kauffman (Revell); *A Christian's Dictionary,* by James S. Kerr and Charles Lutz (Fortress Press).

Absolution: The remission of guilt and penalty for sin by a priest, following confession.

Adoption: A legal term appropriated by theology, originating in Paul and signifying the act by which the privileges of a child of God are conferred upon the believer in Christ.

Adoration: An act of homage to God.

Adventist: A believer in the incarnation of God in Christ, at the time of Christ's birth, or in the Second Coming or Advent.

Affusion: The pouring or sprinkling of water in baptism.

Allah: In Islam, the name of the Supreme Being or all-powerful God.

Anastasis: A Greek word meaning "the resurrection."

Anathema: Anything damned or despised.

Anchorite: A monk or zealous one who lives in isolation.

Antichrist: Against Christ. A powerful evil leader to be conquered at Christ's second coming.

Annunciation: The announcement by the angel Gabriel to the Virgin Mary that she was to be the mother of Christ.

Anointing: The act of consecrating by the application of oil, used in consecrating sacred objects or persons, as preparation for death, or in completing the efficacy of baptism.

Antinomianism: The doctrine that the gospel or the Christian faith does away with the old moral law, so that the Christian is not bound by it.

Apocalyptic: Pertaining to or in the nature of a revelation.

Apocrypha: A group of books excluded by Protestants from the Bible as not authoritative but worthy of study for their religious and historical value.

Apostolic: Of or pertaining to an apostle or according to the belief or practices of the apostles.

Apostolic Succession: The doctrine of an unbroken line of succession in the episcopacy from the apostles to the present time, maintained in Greek, Roman, and Anglican churches.

Arminian: The followers of Arminius (1560–1609), a Dutch Protestant theologian. Arminius denied Calvin's doctrine of unconditional predestination, limited atonement, and irresistible grace, and stood for universal salvation for all.

Athanasian: The belief of Athanasius (193–373), who was a defender of the orthodox view of the divinity of Christ. He opposed and won over Arius at the Council of Nicaea; Arius held that Christ was created by but was essentially different from the Father.

Atonement: The reconciliation of the sinner with God through the sufferings of Jesus Christ.

Autocephalous: Ecclesiastically self-controlling, or having jurisdiction as an independent head. "Autocephali" was a term applied to bishops in early Christian times who recognized no ecclesiastical superior.

Autonomous: Self-governing, or independent.

Ban, The: A sentence which amounts to excommunication or outlawry by the church upon those guilty of an act or speech forbidden by the church.

Baptism: The ceremonial application of water to a person by either sprinkling, immersion, or affusion as a sign of the washing away of sin and of admission into the church as commanded by Christ in Matt. 28:19. Spirit baptism in some sects is a baptism by the Holy Ghost, not with water.

Binitarianism: The doctrine teaching that there are only 2 persons in the Godhead (Father and Son).

Born Again, To Be: The experience of a second birth in the Spirit.

Byzantine: Related to the city of Byzantium.

Calvinists: Those holding the faith of John Calvin (1509-64).

Canon: The books admitted to the Bible as authentic and authoritative.

Catechism: The form or guide of instruction used in instruction of candidates for church membership, preceding baptism. The book containing items for such instruction.

Catholic Epistles: The New Testament Epistles (usually James, I and II Peter, I John and Jude, II and III John) that were addressed to the whole (catholic) church.

Catholicos: An Oriental primate or head of a sect. "Catholikos" was a term assumed by the spiritual head of the Armenian church and later applied to several prelates under him.

Celibacy: The state of being unmarried.

Cenobite: Person in a religious order who lives in a separate cell, but who is also a member of a community of other such persons.

Chalice: A cup used at Communion services resembling the one used at the original Last Supper.

Charisma: An unusual gift or ability (in Greek, it is the word for "grace") enabling one to influence others.

Chastity: The state of refraining from sexual relations in order to obtain religious or moral purity.

Chrism: An ungent, usually olive oil or balm, used in the Greek and Roman Catholic churches for anointing at baptism, confirmation, ordination, and consecration services, and sometimes for extreme unction. Chrismation is the act of anointing.

Christocentric: With Christ as the center.

Christology: Any comprehensive teaching about Christ.

Classis: In some Reformed churches a court made up of ministers and ruling elders with a status between a consistory and a synod, corresponding to the presbytery in Presbyterian churches. It may also mean the district it represents.

Collect: Brief prayer asking for specific blessing. Or, generally, in Roman and Anglican liturgies, a prayer read before the Gospel and Epistle are read, to condense or "collect" their teaching.

Communicant: A church member who participates in the Lord's Supper.

Communion: The Lord's Supper. "Open" Communion is a sacrament open to all Christians; "closed" Communion is closed to all except those of a particular faith or belief. The word is also used occasionally as a synonym for denomination.

Communion of Saints: The spiritual union in the Christian community.

Confession: A statement of the religious beliefs of a religious body, or an admission of sin upon conversion.

Confirmation: The initiatory rite by which persons are inducted into the church, or the approval of authorities by which the election of bishops is ratified by the church.

Congregational: The church polity that makes the authority of the local congregation supreme within its own area.

Consecrate: To set apart as sacred certain persons, animals, places, objects, or times.

Consistory: (1) An ecclesiastical court. The papal (Roman Catholic) consistory is composed of the College of Cardinals, over whom the pope presides, and meets to ratify various measures. (2) The Dutch Reformed consistory corresponds to the Presbyterian session. (3) The French Reformed consistory is similar to the presbytery in Presbyterian polity. (4) The Lutheran consistory (abroad) is appointed by the state. (5) The consistory of the Anglicans has diocesan jurisdiction.

Consubstantiation: The theory that, following the words of institution in the Lord's Supper, the substantial body and blood of Christ join sacramentally with the bread and wine (which remains unchanged), the union remaining only until the purpose of the consecration is fulfilled. Applied often to Lutheran doctrine, it is denied by the Lutherans.

Contrition: Sorrow and/or repentance for sin.

Conversion: Religiously, a radical spiritual and moral change, commonly attending a change of belief, and involving profoundly altered spirit and conduct—"a change of heart."

Covenant: Sacred relationship between God and man. The designations "Old Testament" and "New Testament" indicate the Christian concept of the old covenant of works in Judaism being supplanted by the new covenant of grace through the work of Christ.

Creed: A statement of belief including the fundamentals considered necessary to salvation; a creed differs from a confession in that it may be held by Christians and recited in public worship.

Deacon: A minor church officer; its origin is often identified with the appointment of the 7 in Acts 6:1-6.

Decalogue: The Ten Commandments.

Defrock: The banning of a priest or minister from his office.

Deism: School of philosophy and theology teaching God's relation to man as expressed in universal natural law rather than through revelation.

Diocese: The territory of a church under the jurisdiction of a bishop.

Dispensationalism: The doctrine that the history of the world is divided into specific time periods, or "dispensations"; usually 7 in number.

Doctrine: That which is taught as the belief of a church.

Dogma: Belief authoritatively held by a religious group.

Ecclesiastical: Pertaining to the church or the clergy.

Ecumenical or Oecumenical: General, universal, representing the whole Christian church.

Ecumenical Councils, The: The 7 early church councils of Nicaea (I) in 325, Constantinople (I) in 381, Ephesus in 431, Chalcedon in 451, Constantinople (II) in 553, Constantinople (III) in 680, and Nicaea (II) in 787.

Election: Selection of an individual by God for salvation.

Encyclical: A circular letter sent to local churches, usually a communication from the pope, but more recently used in a broader sense to report the actions or findings of church conferences.

Episcopal: Having to do with bishops, or governed by bishops.

Eschatology: Study of the last things, involving the final coming and triumph of Christ and his Kingdom, and sometimes the resurrection and related topics.

Esoteric: A term based on the custom in the Greek Mystery religions to explain advanced doctrines only to the fully initiated.

Eucharist: Holy Communion, the Lord's Supper.

Evangelical: A word used to denote primary loyalty to the gospel of Christ in contrast to ecclesiastical or rationalistic types of Christianity; spiritual-mindedness and zeal for Christ living as distinguished from ritualism.

Excommunication: Exclusion from the religious fellowship of the church; can be either permanent or temporary.

Extreme Unction: See unction.

Fall of Man: Man's estrangement from God through sin, as symbolized by the disobedience of Adam and Eve.

Fasting: Going without food or certain foods for a specified period.

Feast Day: A day in the church calendar set aside for celebration, for feasting and not fasting, such as Christmas or Easter.

Foot Washing: The practice of washing the feet of fellow church members, sometimes as a ceremonial cleansing from defilement preparatory to worship, sometimes as an ordinace, by Mennonites, Dunkards, the Church of God, and so on.

Fornication: Sexual intercourse outside marriage.

Free Will: Man's power to choose between good and evil without compulsion or necessity.

Fundamentalist: One who believes in the infallibility of the Bible as inspired by God and that it should be accepted literally—as distinguished from the modernist, who interprets the Bible in accordance with more modern scholarship or scientific knowledge—and who accepts the conservative orthodox position in all manner of doctrine and theology.

Future Punishment: The punishment inflicted upon sinners *after death.*

General Confession: A public, congregational confession of sins; among Roman Catholics, a confession in which the individual sums up past sins; among Protestants, a section of the ritual recited in unison by pastor and congregation, modeled on historic Roman Catholic and Anglican forms.

Generationism: The belief that the soul as well as the body is procreated by the parents of the child in the act of propagation. Similar to traducianism, but different from creationism and preexistence.

Genuflection: The act of bending the knee in worship, or in entering the sanctuary or approaching the altar, as an indication of reverence and humility—a custom dating from the early church, still prevalent in many liturgical churches.

Gift of Tongues: Ecstatic speech induced by religious excitement or emotion.

Glossolalia: Speaking in tongues—the psychological and religious phenomenon described in the account of Pentecost in Acts 2.

Grace: The gift of God to man of the divine favor and inner power necessary to salvation.

Heterodox: Not orthodox; contrary to the accepted teachings.

Hierarchy: Government by priests or prelates, as in the Roman Catholic Church.

Holiness: A state of moral and spiritual purity and sinlessness, or a title designating persons set apart for religious service.

Holy Orders: The power granted the ecclesiastical leaders of the church (bishops, priests, ministers, elders, deacons, subdeacons, etc.) to direct the spiritual function of the church.

Immaculate Conception, The: The dogma that the Virgin Mary was conceived free of original sin.

Immanence: A term describing the presence of God in the world, as opposed to his transcendence.

Immersion: Baptism by complete submersion in water.

Impanation: The doctrine that the body and blood of Christ are present in one substance in the bread and wine of the Eucharist after consecration, but without transubstantiation; held to be heretical by the Roman Catholic Church.

Immortality: Life after death, life imperishable.

Incarnation: God's becoming man in Jesus Christ.

Indulgence: In the Roman Catholic Church, a remission "of the temporal punishment due to sins, the guilt of which has already been remitted." Granted only when penance is shown.

Inerrant: The quality of being without fault; applied to the text of the Bible by some Christians.

Infallibility: The authority of the Scriptures as incapable of error, or a term applied to the pope of Rome.

Inspiration, Verbal: Signifying the supernatural influence upon the writers of the Scriptures by which divine authority was given their work and that places the Bible beyond error.

Judgment, Judgment Day: The act of judging by God on the last "judgment day," when reward and punishments are to be declared.

Justification: Freeing or being freed from the guilt or penalty of sin and restored to divine favor. God's Act by which men are declared righteous, because of the merits of Christ.

Kiss of Peace, or Holy Kiss: A religious greeting or ceremony, a kiss of welcome.

Laity: Those members of the church who are not clergy.

Laying on of Hands: A rite of consecration and affirmation.

Litany: Form of prayer made up of a series of petitions by the minister or priest, with congregational responses.

Liturgy, Liturgical: A liturgy is a prescribed form or collection of forms for public worship; in liturgical churches rite and ceremony are more prominent than the emphasis upon preaching or evangelism.

Logos: Christ as the Word, eternally generated from the substance of God the Father; the second Person of the Trinity.

Love Feast: A common devotional meal of the early Christians, culminating in the Eucharist, and sometimes called agape.

Mass, The: The central worship service of the Roman Catholic Church, consisting of prayers and ceremonies; sometimes the Holy Eucharist as a sacrifice.

Mariolatry: The worship of and/or devotion to the Virgin Mary.

Medium: A person through whom supposed messages from the spiritual world are sent, as in Spiritualism.

Metropolitan: A bishop in an Eastern church who has provincial as well as diocesan powers.

Minor Order: Orders below those of bishop, priest, deacon, and subdeacon (such as porters, lectors, lay readers, acolytes). Those in minor orders are not ordained, but act under a benediction from the bishop.

Modernist: See **Fundamentalist.**

Monophysitism: The doctrine that Christ had but one composite divine-human nature.

Monotheism: Belief in one, and only one God, as opposed to polytheism or pantheism.

Mysticism: A type of religion that puts the emphasis on an immediate experience of God, a direct and intimate consciousness of divine reality, without the intermediate stages or means often thought essential.

Nestorian: Member of a Christian sect named after Nestorius, a fifth-century Syrian patriarch of Constantinople condemned as a heretic; still found in Turkey and Persia.

Nicene: Pertaining to Nicaea, when the Nicene Creed was adopted at the famous council of 325, settling the controversy concerning the persons of the Trinity; properly called the Niceno-Constantinopolitan Creed.

Nonconformist: One who does not accept established ways, such as a Protestant in England who does not belong to the established Anglican Church.

Ordinance: A religious rite or ceremony not considered as a sacrament.

Orthodoxy: Belief in doctrine considered correct and sound, or holding the commonly accepted faith.

Pacifism: Opposition to all military ideals, preparedness, war, and so on.

Passover: The Jewish festival commemorating the time in Egypt when God "passed over" Israelite homes but required the death of Egyptian firstborn.

Patriarch: A bishop of highest rank, standing above metropolitans and ruling patriarchates.

Peace Churches: Churches historically holding a pacifist position, such as Friends and Mennonites.

Patriarch: A bishop of highest rank, standing above metropolitans and ruling patriarchates.

Penance: An ecclesiastical punishment inflicted for sin, or a sacrament of the Roman Catholic Church.

Pentecostal: The religious experience of conversion based upon the descent of the Holy Ghost upon the apostles at the biblical Pentecost.

Perfection: The complete realization of moral or spiritual possibilities in personal experience.

Pietism: Specifically, a German Lutheran movement of the seventeenth and eighteenth centuries, in the interests of revival from a stagnant orthodoxy. Generally, a term used to designate those movements in current Christianity emphasizing the personal, spiritual, and practical rather than the institutional, formal, and intellectual aspects of faith.

Plenary: Full, complete; a plenary council is attended by all its qualified members.

Polity: A particular form or system of government.

Predestinarian: A believer in predestinarianism—that all events are predetermined by God and that each person's eternal destiny is fixed by divine decree.

Premillenialism: Belief that the personal visible return of Christ will precede his reign for a thousand years on earth; postmillenarians believe that the return will come at the end of the millennium.

Presbytery: A church court or assembly having the ecclesiastical or spiritual rule and oversight of a district or the district itself.

Reconciliation: The process of being brought back into fellowship with God.

Redemption: God's deliverance of man from sin and death through the sacrificial atonement of Christ.

Regeneration: A new birth, re-creation, a radical renewal of life, or conversion.

Religious: Those in the Roman Catholic Church who are members of an order.

Remission of Sin: Pardon or forgiveness for sin.

Repentance: Turning from a sinful to a godly life.

Reprobation: Eternal condemnation, the fate of those not included in God's election.

Revelation: What God makes known to men, as in Scripture.

Ritual: Religious ceremony or its verbal form.

Sabbatarian: One who believes that the seventh day should be observed as the Christian Sabbath.

Sacerdotal: A term denoting a religious system in which everything is valued in relation to the ministrations of the priestly order.

Sacramental: A religious rite composed of 2 elements, a physical sign and a spiritual good.

Salvation: The rescue of man from evil or guilt by God's power, that he may obtain blessedness.

Sanctification: The work of the Holy Spirit by which the believer is set free from sin and exalted to holiness of life.

Second Coming: The second advent of Jesus. *See* **Premillennialism.**

See: The local seat from which a bishop, archbishop, or the pope exercises jurisdiction.

Speaking in Tongues: *See* **Glossolalia**.

Suffragan Bishop: An episcopal assistant to a diocesan bishop.

Synod: An ecclesiastical council either of regular standing or appointed as needed; in Presbyterian churches a body between the presbyteries and the general assembly.

Total Depravity: The equivalent of original sin, every human faculty having an innate evil taint.

Tonsured: The shaved head of a person admitted to a monastic order or to holy orders.

Tongues, Gift of: An ecstatic utterance induced by religious excitement.

Transcendence: The exaltation of God above the universe and his distinctness from it.

Transfiguration: Change in form or appearance, such as the transfiguration of Jesus (Mark 9:2-10).

Transmutation: The change from one nature, substance, or form to another.

Transubstantiation: The doctrine that there is present in the Eucharist after consecration of the elements the substantial body and blood of Christ, with his whole soul and divinity.

Trine Immersion: A form of baptism in which the candidate is immersed 3 successive times, in the name of the Father, Son, and Holy Ghost.

Trinitarian: A believer in the Trinity—that there is a union of Father, Son, and Holy Ghost in one divine nature.

Triune: Having the quality of three-in-oneness; a reference to the Trinitarian God.

Unction: A ceremonial anointing with oil, as in extreme unction in case of death or imminent death. (Extreme unction is now designated as "the anointing of the sick.")

Uniat: Persons or churches acknowledging the supremacy of the pope but maintaining their own liturgies or rites.

Unitarian: The theology that insists upon the unity of God, denying the doctrine of the Trinity.

Universalism: The universal fatherhood of God and the final harmony of all souls with God.

Unleavened Bread: Bread made without yeast, necessary for Jewish Passover, and often used in Christian eucharistic services.

Varuna: Hinduism's supreme god and creator.

Veadar: Month in the Jewish calendar that falls between Adar and Misan on leap years.

Vehicle: Buddhist term for a way of salvation.

Venerable: Anglican title for archdeacon; Catholic title for one who has reached a particular point in the process of beatification; title of honor for one of unusual sanctity, as the Venerable Bede.

Venial Sin: In Roman Catholic doctrine, a slight offense that does not require the sacrament of penance, a sin that is not mortal (meriting eternal death).

Venite: "O come." Latin version of Psalm 95, used frequently at Matins.

Versicle: Short statement in a worship service followed by a congregational or choral response.

Vestment: Article of clothing worn by religious officiant.

Vicar: Priest or incumbent of a parish; clergyman who serves as the deputy or substitute for another.

Vocation: Call to serve God, in one's work and life.

Vulgate: Latin version of the Bible translated by Jerome.

Warden: Head of an ecclesiastical institution, or official entrusted with the temporal affairs or the protection of property in a parish.

Western Church: Term for Christianity in Europe or America, or for Roman Catholicism as opposed to Eastern Orthodoxy.

Whitsunday: "White Sunday" or Pentecost, Christian festival on the seventh Sunday after Easter.

Works: New Testament term for demonstrable activity.

Yahweh: Jewish name for the Lord.

Yeshiva: Higher Jewish school for rabbinical and talmudic study.

Zionism: The modern movement that seeks the colonizing of the Jews in Palestine. The forming of the state of Israel in 1948 was in part a result of the Zionist movement.

BIBLIOGRAPHY

GENERAL

Included in this listing are titles recommended by scholars and officials within the various denominations, and others added by the editor. They are listed in 2 classifications: *General*, covering the whole field of the church in the United States, and *Denominational*, covering the separate bodies.

Beyond this, and not included here, there are treatises, tracts, memorials, disciplines, yearbooks, theological outlines, confessions, and other statements of belief and organization obtainable from the headquarters of the denominations listed on pages 259-66.

Ahlstrom, Sydney E. *A Religious History of the American People.* New Haven: Yale University Press, 1973.

Bach, Marcus. *Faith and My Friends.* Indianapolis: Bobbs-Merrill, 1951.

———. *Report to Protestants.* Indianapolis: Bobbs-Merrill, 1953.

———. *Had You Been Born in Another Faith.* Englewood Cliffs, N.J., Prentice-Hall, 1961.

Bainton, R. H. *The Church of Our Fathers.* New York: Scribner's, 1950.

Banks, William L. *The Black Church in the U.S.* Chicago: Moody Press, 1972.

Bates, Ernest Sutherland. *American Faith.* New York: W. W. Norton, 1957.

Brauer, J. C. *Protestantism in America.* Philadelphia: Westminster Press, 1953.

Brown, Robert M. *The Spirit of Protestantism.* New York: Oxford University Press, 1961.

Chadwick, Henry, ed. *The Pelican History of Church.* 6 vols. Baltimore: Penguin Books, 1960-70.

Clark, Elmer T. *The Small Sects in America.* Nashville: Abingdon, 1949.

Cobb, John B. *Varieties of Protestantism.* Philadelphia: Westminster Press, 1960.

Dillenberger, John, and Welch, Claude. *Protestant Christianity.* New York: Scribner's, 1954.

Drummond, A. L. *The Story of American Protestantism.* Boston: Beacon Press, 1950.

Gaustad, Edwin Scott. *Historical Atlas of Religion in America.* New York: Harper, 1962.

———. *A Religious History of America.* New York: Harper, 1964.

Herberg, Will. *Protestant-Catholic-Jew.* New York: Anchor Books, 1955.

Hudson, W. S. *American Protestantism.* Chicago: University of Chicago Press, 1961.

———. *The Great Tradition of American Churches.* New York: Peter Smith, 1963.

———. *Religion in America.* New York: Scribner's, 1965.

———. *The Story of the American Church.* New York: Harper, 1958.

Jacquet, Constant H., Jr., ed. *Yearbook of American and Canadian Churches* (annual). Nashville: Abingdon.

Johnson, D. W., and Cornell, G. W. *Punctured Preconceptions: What North American Christians Think About the Church.* New York: Friendship Press, 1972.

Landis, Benson Y. *Religion in the United States.* New York: Barnes & Noble, 1965.

Latourette, Kenneth S. *Christianity in a Revolutionary Age: The 20th Century Outside Europe.* New York: Harper, 1962.

Mayer, F. E. *The Religious Bodies of America*. St. Louis: Concordia Publishing House, 1954.

Neve, J. L. *Churches and Sects of Christendom*. Blair, Nebr.: Lutheran Publishing House, 1952.

Rosten, Leo. *A Guide to the Religions of America*. St. Louis: Bethany Press, 1963.

Schaff, Philip. *The Creeds of Christendom*. New York: Harper, 1919.

Smith, H. Shelton, Handy, Robert T., and Loetscher, Lefferts A. *American Christianity: An Historical Interpretation with Representative Documents*. 2 vols. New York: Scribner's, 1960–1963.

Smith, James W. *Religion in American Life*. 4 vols. Princeton University Press, 1961.

Sohm, Rudolf. *Outlines of Church History*. Boston: Beacon Press, 1958.

Spence, Hartzell. *The Story of America's Religions*. Nashville: Abingdon, 1962.

Sperry, W. L. *Religion in America*. Boston: Beacon Press, 1963.

Stuber, Stanley I. *How We Got Our Denominations*. New York: Association Press, 1948.

Sweet, W. W. *The American Churches: An Interpretation*. Nashville: Abingdon, 1948.

———. *Religion in the Development of American Culture*. New York: Scribner's, 1952.

———. *The Story of Religion in America*. New York: Harper, 1930.

Walker, Williston. *History of the Christian Church*. New York: Scribner's, 1959.

Whalen, William J. *Separated Brethren*. Milwaukee: Our Sunday Visitor Press, 1979.

Williams, J. Paul. *What Americans Believe and How They Worship*. New York: Harper, 1962.

DENOMINATIONAL

Adventism

Froom, Le Roy E. *The Prophetic Faith of Our Fathers*. 4 vols. Washington, D.C.: Review and Herald Publishing Assn., 1946-54.

Hasel, Gerard F. *Old Testament Theology: Basic Issues in the Current Debate*. Grand Rapids: Eerdmans, 1972.

Herndon, Booton. *The Seventh-day: The Story of the Seventh-day Adventists*. New York: McGraw-Hill, 1960.

Johnsen, Carsten. *Man-The Invisible*. Norwegian Research Council for Science and the Humanities. Oslo: Universitetsforlaget, 1971.

Maxwell, Arthur S. *Your Friends the Adventists*. Mountain View, Calif.: Pacific Press Publishing Assn., 1960.

Seventh-day Adventists Answer Questions on Doctrines. Washington, D.C.: Review and Herald Publishing Assn., 1957.

Spalding, Arthur W. *Origin and History of Seventh-day Adventists*. 4 vols. Washington, D.C.: Review and Herald Publishing Assn., 1961.

White, Ellen G. *The Desire of Ages*. Mountain View, Calif.: Pacific Press Publishing Assn., 1940.

————. *The Great Controversy Between Christ and Satan*. Mountain View, Calif.: Pacific Press Publishing Assn., 1927.

Bahá'í

Abdul-Bahá. *Some Answered Questions*. Wilmette, Ill.: Bahá'í Publishing Trust.

Amato'l-Bahá Ruhiyyih Khanum. *The Priceless Pearl*. Wilmette, Ill.: Bahá'í Publishing Trust.

Esselmont, J. E. *Bahaullah and the New Era*. Wilmette, Ill.: Bahá'í Publishing Trust, 1971.

Faizi, Gloria. *The Bahai Faith: An Introduction*. Wilmette, Ill.: Bahá'í Publishing Trust, 1973.

Hofman, David. *Renewal of Civilization*. Wilmette, Ill.: Bahá'í Publishing Trust, 1970.

Nabil. *The Dawn Breakers*. Wilmette, Ill.: Bahá'í Publishing Trust.

Shoghi Effenid. *God Passes By*. Wilmette, Ill.: Bahá'í Publishing Trust.

————. *The World Order of Baha'u'llah*. Wilmette, Ill.: Bahá'í Publishing Trust.

Spears, Wm. *Release the Sun*. Wilmette, Ill.: Bahá'í Publishing Trust.

Baptists

Armstrong, O. K. and Marjorie. *The Indomitable Baptists*. Garden City, N.Y.: Doubleday, 1967.

Campbell, Alexander. *Christian Baptism with Its Antecedents and Consequences*. Bethany, Va.: A. Campbell, 1852.

Cox, Norman W. *Encyclopedia of Southern Baptists*. Nashville: Broadman Press, 1958.

Maring, Norman H., and Winthrop, S. Hudson. *A Baptist Manual of Polity and Practice*. Valley Forge, Pa.: Judson Press, 1963.

Newman, A. H. *History of the Baptist Churches in the United States*. Philadelphia: American Baptists Publication Society, 1913.

Olson, Adolf. *A Centenary History*. (Baptist General Conference of America) Chicago: Baptist Conference Press, 1952.

Pelt, Owen C., and Smith, Ralph Lee. *The Story of the National Baptists*. New York: Vantage Press, 1960.

Ramaker, A. J. *The German Baptists in North America*. Cleveland: German Baptist Publication Society, 1924.

Shelley, Bruce L. *Conservative Baptists: A Story of Twentieth Century Dissent*. Denver: Conservative Baptist Theological Seminary, 1960.

Stealey, S. L. *A Baptist Treasury*. New York: Thomas Y. Crowell, 1958.

Sweet, W. W. *Religion on the American Frontier: The Baptists*. New York: Henry Holt & Co., 1931.

Torbet, R. G. *A History of the Baptists*. Valley Forge, Pa.: Judson Press, 1973.

Tull, James E. *Shapers of Baptist Thought*. Valley Forge, Pa.: Judson Press, 1972.

Black Churches

Frazier, E. Franklin. *The Negro Church in America*. New York: Schocken Books, 1961.

Mays, Benjamin E., and Nicholson, Joseph W. *The Negro's Church*. New York: Institute of Social and Religious Research, 1933.

Nelsen, Hart M., Yokely, Raytha, and Nelsen, Anne. *The Black Church in America*. New York: Basic Books, 1971.

Pelt, O. D., and Smith, Ralph J. *The Story of the National Baptists*. New York: Vantage Press, 1973.

Washington, Joseph R., Jr. *Black Religion: The Negro and Christianity in the United States*. Boston: Beacon Press, 1964.

Woodson, Carter G. *The History of the Negro Church*. 2d ed. Washington, D.C.: Associated Publishers, 1921.

Brethren

Bittenger, Emmert F. *Heritage and Promise*. Elgin, Ill.: Brethren Press, 1970.

Durnbaugh, Donald F. *The Brethren in Colonial America*. Elgin, Ill.: Brethren Press, 1958.

———. *European Origins of the Brethren*. Elgin, Ill.: Brethren Press, 1958.

Garber, Ora W. *The Church of the Brethren*. Elgin, Ill.: Brethren Press, 1967.

Sappington, Roger E. *Brethren and Social Policys 1908–1958*. Elgin, Ill.: Brethren Press, 1961.

Christian Science

A Century of Christian Science Healing. Boston: Christian Science Publishing Society, 1966.

Beasley, Norman. *The Cross and the Crown: The History of Christian Science*. New York: Duell, Sloan & Pearce, 1952.

Canham, Erwin D. *Committment to Freedom: The Story of the Christian Science Monitor*. Boston: Houghton Mifflin, 1958.

———. *Science and Health with Key to the Scriptures*. Boston: Christian Science Board of Directors. Many editions.

Gottschalk, Stephen. *The Emergence of Christian Science in American Religious Life*. Berkeley: University of California Press, 1973.

DeWitt, John. *The Christian Science Way of Life*. Boston: Christian Science Publishing Society, 1971.

Leishman, Thomas. *Why I Am a Christian Scientist*. Camden, N.J.: Thomas Nelson, 1958.

Peel, Robert. *Mary Baker Eddy: The Years of Discovery*. New York: Holt, Rinehart & Winston, 1966.

———. *Mary Baker Eddy: The Years of Trial*. New York: Holt, Rinehart & Winston, 1971.

———. *Christian Science: Its Encounter with American Culture*. New York: Holt, Rinehart & Winston, 1958.

Church of God

Brown, C. E. *When the Trumpet Sounded* (History of the Church of God of Anderson, Ind.). Anderson, Ind.: Warner Press, 1951.

Conn, Charles W. *Like a Mighty Army*. Cleveland, Tenn.: Church of God Publishing House, 1955.

Forney, C. H. *History of the Churches of God*. Harrisburg, Pa.: Christian Publications, Inc., 1914.

Frodsham, S. H. *With Signs Following*. Springfield, Mo.: Gospel Publishing House, 1941.

Riggs, R. M. *The Spirit Himself*. Springfield, Mo.: Gospel Publishing House, 1949.

Church of the Nazarene

Redford, M. E. *The Rise of the Church of the Nazarene*. Kansas City: Nazarene Publishing House, 1951.

Smith, Timothy L. *Called to Holiness: The Story of the Nazarenes, The Formative Years*. Kansas City, Mo.: Nazarene Publishing House, 1962.

Churches of Christ

MacClenny, W. E. *Life of James O'Kelly*. Indianapolis, Ind.: United Christian Missionary Society, 1950.

Stone, B. W. *Biography of Elder Barton Warren Stone*. Cincinnati: Standard Publishing Co., 1847.

West, E. *Search for the Ancient Order*. Indianapolis, Ind.: 1951.

Churches of the New Jerusalem (Swedenborgians)

Barrett, B. F. *The Question, What Are the Doctrines of the New Church? Answered*. Germantown, Pa.: Swedenborg Publication Association, 1909.

Smythe, J. K. *Gist of Swedenborg*. Philadelphia: J. B. Lippincott Co., 1920.

Swedenborg, Emanuel. *Complete Works*. Boston: Houghton Mifflin, 1907.

Disciples of Christ

Beazley, George G., Jr. *The Christian Church (Disciples of Christ): An Interpretative Examination in the Cultural Context*. St. Louis: Bethany Press, 1973.

Campbell, Alexander. *Creative Freedom in Action*. 1832.

Crain, James Andrew. *The Development of Social Ideas Among the Disciples of Christ*. St. Louis: Bethany Press, 1969.

Garrison, W. E., and DeGroot, A. T. *Disciples of Christ, A History*. St. Louis: Bethany Press, 1958.

Garrison, Winifred E. *Heritage and Destiny*. St. Louis: Bethany Press, 1963.

Harrell, David Edwin, Jr. *Quest for a Christian America: The Disciples of Christ and American Society to 1866*. Nashville: The Disciples of Christ Historical Society, 1966.

Humbert, Royal, ed. *A Compend of Alexander Campbell's Theology*. St. Louis: Bethany Press, 1961.

Lair, Loren E. *The Christian Churches and Their Work*. St. Louis: Bethany Press, 1963.

Panel of Scholars. *The Renewal of Church*. St. Louis: Bethany Press, 1963.

Whitley, Oliver R. *The Trumpet Call of Reformation*. St. Louis: Bethany Press, 1963.

Eastern Churches

Benz, Ernst. *The Eastern Orthodox Church: Its Thought and Life*. Trans. Richard and Clara Wonston. Aldine Publishing Co., 1963.

Bespuda, Anastasia. *Guide to Orthodox America*. Tuckahoe, N.Y.: Saint Vladimir's Seminary Press, 1965.

Bogolepov, Alexander A. *Toward an American Orthodox Church: The Establishment of an Autocephalous Orthodox Church*. New York: Morehouse-Barlow Co., 1963.

Bratsiotis, Panagiotis. *The Greek Catholic Church*. Notre Dame and London: University of Notre Dame Press, 1967.

Bulgakov, Sergius. *The Orthodox Church*. Milwaukee: Morehouse Publishing Co., 1935.

Constantelos, Demetrios J. *The Greek Orthodox Church*. New York: The Seabury Press, 1967.

Emhardt, Chauncy, et al. *The Eastern Church in the Western World*. Milwaukee: Morehouse Publishing Co., 1828.

LeGuillou, M. J. *The Spirit of Eastern Orthodoxy*. New York: Hawthorne Books, 1962.

Meyendorff, John. *The Orthodox Church*. London: Darton, Longman and Todd. New York: Pantheon Books (Random House).

Salutos, Theodore. *The Greeks in America*. Cambridge, Mass.: Harvard University Press, 1964.

Schmemann, Alexander. *The Historical Road of Eastern Orthodoxy*. New York: Holt, Rinehart & Winston, 1963.

Ware, Timothy. *The Orthodox Church*. Baltimore: Penguin Books, 1964.

Zernov, Nicholas. *Eastern Christendom: A Study of the Origin and Development of the Eastern Orthodox Church*. New York: G. P. Putnam's Sons, 1961.

Episcopal Church

Addison, J. T. *The Episcopal Church in the United States: 1789–1831*. New York: Scribner's, 1951.

Albright, Raymond W. *History of the Protestant Episcopal Church*. New York: Macmillan, 1964.

Chorley, E. C. *Men and Movements in the American Episcopal Church*. New York: Scribner's, 1946.

Damrosch, Frank, Jr. *The Faith of the Episcopal Church*. New York: Morehouse-Gorham, 1946.

DeMille, George E. *The Episcopal Church Since 1900*. New York: Morehouse-Barlow, 1955.

Manross, W. W. *A History of the American Episcopal Church*. New York: Morehouse-Gorham, 1950.

McConnell, S. D. *History of the American Episcopal Church*. Milwaukee: Morehouse Publishing Co., 1916.

Pittenger, W. Norman. *The Episcopalian Way of Life*. Englewood Cliffs, N.J.: Prentice-Hall, 1957.

Simcox, Carroll E. *Approach to the Episcopal Church*. New York: Morehouse, Barlow, 1961.

Will, Theodore. *The Episcopal Church*. New York: Morehouse-Gorham, 1934.

Wilson, Frank E. *Faith and Practice*. New York: Morehouse-Gorham, 1941.

BIBLIOGRAPHY

Friends

Bacon, M. *Quiet Rebels*. New York: Basic Books, 1969.

Barclay, Robert. *Apology for a True Christian Divinity*. 1959.

Boulding, K. E. *Evolutionary Potential of Quakerism*. Pendle Hill pamphlet, 1964.

Brinton, H. *Quaker Education: In Theory and Practice*. Pendle Hill, 1958. Paper. *Friends for 300 Years*. Pendle Hill.

Bronner, Edwin. *American Quakers Today*. Friends World Committee, 1966.

Comfort, W. W. *The Quaker Way: Just Among Friends*. Philadelphia: American Friends Service Committee, 1968. Paper.

Cooper, C. W., ed. *Break the New Ground: Seven Essays by Contemporary Quakers*. Philadelphia: Friends World Committee, 1969.

de Hartog, J. *The Hospital*. New York: Atheneum, 1964.

Jonas, G. *On Doing Good*. New York: Scribner's, 1971.

Loukes, H. *Quaker Contribution*. New York: Macmillan, 1965.

West, J. *Quaker Reader*. New York: Viking Press, 1969.

Jehovah's Witnesses

Cole, Marley. *Jehovah's Witnesses. The New World Society*. New York: Vantage Press, 1955.

Jehovah's Witnesses in the Divine Purpose. New York: Watch Tower Bible & Tract Society, 1959.

Let God Be True. New York: Watch Tower Bible & Tract Society, 1946.

New World Translation of the Holy Scriptures. New York: Watch Tower Bible & Tract Society, 1961.

The Truth That Leads to Eternal Life. New York: Watch Tower Bible & Tract Society, 1968.

The Truth That Leads to Eternal Life. New York: Watch Tower Bible & Tract Society, 1968.

True Peace and Security—From What Source? New York: Watch Tower Bible & Tract Society. 1973.

Jewish Congregations

Agus, Jacob Bernard. *Guidepost in Modern Judaism*. New York: Bloch Publishing Co., 1954.

Bamberger, B. J. *The Story of Judaism*. New York: Union of American Hebrew Congregations, 1957.

Dimont, Max, I. *Jews, God and History*. Garden City, N.Y.: Doubleday, 1972.

Donin, Rabbi Hayim Halevy. *To Be a Jew*. New York: Basic Books, 1973.

Eben, Abba. *My People: The Story of the Jews*. New York: Random House.

Finkelstein, Louis. *The Jews: Their History, Culture and Religion*. New York: Harper, 1949.

Gay, Ruth. *Jews in America: A Short History*. New York: Basic Books, 1965.

Gaer, Joseph. *Our Jewish Heritage*. New York: Holt, Rinehart and Winston, 1957.

Glazer, Nathan. *American Judaism*. Chicago: University of Chicago Press, 1957.

Goldman, Nahum. *The Jewish Paradox*. New York: Grossett & Dunlap, 1978.

Gross, David A. *1001 Questions and Answers About Judaism*. New York: Doubleday.

Hertzberg, A. *Judaism*. New York: George Braziller, 1961.

Isaacson, Rabbi Benjamin, and Wigoder, Deborah. *The International Jewish Encyclopedia*. Englewood Cliffs, N.J.: Prentice-Hall, 1973.

Jacobs, Louis. *Jewish Thought Today*. New York: Behrman, 1970.

Jewish Encyclopedia. 12 vols. New York: Keter Publishing Co., 1974.

The Jews: Their Religion and Culture. New York: Shocken, 1970.

Karp, Abraham J. *The Jewish Way of Life*. Englewood Cliffs, N.J.: Prentice-Hall, 1962.

Levinger, Lee J. *A History of the Jews in the United States*. New York: Union of American Hebrew Congregations, 1961.

Millgram, A. E. *Jewish Yearbook*. Jewish Publications, 1971.

Pool, David de Sola. *The American Jew*. New York: Harper, 1942.

Roth, Leon. *Judaism: A Portrait*. New York: Viking Press, 1961.

Steinberg, Milton. *Basic Judaism*. New York: Harcourt, 1947.

Wallach, Michael, ed. *Jewish Year Book* (annual). New York: Hartmore, 1970.

Wouk, Herman. *This Is My God*. Garden City, N.Y.: Doubleday, 1959.

Latter-Day Saints (Mormons)

Anderson, Nels. *Desert Saints: The Morman Frontier in Utah*. Chicago: University of Chicago Press, 1966.

Arrington, L. J. *Great Basin Kingdom: An Economic History of the Latter-day Saints*. Cambridge: Harvard University Press, 1958.

Berrett, W. E. *The Restored Church*. Salt Lake City: Deseret Book Co., 1969.

Brodie, F. M. *No Man Knows My History: The Life of Joseph Smith*. New York: Alfred A. Knopf, 1945.

Hill, M. S., and Allen, J. B., eds. *Mormonism and American Culture*. New York: Harper, 1972.

Hinckley, G. B. *What of the Mormons*. Salt Lake City: Deseret Book Co., 1970.

Howells, R. S. *The Mormon Story*. Salt Lake City: Bookcraft, 1963.

Mullen, Robert. *The Latter-day Saints*. Garden City, N.Y.: Doubleday, 1966.

Nibley, Hugh. *An Approach to the Book of Mormon*. Salt Lake City: Council of the Twelve Apostles of the Church of Jesus Christ of Latter-day Saints, 1957.

O'Dea, Thomas F. *The Mormons*. Chicago: University of Chicago Press, 1957.

Richards, F. D., and Little, J. A. *A Compendium of the Doctrines of the Gospel*. Salt Lake City: Deseret Book Co., 1925.

Richards, Legrande. *Marvelous Work and a Wonder*. Salt Lake City: Deseret Book Co., 1972.

Roberts, B. H. *A Comprehensive History of the Church of Jesus Christ of Latter-day Saints*. Provo: Brigham Young University Press, 1965.

Smith, Joseph. *The Book of Mormon*. Salt Lake City: Deseret Book Co., 1972.

———. *The Doctrine and Covenants*. Salt Lake City: Deseret Book Co., 1971.

———. *The Pearl of Great Price*. Salt Lake City: Deseret Book Co., 1971.

———. *Essential in Church History*. Salt Lake City: Deseret Book Co., 1973.

Talmage, James E. *Articles of Faith*. Salt Lake City: Deseret Book Co., 1971.

West, R. B. *Kingdom of the Saints: The Story of Brigham Young and the Mormons*. New York: Viking Press, 1957.

BIBLIOGRAPHY

Lutherans

Allbeck, Willard D. *Studies in the Lutheran Confessions.* Philadelphia: Fortress Press, 1968.

Arden, G. Everett. *Augustana Heritage.* Rock Island: Augustana Press, 1963.

Bainton, Roland. *Here I Stand.* Nashville: Abingdon, 1950.

Bergendoff, Conrad. *The Church of the Lutheran Reformation.* St. Louis: Concordia Publishing House, 1967.

Bodensieck, Julius, ed. *The Encyclopedia of the Lutheran Church.* Philadelphia: Fortress Press, 1965.

Dillenberger, John, ed. *Martin Luther: Selections from His Writings.* Garden City, N.Y.: Doubleday, 1961.

Ebeling, Gerhard. *Luther: An Introduction to His Thought.* Philadelphia: Fortress Press, 1970.

Kerr, H. T., ed. *A Compend of Luther's Theology.* Philadelphia: Westminster Press, 1943 (paperback, 1966).

Lowe, Ralph W. *The Lutheran Way of Life.* Englewood Cliffs, N.J.: Prentice-Hall, 1966.

Nelson, E. Clifford. *Lutheranism in North America: 1914-1970.* Minneapolis: Augsburg, 1972.

Neve, H. T., and Anderson, B. A., eds. *The Maturing of American Lutheranism.* Minneapolis: Augsburg, 1968.

Neve, J. L. *Introduction to the Symbolical Books of the Lutheran Church.* Columbus: Lutheran Book Concern, 1926.

Sasse, Hermann. *Here We Stand,* trans. T. Tappert. New York: Harper, 1938.

Scherer, James A. *Mission and Unity in Lutheranism.* Philadelphia: Fortress Press, 1969.

Schlink, Edmund. *Theology of the Lutheran Confessions.* Philadelphia: Muhlenberg Press, 1961.

Schmidt, John. *The Lutheran Confessions: Their Value and Meaning.* Philadelphia: Muhlenberg Press, 1956.

Swihart, Altman K. *Luther and the Lutheran Church, 1483-1960.* New York: Philosophical Library, 1960.

Tappert, Theodore G., ed. *The Book of Concord: The Confessions of the Evangelical Lutheran Church.* Philadelphia: Muhlenberg Press, 1959.

———. *Lutheran Confessional Theology in America 1840-1880.* (Library of Protestant Thought) New York: Oxford University Press, 1972.

Vajta, Vilmos, ed. *Church in Fellowship, Vol. 1, Pulpit and Altar Fellowship Among Lutheran Churches in Europe and North America.* Minneapolis: Augsburg, 1963.

Watson, Philip S. *Let God Be God!* Philadelphia: Muhlenberg Press, 1948.

Wentz, Abdel Ross. *A Basic History of Lutheranism in America.* Philadelphia: Fortress Press, 1964.

———. *The Lutheran Church in American History.* Philadelphia: United Lutheran Publication House, 1933.

Wentz, Frederick K. *Lutherans in Concert.* Philadelphia: Fortress Press, 1969.

Wolf, R. C. *Documents of Lutheran Unity in America.* Philadelphia: Fortress Press, 1966.

Mennonites

Bender, Harold S. *Conrad Grebel, The Founder of the Swiss Brethren.* Scottdale, Pa.: Herald Press, 1971.

————. *The Mennonite Encyclopedia.* 4 vols. Scottdale, Pa.: Herald Press, 1955-59.

Dyck, Cornelius J., ed. *Introduction to Mennonite History.* Scottdale, Pa.: Herald Press, 1972.

Hershberger, Guy F. *War, Peace and Nonresistance.* Scottdale, Pa.: Herald Press, 1969.

Mennonite Confession of Faith. Scottdale, Pa.: Herald Press, 1968.

Smith, C. H. *The Story of the Mennonites.* Newton, Kans.: Mennonite Publication Office, 1957.

Methodists

Armstrong, James. *United Methodist Primer.* Nashville: Tidings, 1972.

Asbury, Francis. *Journals and Letters,* Elmer T. Clark, ed. Nashville: Abingdon, 1958.

Book of Discipline of the United Methodist Church. Nashville: Abingdon, 1972.

Bucke, Emory S., ed. *History of American Methodism.* Nashville: Abingdon, 1964.

Carter, Henry. *The Methodist Heritage.* Nashville: Abingdon, 1952.

Clark, Elmer; Potts, J. Manning; and Payton, Jacob S. *The Journals and Letters of Francis Asbury.* Nashville: Abingdon, 1958.

Colaw, Emerson. *Beliefs of a United Methodist Christian.* Nashville: Tidings, 1972.

Harmon, Nolan B. *Understanding the Methodist Church.* Nashville: Abingdon, 1977.

Kennedy, Gerald H. *The Methodist Way of Life.* Englewood Cliffs, N.J.: Prentice-Hall, 1958.

Kirkpatrick, Dow, ed. *The Doctrine of the Church* (Oxford Institute on Methodist Theological Studies, 1962). Nashville: Abingdon, 1964.

Methodist Church (Membership Manual). Nashville: Abingdon.

Moore, John M. *The Long Road to Methodist Union.* Nashville: Abingdon, 1943.

Norwood, Frederick A. *The Story of American Methodism.* Nashville: Abingdon, 1975.

Stokes, Mack B. *Major United Methodist Beliefs.* Nashville: Abingdon, 1972.

Sweet, W. W. *Methodism in American History.* Nashville: Abingdon, 1954.

Tuell, Jack Marvin. *The Organization of the United Methodist Church.* Nashville: Abingdon, 1977.

Moravians

deSchweinitz, E. A. *The Story of Unitas Fratum.* Bethlehem, Pa.: Moravian Book Shop, 1885.

Hamilton, J. T., and Hamilton, K. G. *History of the Moravian Church.* (The Renewed Unitas Fratum from 1722-1957) Bethelehm, Pa.: Interprovincial Board of Christian Education, 1967.

Lewis, Arthur J. *Zinzendorf, The Ecumenical Pioneer: A Study of the Moravian Contribution to Christian Mission and Unity.* London: SCM Press, 1962.

Schattschneider, A. W. *Through Five Hundred Years.* Interprovincial Board of Christian Education, 1966.

Weinlick, John R. *The Moravian Church Through the Ages*. Bethlehem, Pa.: Interprovisional Board of Christian Education, 1966.

Old Catholic Churches

Anson, Peter. *Bishops at Large*. London: Faber & Faber, 1964.

Moss, C. B. *The Old Catholic Movement*. New York: Morehouse, 1964.

Pruter, Fr. Karl. *A History of the Old Catholic Church*. Scottsdale, Ariz.: St. Willibrord's Press, 1973.

Pentecostalists

Bennett, Dennis J. *Nine O'clock in the Morning*. Plainfield, N.J.: Logos International, 1970.

Bloch-Hoell, Nils Egede. *The Pentecostal Movement: Its Origin, Development, and Distinctive Character*. New York: Humanities Press, 1964.

Clark, E. T. *The Small Sects in America*. Nashville: Abingdon, 1949.

Conn, Charles. *Like a Mighty Army*. Cleveland, Tenn.: Pathway Press, 1955.

Cunningham, Robert C. *Filled with the Spirit*. Springfield, Mo.: Gospel Publishing House, 1972.

Durasoff, Steve. *Bright Wind of the Spirit*. Englewood Cliffs, N.J.: Prentice-Hall, 1972.

Frodsham, S. H. *With Signs Following*. Springfield, Mo.: Gospel Publishing House, 1946.

Gaver, Jessyca Russell. *Pentecostalism*. New York: Universal Publishing and Distribution Corp., 1971.

Gee, Donald. *Concerning Spiritual Gifts*. Springfield, Mo.: Gospel Publishing House, 1972.

Harper, Michael. *As at the Beginning: The Twentieth Century Pentecostal Revival*. Plainfield, N.J.: Logos International, 1971.

Harris, Ralph W. *Spoken by the Spirit*. Springfield, Mo.: Gospel Publishing House, 1973.

Hollenweger, Walter. *The Pentecostals: The Charismatic Movement in the Churches*. Minneapolis: Augsburg, 1972.

Menzies, William W. *Anointed to Serve, The Story of the Assemblies of God*. Springfield Mo.: Gospel Publishing House, 1971.

Moon, Elmer Louis. *The Pentecostal Church*. (A history of the Pentecostal Church of God of America, Inc.) New York: Carlton Press, Inc., 1966.

Nichol, John Thomas. *The Pentecostals*. Plainfield, N.J.: Logos International, 1971.

Riggs, R. M. *The Spirit Himself*. Springfield, Mo.: Gospel Publishing House, 1949.

Sherrill, John. *They Speak with Other Tongues*. Old Tappan, N.J.: Fleming H. Revell, 1964.

Synan, Vinson. *The Holiness-Pentecostal Movement in the United States*. Grand Rapids: Eerdmans, 1972.

―――. *The Old-Time Power*. Franklin Springs, Ga.: Advocate Press, 1973.

Presbyterians

Armstrong, Maurice W.; Loetscher, Lefferts A.; and Anderson, Charles A. *The Presbyterian Enterprise*. (Presbyterian Historical Society Publications, 1) Philadelphia: Westminster Press, 1956.

Biggs, C. A. *American Presbyterianism.* New York: Scribner's, 1885.

Calvin, John. *Institutes of the Christian Religion.* Philadelphia: Westminster Press, 1960.

Davies, A. Mervin. *The Presbyterian Heritage.* Richmond, Va.: John Knox Press, 1965.

Drury, C. M. *Presbyterian Panorama.* Philadelphia: Westminster Press, 1952.

Jamison, Wallace N. *The United Presbyterian Story, 1858–1958.* Pittsburgh: Geneva Press, 1958.

Lingle, Walter W., & Kuykendall, John W. *Presbyterians: Their History and Beliefs.* Richmond, Va.: John Knox Press, 1978.

Loetscher, Lefferts A. *A Brief History of the Presbyterians.* Philadelphia: Westminster Press, 1978.

———. *The Broadening Church.* Philadelphia: University of Pennsylvania Press, 1954.

Mackay, John A. *The Presbyterian Way of Life.* Englewood Cliffs, N.J.: Prentice-Hall, 1960.

Melton, Julius. *Presbyterian Worship in America.* Richmond, Va.: John Knox Press, 1967.

Miller, Park Hays. *Why I Am a Presbyterian.* New York: Thomas Nelson, 1956.

Reed, R. C. *History of the Presbyterian Churches of the World.* Philadelphia: Westminster Press, 1905.

Slosser, Gaius J., ed. *They Seek a Country. The American Presbyterians.* New York: Macmillan, 1955.

Thompson, Ernest Trice. *Presbyterians in the South.* Richmond: John Knox Press. Vol. I, 1963; Vols II & III, 1973.

Thompson, R. E. *A History of the Presbyterian Churches in the United States.* (American Church History Series, Vol. VI). New York: Scribner's, 1895.

Trinterud, Leonard J. *The Forming of an American Tradition.* Philadelphia: Westminster Press, 1949.

Reformed Bodies

Berts, H. *The Christian Reformed Church in North America.* Grand Rapids: Eastern Avenue Book Store, 1923.

Boettner, Loraine. *Studies in Theology.* Grand Rapids: Eerdmans Publishing Co., 1941.

Brown, W. D. *History of the Reformed Church in America.* New York: Board of Publication and Bible School Work of the Reformed Church in America, 1928.

Brouwer, Arie R. *Reformed Church Roots.* New York: Reformed Church Press, 1977.

Corwin, E. T. et al. *A History of the Reformed Church, Dutch, the Reformed Church, German, and the Moravian Church in the United States* (American Church History Series, Vol. VIII). New York: Scribner's, 1895.

Hoekema, H. *The Protestant Reformed Churches in America.* Grand Rapids: Eerdman's, 1936.

The Word of God and the Reformed Faith. (American Calvinistic Conference) Grand Rapids: Baker Book House, 1942.

BIBLIOGRAPHY

Roman Catholic Church

A New Catechism: Catholic Faith for Adults. New York: Herder & Herder, 1967.

Abbott, Walter M., S.J., ed. Documents of Vatican II. New York: American Press, 1966.

Attwater, Donald, ed. Catholic Dictionary. New York: Macmillan, 1958.

Catholic Almanac. Published annually by Our Sunday Visitor, Huntington, Ind.

Ellis, John Tracy. American Catholicism. 2d ed. Chicago: University of Chicago Press, 1969.

Greely, Andrew. The American Catholic. New York: Basic Books, 1977.

Greenwood, John, ed. Handbook of the Catholic Faith. Garden City, N.Y.: Image Books, 1956.

Hughes, Phillip. A Popular History of the Catholic Church. Garden City, N.Y.: Image Books, 1954.

Kung, Hans. The Church. New York: Sheed & Ward, 1967.

McAvoy, Thomas A. History of the Catholic Church in America. Notre Dame, Ind.: University of Notre Dame Press, 1969.

New Catechism: Catholic Faith for Adults. New York: Herder and Herder, 1967.

New Catholic Encyclopedia. New York: McGraw-Hill Book Co., 1967.

O'Brien, David. The Renewal of American Catholicism. New York: Oxford University Press, 1972.

Official Catholic Directory. New York: P. J. Kenedy & Sons (annual).

Welch, Claude. The Reality of the Church. New York: Scribner's, 1958.

Spiritualists

Bach, Marcus. They Have Found a Faith. Indianapolis: Bobbs-Merrill, 1946.

Braden, Chas. S. These Also Believe. New York: Macmillan, 1949.

Graebner, Theodore T. Spiritism. St. Louis: Concordia Publishing House, 1919.

Hill, J. A. Spiritualism: Its History, Phenomena and Doctrine. New York: Doubleday, 1919.

Leaf, H. What Is This Spiritualism? New York: Doubleday, 1919.

The Spiritualist Manual. Washington, D.C.: National Spiritualist Association of the United States of America, 1944.

Unitarian-Universalist

Cassara, Ernest. Hosea Ballou. Boston: Beacon Press, 1961.

———. Universalism in America. Boston: Beacon Press, 1971.

Darling, Edward. They Cast Long Shadows. Boston: Beacon Press, 1971.

Marshall, George. Challenge of a Liberal Faith. New York: Pyramid Publications, 1971.

Mendlesohn, Jack. Channing: The Reluctant Radical. Boston: Little, Brown, 1971.

Parke, David, ed. The Epic of Unitarianism. Boston: Beacon Press, 1957.

Robinson, Elmo. The Story of American Universalism. New York: Exposition Press, 1970.

Scott, Clinton Lee. The Universalist Church of America. Boston: Beacon Press, 1957.

Wilbur, Earl Morse. A History of Unitarianism. New York: Cambridge University Press, 1952.

———. *Our Unitarian Heritage*. Boston: Beacon Press, 1925.

Williams, George H. *American Universalism*. Boston: Beacon Press, 1971.

Wright, Conrad. *The Beginnings of Unitarianism in America*. Boston: Beacon Press, 1955.

———. *The Liberal Christians*. Boston: Beacon Press, 1970.

———. *Three Prophets of Religious Liberalism*. Boston: Beacon Press, 1961.

United Church of Christ

Atkins, G. G. *History of American Congregationalism*. Boston: Pilgrim Press, 1942.

Burton, C. E. *Manual of the Congregational and Christian Churches*. Boston: Pilgrim Press, 1936.

Horstman, J. H. E., and Wernecke, H. H. *Through Four Centuries*. St. Louis: Eden Publishing House, 1938.

Horton, Douglas. *The United Church of Christ*. New York: Thomas Nelson & Sons, 1962.

Williams, D. D., and Shinn, R. L. *We Believe: An Interpretation of the United Church Statement of Faith*. New York: United Church Press, 1966.

Unity School of Christianity

Bach, Marcus. *The Unity Way of Life*. Lee's Summit, Mo.: Unity Books, 1972.

Cady, H. Emilie. *Lessons in Truth*. Lee's Summit, Mo.: Unity Books, 1896.

D'Andrade, Hugh. *Herald of the New Age*. New York: Harper, 1974.

Fillmore, Charles R. *The Adventure Called Unity*. Lee's Summit, Mo.: Unity Books 1971.

———. *Dynamics for Living*. Lee's Summit, Mo.: Unity Books, 1967.

Freeman, J. D. *The Story of Unity*. Lee's Summit, Mo.: Unity Books, 1972.

———. *The Household of Faith*. Lee's Summit, Mo.: Unity Books, 1951.

INDEX

National Spiritualists Association of
Churches, 236
Netherlands Reformed Congregations,
222
New Carpatho-Russian Orthodox
Greek Catholic Diocese, 113
New Congregational Methodist
Church, 184
New Hampshire Confession, 37, 40,
51, 54
New Lights or Separates (Baptists), 36,
56
New School (Presbyterian), 208, 209
Nitschmann, David, 188
Noble, Drew Ali, 60
Noli, Theophan S., 112
North American Baptist Association, 45
North American Baptist Conference,
53
North American Baptists, 54
North American Old Roman Catholic
Church, 193, 195
Northern Baptist Convention, 38, 47,
49, 58
Northern Presbyterians, 212
Norwegian Lutheran Church, 164
Norwegian Lutheran Church of
America, 158

O'Kelly, James, 100, 247, 248
Olcott, Henry Steel, 237
Old and New Light Groups, 217
Old Catholic Churches, 192
Old German Baptist Brethren, 62, 63,
64
Old Hungarian Reformed Church, 250
Old Lights or Regulars, 24
Old Order Amish Mennonite Church,
168, 169, 170
Old Order (or Yorker) Brethren, 62, 68,
69
Old Order (Wisler) Mennonite
Church, 172
Old Roman Catholic Church in Eu-
rope and America (English Rite),
195
Old School Baptists, 55
Old School (Presbyterian), 208, 209
Open Bible Standard Church, Inc., 196
Open Brethren, 65
(Original) Church of God, 85, 86
Orthodox Church in America, 110
Orthodox Judaism, 150, 152

Orthodox Presbyterian Church, 215,
216, 217
Otterbein, Philip William, 169
Ottersen, Roger W., 74
Oxford Methodists, 173
Oxford Movement, 123
Palmer, Paul, 49
Palmquist, Gustav, 44
Parker, Daniel, 57
Particular Baptist Church, 35
Patriarchal Parishes of the Russian
Orthodox Church in the U.S.A., 119
Peace of Constantine, 112
Pedobaptists, 34
Pendelton, T. M., 52
Penn, William, 62, 135, 167
Pentecost, 149
Pentecostal Assemblies of Jesus Christ,
202
Pentecostal Assemblies of the World,
Inc., 199
Pentecostal Bodies, 197
Pentecostal Church, Inc., 199, 202
Pentecostal Church of Christ, 200
Pentecostal Church of God, 200
Pentecostal Church of the Nazarene, 99
Pentecostal Evangel, 198
Pentecostal Fellowship of North
America, 196
Pentecostal Fire-Baptized Holiness
Church, 199, 200
Pentecostal Free-Will Baptist Church,
Inc., 201
Pentecostal Holiness Church, 106, 200,
201
Pentecostal Union, 202
People's Methodist Church, 185
Pesach (Passover), 149
Peter, Jesse, 41
Philadelphia Confession, 37
Philadelphia Yearly Meeting, 135, 138
Philips, Obbe, 167
Phillips, Bishop W. T., 31
Photius, 109
Pietists, 62, 68
Pilgrim Holiness Church, 257
Pillar of Fire, 202
Pilmoor, Joseph, 174
Plates of Laban, 98
Plymouth Brethren, 62, 65
Polk, Bishop Leonidas, 123
Polish National Catholic Church of
America, 203, 205